AN EXPLORER'S GUIDE

Rhode Island

Kim Grant

AN EXPLORER'S GUIDE

Rhode Island

Phyllis Méras & Katherine Imbrie

SIXTH EDITION

The Countryman Press ✷ Woodstock, Vermont

Sixth Edition

Interior photographs by Katherine Imbrie unless otherwise specified
Maps by Erin Greb Cartography, © The Countryman Press
Book design by Bodenweber Design
Composition by PerfecType, Nashville, TN

Explorer's Guide Rhode Island
978-0-88150-963-2

Published by The Countryman Press, P.O. Box 748, Woodstock, VT 05091

Distributed by W. W. Norton & Company, Inc., 500 Fifth Avenue, New York, NY 10110

Printed in the United States of America

10 9 8 7 6 5 4 3 2 1

EXPLORE WITH US!

Welcome to the sixth edition of *Rhode Island: An Explorer's Guide*, the first statewide guide to the Ocean State. As in every other book in the Explorer's Guide series, all inclusions—attractions, inns, restaurants—have been chosen on the basis of personal experience, not paid advertising.

We hope you find this guide easy to read and use. We've kept the layout fairly simple, but here are some general tips to help you find your way.

WHAT'S WHERE

In the beginning of the book you'll find an alphabetical listing of special highlights and important information that you may want to reference quickly.

LODGING

When making reservations, especially at B&Bs and smaller inns, we suggest that you inquire in advance about policies regarding smoking, children, the use of credit cards for payment, and any minimum-stay requirements.

RESTAURANTS

In most chapters please note a distinction between *Dining Out* and *Eating Out*. Restaurants listed under *Eating Out* are generally inexpensive and more casual; reservations are suggested for restaurants in *Dining Out*.

PRICES

It is difficult to convey current prices, as changes occur frequently and, especially in popular vacation areas, rates are often adjusted to the season. As always, we suggest that you call ahead. There is a 13 percent state room tax in Rhode Island, added to a 7 percent sales tax. The prices indicated by the rating system used in this book do not include taxes or gratuity.

Lodging (double occupancy, per night): $ means under $120; $$ means $120–200; $$$ means $200–300; $$$$ means over $300.

Eating Out and Dining Out (price of an entrée): $ means under $10; $$ means $10–20; $$$ means $20–30; $$$$ means over $30.

KEY TO SYMBOLS

- The "value" symbol appears next to lodgings, restaurants, and activities that combine exceptional quality with moderate prices.
- The dog paw symbol appears next to lodgings that as of press time accept pets (with prior notification), as well as other places where pets are allowed.
- The "child and family interest" symbol appears next to lodgings, restaurants, activities, and shops of special appeal to youngsters and families.
- ♿ The wheelchair symbol appears next to establishments that are partially or fully handicapped accessible.

We would appreciate your comments and corrections about places you discover or know well. Please send your letters to Explorer's Guide Editor, The Countryman Press, P.O. Box 748, Woodstock, Vermont 05091.

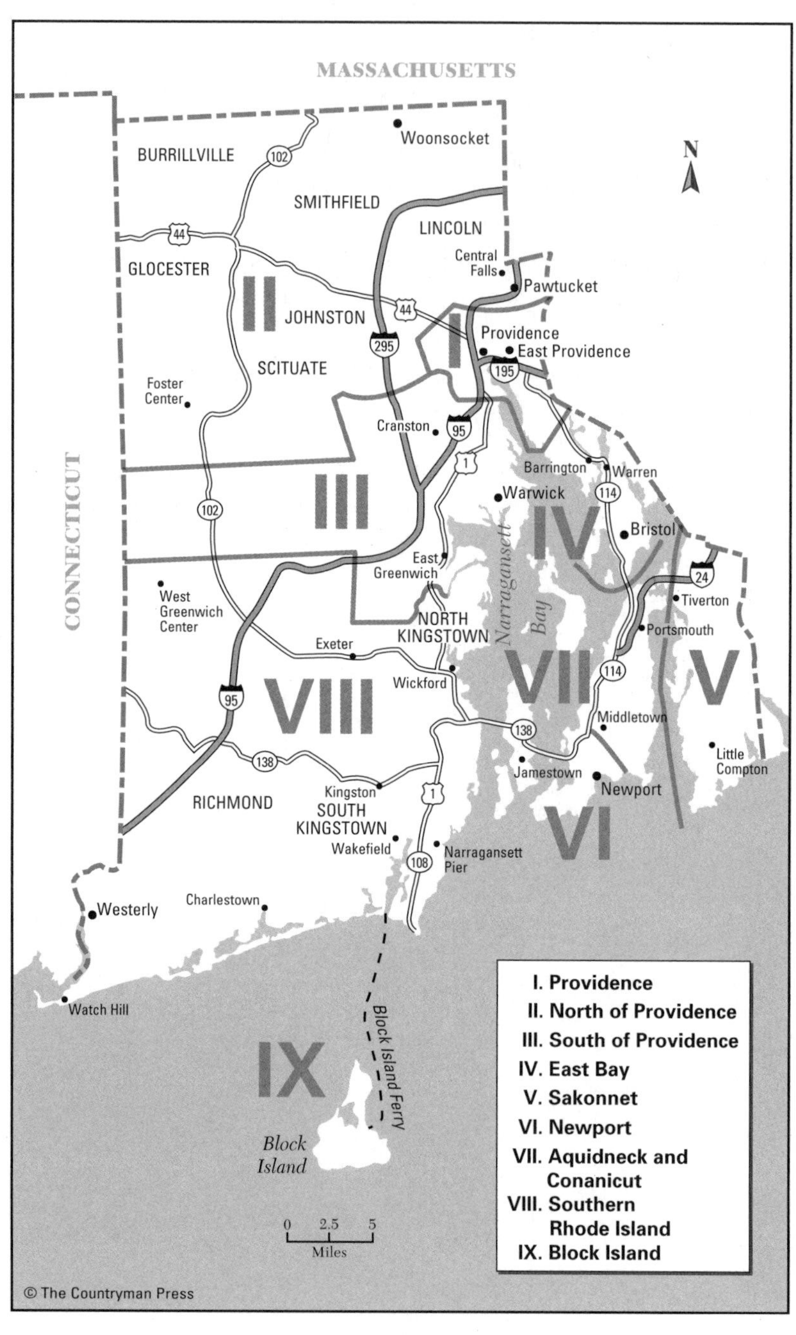
MASSACHUSETTS
CONNECTICUT
N
BURRILLVILLE
Woonsocket
SMITHFIELD
LINCOLN
GLOCESTER
Central Falls
Pawtucket
JOHNSTON
Providence
East Providence
SCITUATE
Foster Center
Cranston
Barrington
Warren
Warwick
Bristol
East Greenwich
West Greenwich Center
NORTH KINGSTOWN
Narragansett Bay
Tiverton
Portsmouth
Exeter
Wickford
Middletown
Jamestown
Newport
Little Compton
Kingston
SOUTH KINGSTOWN
RICHMOND
Wakefield
Narragansett Pier
Westerly
Charlestown
Watch Hill
Block Island Ferry
Block Island
0 2.5 5
Miles
I. Providence
II. North of Providence
III. South of Providence
IV. East Bay
V. Sakonnet
VI. Newport
VII. Aquidneck and Conanicut
VIII. Southern Rhode Island
IX. Block Island
© The Countryman Press

CONTENTS

MAPS

ACKNOWLEDGMENTS

The following people have been most generous with suggestions, information, and advice during the preparation of this book: Bob Billington and Wendy Jenks of the Blackstone Valley Tourist Authority; David de Petrillo of the Rhode Island Tourism Division; Mark Brouder of the Rhode Island Welcome Center; Albert Klyberg of the Rhode Island Historical Society; Leonard Panaggio, formerly of the Rhode Island Tourism Division; the Newport Tourism & Development Council; Deb O'Hara, director of Tiverton Library Services; the Preservation Society of Newport County; Ida Millman, Jean Rossi, the late Nancy Luedeman, Richard J. Walton, Leigh Diakapolous, Lois Hollingsworth, Nancy Whitcomb, Thomas D. Stevens, Jeff Stevens, Sal Laterra, the late Edwin Safford, Richard and Janet Wood, Laurinda Barrett, James Dugan; David Brussart, Donald Breed, Lynne Chaput, Channing and Bianca Gray, Ken Weber, Doug Fellow, Alan Kerr, William K. Gale, Andy Smith, Mikki Catanzaro, Gail Ciampa, Janet Butler, Donna Lee, Janina Fera, Rose Lansing, Donna McGarry, Rick Massimo, Patricia Pothier, Lars Smith, and Jim Seavor of *the Providence Journal.*

Thanks are also due to Brian C. Tefft of the State Division of Fish, Wildlife, and Estuarine Services; Robert and Betsy Dunley, the late Katrina Aldrich, the late Emily Cocroft, Robert Cocroft, William Cocroft, the late Thomas H. Cocroft, the late David Fowler, Frank and Esther Mauran, Mary McGovern, Joan and the late Roger Noone, and B. L. Gordon of the Watch Hill Book & Tackle Shop; Susan Capuano, Wilbur Doctor, Jim and Adelheide Dresser, Carol Hazelhurst, John C. Quinn, Leppy McCarthy, Joan Ress Reeves, Suzanne Jeffers, Caroline Vollmer, Suzanne Vollmer, Paul Carrick, the late Ann Lampson, Laura Katz, Anita Pariseau, Lorraine and Jacques Hopkins, Gregory Del Sesto, Gloria Maroni, Chet Browning, the Rhode Island Department of Economic Development;

Katherine Imbrie

SOUTH COUNTY SHOP

Evan Smith, Newport County Convention & Visitors Bureau; and Kermit Hummel, Jennifer Thompson, Lisa Sacks, Kathryn Flynn, and Melissa Dobson of The Countryman Press, for their extraordinary patience.

INTRODUCTION

Welcome to the Ocean State. That may seem like a grand nickname for the country's tiniest state, which measures a mere 48 miles long by 37 miles wide, but with Narragansett Bay slicing it nearly in two, there's no place within Rhode Island's borders that's more than a 20-minute drive from its 400-mile coastline. In fact, with a total of 36 islands, including Aquidneck, second largest (after Long Island) on the East Coast, Rhode Island could almost be classified as an archipelago.

Very much a New England state in many respects, Rhode Island enjoys its own distinct identity—actually several identities, all of which involve a strong sense of independence. Rhode Island was founded in 1636 by religious refugees fleeing the rigid Puritanism of the Massachusetts Bay Colony, and soon became a haven for outcasts of all sorts—Quakers, Jews, Antinomians. Privateering—preying on enemy ships—grew simultaneously with the colony's shipbuilding industry and often was indistinguishable from outright piracy. All of this combined to earn the colony an earlier nickname, Rogue's Island.

The ports of Providence and Newport were heavily engaged in the unsavory slave trade, but the state could also boast some early abolitionists, including Samuel Hopkins and Ezra Stiles, later president of Yale, who helped enact a ban on slave trading in 1774, the first such law in the colonies. Rhode Island's Black Regiment, the nation's first such unit, routed Hessian mercenaries on Aquidneck in 1778, earning members full citizenship in the process.

Rhode Island and Mother England clashed regularly over trade-related issues, and the colony finally declared itself independent of the Crown on May 4, 1776, two months before the remaining colonies issued the Declaration of Independence. After participating enthusiastically in the Revolution—General Nathanael Greene was a native son—Rhode Island typically refused to join the Union, reluctantly becoming the 13th and last colony to ratify the Constitution in 1790, and only after threats of tariff barriers and invasion. That stubborn streak has continued; in the 1920s, when the rest of the nation was dutifully approving the Volstead Act, Rhode Island was one of just two states to reject it. Once Prohibition was a fact, Rhode Islanders quickly moved into rum-running, taking full advantage of the coast's many hidden coves and inlets.

But the long, colorful history is just one aspect of the Ocean State. Blessed with some swift-running rivers that could be harnessed for waterpower, particularly in the Blackstone River region, the state developed into what has been called the birthplace of the industrial revolution. In Pawtucket, Samuel Slater in 1790 started the nation's first successful cotton-manufacturing operation. Peace Dale in South County was the site of the first power loom, in 1814. The textile industry drew thousands of immigrant workers—French Canadians, Irish, English, and Italians, the same groups who make up much of the population today. Rhode Island also got an early start in the jewelry business, perfecting the plating of pot metals in the 1700s and creating an industry that for years was an important part of the economy.

Divided as it is by water and geography—the colony at one time had four different capitals—Rhode Island offers much diversity in a small space, from the quiet pastures and woods of South County (the popular name for the southwestern part of the state), home to Swamp Yankees and descendants of the Narragansett tribe; to the urban life of revitalized Providence, now one of the most inviting small cities in America and boasting some of the region's finest restaurants. Its entire downtown has

CLIFF WALKERS, NEWPORT

Katherine Imbrie

been placed on the National Register of Historic Places. Then there is the sophistication of Newport, summer home to wealthy visitors from the 1700s to the present. The geography is varied as well, with rugged hillsides in the north, barrier beaches along the southern coast, steep headlands in the east, and rolling pastures in the southeast corner. And there is Narragansett Bay, the second largest estuary on the East Coast (after the Chesapeake Bay), which forms a 28-mile wedge cutting into the state and accounts for the two most popular forms of recreation: swimming and boating.

In this book we have done our best to introduce you to the highlights of the smallest state with the longest name (officially Rhode Island and Providence Plantations)—to its history and legends; its 400 miles of shore; its natural areas and winding country roads; and its grand historic houses, mill villages, and immigrant neighborhoods. We urge you to follow us on our exploration and see for yourself what so many travelers miss in their rush from Boston or New York to Cape Cod and northern New England.

Phyllis Méras, born in New York, came to Rhode Island after Wellesley College and the Columbia Graduate School of Journalism. Although she has traveled from the state many times since then, working for the *New York Times,* the *Vineyard Gazette* on Martha's Vineyard, and a newspaper in Switzerland, she married a Rhode Islander, Thomas Cocroft, and, like the proverbial bad penny, seems always to come back. She has written an earlier guidebook to the state and is the former travel editor of the *Providence Journal.*

Katherine Imbrie has spent summers on the Rhode Island coast since she was a child and came to live in Rhode Island as a teenager. She was a features writer and restaurant reviewer for the *Providence Journal* for more than two decades, and currently writes for *Newport This Week* in Newport.

We hope this guide will help you discover something new in your backyard or plan a holiday in the Ocean State. As you follow some of our recommendations and visit our favorite places, please don't forget to send us your own recommendations, so that future editions of this guide are as complete and accurate as possible.

WHAT'S WHERE IN RHODE ISLAND

AGRICULTURAL FAIRS Each August the agriculturally minded head to Richmond for the annual **Washington County Agricultural Fair.** This is the state's only major old-fashioned country fair, with horse and oxen pulls, animals, fruit and vegetable judging, country-and-western stage shows, and midway games. Smaller fairs include **Foster's Old Home Days** in July and Scituate's **Old Home Day** the same month. There are **Harvest Fairs** held in September at Coggeshall Farm Museum and in October at the Norman Bird Sanctuary in Middletown. For further information, e-mail www.rigrown.ri.gov or call or write the Rhode Island Division of Agriculture (401-222-2781), 235 Promenade Street, Providence 02908.

AIRLINES AND AIRPORTS **T. F. Green State Airport** on Post Road in Warwick, the state's largest airport, is served by major and commuter airlines. **New England Airlines** offers scheduled flights between **Westerly State Airport** and **Block Island State Airport,** and **Action Airlines** has charter flights to Block Island from **Groton/New London Airport** in Connecticut. **Resort Air** on Block Island also offers charter service. **Newport State Airport** in Middletown, **Quonset State Airport** in North Kingstown, and **North Central Airport** in Smithfield are open to charter and private planes.

AMUSEMENT PARKS The waterslides at **Water Wizz** (401-322-0520), at Misquamicut Beach in Westerly, attract adults as well as children. Miniature golf and batting cages, as well as bumper boats, can be found in Narragansett at **Adventureland;** and **Yawgoo Valley Ski Area and Sports Park** (401-295-5366; www.yawgoo.com) in Exeter has a water park, a volleyball court, and horseshoes.

ANTIQUES Like any other New England state, Rhode Island is rich in antiques. And while the dealers are fairly knowledgeable, the prices (especially outside

Newport) will surprise visitors from metropolitan areas. Newport, with its Gilded Age artifacts and China trade connections, not surprisingly has the biggest selection. For more information, contact the **Newport County Antique Dealers Association,** Box 222, Newport 02940. Warren, particularly the downtown waterfront area, is another trove of antique treasures, along with Providence and South County, especially Wickford village in North Kingstown. But that unheralded shop along a country road may be just the place you've been looking for.

AREA CODE The area code for all Rhode Island is **401.**

ART GALLERIES There are art galleries throughout the state, with major public and private galleries in most communities. Further information may be obtained from the **Rhode Island State Council on the Arts** (401-222-3880; www.arts.ri.gov). Many galleries are also listed in the *Rhode Island Summer Guide,* published in May by *the Providence Journal* (401-277-7000).

ART MUSEUMS The **Museum of Art, Rhode Island School of Design** (401-454-6500; www.risd.edu) in Providence, is the state's most important museum of art, with a collection that includes ancient and Oriental art, 19th-century French art, modern Latin American work, American furniture, and decorative arts. The

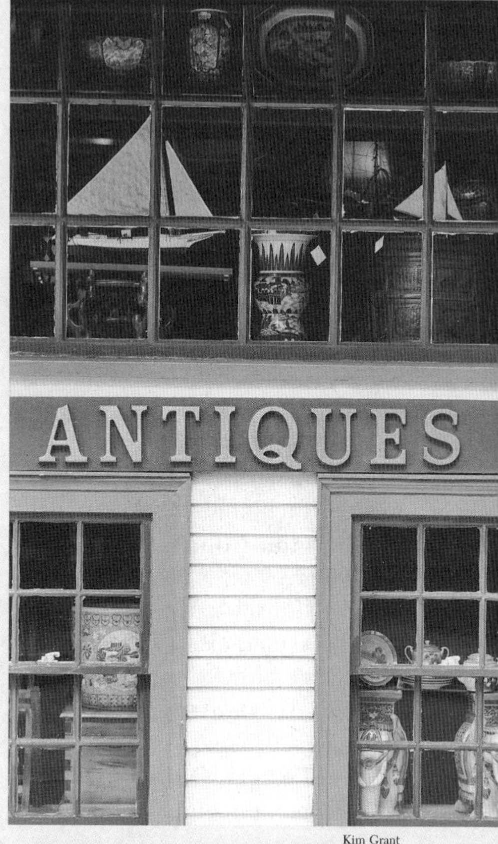

Kim Grant

Newport Art Museum (401-848-8200; www.newportartmuseum.org) offers changing exhibits of historical and contemporary art from Newport and other parts of New England. (See also *Art Galleries and Museums.*)

BEACHES Living up to its nickname of the Ocean State, Rhode Island has more than three dozen saltwater beaches along its hundreds of miles of coastline. Among the largest and most popular of the beaches with surf are **Charlestown Town Beach, Narragansett Town Beach, Watch Hill**

Town Beach, East Matunuck State Beach, and **Green Hill** in South Kingstown; **Misquamicut State Beach** in Westerly; and **Scarborough State Beach** in Narragansett. Less accessible but still popular is **Goosewing Beach** in Little Compton. Bodysurfers find Newport's **First** and **Second Beaches** to their liking, while surfboarders come to ride the waves between the **Narragansett Town Beach** and **East Matunuck State Beach.** Saltwater bathing facilities for families with small children are best at **Roger Wheeler State Beach** and **Salty Brine Beach** in Narragansett and **Fred Benson Town Beach** (Crescent Beach) on Block Island. **Third Beach** in Middletown is also relatively calm and popular with children. Farther inland, the best beaches are **Sandy Point** in Portsmouth and **Fogland** in Tiverton, both on the Sakonnet River, and **Bristol Town Beach** and **Colt State Park,** both along upper Narragansett Bay. There are parking fees for both state and town beaches (anywhere from $14 to $30), and parking is always limited, so it's wise on a hot summer's day to arrive as early as possible. Rates are higher on weekends and for out-of-state residents, and a few beaches charge entrance fees.

BED & BREAKFASTS Rhode Island offers bed & breakfast accommodations by the ocean, in rural villages, and in its capital. A list is printed each year in the **Rhode Island Tourism Division's** *Rhode Island Travel Guide,* available at visitor information bureaus throughout the state or by calling (401-278-9100 or 1-800-556-2484) or emailing (www.visitrhodeisland.com). Reservation services include **Bed & Breakfast**

Kim Grant

of Newport (401-846-5408; www.bbnewport.com); **Bed & Breakfast Referrals of South Coast Rhode Island** (1-800-853-7479; www.bandbsocoastri.com); **Block Island Chamber of Commerce** (401-466-298 or 1-800-383-BIRI; www.blockislandchamber.com), or Block Island Reservations (401-466-2605 or 1-800-825-6254; www.blockislandreservations.com); the **Narragansett Chamber of Commerce** (401-783-7121; www.narragansettcoc.com) and **Taylor-Made Destinations** (401-848-0300 or 1-800-848-8848; www.citybythesea.com).

BIKING Though Rhode Island is a small state, its terrain varies widely—with dense woodlands, sea and bay coastline, flatlands, hills, and rolling farmland. Much of it is interesting for the cyclist to explore. Among the best areas for cycling are along the 14.5-mile **East Bay Bike Path** between Providence and Bristol, which sometimes edges Narragansett Bay and at other times passes through towns and villages. A map of the bicycle path is contained in the **Rhode Island Tourism Division's** *Rhode Island Travel Guide.* **Block Island's** unspoiled, winding roads are also popular with cyclists. A ride along Newport's 15-mile-long **Bellevue Avenue** and **Ocean Drive** will take you past mansions on one side and the ocean on the other. Bristol's **Colt State Park** and remote **Tiverton** and **Little Compton** afford picturesque rides as well. We also recommend Warwick's **Goddard State Park,** the **Greenville** area of Smithfield, and the island of **Jamestown.**

BIRDING Situated as it is directly under the Atlantic Flyway, **Block Island** lures many a birder, especially in fall. There are many other fine birding sites in the state as well: in Middletown, the **Sachuest Point National Wildlife Refuge** and the **Norman Bird Sanctuary;** in South Kingstown, the **Trustom Pond National Wildlife Sanctuary;** in Charlestown, the **Ninigret National Wildlife Area;** in Providence, the **Swan Point Cemetery;** and the many state management areas. Further information is available from the **Audubon Society of Rhode Island** (401-949-5454).

BUS SERVICES **Peter Pan/Bonanza** (401-751-8800 or 1-800-556-3815; www.peterpanbus.com) serves Providence from New York, Boston, Cape Cod, and Albany (via Springfield, Massachusetts). **Greyhound** (401-454-0790 or 1-800-231-2222; www.greyhound.com) also links Providence with Boston and New York. On both lines there can be intermediate stops in Connecticut.

CAMPING Both private and state camping areas—some sophisticated, some quite primitive—are scattered throughout the rural sections of the state. Information on *Rhode Island outdoor activi-*

ties, including camping, is available in the Rhode Island Travel Guide issued by the **Rhode Island Tourism Division** (401-278-9100 or 1-800-556-2484, www.visitrhodeisland.com).

CANOEING AND KAYAKING

Canoe and kayak rentals, lessons, and guided trips are offered by the **Kayak Centre** (401-295-4400; www.kayakcentre.com) in Wickford, **Hope Valley Bait and Tackle Shop (rentals only)** (401-539-2757) in Wyoming, **Narrow River Kayaks** (401-789-0334; www.narrowriverkayaks.com) in Narragansett, **Quaker Lane Bait and Tackle** (401-294-9642; www.quakerlanetackle.com) in North Kingstown. Further information on canoeing routes and facilities can be obtained from the **Rhode Island Canoe and Kayak Association** (401-725-3344). A guide to canoeing the Blackstone River is available from the **John H. Chafee Blackstone River Valley National Heritage Corridor** (401-762-0250), Depot Square, Woonsocket 02895. Information on canoeing the Wood and Pawcatuck Rivers is available from the **Wood-Pawcatuck Watershed Association** (401-539-9017), 203 Arcadia Road, Hope Valley 02832.

CHILDREN, ESPECIALLY FOR

Throughout this book we have marked a number of sites with particular appeal to children and families with a "✐." In Providence, the **Providence Children's Museum** (401-273-5437; www.childrenmuseum.org) is a hands-on museum for children 2 to 11 years old. The Newport area's

Jim McElholm/South County Tourism

attractions for children include the **Old Colony and Newport Railway** (401-849-0546) and **Green Animals** topiary garden in Portsmouth (401-847-1000). There are children's carousels at **Roger Williams Park** (401-785-9450) in Providence, **Slater Memorial Park** (401-728-0500, ext. 257) in Pawtucket, and at the site of the former **Crescent Park** (401-433-2828) in East Providence. In Providence, **Roger Williams Park** (401-785-3510) has a zoo. In Jamestown at the **Watson Farm** (401-423-0005), there are horses, cows, chickens, and sheep, as well as the recently restored **Windmill** (401-423-1798).

CLAM CAKES A Rhode Island phenomenon, the clam cake, or fritter, is an irregular sphere of dough containing bits of clam or, more properly, quahog meat, along with salt and pepper. The cakes are fried so that they are crispy brown on the outside and soft and chewy within. Clam cakes, sold by the dozen or half dozen, are synonymous with summer hereabouts and often served as a complement to chowder, also made from the meat of the quahog.

CLIMATE Narragansett Bay and the Atlantic Ocean play a major role in the climate of the state. During winter the proximity of the water quickly changes many snowstorms to rain, and many hot summer days are cooled by ocean and bay breezes. Extreme temperatures are infrequent in either summer or winter: In January the average temperature is 30 degrees; in July, 72 degrees. Temperatures generally exceed 90 degrees only two or three days a year.

CRUISES With the water playing such a prominent part in the state, cruises abound. Among them are ***La Gondola*** (401-421-8877; www.gondolari.com) in Providence, offering river gondola trips; and Newport **Majestic Cruises** (401-649-3575; www.newportmajestic.com) in Newport, offering sightseeing, dinner dances, and theme cruises to such special events as Bristol's Fourth of July Parade. Both Newport Majestic Cruises and **Sight Sailing of Newport** (401-849-3333; www.sightsailing.com) provide narrated tours of Newport's historic harbor during summer, and Newport Majestic Cruises also has trips around Warren harbor. The ***Blackstone Valley Explorer*** (401-724-1500 or 1-800-619-BOAT; www.rivertourblackstone.com) cruises the Blackstone River. A complete listing of excursion and sightseeing boats is contained in the *Rhode Island Travel Guide,* published annually by the **Rhode Island Department of Economic Development,** Rhode Island Tourism Division (401-278-9100; 1-800-556-2484; www.visitrhodeisland.com).

EVENTS Major events in the state are listed at the end of each

Kim Grant

chapter, but seasonal-events booklets are published by the **Rhode Island Tourism Division** (401-278-9100 or 1-800-556-2484). Events are also listed in each year's *Rhode Island Travel Guide,* available from the Tourism Division. (See also *Newspapers.*)

FALL FOLIAGE For much of September and October the Blackstone River Valley and the western part of the state are ablaze with color. This is one of the most popular seasons for a boat trip on the ***Blackstone Valley Explorer*** (401-724-1500 or 1-800-619-BOAT; www.rivertourblackstone.com).

FARMERS' MARKETS Farmers offer their produce for sale not only at roadside stands but also at seasonal markets such as the **Aquidneck Growers Market next to Newport Vineyards in Middletown on Saturdays in-season, 9–1**; the **South Kingstown Farmers' Market** on Flagg Road at the University of Rhode Island in Kingston on Saturday morning; the **Westerly Farmers' Market** on Main Street opposite the Westerly Sun on Thursday, noon–4; and the **Block Island Farmers' Market** at Manisses Corner on Block Island on Wednesday morning and at Negus Park on Saturday morning. For further information, call or write the **Rhode Island Division of Agriculture** (401-222-2781), 235 Promenade Street, Providence 02903.

FERRIES The **Interstate Navigation Company** (401-783-4613 or 1-866-783-7996; www.blockislandferry.com) has ferries year-round sailing between Galilee and Block Island and in summer linking Providence, Newport, and New London with Block Island. The **Block Island Hi-Speed Ferry** (401-783-4613; 1-866-783-7996), sailing in summer, cuts sailing time between Galilee and Block Island to about 30 minutes. Ferry service (401-253-9808) also links Bristol with Prudence and Hog Islands in Narragansett Bay.

FISHING Fish are plentiful in Rhode Island waters and streams where largemouth bass, northern pike, crappies, trout, and landlocked salmon are stocked. Coastal waters abound with striped bass, bluefish, tuna, and sharks. Licenses are required of everyone between 16 and 65. A three-day resident tourist license is a bargain for short-term visitors. For a complete set of rules and regulations pertaining to Rhode Island fishing, contact the Division of Licensing of the Department of Environmental Management (401-789-3094; 401-277-3075). Licenses can be obtained at 235 Promenade Street, Providence 02908 (401-222-3576).

FLORAL EVENTS Spring comes busting out in February when the **Rhode Island Spring Flower and Garden Show** opens at the Rhode Island Convention Center (401-458-6000; 1-800-858-5852) on Sabin Street in Providence. During **Daffodil Week** more than 50,000 daffodils bloom at Blithewold, making it one of the largest daffodil displays in New England. In mid-May, find the

Kim Grant

Arbutus Garden Annual Plant Sale at the South Kingstown American Legion Hall in Wakefield. The annual plant sale on Water Street on Block Island is also held in mid-May. In early June and late September a highlight is Newport's **Secret Gardens Tour;** Block Island offers its **House and Garden Tour** in August. The Indian Run Garden Club presents **Herb Garden Day** in midsummer and an **Herbal Wreath Day** in mid-September, both held at the South County Museum in Narragansett. Also in September see the **Dahlia Society Flower Show** at the Cold Spring House in Wickford.

GENEALOGY Although the historical societies of most Rhode Island towns have genealogical records that are open to the public, the best place to begin a quest for genealogical information is at the **Rhode Island Historical Society Library** (401-273-8107) in Providence.

GOLF A list of public golf courses, including addresses, telephone numbers, and facilities, is contained in the **Rhode Island Tourism Division's** *Rhode Island Travel Guide* (401-278-9100 or 1-800-556-2484; www.visitrhodeisland.com).

HISTORIC HOUSES The **Rhode Island Tourism Division** (401-278-9100 or 1-800-556-2484; www.visitrhodeisland.com) provides some information on historic houses in its *Rhode Island Visitor Guide.* Town historical societies and the **Rhode Island Historical Preservation Commission** (401-222-2678) in Providence are other good sources.

HORSEBACK RIDING **Newport Equestrian Center** (401-848-5440) in Middletown and **Sandy Point Stables** (401-849-3958) in Portsmouth offer riding on Aquidneck Island. In West Greenwich there is year-round trail riding at **Stepping Stone Ranch** (401-397-3725). **Sunset Stables** (401-722-3033) offers trail rides through Lincoln Woods State Park, just a 10-minute drive from Providence.

HOTELS/MOTELS In this guide, hotels and motels are listed only for areas in which where they are the principal accommodation and there is little else to offer. Most listings are B&Bs and small, attractive New England inns.

HUNTING Rhode Island offers plenty of opportunity for hunting, with seasons for small game, deer, and waterfowl. Special hunting licenses are required and there are various restrictions, including type of firearms permitted and use of reflective clothing (either 200 or 500 square inches of fluorescent orange, depending on the season). In addition, certain towns have their own ordinances governing hunting. Licenses are available at local town halls and certain authorized agents. For more information, contact the Division of

Licensing of the **Department of Environmental Management** (401-222-3576), 235 Promenade Street, Providence 02908. Further information is available from the **State Division of Fish and Wildlife** (401-789-3094) in Wakefield.

INFORMATION The **Rhode Island Tourism Division** (401-278-9100 or 1-800-556-2484; www.visitrhodeisland.com), 315 Iron Horse Way, Suite 101, Providence 02908, publishes an annual *Rhode Island Travel Guide with information on* boating and fishing, camping, and special events. It can be ordered online. There are also regional tourism organizations: the **Blackstone Valley Tourism Council** (401-724-2200), 175 Main Street, Pawtucket; the **Providence-Warwick Convention & Visitors Bureau** (401-274-1636 or 1-800-233-1636; www.goprovidence.com), 1 Sabin Street, Providence 02903; the **Newport and Bristol County Convention and Visitor's Bureau, Visitor's Center** (401-845-9110 or 1-800-326-6030; www.gonewport.com), 23 America's Cup Avenue, Newport 02840; the **South County Tourism Council** (401-789-4422; 1-800-548-4662), 4808 Tower Hill Road (in the Oliver Stedman Government Center), Wakefield 02879; and the Warwick Department of Tourism, Culture, and Development (401-738-2000 ext. 5402 or 1-800-482-7942; www.visitwarwick.com), Warwick City Hall, 3275 Post Road, Warwick 02886.

INNS There are many country inns and bed & breakfasts in Rhode Island. A list of these accommodations, as well as hotels, is included in the **Rhode Island Tourism Division's** *Rhode Island Travel Guide,* available by calling 401-276-9100 or 1-800-556-2484 or on the web at www.visitrhodeisland.com. (See also *Bed & Breakfasts.*)

INTERSTATES Rhode Island is served by I-95 from Westerly to Pawtucket; I-295 from Warwick around Providence to Attleboro, Massachusetts; and I-195 from Seekonk, Massachusetts, to Providence.

ISLANDS **Block Island** is the most populous and popular of the state's offshore islands, and it remains truly cut off from the mainland. (Aquidneck, site of Portsmouth, Middletown, and Newport, and the island of Conanicut are linked to the mainland by bridges.) Block Island is served by ferry from Galilee year-round and from Newport and New London, Connecticut, and Montauk, New York, in summer. **Prudence** and **Hog Islands** have summer ferry service from Bristol, but—except for the National Marine Estuarine Reserve on the northern part of Prudence—these islands are largely of interest only to their own small summer populations.

Katherine Imbrie

SPRING HOUSE HOTEL, BLOCK ISLAND

Patience Island also has an estuarine reserve, but it is accessible only by private boat.

JONNY CAKES (OR JONNYCAKES) The recipe for these flat cornmeal cakes was originally based on white flint corn, which grows almost exclusively in the acid, salt-tinged soil of Rhode Island. (These days midwestern white dent corn is usually substituted.) Called "journey cakes" by early settlers—who stuffed them in their pockets or saddlebags for sustenance on long treks—jonny cakes are now served warm, often with a coating of maple syrup. According to the Society for the Propagation of the Jonnycake (yes, there is one), there are two versions: The West Bay/South County cake, formed thick, is made with scalding water; the East Bay/Newport preference is for a thinner, crêpelike cake made with cold milk. The cakes are served at area restaurants and at May Breakfasts (in honor of Rhode Island Independence Day) at halls around the state.

LAKES Beside the spectacular Narragansett Bay, Rhode Island's lakes are bound to pale, but there are several that are popular with anglers, many that are enjoyed by boaters, and the largest inland body of water in the state—the **Scituate Reservoir**—is loved simply for its beauty. Among the larger of the state's lakes (though they are sometimes called ponds, their size notwithstanding) are **Worden's Pond** in South Kingstown, **Watchaug Pond** in Charlestown, **Wallum Lake** in Pascoag, **Tiogue Lake** and **Johnson's Pond** in Coventry, **Olney Pond** in Lincoln, **Lake Washington** in Glocester, and **Echo Lake** in Burrillville.

LIGHTHOUSES Twelve working lighthouses blink along the 400 miles of Rhode Island coastline, marking harbor entrances and warning mariners of shoals and rocks. For the most part they are not open to the public except by special request, but two—**Watch Hill** and Block Island's **North Light**—have museums of lighthouse history. **Southeast Light** on Block Island has a museum as well. At **Castle Hill** in Newport the Coast Guard station is open to the public by request. The other Rhode Island lighthouses are **Beavertail,** off Jamestown, and facilities at Hog Island, Point Judith, Conimicut, Sakonnet, Warwick, Sandy Point, and Goat Island.

MUSEUMS Providence, in particular, is rich in museums and libraries with special exhibits on permanent display. Most notable among them are the **Museum of Art, Rhode Island School of Design** (401-454-6500); the **John Hay Library** (401-863-2146), the **Annmary Brown Memorial** (401-863-2942), and the **John Carter Brown Library** (401-863-2725) at Brown University; the **John Brown House Museum** (401-273-7507); the **Governor Henry Lippitt House Museum** (401-453-0688); the **Johnson & Wales Culinary Arts Museum** (401-598-2805); **Rhode Island Historical Society Library** (401-273-8107) at Aldrich House; the **Rhode Island Black Her-**

Michele Rajotte

itage Society (401-751-3490); and **Roger Williams Park Museum of Natural History** (401-785-9450).

Other major museums include the **Herreshoff Marine Museum** (401-253-5000) in Bristol; the **South County Museum** (401-783-5400) in Narragansett; the **Newport Art Museum** (401-848-8200), the **Newport Historical Society Museum** (401-846-0813), the **Redwood Library and Athenaeum** (401-847-0292), the **International Tennis Hall of Fame** (401-849-3990), and the **Museum of Yachting** (401-847-1018) in Newport; and the **Providence Children's Museum** (401-273-5437) and the **Slater Mill Historic Site** (401-725-8638) in Pawtucket. The **US Naval War College** (401-841-4052), part of the Naval Education Training Center in Newport, maintains an excellent **Naval War College Museum,** with many exhibits on the art and science of naval warfare and local seafaring history.

MUSIC SERIES, SUMMER The **Newport Music Festival,** founded in 1969, presents some of the world's finest chamber musicians and introduces important new musical talent each July. More than 50 concerts are held over the course of two weeks in Newport's historic mansions. The **Jazz Festival Newport** and the **Newport Folk Festival** are outdoor events held each August at Fort Adams State Park. The folk festival brings national talents. The University of Rhode Island in Kingston holds the **Summer Chamber Music Festival** in June and July. In July and August there are **Carousel Bayside Concerts** outdoors at Rose Larisa Park in East Providence, **Summer-Concerts-by-the-Bay** at Blithewold Mansion and Gardens in Bristol, and the **Lafayette Band** plays pop music at both indoor and outdoor concerts in North Kingstown. These are among the summer events listed in the events calendar of the **Rhode Island Tourism Division's** *Rhode Island Travel Guide* (401-278-9100 or 1-800-556-2484; www.visitrhodeisland.com). (See also *Special Events* listed at the end of each chapter.)

NATURE PRESERVES, COASTAL **Block Island's Scenic Natural Areas** in New Shoreham encompass 175 acres in different locales, offering various activities such as hiking and historical and nature programs. **East Beach/Ninigret Conservation Area** in Charlestown covers 174 acres. Activities include swimming, naturalist programs, fishing and shellfishing, hunting (rabbits, waterfowl), and camping. **Narragansett Bay National Estuarine Research Reserve** in Portsmouth preserves thousands of acres on Hope, Patience, and Prudence Islands. Hope Island is closed during spring and fall because of nesting birds. Naturalist programs are offered in summer at the

Kim Grant

north and south ends of Prudence, which is accessible by public ferry from Bristol. There is no public transportation to either Patience or Hope. **Norman Bird Sanctuary** in Middletown contains 450 acres; hiking, bird-watching, and naturalist programs are popular activities there. Other nature preserves that are ideal for hiking and birding include **Emilie Ruecker Wildlife Refuge** in Tiverton; **Sachuest Point National Wildlife Refuge** in Middletown, with 242 acres of salt marsh, beaches, and grasslands; and the 641-acre **Trustom Pond National Wildlife Refuge** in South Kingstown.

NATURE PRESERVES, INLAND **Fisherville Brook Wildlife Refuge** in Exeter contains 70 acres. Hiking is popular here, with wooded trails to a pond with a waterfall. **Great Swamp Wildlife Management Area** in South Kingstown preserves 3,293 acres for hiking, fishing, and hunting. Hikers enjoy 550 acres at **Parker Woodland** in Coventry, and **Powder Mill Ledges Refuge** in Smithfield, headquarters of the Audubon Society of Rhode Island, is open to the public daily for hiking through field and forest. The second largest natural pond in Rhode Island is at **Kimball Wildlife Refuge** in Charlestown.

NEWSPAPERS The ***Providence Journal*** is the statewide newspaper, although many communities have their own dailies and/or weeklies, such as *Newport This Week* (online www.newport-now.com) in Newport, which includes updated calendar listings for events in the City by the Sea. In Providence, the free ***Providence Phoenix,*** a cousin of the *Boston Phoenix,* is for the younger crowd and is an excellent source of entertainment (concerts, bar bands, literary events) listings.

OBSERVATORIES **Frosty Drew** (401-364-9508), Ninigret Park, off RI 1A, Charlestown. Open on clear Friday nights, year-round. **Ladd Observatory** (401-863-2323), 210 Doyle Avenue, corner of Hope Street in Providence. Open one or two nights weekly for viewing. Located on the highest point in Providence and with a powerful refractor telescope, Ladd Observatory, which is affiliated with Brown University, is an excellent facility for viewing planets. All observatories are free.

PARKS AND FORESTS Rhode Island has a number of state parks open to the public for hiking, swimming, boating, fishing, picnicking, and in-line skating. Many offer naturalist and recreational programs. Hunting is possible at **Arcadia Management Area** in West Greenwich, Exeter, and Hopkinton, which also provides forestry demonstrations. **Goddard Memorial State Park** in Warwick contains 472 acres, and saltwater fishing is among the activities available there. Other state parks include: **Beavertail State Park** in Jamestown, 153 acres; **Brenton Point State Park** in Newport, 89 acres; **Burlingame State Park** in Charlestown, 2,100 wooded acres; **Colt State Park** in Bristol, 466 acres; **Haines Memorial State Park** in Barrington, 85 acres; and **Lincoln Woods State Park** in Lincoln, 627 acres.

POPULATION According to the latest census information, Rhode Island's population stands at 1,052,567, considerably more than in 1790, when 68,825 souls were counted. Rhode Island is the country's smallest and most densely populated state, with more than 900 people per square mile. Because most of the population is centered on Providence, however, the state seems predominantly rural.

QUAHOG The quahog is the official shellfish of Rhode Island. This large, hard-shell clam (pronounced *co-hog*) is used in chowder or mixed with bread, spices, and sometimes chourico, the Portuguese sausage, to make stuffed clams, or "stuffies," as they're known. Stuffies are available at clam shacks everywhere. An annual festival devoted to the quahog is held in Wickford in early October.

RATES, LODGING AND DINING Prices change frequently, and the value of your dollar will vary significantly from one part of the state to another (expect to pay more for a meal or a bed in Newport, for example). Dollar-sign symbols are provided throughout the guide to give you a general sense of what you can expect to pay. Please refer to "Explore with Us" on page 6. Such a rating method, though commonly used, is imprecise, and we always recommend calling ahead to check rates and reservations. We have highlighted inns and restaurants that offer unusual value with the symbol "💲."

SAILING LESSONS Newport is the sailing center, and there are many sailing schools and programs to choose from: **Fort Adams Sailing Association** (401-849-8385; www.sailnewport.org) is a nonprofit group offering lessons for juniors and adults; **J World Sailing School** (401-849-5492) provides cruising and racing instruction by the makers of J-boats; **Newport Sailing School** (401-848-2266) offers two- and three-day learn-to-sail programs; **Shake-a-Leg Sailing Center** in Middletown (401-849-8898) has special 20-foot sloops equipped for the physically challenged.

SCENIC DRIVES With 400 miles of coastline and a rural interior, Rhode Island offers many scenic routes. Among those officially designated as scenic routes are **RI 1A,** which runs from Narragansett to Wickford along the coast; **RI 3,** leading from the coast in East Greenwich inland to Hope Valley; **RI 77,** following the Sakonnet River through Tiverton to Little Compton; and **RI 138,** which takes you over the Jamestown Bridge to the island of Conanicut.

Kim Grant

SKIING, CROSS-COUNTRY Cross-country skiing can be found at **Goddard State Park** (401-884-2010) in Warwick; **Norman Bird Sanctuary** (401-846-2577) in Middletown; **Pulaski State Park** (401-568-2085) in Burrillville; and **Slater Memorial Park** (401-728-0500) in Pawtucket.

SKIING, DOWNHILL **Yawgoo Valley** (401-295-5366; www.yawgoo.com) in Exeter is the state's only remaining downhill ski area. It is quite small, with basic services.

STEAMERS These clams form the basis of the Rhode Island clamboil, or are just served steamed on a platter with clarified butter or clam broth (or both) for dipping. You'll get an occasional argument about exactly what a steamer is—small quahog, littleneck, cherrystone—but most natives agree that it is simply a small, soft-shell clam normally found in tidal flats. Littlenecks are, in fact, small quahogs (steamers have long necks); cherrystones are larger (older) members of the family, followed by the largest quahogs, called "chowders."

TAXES Rhode Island has a sales tax of 7 percent, which does not apply to clothes, food, or drugs. Lodgers are subject to a state room tax of 13 percent.

THEATER, SUMMER Matunuck's **Theatre-by-the-Sea** (401-782-8587; www.theatrebythesea.com) is a summer tradition in South County. It is known for energetic performances of musicals and other light Broadway fare. **The Colonial Theatre** (401-596-7909; http://thecolonialtheatre.org) offers outdoor performances such as Shakespeare in the Park in Westerly.

THEATER, YEAR-ROUND The **Granite Theatre** (401-596-2341; www.granitetheatre.com) in Westerly serves up contemporary plays in a beautifully restored 19th-century church. In Warren, **2nd Story Theatre** (401-247-4200; www.2ndstorytheatre.com) offers classics like Shakespeare and Ibsen as well as contemporary plays, and in Pawtucket the **Sandra Feinstein-Gamm Theatre** (401-723-4266; www.gammtheatre.org) productions are sometimes traditional and sometimes politically charged. The Tony Award–winning **Trinity Repertory Theater** (401-351-4242; www.trinityrep.com) in downtown Providence is widely regarded as one of the best regional theaters in the country. There is plenty of theater at area colleges, some of it quite good, and touring companies performing Broadway shows *(Les Mis, Mary Poppins)* make regular stops at the **Providence Performing Arts Center** (401-421-2997). Smaller Providence theaters presenting less mainstream, sometimes original, works include **Newgate Theatre** (401-454-0454), **Perishable Theatre** (401-331-2695), and **Brown**

University Theater (401-863-2838). Two popular dinner theaters are the **Newport Playhouse & Cabaret** (401-848-7529) and **Mill River Dinner Theater** (401-721-0909) in Central Falls. It's worth calling ahead for schedules and special performances if you know you'll be in the area.

TRAIN SERVICE **Amtrak** (1-800-USA-RAIL) makes stops at Westerly, Kingston, and Providence on its Boston–New York runs. The Kingston stop is convenient for those traveling to Newport or South County.

Kim Grant

VINEYARDS **Sakonnet Vineyards** in Little Compton (401-635-8486; www.sakonnetwine.com) lets you sample some of its award-winning vintages during guided tours Wednesday through Sunday noon–4 in-season. **Newport Vineyards** (401-848-5161; www.newportvineyards.com) operates a retail store in Middletown and also offers tours of its nearby vineyard. **Diamond Hill Vineyards** (401-333-2751; www.favorlabel.com) offers tours in Cumberland. Greenvale Vineyards (401-847-3777; www.greenvale.com) offers tours in Portsmouth.

WHALE-WATCHING The best whale-watching is out of Galilee in Narragansett. Contact either the **Frances Fleet** (401-783-4988 or 1-800-662-2824; www.francesfleet.com) or **Seven B's** (401-789-9250; www.sevenbs.com).

WINDJAMMERS Newport is the premier port for windjammer-type sailing cruises. Boats 70 feet and longer make regular half-day, day, and evening sails, among them the ***Adirondack*** (401-647-0000; www.sail-newport.com), a 78-foot schooner departing from the end of Bowen's Wharf; and ***Madeleine*** (401-849-3033), a 72-foot schooner sailing from Bannister's Wharf.

YACHTING The popularity of yachting in Rhode Island is well known—the America's Cup was traditionally held in Newport until the American loss in 1983. In addition to weekly local and statewide events, Newport, in particular, plays host to a number of national and international regattas and ocean races, including the **Annapolis to Newport Race,** the biennial **Newport to Bermuda Race,** and the **Classic Yacht Regatta.** For information, contact Sail Newport (401-846-1983; www.sailnewport.org). Not surprisingly, Rhode Island has several excellent museums devoted to yachting, including the **Museum of Yachting** in Newport (401-847-1018; www.moy.org) and the **Herreshoff Marine Museum** and **America's Cup Hall of Fame** in Bristol (401-253-5000; www.herreshoff.org), both well worth visiting.

ZOO **Roger Williams Park Zoo** (401-785-3510; www.rwpzoo.org), 950 Elmwood Avenue, exit 17 off I-95 in Providence, is the only zoo in Rhode Island. A serious attempt is made to create natural habitats for its various critters, and a multi-million-dollar renovation and expansion is under way.

1 Providence

Kim Grant

PROVIDENCE

It was January 1636, and colonial officials of the Puritan Massachusetts Bay Colony were eager to be rid of the reformer-clergyman Roger Williams. He believed in the separation of church and state, and loudly criticized civil authorities of the colony, who were decreeing punishments for infractions of church rules. Williams associated enthusiastically with the Native Americans most colonists feared, and indeed he insisted that the king of England had no right to give away Native American lands. When a vessel was readying for departure to England, the officials made secret arrangements to deport the independent-spirited clergyman. But word of the plot reached Williams just before the vessel was to sail, and with only one companion, Thomas Angell, he fled.

That winter was stormy, and snows were heavy. For 14 weeks the two refugees wandered the woods, seeking a place outside the Massachusetts Bay Colony to settle.

As spring came, their wandering brought them to the banks of the Seekonk River. The land bordering the river looked fertile, and the men felt sure that they were outside Massachusetts's jurisdiction. The Native Americans they met seemed friendly. As the two men prepared to settle down, they sent word back to their Massachusetts Bay friends that they would welcome any who chose to join them. More refugees began to arrive. Building was under way when suddenly a warning came from the governor of the neighboring Plymouth Bay Colony: Williams's site, which today is East Providence, was on Plymouth lands, and Williams's presence would not be tolerated.

Grimly, the settlers packed up their belongings, piled them into their one canoe, and launched it on the river, heading toward what they hoped would be friendlier territory on the opposite shore. Fortunately for the settlers, it belonged to the Narragansett chief Canonicus. Williams had known Canonicus during the time he had spent in Plymouth, and the chief made Williams and his companions welcome.

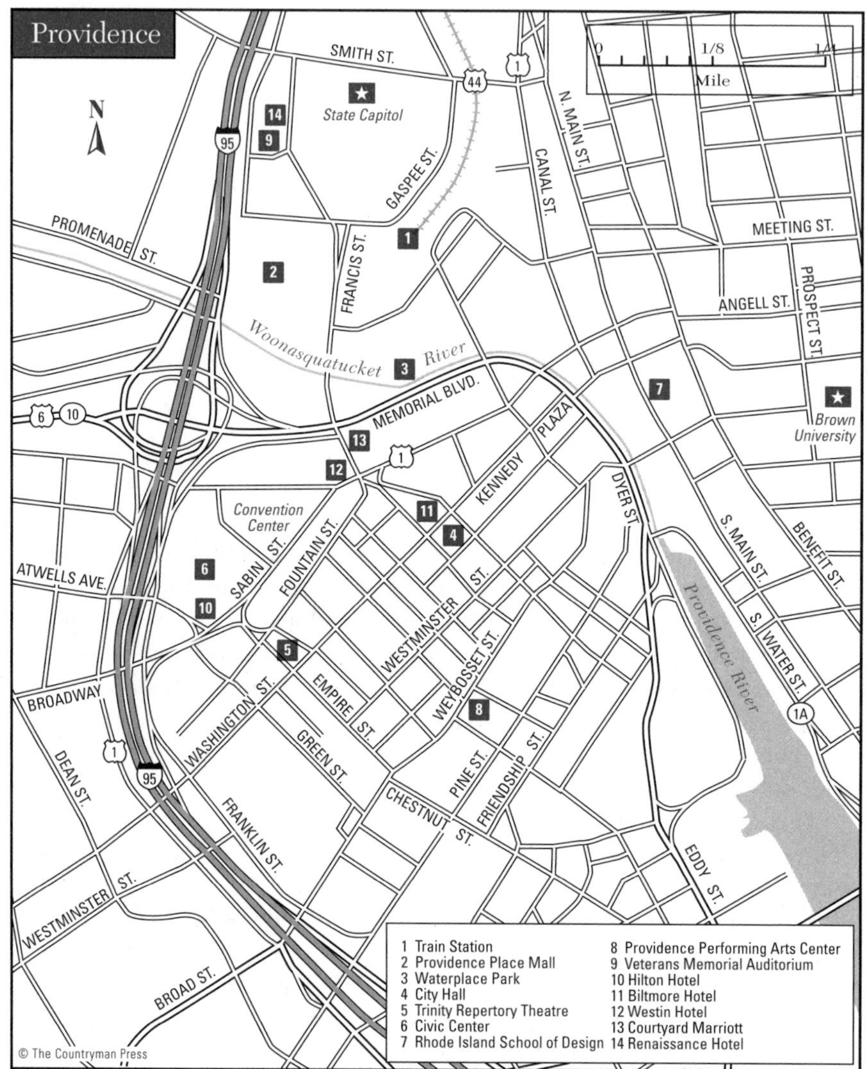
Providence
N
0
1/8
1/4
Mile
SMITH ST.
State Capitol
GASPEE ST.
FRANCIS ST.
PROMENADE ST.
CANAL ST.
N. MAIN ST.
MEETING ST.
ANGELL ST.
PROSPECT ST.
Woonasquatucket River
MEMORIAL BLVD.
KENNEDY PLAZA
DYER ST.
Brown University
Convention Center
SABIN ST.
FOUNTAIN ST.
ATWELLS AVE.
WESTMINSTER ST.
WEYBOSSET ST.
EMPIRE ST.
WASHINGTON ST.
GREEN ST.
BROADWAY
DEAN ST.
FRANKLIN ST.
CHESTNUT ST.
PINE ST.
FRIENDSHIP ST.
S. MAIN ST.
BENEFIT ST.
S. WATER ST.
Providence River
EDDY ST.
WESTMINSTER ST.
BROAD ST.
1 Train Station
2 Providence Place Mall
3 Waterplace Park
4 City Hall
5 Trinity Repertory Theatre
6 Civic Center
7 Rhode Island School of Design
8 Providence Performing Arts Center
9 Veterans Memorial Auditorium
10 Hilton Hotel
11 Biltmore Hotel
12 Westin Hotel
13 Courtyard Marriott
14 Renaissance Hotel
© The Countryman Press

The settlers wasted no time in clearing the land, which the clergyman named Providence in gratitude for God's providence to him in his distress, and which, Williams declared, would ever afterward be a place of refuge for the oppressed. By 1675 there were 1,000 residents and some 75 houses. More than two dozen of these were burned to the ground in a Native American attack in 1676, but, determinedly, the settlers rebuilt. In 1680 a wharf was added to facilitate trade, and Providence's days of prosperity began.

Today, with a population of about 180,000, Providence is the capital of Rhode Island and New England's second-largest city, after Boston. Like so many other New England cities, its downtown suffered noticeably in the era of the suburban mall. In recent years, however, the heart of the city has undergone a near-miraculous renewal.

New hotels—boutique, high-style, and grand gathering places for conventioneers—have risen. Long-abandoned department stores have been transformed into apartments and elegant condos attracting new urbanites. Students are everywhere. Where the city's largest department store, The Outlet Company, once stood, Johnson & Wales University has a pretty urban campus. Another former department store has become the site of continuing-education classes for the University of Rhode Island. In an early-20th-century bank building, the Rhode Island School of Design now has both its library and a dormitory. New shops selling gifts, home

THE CRAWFORD STREET BRIDGE CROSSES THE PROVIDENCE RIVER IN THE REVITALIZED DOWNTOWN AREA.

Kim Grant

furnishings, and designer clothes have opened. So, too, have new restaurants.

The city's old commercial area along Westminster, Weybosset, and Washington Streets is the only metropolitan commercial district in the nation to be listed in its entirety on the National Register of Historic Places.

Walkways wind along Providence's downtown rivers. On WaterFire nights in spring, summer, and fall, 100 ritual fires glow in the rivers' midstream. The pyres burn from sunset to after midnight, and exotic otherworldly music—sometimes chants, sometimes folk music, sometimes opera—plays. It's a spectacle that attracts thousands. Gondolas and water taxis can be rented for a closer view of WaterFire.

Here and there along the rivers, illustrated signs recount the colorful history of the city. Restaurants and cafés line the riverfront. On South Main Street, a World War II memorial has joined World War I and Korean War memorials at Monument Square.

Since its construction in the mid-1990s, the Rhode Island Convention Center has been attracting boat, garden, home, car, and pet shows, as well as major conventions. Pop concerts, sporting events, and other entertainments such as Ringling Bros. and Barnum & Bailey Circus shows fill the Dunkin' Donuts Center with viewers year-round.

The state's largest indoor shopping center, Providence Place—with 150 retail stores including Macy's and Nordstrom, an IMAX theater, and several full-service restaurants—is next to the State House. Close by, a new Marriott Renaissance Hotel was created in 2007 from a derelict 1920s neoclassical Masonic temple.

The Providence art scene has been enlivened with the opening of The Steel Yard near Eagle Square. There, old factory spaces have been turned into workshops and studios for glassblowers, welders, and sculptors who fashion art out of recycled industrial materials.

Meanwhile, in old Providence, Benefit Street is considered by many to have the richest concentration of 18th- and 19th-century architecture in America. All along the streets of the city's East Side, tall brick and clapboard mansions proclaim the wealth that the shipping trade brought to the city during those centuries. When the British occupied Newport in Revolutionary War days, many Newport merchants fled to Providence with their money and goods to establish themselves in trade there. Foremost among them was James Brown, who established a distillery and a slaughterhouse and entered the shipping trade, and whose sons John, Nicholas, Joseph, and Moses brought wealth and fame to the city.

John, merchant and shipbuilder, opened trade with China. Joseph became an architect and built many of the city's most handsome edifices. Nicholas provided land and money to establish the university that bears the family's name. Moses gave land for the establishment of a Quaker school and helped William Slater introduce the first water-powered cotton mill in the nation in neighboring Pawtucket.

GUIDANCE **Rhode Island Tourism Division** (401-278-9100; 1-800-556-2484; www.visitrhodeisland.com), 555 Valley Street, Suite 101. Open Monday through Friday 8:30–4:30. This central tourist office has a limited supply of booklets and brochures about travel in all parts of the state, including the capital, but access to more material is on the website.

Roger Williams National Memorial (401-521-7266; www.nps.gov/rowi), North Main and Smith Streets. Open daily 9–4:30 except major holidays. An interpretation of the life and times of Roger Williams and the city he founded is offered through exhibits, videos, booklets, and brochures and by National Park Service guides. On-site parking.

Providence-Warwick Visitor Information Center (401-274-1636; 1-800-233-1636; www.goprovidence.com), Rhode Island Convention Center, 1 Sabin Street, in the rotunda on the ground floor. Open Monday through Saturday 9–5. Booklets and brochures about the city are available at this usually staffed facility. Parking is limited to 15 minutes.

GETTING THERE *By car:* The major roads into the city are I-95 north and south, I-195 east and west, RI 146 north and south, RI 10 north and south, US 1 north and south, US 44 east and west, and US 6 east and west.

By air: **T. F. Green State Airport** (401-737-4000) is located 7 miles south of Providence in Warwick and is served by major airlines.

By rail: **Amtrak** (401-727-7380; 1-800-USA-RAIL; www.amtrak.com) links Boston and New York through Providence, and at peak commuter times there is also **MBTA** (617-222-6020) commuter rail service with Boston. All trains use the station at 100 Gaspee Street across from the State House.

By bus: **Peter Pan Bonanza** (401-751-8800; www.peterpanbus.com), 1 Bonanza Way. **Greyhound** (401-454-0790; 1-800-231-2222), 1 Kennedy Plaza. The bus terminal is on the outskirts of the city, and a 10-minute shuttle bus links it with downtown.

MEDICAL EMERGENCY The statewide emergency number is **911.**

Miriam Hospital (401-331-8500), 164 Summit Avenue.

Rhode Island Hospital (401-444-4000), 593 Eddy Street.

Roger Williams Medical Center (401-456-2000), 825 Chalkstone Avenue.

St. Joseph's Hospital (401-456-3000), 200 High Service Avenue, North Providence.

Women & Infants Hospital (401-274-1100), 101 Dudley Street.

✷ To See

HISTORIC HOMES AND SITES The Arcade, 65 Weybosset Street. In 1850 *Guyot's Geography* listed this shopping arcade (temporarily closed as this book went to press) as one of the Seven Wonders of the United States. Architecturally, the Arcade remains a memorable building. In 1827 Providence banker and investor Cyrus Butler conceived the idea of a covered shopping arcade with colonnaded facades that would recall l'Église de la Madeleine in Paris. Wealthy man though he was, Butler faced problems with its construction. Although he owned half the land on which the proposed arcade was to be built, Benjamin and Charles Dyer owned the other half. They were interested in such a building, but they wanted a say in its design. Butler hired architect Russell Warren to design his half, and the Dyers hired James C. Bucklin to design theirs. Fortunately, both architects admired Greek Revival, so there was no altercation—until it came to the facade. Bucklin wanted a series of stone panels to decorate the pediment; Warren favored a simple triangle. The problem was solved by placing Warren's pediment on the Westminster Street end and Bucklin's panels on the Weybosset Street end. They agreed on 22-foot-tall granite monoliths to support the pediments on both sides. At the time of construction, these 12- to 15-ton pillars were the largest monoliths in the country. Hauling them from the quarry in Johnston, Rhode Island, required 12 to 18 oxen. In addition to the pillars, architectural high points of the Arcade are the ironwork on the upper stories of the three-tiered edifice and the cantilevered stairs between the street and the second floor.

ANGELL STREET BY THOMAS H. COCROFT

Beneficent Congregational Meeting House (401-331-9844), 300 Weybosset Street. For years the large gilded dome of this church was a landmark on the Providence skyline. Built in 1809, its dome is unusual for a Congregational church of its day. It was the choice of the congregation's second pastor, the Reverend James Wilson, who came to Providence from Ireland in 1791. Classical Revival was popular in Dublin at that time, and to some extent the church imitates the Customs House in Dublin. In 1836 architect James C. Bucklin supervised renovations.

John Brown House Museum (401-273-7507; www.rihs.org), 52 Power Street (at the corner of Benefit Street). Call for hours. This museum of Federal-period life in Rhode Island, as seen through the Brown family, can be viewed on guided tours only, and these vary with the season, so it is best to call for details. Mannequins in period costume help bring the house and the period to life. Joseph Brown designed this three-story brick house with brownstone trim for his shipowner brother John, but died before it was completed in 1788. John Quincy Adams called it "the most magnificent and elegant private house I have seen on this continent." At the time of its construction, it had an uninterrupted view of the harbor below and of John Brown's vessels arriving from the Orient laden with tea, silk, and china. Brown's fortuitous decision to trade in the Orient came as a result of failures in the slave trade. After one vessel carrying slaves was lost and half the slaves on a second died of scurvy, Brown's abolitionist Quaker mates encouraged him to substitute canisters of tea and bolts of silk for human cargo. Before long, Brown was the city's wealthiest merchant.

George Washington was among the guests here, for Brown was devoted to the rebel cause, providing ships from his shipyard and cannon from the family foundry for the Revolutionary army. Furnishings include Hepplewhite, Sheraton, Townsend, and Goddard pieces. There is Chinese export ware, Sandwich glass, Staffordshire earthenware, and, in the coach house, a chariot made in Philadelphia in 1782 that is reputedly the earliest "fancy" vehicle made in America.

Brown University, Prospect and Waterman Streets. Turn right on Benevolent Street and left at the first corner to begin exploring this extensive campus. The privately owned redbrick **Candace Allen House,** where you turn, was built by Providence industrialist Zachariah Allen to soften the heartache his daughter suffered when her fiancé was killed in the War of 1812. **University Hall,** off Prospect Street, is the university's oldest building, constructed in 1770 when the college was moved from Warren. During the Revolution, University Hall became a barracks for the colonial troops and their French allies. The seventh-oldest college in the nation, Brown was founded in 1764 and took its name, after its move to Providence, from Nicholas Brown, who gave it extensive funds and land.

Kim Grant

THE HILLTOP CAMPUS OF BROWN UNIVERSITY ABOVE THE CITY OF PROVIDENCE

General Ambrose Burnside House, 314 Benefit Street. When it was completed in 1867 for General Burnside (after whom sideburns were named), this privately owned, sprawling redbrick house with stone, wood, and cast-iron trim, plus a curved corner and a wraparound porch, was lauded as one of the finest "modern" houses in Providence. At the time of its construction, Burnside, just back from the Civil War, had been elected governor of Rhode Island. Later he became a US senator.

Edward Carrington House, 66 Williams Street. This three-story Federal-style brick mansion was built as a two-story house in 1810 by John Corliss. Edward Carrington, one of the city's wealthiest merchants and American consul in China from 1808 to 1811, purchased it and added the third story and the richly decorated entrance porch. The house is considered one of the city's great architectural monuments, but it is not open to the public.

Cathedral of St. John (401-331-4622), 271 North Main Street. Under the inspiration of Charles Bulfinch, Providence architect John Holden Greene designed this white-and-brown 1810 cathedral, combining a basically Georgian-style structure with a Gothic Revival tower and Gothic decoration.

Captain Edward Dexter House, 72 Waterman Street. Built in 1799, this is one of the most elaborate Federal-style houses in the city. It was once the home of Charles Pendleton, and its original interior has been re-created at Pendleton House, adjoining the RISD Museum.

Sullivan Dorr House, 109 Benefit Street. This imposing house was built in 1810 for a China-trade merchant. One of Providence's finest examples of Federal architecture, its facade is supposedly a copy of Alexander Pope's villa at Twickenham, England. It was Thomas Wilson Dorr, Sullivan's son, who instigated the Dorr Rebellion of 1842, seeking suffrage for all freemen, not only property owners. The house, now privately owned, is built on the lot that originally belonged to Roger Williams. He was first buried behind where the house stands, but his remains were later removed to the city's North Burial Ground and after that to Prospect Terrace.

East Providence. Both East Providence and the **Fox Point** section of Providence are largely Portuguese enclaves, with ethnic bakeries, other food shops, and—especially in East Providence—a number of Portuguese restaurants.

Federal Hill. The entrance to the Italian section of Providence, located on Federal Hill just above the heart of the city, is marked by a cement arch topped with a pinecone expressing hospitality. Restaurants, bakeries, cafés, and food shops line the main thoroughfare—Atwells Avenue—and many of its side streets. As in downtown Providence, the last 15 years have marked a revival on Federal Hill. New restaurants, boutiques, and upscale food markets now line the avenue, attracting a younger clientele from all over the city. At De Pasquale Square, once the place where older men of the neighborhood gathered around the fountain on sunny afternoons, there are now outdoor cafés and restaurants along with a boutique hotel. For the visitor interested in architecture, there are a number of large and interesting turn-of-the-century and early-20th-century structures on the Hill.

First Baptist Meeting House (401-454-3418), 75 North Main Street. This graceful, simple structure was designed by Joseph Brown and is topped with a steeple inspired by St. Martin-in-the-Fields in London. This 1775 church succeeded two earlier ones that had been used for the Baptist worship introduced by Roger Williams in 1638. Ships' carpenters from Boston, out of work because Parliament had closed the port after the Boston Tea Party, constructed it. Familiar with masts and rigging, the builders knew to allow the steeple sufficient give; it swayed just enough not to topple in either the gale of 1815 or the hurricane of 1938. This was the first Baptist church in America and is the mother church for Baptists in this country. Notable in its pale gray interior barely touched with gold are the Ionic columns and the Waterford glass chandelier, first lit in 1792 for the wedding of the architect's niece, Hope. Guided tours are offered from June through the Columbus Day weekend, 10–noon and 1–3.

Kim Grant

IN DOWNTOWN PROVIDENCE

First Unitarian Church (401-421-4970), Benefit and Benevolent Streets. John Holden Greene, who built this tall stone church in 1816 to replace a two-towered wooden structure that had burned, considered it his masterpiece. Its steeple holds the largest bell ever cast in the Paul Revere and Sons Foundry.

Grace Church (401-331-3225), Mathewson and Westminster Streets. This Victorian Gothic brownstone church was built in 1846. Designed by Richard Upjohn of New York, it is notable for its chimes.

Handicraft Club, 42 College Street. Banker and cotton merchant Thomas Beckwith commissioned John Holden Greene to build this Federal-style brick mansion in 1826, much to the horror of Beckwith's family, who felt that the site selected was much too "far out in the sticks" for respectable city people. Today it's open to club members and occasionally to the public.

Governor Stephen Hopkins House (401-421-0694), 15 Hopkins Street. Open May through October, Friday and Saturday 1–4 and by appointment. Stephen Hopkins, one of Rhode Island's two signers of the Declaration of Independence, lived in this house from 1742 to 1785. Long an outspoken opponent of royal oppression in the colonies, Hopkins, his hand stricken by palsy, reportedly said as he prepared to sign the Declaration, "My hand trembles, but my heart does not." Hopkins was governor of the colony of Rhode Island 10 times, chief justice of the Superior Court, and the first chancellor of Brown University. He is credited with moving Brown (then Rhode Island College) from Warren, where it was founded.

Thomas Poynton Ives House, 66 Power Street. Built in 1805 for Thomas Poynton Ives and his wife, Hope Brown (for whose marriage the chandelier in the First Baptist Meeting House was first lit), this privately owned Federal house is similar in design to the John Brown House.

Governor Henry Lippitt House (401-453-0688; www.preserveri.org), 199 Hope Street. Open May through October, Friday 11–3 or by appointment. From its construction in 1863 until 1981, this brownstone-trimmed brick Italianate dwelling remained in the Lippitt family. Henry Lippitt, for whom it was built, was Rhode Island's governor from 1876 to 1877. Its interior boasts the finest mid-19th-century Renaissance Revival decorations by local craftsmen in the city. Most notable are the marbleized center hall and the faux-bois ceilings and paneling in both the hall and the billiard room, as well as the stenciling. The house is furnished with Victorian antiques that largely belonged to the family.

Market House, Market Square. This square redbrick building with its fanlights is a design of Joseph Brown's. In 1771, when its construction began, it was carefully sited on a bank of the Providence River so that produce could be brought directly to and from it by ship. In the years immediately preceding the Revolution, this was a center of much intrigue, and in March 1775 tea was angrily burned nearby in response to the tea tax. A plaque marks the spot. Another plaque marks the height reached by the floodwaters of the devastating hurricane of 1938. From 1832 until 1878, this was the seat of Providence city government.

Nightingale-Brown House, 357 Benefit Street. One of the largest colonial frame houses in existence, this three-and-a-half-story clapboard home, half hidden behind a wall, was built for Providence merchant Colonel Joseph Nightingale in 1792. He died soon after its completion, and his widow sold it to Nicholas Brown, for whom Brown University, previously Rhode Island College, was named. (Legend has it that Nicholas Brown, on the board of Rhode Island College and seeking funds for it, proposed that it be named for the donor of a substantial gift. He subsequently became that donor.) Until the 1980s the house remained the residence of succeeding generations of the Brown family. The last family member to occupy it was Anne Kinsolving Brown, widow of John Nicholas Brown, who, when he was born in 1900, was described by the *New York Post* as "the world's richest baby." In the 1930s, after the Lindbergh kidnapping and when John Nicholas's children were growing up, a curious cagelike structure was constructed on top of the house so that the children could play outdoors in safety. The house is now the home of the master's program in public humanities at Brown University.

The Old Arsenal, 176 Benefit Street. James Bucklin designed this Gothic Revival, fortress-like stone structure in 1840 for the Providence Marine Corps of Artillery, the first volunteer artillery battery in the country.

The Old State House (401-222-2678), 150 Benefit Street. Open Monday through Friday 8:30–4:30, visits preferably by appointment. From 1762 until 1900 this was the meeting place of the General Assembly, where on

May 4, 1776, the act was passed "constituting Rhode Island the first free and independent republic in America and asserting her absolute independence of England." Two months later the Declaration of Independence was signed in Philadelphia. Today, this is the headquarters of the Rhode Island Historical Preservation Commission.

South Main Street. Two fine old mansions along this street may be viewed from the outside: the Federal-style Benoni Cooke House at no. 110, with its side entrance, and the Joseph Brown House at no. 50, with its gracefully curved white pediment. A tale is told of how in the 18th century, when the entrance to the Brown House was on the second floor, an officer of the French army billeted there gaily rode his horse up the stairs and into the front hall. The horse refused to walk back down the stairs and had to be led out a direct exit into the garden.

South Water Street. Once the site of the Providence Steam Engine Company, a mid-19th-century complex of stone and brick buildings, today this area is filled with trendy restaurants, bars, galleries, and nightclubs. There is an incomparable view of the river and cityscape from many of them and from walkways in front of them.

State House (401-222-2080), 90 Smith Street. Open Monday through Friday 8:30–4:30. The white marble dome of this imposing early-1900s capitol is said to be one of the largest unsupported domes in the world.

THE WHITE MARBLE DOME OF THE RHODE ISLAND STATE HOUSE IS SAID TO BE ONE OF THE LARGEST UNSUPPORTED DOMES IN THE WORLD.

Sal Laterra

The State House holds two notable works of art: in the Governor's Reception Room, a full-length portrait of George Washington painted by Saunderstown native Gilbert Stuart; and on the first floor, a portrait of Civil War general Ambrose Burnside by Emanuel Leutze, the artist noted for his painting *Washington Crossing the Delaware*. Also of interest is the original parchment charter granted by Charles II to the colony of Rhode Island in 1663, and the sword, epaulets, field desk, locket, and signets of Warwick-born Nathanael Greene, Washington's second-in-command.

Thomas Street. The redbrick Providence Art Club, built in 1791 for Seril Dodge, Providence's first jewelry maker, is at no. 11 on this steep little street. His brother Nehemiah, also a Providence jeweler, developed the gold-plating process that made Rhode Island a major jewelry center. The half-timbered Fleur-de-Lys Building at no. 7 was constructed as a studio for Rhode Island artist Sidney R. Burleigh in 1886. Much of the molded, painted, and carved exterior studio decoration is of his design and was executed by Burleigh and fellow artists. The building continues to house studios.

Wickenden Street. Boutiques, art galleries, coffee shops, ethnic restaurants, antiques and collectibles stores, all in old buildings—some restored and some not-so-restored—make this an attractive, lively street by day or night for young singles and couples.

Betsey Williams Cottage (401-785-9457), Roger Williams Park, near the Elmwood Avenue entrance. This little gambrel-roofed house, built in 1785, belonged to a descendant of Roger Williams, who gave the first 100 acres for the establishment of the park. It is closed to the public.

LIBRARIES **John Carter Brown Library** (401-863-2725), Brown University campus, George and Brown Streets. Open Monday through Friday 8:30–5, Saturday 9–noon. The first printed accounts of Columbus's arrival in the New World are among the library's collection of 40,000 books and pamphlets describing the development of the New World.

John Hay Library (401-863-3723; http://library.brown.edu/about/hay/), Prospect and College Streets. Open Monday through Thursday 10–6 and Friday 10–5 during the school year. Otherwise 10–5 Monday through Friday. Brown University's special collections are kept here; call for an appointment to see them. Among them is the third-largest collection of Lincoln material in the world (after those at the Illinois Historical Society and the Lincoln National Life Insurance Company of Fort Wayne, Indiana), including some 900 Lincoln manuscripts. Also among the library's treasures are more than 500,000 pieces of American sheet music, thousands of miniature soldiers (including a 20th-century Indian army with elephants and a Nazi motorcycle unit), and letters written by Rhode

Island Gothic writer H. P. Lovecraft, who stalked Benefit Street in the dark for inspiration for his eerie stories.

Providence Athenaeum (401-421-6970), 251 Benefit Street. Open Monday through Thursday 9–7, Friday and Saturday 9–5; also winter Sundays 1–5 and summer Saturdays 9–1. This 1850 Doric Greek granite building houses one of the oldest libraries in the nation—it began as a subscription library in 1851. Among its treasures is an 1801 ivory miniature by Newport artist Edward Malbone that is generally considered the most valuable miniature in the United States. It is in the alcoves here that Edgar Allan Poe courted a fellow poet, the widow Sarah Helen Whitman. The couple met when Poe came to Providence to lecture at Brown University. It's said that Mrs. Whitman was his inspiration for "To Helen" and "Annabel Lee." They became engaged, but the engagement was broken because of Poe's penchant for drink. Broken betrothal notwithstanding, she remained the poet's staunch supporter, writing a notable defense of him. Next to the library, the five brick houses of Athenaeum Row, from 257 to 276 Benefit Street, are of interest. Built in 1845, they are among the city's first row houses.

Rhode Island Historical Society Library (401-331-8575; www.rihs.org), 121 Hope Street. Open Wednesday and Friday 10–5, Thursday noon–8. The second-largest genealogical collection in New England (after Boston's), it includes such materials as birth, death, and marriage records from 1636 to 1850 and 1853 to 1900; maps; census records; books; and historical documents.

MUSEUMS **John Brown House Museum.** See *Historic Homes and Sites.*

Johnson & Wales Culinary Arts Museum (401-598-2805; www.culinary.org), 315 Harborside Boulevard, off Narragansett Boulevard. Open Tuesday through Sunday 10–5. Call for driving directions. There are half a million items of interest in this little museum, the world's largest culinary collection. On display are cooking utensils from the third millennium BC to the present; favorite recipes of American presidents; presidential china; letters of potentates, writers, artists, and composers on culinary matters; hotel and restaurant silver through the centuries; a diner and a history of the New England diner; student-decorated wedding cakes and fancy breads; and pictures and memorabilia of the world's great chefs.

Providence Children's Museum (401-273-5437; www.childrenmuseum.org), 100 South Street. Open Tuesday through Sunday 9–6. Admission is free all day the first Sunday and 5–8 the third Friday of each month. This is a hands-on museum for children 1 to 11 years old, with emphasis on both fun and learning. Young visitors can create their own plays with puppets, props, and costumes; pretend to cook in a 1640 kitchen; sit on a giant's lap; and build bridges, operate a child-sized crane, and lift Styrofoam beams to build a highway.

RISD Museum (Museum of Art, Rhode Island School of Design) (401-454-6500; www.risdmuseum.org), 224 Benefit Street. Open Tuesday through Sunday 10–5; until 9 the third Thursday of each month. Free admission Sunday 10–1 and the last Saturday of each month. Sometimes referred to as "the jewel box of Providence," the RISD (*Riz-dee,* as it's known colloquially throughout the state) Museum is exceptionally rich in Newport silver and cabinetwork, French impressionist painting, and ancient Egyptian and Asian art. There is also a modern wing. The adjoining Pendleton House was built in the Georgian style, according to the stipulations of lawyer-collector Charles Pendleton as a condition for housing his collection there. The collection includes Chinese export ware, English and European porcelain and glassware, rugs, and antique furniture.

✷ To Do

BICYCLING East Bay Bike Path (401-253-7482). Starting in Providence near India Point Park, this bicycle path runs on the bed of a former railroad line along the shore of Narragansett Bay to Bristol. More than 14 miles long, it has two picnic areas (at Haines Memorial State Park in Barrington and Colt State Park in Bristol), restrooms, and telephones along the route, which sometimes passes through towns, sometimes through woods and fields along the bay.

BOAT EXCURSIONS La Gondola (401-421-8877; 508-984-8264; www.gondolari). Forty-minute excursions from May through October on the Woonasquatucket and Providence Rivers aboard 36-foot, six-person gondolas—one made in America from a 19th-century Venetian design, the other made in Venice. Both are decorated with hand-sculpted wooden carvings. Reservations suggested.

FOR FAMILIES ✐ **Bank of America Skating Center** (401-331-5544), 2 Kennedy Plaza. Open Monday through Friday 10–10, and Saturday and Sunday 11–10. Modeled after New York City's Rockefeller Center outdoor ice rink, this facility in the heart of downtown Providence offers skating opportunities for everyone in the family. In winter the skating is on ice; in summer, in-line skating is offered. Both in-line and ice skate rentals are available.

✐ **Charles I. D. Looff Carousel** at Crescent Park (401-433-3238; 401-435-7518), 700 Bullocks Point Avenue, Riverside. The largest and most elaborate of Looff's 62 hand-carved, early-1900s figures spins weekends noon–9 from Memorial Day to mid-June, then Wednesday through

Sunday until Labor Day. Carousel hours then revert to noon–9 weekends plus Mondays until Columbus Day.

See also the **Providence Children's Museum** under *Museums* and **Roger Williams Park and Zoo** under *Green Space.*

GOLF **Triggs Memorial Golf Course** (401-521-8460), 1533 Chalkstone Avenue. This 18-hole, par-72 course was laid out in 1930 in links style, on rolling terrain with many ponds. There is a restaurant and bar, and golf carts and clubs can be rented.

STARGAZING **Ladd Observatory** (401-863-2323), 210 Doyle Avenue, corner of Hope Street in Providence. Open on clear Tuesday evenings 7–9, but call in advance. Located on the highest point in Providence and with a powerful refractor telescope, Ladd Observatory, which is affiliated with Brown University, is an excellent facility for viewing planets.

TENNIS **Roger Williams Park** (401-785-9450), Elmwood Avenue. There are eight outdoor tennis courts in the park.

TOURS **Carriage Rides of Providence** (401-377-2426), Side Hill Farm, 60 Clarks Falls Road, Hopkinton. Minimum two-hour carriage rides through downtown Providence can be arranged.

The Gallery Night Art Bus (401-490-2042; www.gallerynight.info) On the third Thursday of each month from March through November, a bus leaves the corner of Stillman and Canal Streets behind Citizens Plaza in downtown Providence for a free tour of the city's art galleries and special art events from 5 to 6:40 PM. It's a good way to take in an overview of the city's vibrant art scene. Tour takers can get on and off at galleries as they please and reboard later buses to continue.

The Providence Link (401-781-9400; www.ripta.com), Providence Link Trolley Pavilion, north side of Kennedy Plaza. While not exactly a tour, these trolleys transport visitors to places of interest around the city—the Green Line to the Convention Center and the restaurants of Italian Federal Hill and the East Side (site of Brown University and Rhode Island School of Design). Various passes are available.

WALKING A **riverwalk pathway** edges the east embankment of the Providence River between Waterplace Park and the Point Street Bridge. Here and there along the way, placards recount the history of the city, and benches provide resting places. In the warm seasons, picnic tables are set out where the riverwalk passes Rhode Island School of Design. On the river itself, bonfires burn and music plays from sunset to midnight on many summer weekends during free WaterFire events.

Summer Walks (401-273-7507, ext. 60). From June into early October, Summer Walks offers guided walking tours of various parts of the city.

Walking tours of Benefit Street (401-273-7507) are conducted in summer from the Rhode Island Historical Society's John Brown House Museum.

✷ Green Space

Blackstone Boulevard and **Blackstone Park.** Handsome late-19th- and early-20th-century houses in varying styles and a few intriguing, more modern homes edge this boulevard, which has a parklike green center strip that's popular with strollers and joggers. Pretty plantings brighten the strip in spring. The 1.6-mile boulevard extends below Blackstone Park to the Seekonk River, where the Narragansett Boat Club has its boathouses. Crews are often seen rowing their shells on the river early in the morning and during the evening.

City Hall Park, Kennedy Plaza. An equestrian statue of General Ambrose Burnside is one of the centers of attention in this little city park edged by the post office, Kennedy Plaza, and the gold-brick former railroad station.

College Green (front campus), Brown University, Prospect Street. The wrought-iron Van Wickle Memorial Gates that mark the entrance and exit to the university grounds are opened outward each spring, and the graduating seniors march through to their commencement ceremonies held in the First Baptist Meeting House. In fall, in time-honored tradition, the gates are opened inward to welcome incoming freshmen. The green itself, though small, is a pleasant place for sunning on spring and summer days.

Collier Point Park, Allens Avenue and Henderson Street. This little park with a small boat landing offers a view of Providence Harbor. The property was formerly owned by the Narragansett Electric Company, and the old hoppers for the coal that used to fire the plant have been restored as a historic attraction.

India Point Park, George M. Cohan Boulevard, India Point. Currently marred by a highway construction project, this waterfront park—with a few trees, a little grass, and paved paths for cyclists and walkers—still affords a fine south-facing view of Narragansett Bay. The park is the start of the East Bay Bike Path.

Memorial Park, South Main Street. Shaded by oak trees in front of the Providence County Courthouse, this small park filled with war memorials is dedicated to the memory of courthouse designer F. Ellis Jackson and World War II naval officer Henry B. Gardner Jr.

Prospect Terrace, Congdon Street. From this lovely park, a statue of city founder Roger Williams looks down upon his city and the gleaming white dome of the capitol. Williams is buried here, too. This is a favorite picnic spot and a great place for sunset-watching.

Swan Point Cemetery, Blackstone Boulevard. More than 200 acres of land here overlook the Seekonk River. The picturesque and historic cemetery is filled with winding lanes, 18th- and 19th-century monuments, and trees, which have made it a prime place for birders.

Waterplace Park, Memorial Boulevard. This award-winning 4-acre urban park is set around a tidal basin fed by the Woonasquatucket River. It includes landscaped terraces, an amphitheater for outdoor entertainment, and boat landings for water taxis that carry summer visitors downriver to dining and shopping areas in the South Main Street part of the city. A terraced restaurant overlooks the basin.

Roger Williams National Memorial Park, North Main Street. Open year-round, daily 9–4:30. According to legend, a spring that bubbled on this site in 1636 prompted Roger Williams to establish his settlement of Providence here. This informal 4-acre park is a National Park Service property with a visitor center and exhibits.

✐ **Roger Williams Park** (401-785-9450) **and Zoo** (401-785-3510), Elmwood Avenue. Open daily 7 AM–9 PM. Betsey Williams, great-great-

THE VIEW FROM PROSPECT TERRACE

Katherine Imbrie

granddaughter of Providence's founder, gave the first 100-acre tract from what was the Williams family farm to the city in 1871 for the establishment of a public recreation area. Today the 430-acre Victorian park has a zoo (open 9–4) with more than 1,000 animals—bison, elephants, and giraffes among them; an Australasian collection, including rare mynah birds, wallabies, and tree kangaroos; a museum of natural history; a small planetarium; a carousel; lakes for boating; a Japanese garden; two rose gardens; and a new botanical center including a conservatory and greenhouses containing a tropical garden featuring orchids, insect-eating plants, Mediterranean plants, and cacti.

✷ Lodging

HOTELS **Courtyard by Marriott** (401-272-1191; 1-888-887-7955; www.courtyard.com), 32 Exchange Terrace. ($$–$$$) This centrally located hotel with 216 rooms overlooks Waterplace Park.

♿ **Hotel Providence** (401-861-8000; 1-800-861-8900; www.thehotelprovidence.com), 311 Westminster Street. ($$–$$$) This 80-room boutique hotel in the heart of downtown has a re-created Belle Epoch–style lobby, restaurant, and complimentary workout room.

♿ **Providence Biltmore** (401-421-0700; 1-800-294-7709; www.providencebiltmore.com), 11 Dorrance Street. ($$$–$$$$) Built in 1922 as the city's premier lodging place, its situation in the heart of downtown is still ideal, but despite frequent renovations over the years, its look needs updating.

Providence Hilton Hotel (401-831-3900; 1-800-445-8667; www.hilton.com), 21 Atwells Avenue. ($$–$$$) This 224-room, recently renovated hotel, a former Holiday Inn, is conveniently situated at the edge of downtown near both the Rhode Island Convention Center and the Dunkin' Donuts Civic Center. A short walk in the other direction brings you to the restaurants of Federal Hill.

♿ **Providence Marriott Downtown** (401-272-2400; 1-800-228-9290; www.marriott.com), 1 Orms Street. ($$–$$$) Located near the State House, this is a modern, business-friendly hotel. Its Bluefin Grille serves breakfast, lunch, and dinner.

Wyndham Garden Hotel (401-272-5577, 1-800-388-1213 www.wyndham.com), 220 India Street. ($$–$$$) Plain but moderately priced, this boxy hotel overlooks India Point Park and I-195.

♿ **Renaissance Providence Hotel** (401-919-5000, 1-800-468-3571; www.marriott.com), 5 Avenue of the Arts. ($$$–$$$$) Back in 1926, the Masons began building an impressive limestone-and-brick neoclassical temple next to the State House, but they ran out of money and had to abandon the project. In time, the structure's

Sal Laterra

AN UNFINISHED MASONIC TEMPLE FOR MORE THAN 60 YEARS, THIS PAINSTAKINGLY RENOVATED 1920S STRUCTURE HAS BECOME THE HANDSOME RENAISSANCE PROVIDENCE HOTEL.

copper roof was stolen. Graffiti covered the temple walls. The unfinished building deteriorated, but tearing it down would have been costly, so it simply stood, its impressive facade empty and dilapidated. Then, in 2006, following an $87 million renovation, it opened as a 272-room luxury Marriott hotel with a restaurant and lounge, a fitness center, meeting rooms, and a grand view of the State House. Veterans Memorial Auditorium, where the Providence Symphony Orchestra plays, is right next door.

♿ **Westin Hotel Providence** (401-598-8000; 1-800-228-3000; www.westin.com), 1 West Exchange Street. ($$$–$$$$) This soaring 25-floor hotel catering to business travelers has 564 rooms and suites, a health club, two bars and a cocktail lounge, a breakfast café, and Centro, a highly rated restaurant (see *Dining Out*).

BED & BREAKFASTS **Annie Brownell House** (401-454-2934; www.anniebrownellhouse.com), 400 Angell Street. ($$–$$$) This 1899 Colonial Revival house is tastefully furnished with period pieces. There are three rooms with baths, along with a downstairs suite with bath. A full breakfast is served.

Christopher Dodge Inn (401-351-6111; www.providence-inn.com), 11 West Park Street. ($$–$$$) An 1858, 15-room Federal-style house furnished with early American reproductions and marble fireplaces. A 10-minute walk to the city center, a five-minute walk to Providence Place Mall. Full breakfast.

Old Court Bed & Breakfast (401-751-2002; www.oldcourt.com), 144 Benefit Street. ($$–$$$, depending on the season) This 10-room, 10-bath bed & breakfast in an 1863 redbrick house near Rhode Island School of Design has been decorated in Victorian style.

✷ Where to Eat

DINING OUT Al Forno (401-273-9760; www.alforno.com), 577 South Main Street. ($$$) Open Tuesday through Saturday for dinner. Reservations for six or more only, so be prepared to wait. Wood-grilled pizzas, crisp and thin, are a favorite appetizer at this nationally renowned, award-winning restaurant where wood grilling is the specialty. Desserts, which you order as you start your meal so they can be prepared to perfection, are another hallmark. As a mark of cool, there is little in the way of signage to identify this two-floor brick building, but it's close to the hurricane barrier at the short end of South Main south of Wickenden Street.

Asian Bistro (401-383-3551; www.asianbistrodining.com), 123 Dorrance Street. ($-$$) Open daily for lunch and dinner. There's Thai, Japanese, and Chinese food served in this welcoming restaurant.

♿ **Bluefin Grille** (401-272-5852), in the Providence Marriott, Charles and Orms Streets. ($$–$$$) Open daily for all breakfast, lunch, and dinner. As its name suggests, fresh seafood is the specialty here, but the grilled T-bone steaks and pork chops will satisfy carnivores.

♿ **Blue Grotto** (401-272-9030; www.bluegrottorestaurant.com), 210 Atwells Avenue. ($–$$) Lunch and dinner Monday through Saturday; Sunday dinner noon–9. Very romantic, old-school Italian with thoughtfully prepared dishes, graciously served.

Bravo Brasserie (401-490-5112; www.bravobrasserie.com), Empire and Washington Streets. ($$) Open daily for lunch and dinner; Sunday brunch. Stylishly upscale casual dining has a French accent

OUTDOOR DINING AT ALFORNO

Katherine Imbrie

in a location across the street from Trinity Repertory Theatre.

Café Nuovo (401-421-2525; http://cafenuovo.com/cafenuovo), 1 Citizens Plaza. ($$$–$$$$) Open Monday through Friday for lunch and dinner; Saturday, dinner only. Closed Sunday. A handsome—though small—restaurant in an equally handsome riverfront bank building. In fine weather you can eat outdoors and watch the action on the river. The portions of the trendy Italian cuisine are enormous.

ALONG ATWELLS AVENUE ON FEDERAL HILL

Kim Grant

Capriccio (401-421-1320; www.cafenuovo.com/capriccio), 2 Pine Street. ($$$–$$$$) Open Monday through Friday for lunch and dinner; weekends, dinner only. An over-the-top elegant and somewhat pretentious Italian restaurant serving carefully prepared fare with style. Definitely not for a casual family night out.

CAV (401-751-9164; http://cavrestaurant.com), 14 Imperial Place. ($$–$$$) Open Monday through Friday for lunch and dinner; on Saturday and Sunday, brunch, lunch, and dinner are served. An innovative, imaginative restaurant decorated with African masks and American antiques, which are also for sale. The menu is eclectic, including Middle Eastern, Greek, Italian, French, and Oriental dishes. A wide selection of coffees and teas.

Centro (401-598-8011; www.centroprovidence.com), 1 West Exchange Street ($$–$$$). Open daily for breakfast, lunch, and dinner. This sumptuous Westin Hotel restaurant specializes in Italian food and seafood prepared in unusual ways.

Chez Pascal (401-421-4422; www.chez-pascal.com), 960 Hope Street. ($$$) Open Monday through Saturday for dinner. Duck confit, hanger steak frites, and escargots are the sort of French dishes offered at Chez Pascal, where a quiet, civilized atmosphere prevails and the food is as sophisticated as any in the city.

Costantino's Ristorante (401-528-1100; www.costantinos ristorante.com), 265 Atwells Avenue. ($$$) Call for hours. Northern and southern Italian fare, prepared with care, is offered in elegant surroundings. In spring, summer, and fall you can dine outdoors on dishes like filet mignon rubbed with black truffle butter, or simply have a light antipasto of baby littleneck clams in a spicy pomodoro sauce with garlic, white wine, and herbs, topped with grilled Tuscan bread.

Fleming's Steak House (401-533-9000), 1 West Exchange Street, in the Westin Hotel. ($$$) Open daily for dinner. An upscale beef palace with a comfortably clubby atmosphere.

♿ **Gracie's** (401-272-7811; http://graciesprovidence.com), 194 Washington Street. ($$–$$$) Open Monday through Saturday for lunch and dinner. Exquisitely prepared food served in a mellow atmosphere.

Hemenway's Seafood Grill & Oyster Bar (401-351-8570; www.hemenwaysrestaurant.com), 121 South Main Street ($$–$$$) Open Monday through Saturday for lunch and dinner, Sunday for dinner only, starting at noon. Fresh fish, a spacious, attractive decor, and a view of the Providence River attract diners to this stylish casual restaurant.

Il Piccolo (401-421-9843; www.ilpiccolo-ristorante.com), 1450 Atwood Avenue, Johnston. ($$) Open Tuesday through Friday for lunch and dinner; Monday and Saturday for dinner only. This small restaurant offers fine food, wine, and service. Grilled chicken breast with baby greens, sweet onions, and peppers, and fresh vegetables al dente are highlights.

Jacky's Waterplace and Sushi Bar (401-383-5000; www.jackys waterplace.com), 200 Exchange Street. ($$$) Chinese, Japanese, Vietnamese, Thai, and Singaporean cuisine served in a sumptuous setting overlooking the Providence River. An outdoor terrace looks directly down on the river, making it the ideal place to dine on summer WaterFire nights.

Julian's (401-861-1770; www.juliansprovidence.com), 318 Broadway. ($–$$) Open Monday through Friday for breakfast, lunch, and dinner; Saturday for brunch and dinner; Sunday for brunch and dinner. Endlessly creative combinations of fresh seasonal ingredients make this offbeat and funky place a particularly popular spot among locals.

♿ **Local 121** (401-274-2121; www.local121.com), 121 Washington Street. ($$-$$$) Open Monday for dinner, Tuesday through Sunday for lunch and dinner. Local 21 specializes in serving locally raised beef, locally grown vegetables, and locally caught fish, making the dishes on the menu both tasty and seasonal. The dining room is handsome, too.

Loie Fuller's (401-273-4375; www.loiefullers.com), 1455 Westminster Street. ($$–$$$) A relative newcomer to the ever-evolving Providence dining scene, this art nouveau–style place is creating buzz way out on the West Side, where the cutting-edge places like to start up. Only the intertwined letters *L* and *F* identify it on the outside. Named for a belle epoque artiste, it's French-bistro-style food, open for dinner until midnight every night but Tuesday.

♿ **Lucky Garden** (401-231-5626; www.luckygardenri.com), 1852 Smith Street, North Providence. ($–$$) Open daily except Monday for lunch and dinner. Cantonese chefs prepare a remarkable Hong Kong menu with such special items as sea cucumber with duck feet. There is also a Chinese menu.

♿ **Madeira** Restaurant (401-431-1322; www.madeirarestaurant.com), 288 Warren Avenue, East Providence. ($–$$) Lunch and dinner daily except Sunday, when only dinner is served. Portuguese fare, including an all-beef shish kebab that is a specialty; bacalhau (dried codfish) that is fried, boiled, or broiled; and Portuguese steak topped with eggs and ham.

♿ **McCormick & Schmick's** (401-351-4500), 11 Dorrance Street in the Providence Biltmore hotel. ($$–$$$) Lunch and dinner daily. One of a national chain of upscale seafood restaurants, its central location in the city makes it a popular meeting place for businesspeople as well as tourists. Seafood is flown in from all over the country. The atmosphere is men's clubby, the service good, and the seafood among the best you'll find in Providence.

♿ **Mediterraneo** (401-331-7760; www.mediterraneocaffe.com/restaurant), 134 Atwells Avenue. ($$–$$$) Open Monday through Saturday for lunch and dinner and Sunday for dinner. Luncheon offerings of pizza, pasta, and salads, as well as grilled chicken, fish, and steak, are very reasonable in this spacious Federal Hill restaurant that has sidewalk dining in summer. At dinnertime the prices go up considerably, but the fare is genuinely Italian.

♿ **Mills Tavern** (401-272-3331; www.millstavernrestaurant.com), 101 North Main Street. ($$–$$$) Open daily for dinner. Fine restaurant specializes in wood-fired cooking and thoughtful service. Considered one of the best dining spots in the city.

New Rivers Restaurant (401-751-0350; www.newriversrestaurant.com), 7 Steeple Street. ($$–$$$) Open Monday through Saturday for dinner. Eclectic cooking featuring fresh local ingredients is offered at this American bistro. It's very small, with tables set close together, and the bar is popular for dining.

Old Canteen (401-751-5544; http://theoldcanteen.com), 120 Atwells Avenue. ($$–$$$) Open daily except Tuesday for lunch and dinner; Sunday dinner from 3 PM on. An old-fashioned Italian restaurant with meticulous service and a loyal following.

Pane e Vino (401-223-2230; www.panevino.net), 365 Atwells Avenue. ($$–$$$) Open daily for dinner. Veal, in its many forms, is one of the favorites here.

♿ **Paragon** (401-331-6200; http://paragonandviva.com), 234 Thayer Street. ($$) Open daily for lunch and dinner. Lobster, crabcakes, and calamari are among the appetizers, and cheesecake with strawberries flambé is one of the exotic desserts at this popular, lively, reasonably priced Thayer Street restaurant. You can also have just a simple burger or a fresh salad for lunch. A favorite of the student crowd.

Pizzico (401-421-4114; www.pizzicoristorante.com), 762 Hope Street. ($$–$$$) Open Monday through Friday for lunch and dinner; weekends for dinner only. The northern Italian cuisine at this pleasant East Side restaurant might include pistachio-crusted fried sole, and pumpkin ravioli.

Pot au Feu (401-273-8953; www.potaufeuri.com), 44 Custom House Street. ($$–$$$) The dining is elegant on the second floor of this authentic French restaurant serving dinner nightly. In the downstairs bistro it's more casual and less expensive, but the food is equally well prepared. The Parisian-style bistro is also open nightly. One of the oldest restaurants downtown, it's still one of the best.

♿ **Providence Oyster Bar** (401-272-8866; www.providenceoysterbar.com), 283 Atwells Avenue. ($$$) Open Monday through Saturday for dinner; Friday and Saturday for lunch as well. Closed Sunday. You can get oysters from Maine, British Columbia, Prince Edward Island, or Rhode Island at this welcoming, laid-back raw bar. Other well-prepared seafood is also on offer.

♿ **Providence Prime** (401-454-8881; http://providenceprime.com), 279 Atwells Avenue. ($$$) Open Monday through Saturday for dinner. Closed Sunday. Filet mignon, porterhouse, roast prime rib of beef—Providence Prime is a beef eater's delight, but there are also grilled lamb chops and pork chops, and fish and lobster on the menu.

Ran Zan (401-276-7574; www.ranzan.net), 1084 Hope Street. ($$) Open Tuesday through Friday for lunch and dinner; Saturday and Sunday for dinner only. One of the best casual sushi restaurants in the city is also the only one on this stretch of upper Hope Street.

♿ **Red Fez** (401-272-1212), 49 Peck Street. ($$) Open Monday through Saturday for dinner. An eclectic bistro menu that might feature a dish like lamb tagine with couscous or something much simpler. The menu changes regularly.

♿ **Red Stripe** (401-437-6950; www.redstriperestaurants.com), 465 Angell Street. ($$–$$$) Open daily for lunch and dinner, and on Sunday for brunch as well. Noisy brasserie evokes Paris in the heart of sedate Wayland Square. Mussels are a specialty, along with new twists on comfort classics. Large portions are a hallmark.

Rue de l'Espoir (401-751-8890; www.therue.com), 99 Hope Street. ($$$) Open daily for breakfast, lunch, and dinner; Saturday and Sunday for brunch as well. There's variety aplenty here—from comfort food like French toast made with honey-oat bread to sophisticated seafood dishes. Its location near Brown University and Rhode Island School of Design gives it an avant-garde air.

Ruth's Chris Steak House (401-272-2271), GTECH Center, 10 Memorial Boulevard. ($$$–$$$$) Open daily for dinner. Like Fleming's, Ruth's is a link in a chain of upscale steak palaces catering to corporate expense accounts.

Sawaddee (401-831-1122; www.sawaddeerestaurant.com), 93 Hope Street. ($$) Open daily for lunch and dinner. Spicy Thai cuisine at reasonable prices is offered in this pleasant East Side restaurant.

Siena (401-521-3311; www.sienari.com), 238 Atwells Avenue. ($$$) Open daily for dinner only. Updated take on Tuscan food in a stylishly modern yet warm environment. This is one of the best Italian restaurants in the city.

♿ **Taste of India** (401-421-4355; www.tasteofindiari.com), 230 Wickenden Street. ($) Open daily for lunch and dinner. Fine curry and tandoori cooking in an unpretentious atmosphere.

♿ **Tazza** (401-421-3300; www.tazzacaffe.com), 250 Westminster Street. ($-$$$). Open Monday through Friday for breakfast, lunch, and dinner, Saturday and Sunday for brunch and dinner. Tazza cold and hot small plates are inexpensive and enticing ($6–14). Then there are such elegant—and pricier—entrées as caramelized pineapple-wrapped salmon with lobster-scented risotto or osso buco.

♿ **Temple** (401-919-5050; www.templedowntown.com), 120 Francis Street. ($$$) Breakfast, lunch, and dinner daily. The restaurant within the high-style Renaissance Hotel is named for the Masonic temple that the building originally was designed to be. American bistro with creative modern takes on solid entrées. The Mediterranean menu features Italian, Greek, and Moroccan dishes—among others.

Ten Prime Steak & Sushi (401-453-2333; www.tenprimesteakandsushi.com), 55 Pine Street. ($$$–$$$$) Open daily for lunch and dinner, except Saturday, Sunday, and Monday, when there is no lunch. Nigiri and sashimi and sushi rolls featuring such delights as scallops and cilantro in a spicy peanut sauce are on the inviting menu at this hip, loud downtown restaurant. For meat eaters there is bacon-wrapped filet mignon or a veal chop with portobello mushrooms and truffle oil.

Tini (401-383-2400; http://thetini.com), 200 Washington Street. ($-$$) Open Tuesday through Friday for lunch and dinner, Saturday for dinner only. This teeny, tiny restaurant where there's only room for stools around the bar is an offshoot of Al Forno's, and its fare, though not on such a grand scale in terms of portions, is just as delicious as its older relative's.

Trinity Brewhouse (401-453-2337; www.trinitybrewhouse.com), 186 Fountain Street. ($$–$$$) Lunch and dinner daily. Brewpub offers great food like bratwurst and sauerkraut and fat hamburgers as well as grander fare in a sprawling room located between the Civic Center and Trinity Repertory Company.

♿ **Union Station Brewery** (401-274-2739), 36 Exchange Terrace. ($$) Open daily for lunch and dinner. Along with the home-brewed beers and ales served at this brewpub, there is a tempting casual menu—including pizza dough flavored with the leftover ingredients of the brewing process.

♿ **XO Café** (401-272-2116; www.xocafe.com), 125 North Main Street. ($$–$$$) Open seven nights a week for dinner, and on Sunday for brunch also. Inventive, sophisticated fare served in an arty, stylish setting. The Bento Box appetizer includes calamari, mushrooms, beef, and lobster.

♿ **Zooma Trattoria** (401-383-2002; http://trattoriazooma.com), 245 Atwells Avenue. ($$$) Lunch and dinner daily. Cosmopolitan, high-energy spot for Neapolitan food and a late-night bar menu.

EATING OUT **Abyssinia** (401-454-1412; www.abyssinia-restaurant.com), 333 Wickenden Street ($–$$) There's genuine eat-with-your-fingers injera (an Ethiopian sourdough flatbread) as well as such East African favorites as deep-fried yam cakes with tomatoes, onions, and cilantro. There are vegan dishes aplenty served, but also fish, lamb, beef, and chicken dishes for carnivores.

Angelo's (401-621-8171; www.angelosonthehill.com), 141 Atwells Avenue. ($–$$) Open Monday through Sunday for lunch and dinner. This is a longtime favorite for home-style, unpretentious Italian cooking.

Brickway on Wickenden (401-751-2477; www.brickwayonwickenden.com), 234 Wickenden Street. ($) Serving the best casual breakfasts in the city, Brickway has great omelets, pancakes, and specials at modest prices. Lunch, too. Funky student favorite is noisy but fun.

The Butcher Shop (401-861-4627), 157 Elmgrove Avenue. ($$) Open Monday through Friday 8–7; Saturday 7–6; Sunday until 3. Deli sandwiches and salads, good hamburgers and coffee, but no ambience. A good spot for take-out.

Caserta Pizzeria (401-272-3618; www.casertapizzeria.com), 121 Spruce Street. ($) Open Tuesday through Friday until 10; weekends until 11. Thick-crust pizzas with old-fashioned toppings.

Cilantro Mexican Grill (401-421-8226), 127 Weybosset Street. Just the right place to go for a quick burrito.

Cuban Revolution (401-331-8829), 50 Aborn Street. ($) Cuban food in a casual environment. Sangrias and pork sandwiches are specialties.

East Side Pockets (401-453-1100), 276 Thayer Street. ($) Open daily 9 AM–2 AM. Primarily eat-on-the-street falafel, gyros, chicken kefta, and the like. Popular with the college crowd.

♿ **Fellini Pizzeria** (401-751-6737; www.fellinipizzeria.com), 166 Wickenden Street. ($) Open daily for lunch and dinner. Great selection of creative toppings for thin-crust pizza to eat in or take out.

Kabob and Curry (401-273-8844; www.kabobandcurry.com), 261 Thayer Street. ($–$$) Call for hours. A casual and inexpensive eatery for Indian food. Popular with the college crowd.

Meeting Street Café (401-273-1066), 220 Meeting Street. ($$) Open daily 8 AM–11 PM. Big fat deli sandwiches and soups are the specialty here.

♿ **Mexico Garibaldi** (401-331-4985; www.resmexgaribaldi.com), 948 Atwells Avenue. ($) Open daily except Monday for lunch and dinner. You could almost be in Mexico City in this little restaurant frequented by Mexican residents of Providence. It's just a hole-in-the-wall, but the tamales, burritos, and enchiladas are splendid.

♿ **Olga's Cup and Saucer** (401-831-6666), 103 Point Street. ($–$$) Open Monday through Saturday for breakfast and lunch. Healthy, imaginative light fare includes salads and grilled thin-crust pizzas. Tantalizing home-baked breads and pastries, too. There is outdoor dining in a charming urban garden during the warm months.

♿ **Ribs and Company** (401-944-5432; www.yourribsandcompany.com), 1383 Atwood Avenue, Johnston. ($–$$) Open daily for lunch and dinner. Baby back ribs, barbecued chicken, and steaks are served in an informal, down-home atmosphere.

Seaplane Diner (401-941-9547), 307 Allens Avenue. ($) Open Monday through Friday 5 AM–3 PM, Saturday 5 AM–2 PM, Sunday 7 AM–1 PM. This is a 1940s diner serving all the usual diner fare, as well as such Rhode Island favorites as linguica and eggs, coffee milk, snail salad, and clam cakes.

Spike's Junkyard Dogs (401-861-6888), 485 Branch Avenue. ($) Open daily from 11 AM to 11 PM daily. The hot dogs here are something special—baked, not grilled, and served in fresh hot rolls topped with spicy mustard, tomato, pickle, and hot peppers, or your choice of other toppings.

Venda Ravioli (401-421-9105; www.vendaravioli.com), 265 Atwells Avenue. ($–$$) Open Monday 9–6; Tuesday through Saturday 8:30–6; Sunday 8:30–5. On a summer weekend there may be lines outside waiting for a table at this stylish market and eatery, where the pasta has been homemade for generations and may be simply prepared in a tomato-basil sauce or done in more complicated ways. A local favorite is linguine with hot pepper seeds, but veal cutlets and grilled shrimp are also on the menu. After you've finished eating, you can stroll about and admire the shelves of fresh Italian breads, the cases of sausages and cheeses, as well as an array of kitchen utensils, take-out foods, and pantry foods. The market remains open until 6, except on Sunday when it closes at 5.

Wes' Rib House (401-421-9090; http://wesribhouse.com), 38 Dike Street. ($–$$) Lunch and dinner daily. The specialty is Missouri-style barbecue with corn bread, baked beans, and slaw.

Z Bar & Grill (401-831-1566), 244 Wickenden Street. ($–$$) Open daily for lunch and dinner. Wood grilling is a specialty, and there is a pleasant garden for summer dining at this comfortably sophisticated and modestly priced neighborhood bistro.

CAFÉS **Cable Car Cinema Cafe** (401-272-3970), 204 South Main Street. Open daily for breakfast, lunch, and supper. A café-and-cinema combo that's distinctly for the young at heart. Much frequented by Rhode Island School of Design and Brown University students, its fare is basic sandwiches, salads, coffee, and brownies.

♿ **Café Choklad** (401-383-4764), 2 Thomas Street. On a cold day, this is the perfect spot for hot chocolate and a brownie or a tasty sandwich.

Coffee Exchange (401-273-1198), 297 Wickenden Street. Open 6:30 AM–11 PM daily. Coffee lovers read newspapers or converse while lingering over espresso drinks on the porch, or huddle over their laptops inside at this classic coffeehouse that roasts its own beans. For many locals, a stop at the Exchange is part of a daily routine.

The Duck & Bunny (401-270-3300; www.theduckandbunny.com), 312 Wickenden Street. ($–$$) Open Tuesday through Sunday 10–1 AM. Afternoon tea with finger sandwiches, scones and jam and Devonshire cream, mini-cupcakes—and of course a pot of tea—is served anytime at this tiny, charming restaurant with a garden for outdoor summer dining. A breakfast, lunch, or supper offering might be smoked salmon with capers, dill, green onion, and crème fraiche in an herbed crepe.

La Laiterie at Farmstead (401-274-7177; www.farmsteadinc.com), 184-188 Wayland Avenue. ($$-$$$) The world's best cheeses are on sale at Farmstead, an American version of a French cheese shop, while La Laiterie, its abutting bistro, serves soups, salads, and sandwiches made of the freshest local ingredients.

♿ **L'Elizabeth** (401-861-1974), 285 South Main Street. Open daily afternoon and evening. Subdued elegance is the mark of this lovely European-style café sporting needlework on its chair seats and pretty round tables. Irish coffee, specialty spirits, sherries and cognacs (or nonspirited drinks), and pound cake and cheesecake are served in a most civilized way.

Pastiche (401-861-5190; www.pastichefinedesserts.com), 92 Spruce Street. Open Tuesday through Thursday 8:30 AM–11 PM; Saturday until 11:30; Sunday 10–10. The best pastries in Providence and fine coffees are offered to take out or eat in a charming dining space warmed by a fireplace in cold months. Try the all-American chocolate layer cake, feather-light lemon soufflé cake, or cream-cheese-frosted carrot cake, among many others.

Seven Stars Bakery (401-632-4496), 342 Broadway, and (401-521-2200), 820 Hope Street. At both locations, you'll find Parisian ambience plus the best baked goods in town and excellent espresso drinks. The muffins are good, but the sticky buns are out of this world.

Small Planet Café (401-521-2000), 232 Westminster Street. Vegan treats and calzones, muffins and pastry are accompaniments to this café's inviting coffee.

Sura (401-277-9088; www.surap rovidence.com), 232 Westminster Street. ($-$$$) Open daily 11:30 AM–2 AM. Korean barbecue and stews, Japanese sushi and teriyaki.

ICE CREAM AND SNACKS

Three Sisters (401-273-7230), 1074 Hope Street. Open weekdays 6:30 AM–9 PM, later on weekends. Coffees of all sorts are served along with imaginative ice cream flavors that are invented and created right on the premises. Try green tea or Guinness flavor on a warm night.

✱ Entertainment

FILM **Avon Cinema** (401-421-3315; www.avoncinema.com), 260 Thayer Street. A college-town movie house featuring art films and offbeat movies on double bills that change frequently.

Cable Car Cinema (401-272-3970; www.cablecarcinema.com), 204 South Main Street. Another art house popular with students from nearby Brown and Rhode Island School of Design.

IMAX (401-453-4629; www.nationalamusements.com), Providence Place Mall. In this enormous theater with realistic 3-D

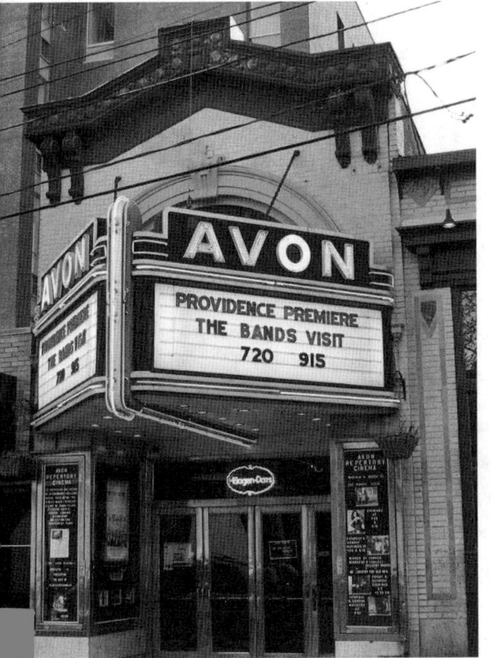

Katherine Imbrie

THE AVON CINEMA

effects, you feel you are part of the film you're seeing.

MUSIC AND DANCE **Festival Ballet Providence** (401-353-1129; www.festivalballet.com), 825 Hope Street. One of the largest ballet companies in New England, the Festival Ballet dances principally at the Veterans Memorial Auditorium.

Opera Providence (401-331-6060; www.operaprovidence.org), 585 Elmgrove Avenue. It might be *Die Fledermaus,* It might be a cheery musical. It could be a Valentine's Day or Christmas event. Opera Providence sometimes performs at the Rhode Island Center for Performing Arts in Cranston, sometimes at country clubs, sometimes at historic sites.

Providence Singers (401-683-1932; http://providencesingers.org). A 100-plus-voice choral group that has been giving concerts in church and college venues for 40 years.

Rhode Island Chamber Music Concerts (401-863-2416; www.ricmc.org), 1 Benevolent Street, First Unitarian Church. Four or five chamber music programs are presented annually.

Rhode Island Civic Chorale and Orchestra (401-521-5670; www.ricco.org). Three programs a year in various downtown churches.

Rhode Island Philharmonic Orchestra (401-248-7000; www.riphil.org), Veterans Memorial Auditorium, 1 Avenue of the Arts. This 61-year-old symphony orchestra, which ranks among the best in New England, offers eight classical programs from October through May. Occasional summer pops concerts, too.

NIGHTLIFE **Hot Club** (401-861-9007; www.hotclubprov.com), 575 South Water Street. This no-frills waterfront bar has a loyal local following.

Lupo's Heartbreak Hotel (401-272-5876; www.lupo.com), 79 Washington Street. Live music of all sorts is offered here.

Nick-A-Nees (401-861-7290), 75 South Street. It's mainly blues at this funky neighborhood bar, with

Sal Laterra

VETERANS MEMORIAL AUDITORIUM IS HOME TO THE RHODE ISLAND PHILHARMONIC ORCHESTRA. FESTIVAL BALLET PROVIDENCE AND OPERA PROVIDENCE ALSO PERFORM THERE.

live music on Monday, Thursday, and most weekend nights.

Olive's (401-751-1200; www.olivesrocks.com), 108 North Main Street. James Bond martinis, blue martinis, burgers, pizza, and bands playing rock and Top 40 music Friday and Saturday.

Patrick's Pub (401-751-1553; www.patrickspub.com), 381 Smith Street. Live Irish music on Tuesday. Trivia on Thursday. Bands on Friday. DJs other nights.

Roots Cafe (401-272-7422; www.rootscafeprovidence.com), 276 Westminster Street. Sometimes there's a comedy night on stage. Sometimes there's a blues jam or a band playing salsa. Whatever the music is, it makes for a great night out.

Snookers Pool Lounge (401-351-7665; www.snookersri.com), 53 Ashburton Street. A good place to escape the crowds and enjoy food and music.

The Spot Underground (401-383-7133; http://thespotprovidence.com), 15 Elbow Street. Live music nightly.

SPECTATOR SPORTS **Providence Bruins** (401-273-5000; www.providencebruins.com), Dunkin' Donuts Center, West Exchange Street. This top development affiliate for the Boston Bruins hockey team plays at the "Dunk" from September through April.

THEATER **Brown University Theater** (401-863-2838), Catherine Bryan Dill Center for the Performing Arts, Waterman Street. A variety of performances are offered throughout the year.

Perishable Theatre (401-331-2695; www.perishable.org), 95 Empire Street. Productions at this little theater are alternative and experimental.

Providence Performing Arts Center (401-421-2997; www.ppacri.org), 220 Weybosset Street. Touring companies bring Broadway shows to this handsomely renovated onetime movie theater.

Rhode Island College Performing Arts Series (401-456-8000; www.ric.edu/pfa/pas.php), Roberts Hall, Rhode Island College, 600 Mount Pleasant Avenue. This group presents programs of theater, dance, and pops and classical music.

Trinity Repertory Company (401-351-4242; www.trinityrep.com), 201 Washington Street. This Tony Award–winning repertory company is among the outstanding theaters of its kind in the country.

✷ Selective Shopping

ANTIQUES SHOPS Antiques & Interiors (401-272-4441; www.antiquesandinteriors.biz), 65 Ashburton Street. High-style and very high-quality European and American antique furniture, rugs, and home accessories are beautifully displayed in a former fire station. A courtyard in back has sculptures and furniture for the garden.

Benefit Street Antiques (401-751-9109; www.benefitstreetantiques.com), 243 Wickenden Street. A wide selection of antique furniture, china, and glass.

Ferguson and D'Arruda (401-273-5550; www.ferguson-darruda.com), 409 Wickenden Street. 10th-century American items, garden ornaments, cast-iron mantels and grills, and much, much more of other periods.

TRINITY REPERTORY HAS A NATIONAL REPUTATION.

Kim Grant

ART GALLERIES **AS220** (401-831-9327), 115 Empire Street; 95 Mathewson Street; and 131 Washington Street. A gallery for alternative art that also offers performances and has its own café.

Bannister Gallery (401-456-9765), 600 Mount Pleasant Street. This Rhode Island College gallery exhibits works largely by Rhode Island artists, with some pieces by students.

David Winton Bell Gallery (401-863-2932), List Art Center, Brown University, 64 College Street. Cutting-edge works by national and international artists.

Buonacorsi+Agniel Gallery (401-484-7566; www.theheadlight.com/gallery), 1 Sims Avenue #102. Works of Rhode Island painters, sculptors, printmakers and photographers.

Bert Gallery (401-751-2628; http://brown.edu/Facilities/David_Winton_Bell_Gallery), 540 South Water Street. Works of 19th- and 20th-century New England artists.

Chabot Fine Art Gallery (401-432-7783; www.chabotgallery.com), 379 Atwells Avenue. Contemporary, abstract, and traditional painting.

Chazon Gallery at Wheeler (401-421-9230; http://chazangallery.org), 228 Angell Street. Contemporary art. Changing exhibits.

Copacetic Rudely Elegant Jewelry (401-273-0470), 65 Weybosset Street. A gallery of contemporary jewelry.

Sarah Doyle Gallery (401-863-2189), 185 Meeting Street. Rotating shows are generally of high caliber and with a feminist slant.

Gallery Z (401-454-8844; www.galleryzprov.com), 259 Atwells Avenue. Paintings by local artists, many of Armenian background.

Lenore Gray Gallery (401-274-3900), 25 Meeting Street. Painting and sculpture by Rhode Island artists.

Krause Gallery at the Moses Brown School (401-831-7350; www.mosesbrown.org/krausegallery), 250 Lloyd Avenue. Exhibits of jury-selected work. Closed weekends.

Providence Art Club (401-331-1114; www.providenceartclub.com), 11 Thomas Street. Painting and sculpture primarily by Rhode Island artists.

Providence College Galleries (401-865-2400), East Campus, Eaton Street Gate. Emerging artists.

Woods-Gerry Gallery (401-454-6141), 62 Prospect Street, 1st floor. When Rhode Island School of Design acquired the Woods-Gerry House, a redbrick Italianate mansion, and sought to demolish it, the Rhode Island Historic Preservation Commission intervened. An outstanding example of the architectural work of Rhode Island native Richard Upjohn, the building was constructed in 1860.

The gallery displays student and faculty work. Outside, there is a lovely garden.

BOOKSTORES **Ada Books** (401-432-6222; http://ada-books.com), 717 Westminster Street. Secondhand and some new books, with an emphasis on poetry.

Books on the Square (401-331-9097; www.booksq.com), 471 Angell Street. General fiction and nonfiction, hardcover and paperback.

Brown University Bookstore (401-863-3168; www.shopbrown.com), 244 Thayer Street. A full-service college bookstore selling remainders, used books, professional books, and textbooks.

Cellar Stories (401-521-2665; www.cellarstories.com), 111 Mathewson Street. Used, hard-to-find, out-of-print, old, and rare books; much Rhode Island history. There is also a search service.

Johnson & Wales Harborside Bookstore (401-598-1445; www.efollett.com), 265 Harborside Boulevard. Books on culinary arts along with college books and supplies.

Johnson & Wales University Downtown Campus Bookstore (401-598-1105; www.efollett.com), 1 Cookson Place. Open weekdays. Best sellers, children's books, coffee-table books, T-shirts, mugs, and other souvenirs of Johnson & Wales.

Map Center (401-421-2184; www.mapcenter.com), 671 North Main Street. Maps, atlases, charts.

Myopic Books (401-521-5533; www.myopicbooks.com), 5 South Angell Street. Browse outside in the garden or inside this comfortable shop dealing in used, out-of-print, first-edition, and rare books.

Rhode Island College Bookstore (401-456-8025), 600 Mount Pleasant Avenue. Open Monday through Thursday 8:45–7, until 4:15 on Friday during the academic year; open Monday through Friday 8:15–3:45 in summer. Hardcovers, paperbacks, remainders, gifts, greeting cards, jewelry, and stationery.

RISD Store (401-454-6465; www.risdstore.com), 30 North Main Street. Open Monday through Thursday 8:30–7, Friday until 5:30, Saturday 10–6, and Sunday noon–5 during the academic year; open Monday through Friday 8:30–5:30 in summer. Books on photography, architecture, graphic arts, fine arts. School supplies.

Symposium Books (401-273-7900; www.symposiumbooks.com), 240 Westminster Street. Open daily. New books that are publishers' returns and remainders are sold at lower prices than most new books.

SPECIAL SHOPS **Bambini** (401-490-6952), 251 South Main Street. Everything cuddly and tasteful you could possibly want for a newborn or children who are a little bit older.

Belleau Art Glass (401-456-0011), 424 Wickenden Street. When the daffodils and lilies are no longer in bloom in your garden, this is the place to come for a hand-blown substitute. There are hand-blown vases and Christmas tree ornaments, too.

Craftland (401-272-4285; www.craftlandshop.com), 235 Westminster St. Local artists' cheery handmade towels, pillows, notepaper, jewelry, imaginative stuffed animals, and silkscreen and woodblock prints are delights of this spacious down-city store.

Creatoyvity (401-351-5718; www.creatoyvity.com), 736 Hope Street. A wide assortment of books, puzzles, and scientific toys.

Curatorium (401-453-4080; www.thecuratorium.com), 197 Wickenden Street. Goofy, wacky, imaginative gifts—kitchen items, glass, bowls, jewelry, scarves.

Fresh Purls (401-270-8220; www.freshpurls.com), 769A Hope Street. Hand-spun and hand-dyed yarn from South Africa, weaving from India, decorative buttons, knitting and crocheting notions.

Frog and Toad (401-831-3434), 795 Hope Street. You can buy hats and mittens from Nepal, kimono scarves from Japan, ginkgo shell magnets from China, gourd birdhouses, as well as local creations and more in this attractive corner gift shop.

Green River (401-621-9092; www.greenriversilver.com), 735 Hope Street. Find sterling silver from Mexico, Bali, and India alongside amber from Poland in this fun and inviting jewelry shop.

Homestyle (401-277-1159; www.homestyleri.com), 229 Westminster Street. Decorator-owned shop has a good selection of hostess gifts and baby gifts along with such offbeat items as handblown glass golf putters, Haitian steel-drum wall decorations, and family photos transformed into pop art.

Mignonette (401-272-4422; www.mignonette.net), 301 Wickenden Street. The fragrance of lavender mingles with perfume from the French flower fields of Grasse here. For the discerning, there are also Italian lingerie and jewelry from the Czech Republic.

Mod Mama (401-273-7800; www.modmama.com), 16 Angell Street. Funky clothes with an urban feel for children up to 6.

The Peaceable Kingdom (401-351-3472), 116 Ives Street. Folk art from around the world, African textiles and masks, dolls, rugs.

Providence Place Mall (401-270-1000), Providence Place. Department stores, specialty shops, jewelers, restaurants, a food court—all in one place in the state's largest mall.

Queen of Hearts (401-421-1471), 222 Westminster Street. Ceramics, jewelry, knitwear, paintings, and clothes by local designers and artists.

RISDworks (401-277-4949; www.risdworks.com), 20 North Main Street. Vases, handbags, lamps, toys, wallets, frames, umbrellas, glass, pottery, jewelry, textiles, and more—all designed by RISD alumni and faculty.

Rock Paper Flowers (401-454-4400; www.rockpaperflowers.net), 174 Wickenden Street. In this three-section shop, Dugan Custom Jewelers will reproduce a missing earring or cufflink for those who have just one of a pair, while Paper Moss has its own letterpress for hand-printing cards and invitations, and Studio 539 specializes in floral arrangements and bouquets.

Simple Pleasures (401-331-4120; www.simplepleasures providence.com), 6 Richmond Square. In 1895 this redbrick building was Mahoney's Forge on the banks of the Seekonk River. Today it houses this charming shop of tastefully selected eclectic gifts from all over the world. There are traditional Kantha Indian hand-stitched quilts, artisan chocolates, Japanese and Nepalese and Japanese silk scarves, and handcrafted jewelry.

Southwest Passage (401-751-7587; www.southwestpassage.net), 180 Wayland Avenue. Silver and turquoise in stunning Navajo, Zuni, Hopi, and Pueblo-designed jewelry, as well as pottery and fetishes from the Southwest fill this little Wayland Square shop.

Studio Hop (401-621-2262), 810 Hope Street. Artist-made ceramics, jewelry, handbags, paperweights, wooden boxes—creative gifts of all sorts.

Three Wheel Studio (401-580-0936), 406 Wickenden Street. The eclectic-style teapots and bowls and vases sold here are all the work of RISD-trained potter Dwo-Wen Chen.

Touched by Green (401-223-4420; www.touchedbygreen.com), 271 South Main Street. Panama hats and palm tree jewelry fashioned by independent overseas artisans.

Zop (401-751-4967; www.zop soap.com), 186 Union Street. The handmade vegetable oil soaps made here may have the fragrance of green tea or cut grass or fern, as well, of course, as the usual floral fragrances.

ZuZu's Petals (401-331-9846), 288 Thayer Street. Perky, boutique-style dresses for the young and trendy for special occasions. The accessories to go with them, too.

✱ Special Events

January: **Boat Show** (401-458-6000; www.providenceboatshow .com), Rhode Island Convention Center.

February: **Rhode Island Spring Flower and Garden Show** (401-458-6000; www.flowershow.com), Rhode Island Convention Center. Northeast International Auto Show, Rhode Island Convention Center.

March–November: **Gallery Night Providence** (401-490-2042; www .gallerynight.info). Third Thursday of the month.

April: **RISD Alumni Sales** (401-351-6379), Benefit Street.

May–October: **WaterFire** (401-272-3111; www.waterfire.org), Waterplace Park. Generally two Saturdays a month in summer and fall, and occasionally midweek. Floating bonfires are lit in the Providence River and accompanied by taped music.

June: **Festival of Historic Houses** (401-831-7440), Benefit Street. Open houses are hosted by the Providence Preservation Society at some of the city's finest restored private houses. Providence Art Festival (http://provideneart festival.com), Westminster Street.

June–July: **Thursday evening band concerts,** Rose Larisa Park, East Providence.

June–October: **Hope Street Farmers' Market** (401-312-4250; www.farmfresh.org), Lippitt Park, Hope Street at Blackstone Boulevard, Saturdays 9:30–12:30. Whole Foods–University Heights Farmers' Market (401-621-5990), 601 North Main Street, Mondays 3 until dusk; Parade Street Farmers' Market (401-312-4250), next to Cranston Street Armory, Thursdays 4–7; Downtown Farmers' Market (401-312-4259, www.farm freshri.org), Kennedy Plaza, Fridays 11–2.

July into the fall: Hartford Avenue Farmers' Market, 370 Hartford Avenue, Wednesdays 3–6. Capitol Hill Farmers' Market (401-222-2781), 3 Capitol Hill, behind the Dept. of Health Building, Thursdays 11–2. Broad Street Farmers' Market (401-312-4250), 697 Broad Street, Saturdays 9–12.

July: **Providence Independence Day Celebration and Fireworks at India Point Park**. **Summer Concert Series.** These Friday-evening concerts are held at Waterplace Park. East Providence Heritage Festival (www .epheritagefest.com), Pierce Memorial Field. East Providence. Three-day outdoor festival featuring ethnic food, crafts, and concerts.

August: **Foo Fest** (401-831-9327). An afternoon and evening of art and music on Empire Street. Puerto Rican Cultural Festival and Parade (401-415-5563), Roger Williams Park. A family festival of food, music, and entertainment. Providence Arts Festival (http: //provideneartfestival.com), Westminster Street.

August–October: **Fruit Hill Farmers' Market** (401-228-8261), Rhode Island College Road and Mount Pleasant Avenue, Fridays 3:30–6.

September: **Dominican Festival** (401-941-0536), Roger Williams Park Temple to Music, 1000 Elmwood Avenue. A family festival of food, music, and other entertainment. **Annual Heritage Day Festival** (401-222-2000), Roger Williams National Memorial, 282 North Main Street. Ethnic groups celebrate their heritages and cultures with song, dance, food, and entertainment.

September–mid-November: **Brown University Farmers' Market** (401-312-4250, www .farmfreshri.org), Thayer Street and George Street, Wednesdays 11–2.

October: **Columbus Day Festival,** Federal Hill. Parade and street festival with vendors selling Italian specialties. **Great Northeast International Beer Festival** (401-458-6000), Rhode Island Convention Center. More than 250 local breweries offer their beers to sample. **Jack-o'-Lantern Spectacular,** Roger Williams Zoo. Halloween event with more than 5,000 jack-o'-lanterns on display. RISD Alumni Sales (401-454-6379), Benefit Street.

November: **Santa arrives at the Roger Williams Park Zoo** (www.rwpzoo.org).

November–December: **Trinity Repertory Company's annual staging of A *Christmas Carol*** (401-351-4242) www.trinity rep.com).

December–January: **Christmas Tree Lighting and Ice Show at Kennedy Plaza (401-421-7740). Annual Latin Christmas Carol Celebration** (401-863-2123), First Baptist Church. Christmas carols sung in Latin, readings from Latin texts by Brown University classics students, organ music. **Winter Festival, Senior Center,** 610 Waterman Avenue, East Providence (401-435-7500). **State Ballet of Rhode Island's annual staging of *Coppélia*** (401-334-2560), Roberts Hall Theater, Rhode Island College, 600 Mount Pleasant Avenue.

North of Providence

2

BLACKSTONE RIVER VALLEY, FOSTER, AND SCITUATE

Kim Grant

BLACKSTONE RIVER VALLEY, FOSTER, AND SCITUATE

Thirty-five miles south of Boston, on a spot overlooking a bend in the river that today bears his name, the Reverend William Blackstone erected a cottage in 1635. He was a Church of England clergyman who came to the New World for greater religious freedom, and his cottage began the settlement of the Blackstone River Valley.

This "Sage of the Wilderness," as Blackstone was called, was the first white settler in the area. He had made his journey from Boston on the white bull that he always rode, carrying with him nearly 200 books—probably the largest library in the New World at that time. A stone monument marks the spot across from the Ann & Hope Specialty Shops in Cumberland where, presumably, Blackstone lived.

There are now three cities in the Blackstone River Valley—Pawtucket, Central Falls, and Woonsocket—as well as several towns, many mill villages, and some rural areas. Pawtucket, "Place by the Waterfall," is the oldest of the three cities and was the birthplace, in the 1790s, of America's industrial revolution.

When Roger Williams was negotiating with the Narragansetts for land to settle in the 1630s, he was uninterested in the wooded, stony terrain of what is now Pawtucket; it was not deemed suitable for farming. But in 1655 blacksmith Joseph Jenks Jr. took advantage of the wood in Pawtucket's forests to fire his forge, establishing a smithy where the Blackstone River tumbles over Pawtucket Falls and becomes the Pawtucket River.

Soon Jenks was producing plows, harrows, and scythes for the farmers of Providence, and business was good enough to attract other blacksmiths. Though Native Americans destroyed the settlement of Pawtucket in King Philip's War, it was rebuilt, and the replacement forges, like their predecessors, flourished.

Samuel Slater began producing cotton yarn in his Pawtucket mill with Blackstone River–powered machinery in 1793. At about the same time, a

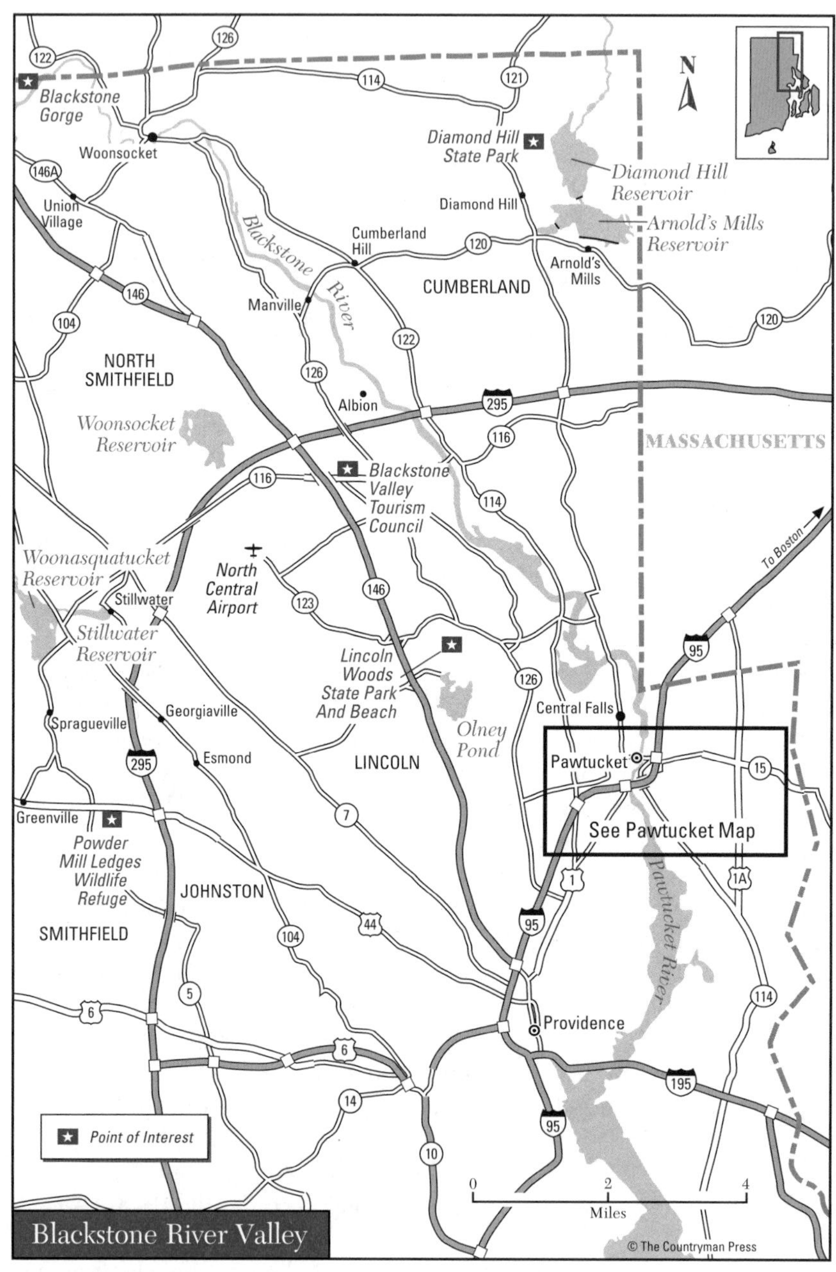
Blackstone Gorge
Woonsocket
Union Village
Diamond Hill State Park
Diamond Hill Reservoir
Diamond Hill
Arnold's Mills Reservoir
Cumberland Hill
Arnold's Mills
Blackstone River
Manville
CUMBERLAND
NORTH SMITHFIELD
Albion
Woonsocket Reservoir
MASSACHUSETTS
Blackstone Valley Tourism Council
Woonasquatucket Reservoir
North Central Airport
Stillwater
Stillwater Reservoir
To Boston
Lincoln Woods State Park And Beach
Olney Pond
Central Falls
Spragueville
Georgiaville
Esmond
LINCOLN
Pawtucket
See Pawtucket Map
Greenville
Powder Mill Ledges Wildlife Refuge
JOHNSTON
SMITHFIELD
Pawtucket River
Providence
Point of Interest
Miles
© The Countryman Press
Blackstone River Valley

mile above Pawtucket Falls a chocolate mill was established—also using Blackstone waterpower—at what today is Central Falls.

Woonsocket, the third of the Blackstone Valley cities and the northernmost city in Rhode Island, had its beginning in 1666 with a sawmill built at a spot that Native Americans called Miswoosakit—"At the Very Steep Hill." The earliest settlers of Woonsocket chose farming as their livelihood, but after Slater proved so successful with his water-powered cotton mill, Woonsocket residents decided to build their own mill. The first Woonsocket cotton mill was established in 1810, and more followed. Spinning and weaving woolens became the city's specialty.

By the second half of the 19th century, Woonsocket's mill industry had gained considerable renown, and many Eastern European and Russian immigrants found their way to Woonsocket's mills. French Canadian immigrants also came in great numbers, and by the 1930s nearly three-quarters of the city's population was first- or second-generation French Canadian. French was heard on the city's streets, and the radio station and newspapers were French. Even today the French influence remains widespread.

Mill villages sprang up all along the river's length, also nourished by the Blackstone's waterpower. As a result, much of the Blackstone River Valley is heavily populated today, even though the mills are largely gone. To some extent factory outlets have replaced the mills, and these provide some interest to the tourist, but until recently there was little to lure the visitor. Indeed, the Blackstone River and the Pawtucket and Seekonk Rivers that it flows into were long victims of industrial pollution. But in recent years these waterways have been cleansed and revived, and waterfront parks provide public access to the rivers where anglers now find sunfish, trout, pickerel, catfish, and bass. On weekends during the warmer months an open vessel, the *Blackstone Valley Explorer*, travels the rivers, offering glimpses of the flora and fauna that are flourishing again.

And then there are those parts of the valley that have always remained rural—where hills rise and fall and apple blossoms perfume the air in spring. (According to legend, William Blackstone developed the first purely American apple: the Yellow Sweeting.)

The Pawtucket Red Sox—a Triple-A farm team of the Boston Red Sox—play their games in Pawtucket's McCoy Stadium. The state's largest gaming facility is in Lincoln. Roast chicken dinners at poultry farms entice travelers on weekend outings to the area.

Though the glory days of the valley's cities have largely come and gone, architectural structures that testify to this bygone era still stand. Of all Rhode Island, it is the Blackstone River Valley that is experiencing the greatest revival of tourism. The traveler must bear in mind, however, that the process is just beginning. Sites of interest to tourists are often unmarked. Obtaining maps and detailed information from the local tourist office is essential.

Rural western Rhode Island lies between Connecticut and the Blackstone River Valley watershed area of Glocester. Forests of white pine, oak, and birch edge its miles of winding, hilly roads. Every now and then the traveler will come upon a cluster of old houses or a farmhouse set far back from the road. There are beautiful fieldstone walls along some stretches, and in spring apple blossoms bloom in old orchards. One of the state's two covered bridges is on Central Pike in Foster. It was rebuilt in authentic 19th-century style after its predecessor was destroyed by fire.

Two Foster villages worth a visit are Foster Center and Moosup Valley. The white spire of the 1882 Greek Revival Second Baptist Church rises above Foster Center, reached by Foster Center Road (RI 94). Twice a month the town council meets in the white-clapboard 1796 Town Meeting House. The oxblood-red library was originally a one-room schoolhouse. In the village of Moosup Valley, the white Congregational church, the Grange, and the library form a picturesque scene near Green Acres Pond, notable for its trout.

Scituate, along with its administrative center of North Scituate, lies on the 6-mile-long Scituate Reservoir on RI 116. With its bandstand-graced green, 1831 Baptist church, a few shops, and yellow and white 18th-century clapboard houses, North Scituate presents a traditional New

THE 6-MILE-LONG SCITUATE RESERVOIR IS A POPULAR DESTINATION FOR FALL FOLIAGE DRIVES.

Sal Laterra

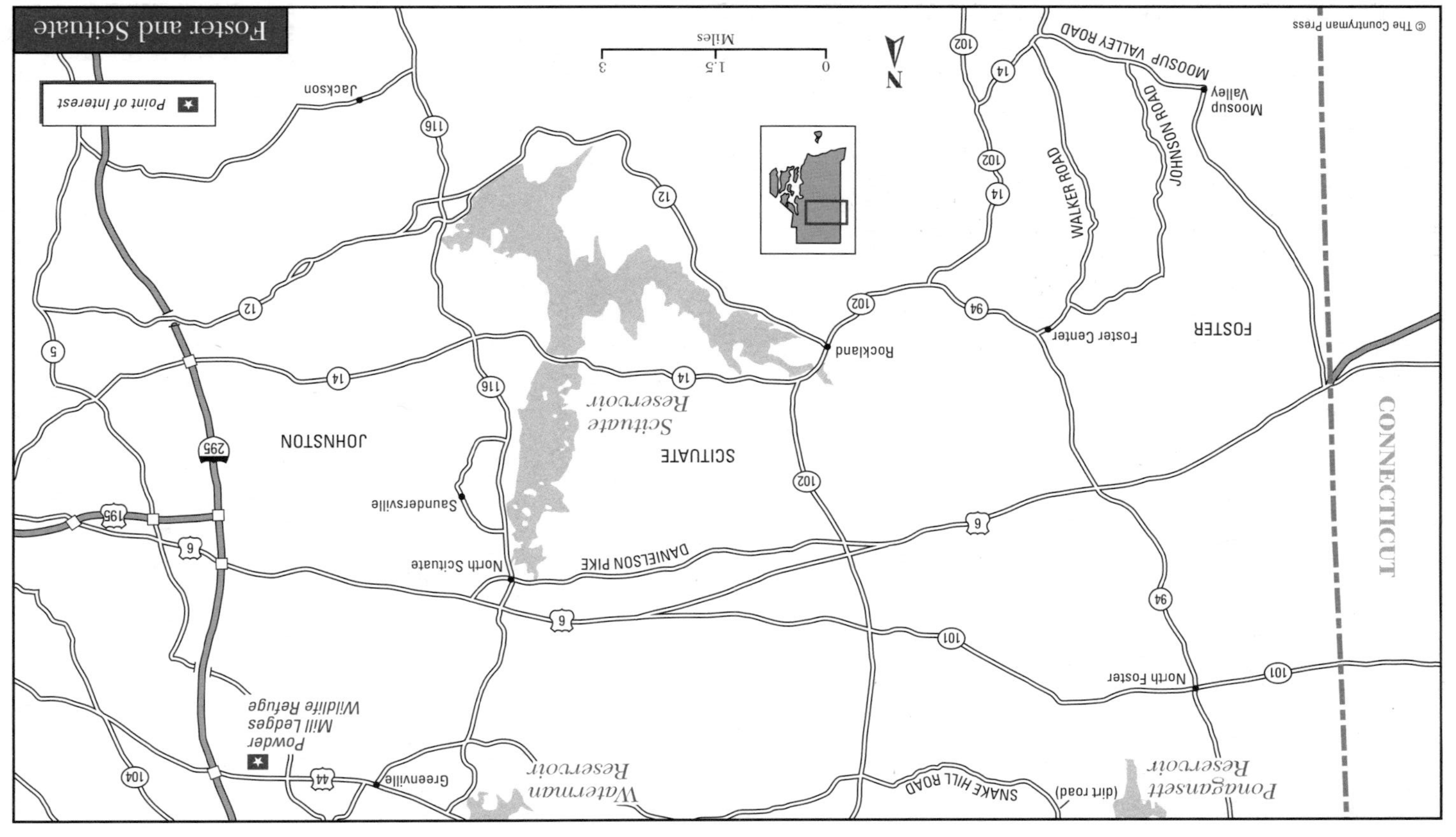
Foster and Scituate
Point of Interest
0
1.5
3
Miles
N
Jackson
Johnston
Saundersville
North Scituate
Danielson Pike
Scituate
Scituate Reservoir
Rockland
Powder Mill Ledges Wildlife Refuge
Greenville
Waterman Reservoir
Snake Hill Road
(dirt road)
Ponaganset Reservoir
North Foster
Foster
Foster Center
Walker Road
Johnson Road
Moosup Valley Road
Moosup Valley
Connecticut
© The Countryman Press
5
12
14
116
102
295
195
6
104
44
94
101

England picture. On the outskirts of the village are apple orchards where picking your own in fall is always a treat, as is finishing with a cup of coffee and hot apple pie at the orchard shop.

Western Rhode Island is for rambling on a pretty summer's day or in crisp, colorful autumn. Though the area lacks spectacular sights, it does offer beautiful scenery and some good examples of 18th-century New England villages.

GUIDANCE **Blackstone Valley Tourism Council and Visitors' Center** (401-724-2200; 1-800-454-2882), 175 Main Street, Pawtucket. Open daily 9–5. Not only are booklets and brochures about the Blackstone Valley available here, but you can also browse in an exhibition gallery with changing displays on the history and crafts of the region. Visitors also can see an orientation film on the Blackstone Valley in a new movie theater with art deco touches—velvet seats and stained-glass decor—that come from the 1920s LeRoy Theater, which was demolished a few years ago.

Blackstone River State Park Visitor Center (401-334-6723), off I-295 north, Lincoln, between exits 9 and 10.

GETTING THERE *By car:* Automobile is by far the best way to explore the Blackstone River Valley and western Rhode Island, but travelers should bear in mind that tourism is just getting established here. From Providence take I-95 north to Pawtucket and Central Falls. To reach Woonsocket, take RI 146 north from Providence.

By bus: **Peter Pan/Bonanza** (617-720-4110), from Boston, serves Providence-Pawtucket. **Rhode Island Public Transit Authority, or** RIPTA (401-781-9400; www.ripta.com), has minimal service to most of the communities of the Blackstone River Valley.

MEDICAL EMERGENCY The statewide emergency number is **911.**

Pawtucket Memorial Hospital (401-729-2000), 111 Brewster Street, Pawtucket.

✷ Villages

Albion, RI 146, Lincoln. Though the English settled this little town in the early 1800s, French Canadian immigration transformed it into a predominantly French-speaking area after the Civil War. Several imposing mansard-roofed tenements for mill workers still stand, as does a curious World War I memorial statue of a doughboy, with the inscription in both French and English.

Chepachet, US 44, Glocester. The village was settled in the early 18th century by descendants of English Dissenters who came to this then-wilderness area from Providence and constructed one-story clapboard houses. Although it was agricultural in its early days, the land was rocky and the village only came into its own at the turn of the 19th century. Then factories began to be built. First there was a hat factory, then a tannery, then a woolen mill on the banks of the Chepachet River, and before long hotels had been built for commercial travelers. But Chepachet's boom was short-lived. Its mills were too small to compete with larger ones in other areas, and by the 20th century, Chepachet's heyday had come and gone. Happily, however, many of its original structures remain, making it, historically speaking, an enticing village.

Harrisville, RI 107, Burrillville. The worsted mill around which this picturesque village grew was built about 1857, utilizing the waterpower from Mill Pond for its dam in the center of the community. Now on the National Historic Register, Harrisville owes its charm to Austin T. Levy, a New Yorker who became the owner of the Stillwater Worsted Mill in the 1930s. Levy planned to settle in Harrisville and wanted to make the hamlet more his idea of a "typical" New England village. To do so, he renovated Harrisville's two churches, the Berean Baptist Church on Chapel Street and the white-spired Universalist church in the village center on Main Street. He hired the architectural firm that had built the Providence County Courthouse to design a redbrick assembly hall in pseudo-colonial style as well as a town hall and a library. A post office was later built in the same style (and presented with much fanfare to the federal government, which had never had a post office building donated to it before). Exceedingly proud of his village creation, Levy, a winter resident of the Bahamas, invited his neighbor there, the duke of Windsor, to come see his New England mill village.

Manville, Lincoln. A handful of old brick mill houses remain here on Old River Road (RI 126).

Quinnville, Lincoln. Six early-19th-century clapboard mill houses and an old farmhouse still stand here along the Blackstone River on River Road.

Slatersville, RI 102, North Smithfield. Fifteen years after the construction of the cotton mill that bears his name in Pawtucket (see *Museums*), Samuel Slater, his brother John, William Almy, and Smith Brown bought water rights and established two mills here. They built houses, churches, and schools for their workers in what was to become an example of paternalistic industry. Thanks to a 20th-century preservationist, Henry P. Kendall, the pretty little white-clapboard houses of Slatersville still stand under leafy trees. There is a pleasant village green with a Greek Revival Congregational church at its head. On both sides of Greene Street stand the mill workers' and mill owners' houses, all with the Greek Revival decoration that Kendall added. He made this addition both to bring more charm to the little village and, in the 20th century, to erase the visible difference between workers' and owners' homes.

Union Village, RI 146, North Smithfield. This village was once known as the Cross Roads. The white-clapboard Friends Meeting House here dates only from 1881, but it stands on the site of an earlier meetinghouse where the mothers of two Rhode Island heroes—Declaration of Independence signer Stephen Hopkins and Continental army general Nathanael Greene—both worshipped.

✷ To See

MUSEUMS

In the Pawtucket area

Lysander and Susan Flagg Museum and Culture Center (401-727-7440), 209 Central Street, next to the public library, Central Falls. Open by appointment. In the Ballou Room, named for Civil War Union major Sullivan Ballou, killed at the battle of Bull Run, is memorabilia of many US wars—the Civil War, World Wars I and II, the Korean and Vietnam conflicts, the engagements in Panama. A full-figure autographed painting of baseball great Ted Williams by Central Falls painter Lorenzo Denevers is in the library next door.

Slater Mill (401-725-8638), 67 Roosevelt Avenue, Pawtucket. Open May through October, Tuesday through Sunday 10–4; November through February, tours by appointment; March and April. Saturday and Sunday 11–3. It was in the old mill here in 1793 that Samuel Slater, a manufacturer's apprentice from Derbyshire, England, used water-powered machines to produce the first cotton yarn made in America. Slater, it is said, carried the plans in his head when he emigrated across the ocean. (Because of English fears that the secrets of their machinery would leave the country, Slater had to disguise himself as an agricultural laborer to obtain passage.) Once in the New World, he elected to settle in Pawtucket after learning that businessman Moses Brown (see the introduction to the "Providence" chapter) was interested in improving some machinery he had purchased. Brown was impressed with Slater's ability and hired him. With Brown's son-in-law William Almy and nephew Smith Brown, Slater built the mill that stands today to house that improved machinery. The mill now displays a replica of an original carding engine and drawings of the other machines (the originals are in the Smithsonian Institution in Washington, DC), as well as a series of textile machines—some very rare—that date from 1838 to 1960. Also open to visitors is the 1758 **Sylvanus Brown House.** Once the home of a millwright and carpenter who worked at the mill, it is furnished with his early-19th-century belongings. On guided tours, costumed docents demonstrate spinning and weaving, and guests are sometimes invited to try their hand at this work, too. In the adjoining **Wilkinson Mill** of 1810, a 19th-century machine shop operates, powered by a 16,000-pound waterwheel.

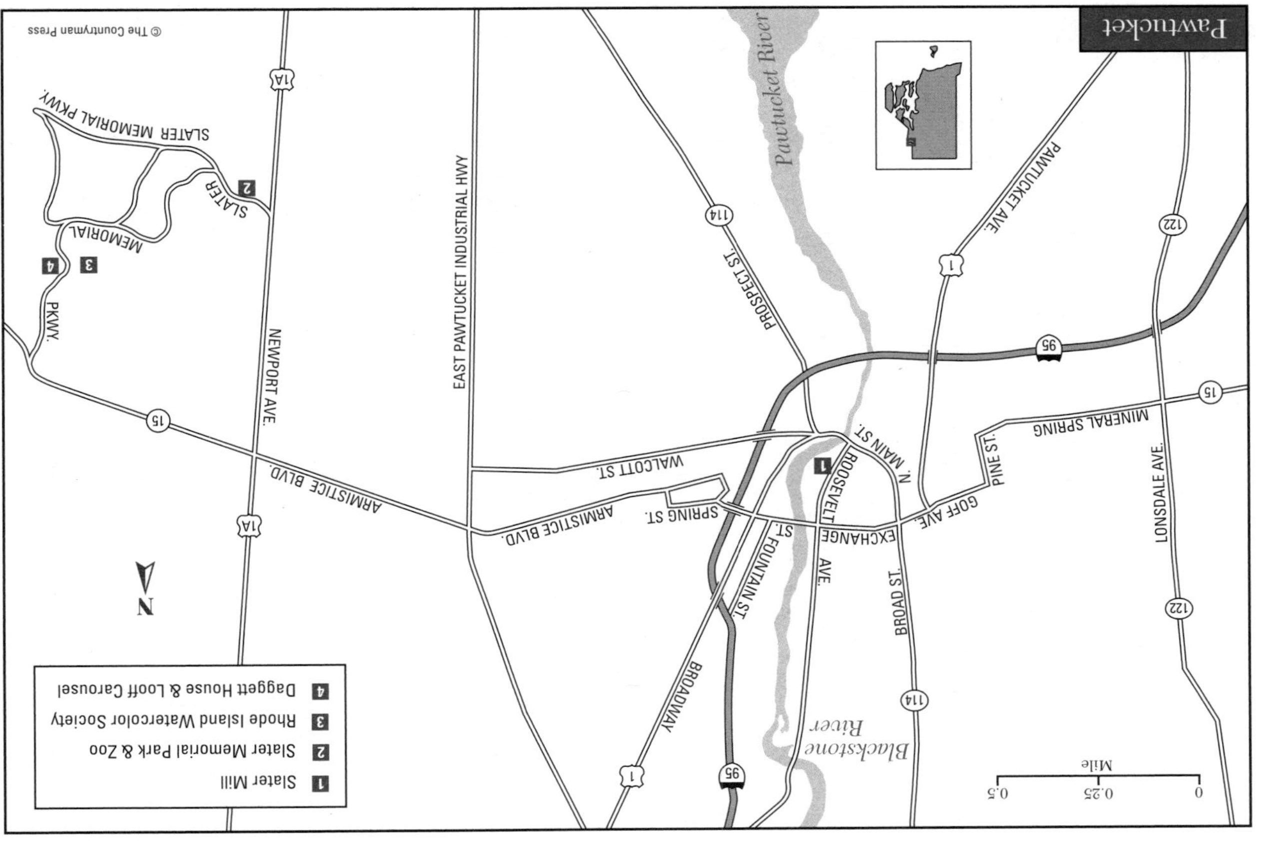
Pawtucket
1 Slater Mill
2 Slater Memorial Park & Zoo
3 Rhode Island Watercolor Society
4 Daggett House & Looff Carousel
N
0
0.25
0.5
Mile
Blackstone River
Pawtucket River
NEWPORT AVE.
ARMISTICE BLVD.
EAST PAWTUCKET INDUSTRIAL HWY
SLATER MEMORIAL PKWY.
SLATER
MEMORIAL
PKWY.
BROADWAY
FOUNTAIN ST.
SPRING ST.
WALCOTT ST.
EXCHANGE ST.
ROOSEVELT AVE.
N. MAIN ST.
BROAD ST.
PROSPECT ST.
GOFF AVE.
PINE ST.
MINERAL SPRING
PAWTUCKET AVE.
LONSDALE AVE.
© The Countryman Press

In Woonsocket

Museum of Work and Culture and Woonsocket Visitors Center (401-769-9675), 42 South Main Street at Market Square. Open Tuesday through Friday 9:30–4, Saturday 10–4, Sunday 1–4. Small admission fee. From 1915 to 1925 this redbrick building housed the Barnai Worsted Company, which manufactured woolen goods for military uniforms and men's fashions. Re-created in the museum are the shop floor of the mill itself, part of a three-family tenement replica such as Quebecois immigrant workers would have occupied in the early years of the 20th century, a church interior, a 1914 union hall, and the classroom of a parochial school.

HISTORIC HOMES AND SITES

In Glocester

Job Armstrong Store (401-568-4077), 1181 Main Street (part of a village commercial block), Chepachet Village. Open Saturday 11–3 in summer and early fall. Exhibits of artifacts from the Glocester of yesteryear. Antique postcards and history-related items are for sale for the benefit of the historical society. This circa-1800 building is the headquarters of the Glocester Heritage Society.

In the Pawtucket area

Eleazer Arnold House (401-728-9696), 487 Great Road, Lincoln. Open year-round Saturday and Sunday 11–5. Of principal interest to those with a bent for architecture, this late-17th-century, stone-ended house with its huge chimney is the best example of its period in Rhode Island. In its heyday, it was known as "Eleazer's splendid mansion" and served as a tavern. Travelers on the Great Road that extended from Providence to Mendon, Massachusetts, one of the earliest colonial roads, recognized it from a distance by its chimney.

Daggett House (401-722-6931; 401-723-0145), Slater Park off US 1A, Pawtucket. Open during city events or by appointment. This gable-roofed house, built by farmer John Daggett in 1685, replaced a smaller one destroyed by Native Americans in King Philip's War. The Daggetts were slaveholders, and the cellar still has the rings from which a slave would swing his hammock. The house is notable for its 17th-century antiques, colonial pewter, the china that belonged to General Nathanael Greene, and two bedspreads that belonged to Samuel Slater's family. This is a DAR-operated property.

Friends Meeting House (401-245-5860), Great Road, Lincoln. Call for hours. This gray-clapboard meetinghouse, part of which dates from 1703, was one of the earliest gathering places of Friends in New England.

Hannaway Blacksmith Shop (401-333-1100, ext. 8424), 671 Great Road, Lincoln. Call for hours. This reconstructed, 19th-century barnlike structure is open for blacksmithing demonstrations one Sunday each month between April and November.

Hearthside (401-726-0597), Great Road, Lincoln. In 1810, using money won in a Louisiana lottery, mill owner Stephen Hopkins Smith built this Federal-style stone house in the hope it would win over a young Providence woman he wished to wed. Unfortunately, it didn't. She found the house too remote, and Smith lived on in it alone. Today, the house is owned by the town and can be visited by appointment.

Kelly House (401-725-2847), Quinnville, on the bikeway of the Blackstone River Park, Lincoln. Open April through October, daily 9–4:30. Audios, videos, and photographic displays recount the story of the Blackstone Canal, which lasted barely 20 years in the early 19th century. Then the railroad took over the transportation of goods from Worcester to Providence. Built in 1835, the Kelly House was the home of the superintendent of the Kelly Cotton Mill, whose owner, Captain Wilbur Kelly, was a leader in the plans for the canal construction.

Looff Carousel (401-728-0500, ext. 251), Slater Park, Pawtucket. Open 11–5 weekends and holidays April through June and Labor Day through November 1. Open daily 11–5 July through Labor Day. Also open the first two weekends in December. It is wise, however, to call in advance to verify hours. Soon after his arrival in America in the 1870s, Danish-born furniture maker Charles Looff carved the figures of this carousel from pieces of leftover wood in his free time. These are the earliest examples of Looff work extant and include 42 horses, three dogs, a lion, a camel, and a giraffe. Looff went on to achieve fame as the carver of the carousel at New York's Coney Island. One of the last examples of his work is at Crescent Park in Riverside.

Moffitt Mill, Great Road, Lincoln. This pretty little stone-and-clapboard mill on the Moshassuck River was built in 1812 as a machine shop. Later it was used for the manufacture of shoelaces and braid. Though not open to the public, it's one of the most attractive old mill buildings still standing in Rhode Island.

In Woonsocket

Church of the Precious Blood (401-766-0326), Park and Carrington Avenues. This redbrick, gable-roofed Victorian Gothic church was erected in 1880.

Congregation B'nai Israel (401-762-3651), 224 Prospect Street. Founded in 1893, this is the oldest Conservative synagogue in Rhode Island. The current striking building was designed by synagogue architect

Samuel Glazer and is brightened by stained-glass windows depicting biblical events. They are the work of Israeli Avigdor Arikha, who learned his art in the workshop of Marc Chagall.

Globe Mill Tenements, 810–816 Front Street. Built about 1830, this Federal-style four-family structure is the city's largest remaining collection of old mill houses.

Harris Block and City Hall (401-762-6400), 169 Main Street. Open Monday through Friday 8:30–4. Edward Harris arrived in the 1830s and found a collection of six mill villages here that he eventually turned into the town of Woonsocket. He built one factory to make cashmeres, and another, completed during the Civil War, was considered the finest woolen mill in the country. He built the Harris Block, initially known as the Harris Institute, in 1856. On the lower level were shops whose rents went to finance the free school he established for his mill workers on the second floor, where on Sundays they learned to read and write. On the third floor was an assembly hall where, in 1860, Abraham Lincoln gave a campaign address. Eventually a public library, one of the first of its kind in the state, took the place of the second-floor school. The city now owns the Harris Block, and city council meetings are held there.

St. Ann's Church (Dominique Doiron, 401-447-0823 or 401-356-0713), 84 Cumberland Street. Inside this buff-colored stone church, completed in 1918 for the rapidly growing French Canadian population of the city, are religious frescoes painted by Italian-born artist Guido Nanchieri. Nanchieri had studied in Florence, then moved to Montreal in 1914 to open a stained-glass business. After he had contracted with the pastor of St. Ann's, the Reverend Ernest Morin, to do the frescoes, it was discovered in Canada that Nanchieri had once painted the figure of Mussolini astride his horse. It was 1940, and anti-Mussolini sentiment was strong in Canada and the United States. Because he had created such a work, Nanchieri was arrested and sent to an Ontario concentration camp. It was only with the help of Father Morin that he was released. He used pre–World War I members of the community as models for such scenes as *The Temptation of Adam and Eve* and *The Life of St. Anne.*

St. Charles Church (401-766-0176), North Main and Daniel Streets. This square-towered granite Gothic church, erected in 1868, is another of Woonsocket's early Catholic churches.

Train Station (401-762-0440), 1 Depot Square. Open Monday through Friday 8–4. Now National Park Service headquarters, this brick-and-terracotta building was constructed in 1882 as a depot for the Providence & Worcester Railroad. It replaced an 1847 structure that Edward Harris had erected when he brought in the first railroad. For many years its clock tower was renowned for the copper locomotive weathervane on top. The original one was sold—and its replacement stolen. Discussions continue about the possibility of another replacement.

Union Saint–Jean Baptiste d'Amerique Building (401-769-0520), 1 Social Street. This Indiana-limestone structure was designed in 1926 by Woonsocket's leading early-20th-century architect, Walter F. Fontaine, to house the nation's largest Franco-American insurance society.

An **outdoor mural** of old Woonsocket's mills and churches by Ron Deziel can be found at 547 Clinton Street, behind the Kennedy Manor Senior Housing complex.

SCENIC DRIVES *In Burrillville:* **East Avenue** (RI 107) winds through the pretty little mill village of Harrisville, and Sherman Farm Road unfolds along the rolling fields of northern Rhode Island farm country.

In Foster: **Johnson Road** offers fine vistas over Moosup Valley.

In Glocester: **Reynolds Road** (RI 94) meanders through rich, hilly farmland; **Wallum Lake Road** (RI 100) goes up hill and down dale past reservoirs and lakes; and **Cucumber Hill Road** dives down into Moosup Valley past horse farms.

In Lincoln: **Breakneck Hill Road** affords vistas of horse farms and fields edged with stone walls; **Great Road** passes through rolling, wooded countryside, including the extensive Chase Farm acreage; **Limerock Road,** narrow and wooded, is a fine route for viewing the Blackstone Valley's fall foliage; and **I-295,** passing through Cumberland, Lincoln, and Smithfield, offers long vistas over the Blackstone River Valley.

In Smithfield: **Snake Hill Road** winds through woods and fields, past farms and orchards bright with apple blossoms in spring. **Swan Road** runs through fragrant apple-orchard country.

WINERY **Diamond Hill Vineyards** (401-333-2751), 3145 Diamond Hill Road, Cumberland. Call for hours. The "new tradition" wines of this 34-acre vineyard are made from the apples, pears, peaches, and blueberries grown on the property. Traditional grape wines are pinot noir, chardonnay, and blush. The wines, with an alcohol content reaching up to 11 percent, are sold only at the vineyard, and buyers can have their own names affixed to their bottles.

✳ To Do

ANIMAL FARMS ✐ Daggett Farm (401-728-0500, ext. 251), Slater Park off US 1A, Pawtucket. Open 9–3:30. There are cows and horses, chickens and sheep, rabbits and donkeys to view on this 6-acre working farm.

APPLE PICKING AND FARM STANDS You'll find good apple picking in late summer and fall at the following farms: **Snowhurst Farm** (401-568-8900), 421 Chopmist Hill Road, Chepachet; **Moosup River Farm** (401-949-7898), 1 Snake Hill Road, Glocester; **Barden Family Orchard** (401-934-1413), 56 Elmdale Road, North Scituate (also pumpkins and blueberries in-season); **Sunset Orchards** (401-934-1900), Gleaner Chapel Road, North Scituate. Open daily 9–5 August through December. Also:

Appleland Orchard (401-949-3690), 135 Smith Avenue, Greenville. Open daily 9–5 summer and fall, selling apples, peaches, and pears.

Harmony Farms (401-934-0741), 359 Sawmill Road, Harmony. Call for hours. Pick-your-own blueberries.

Jaswell's Farm (401-231-9043), 50 Swan Road, Smithfield. Open daily 8–5 from mid-May through December. Pick-your-own apples, strawberries, blueberries, pumpkins, and raspberries in-season. The stand sells homemade cider, honey, and seasonal vegetables.

Phantom Farms (401-333-2240), Diamond Hill Road, Cumberland. Open daily year-round 7 AM–6 PM. Pumpkins, apples, and chrysanthemums brighten this roadside stand in fall, when you can pick your own apples, too. Inside, the treats include such apple confections as pies and muffins. Sometimes there are hayrides for visitors. Honey from farm hives is available for purchase, and in spring and summer fresh vegetables abound.

Wright's Dairy Farm (401-767-3014), Woonsocket Hill Road (off RI 146A), North Smithfield. Open Monday through Saturday 8–7, Sunday 8–4. Dairy-fresh milk, cream, eggs, and whipped cream pastries are sold in the farm bakery; tours of the dairy are offered in summer. Cows are milked daily 3–5.

BICYCLING **Blackstone River Bikeway** (401-724-2200). A 10-mile bike path starts at John Street and Lonsdale Avenue in Cumberland and continues into Woonsocket.

BOATING ***Blackstone Valley Explorer*** (401-724-1500; 1-800-619-BOAT), Blackstone Valley Tourism Council, 175 Main Street, Pawtucket. The 34-foot-long, 49-passenger open riverboat *Blackstone Valley Explorer* takes 45-minute trips on the Blackstone River from Central Falls June through early October.

CANOEING AND KAYAKING Now that the **Blackstone River** is clearer, it's becoming an increasingly attractive waterway for canoeists. The stretch from Albion to Lonsdale is particularly accessible and pretty.

Wildlife that can be seen in the environs of Manville include sandpipers, herons, and snapping turtles.

Blackstone Valley Outfitters (401-312-0369), 25 Carrington Street, Lincoln. Rents canoes, kayaks, and bicycles, and offers guided kayak tours on the Blackstone River. Open Monday through Thursday 9–7, Friday 9–6, Saturday and Sunday 6–5.

Friends of the Blackstone (401-699-1542), 6 Valley Stream Drive, Cumberland. Canoe trips on the Blackstone River between Woonsocket and Valley Falls, Cumberland, are offered by appointment.

FISHING *In Burrillville:* The **Clear River** access is north of Pascoag on RI 100 in White Mill Park. Offers good trout fishing. Access **Roundtop Pond** off RI 96. Stocked with trout. **Spring Lake** (also called Herring Pond) is full of largemouth bass. Access by Black Hut Road. The **Wakefield Pond** access is by the state boat ramp and parking area. Panfish and largemouth bass are plentiful there.

In Cumberland: The **Blackstone River** is accessible in many places, where you can fish for trout. **Howard Pond** is known for panfish and largemouth bass. The access is from Howard Road.

CANOEING THE BLACKSTONE RIVER

Blackstone Valley Tourism Council

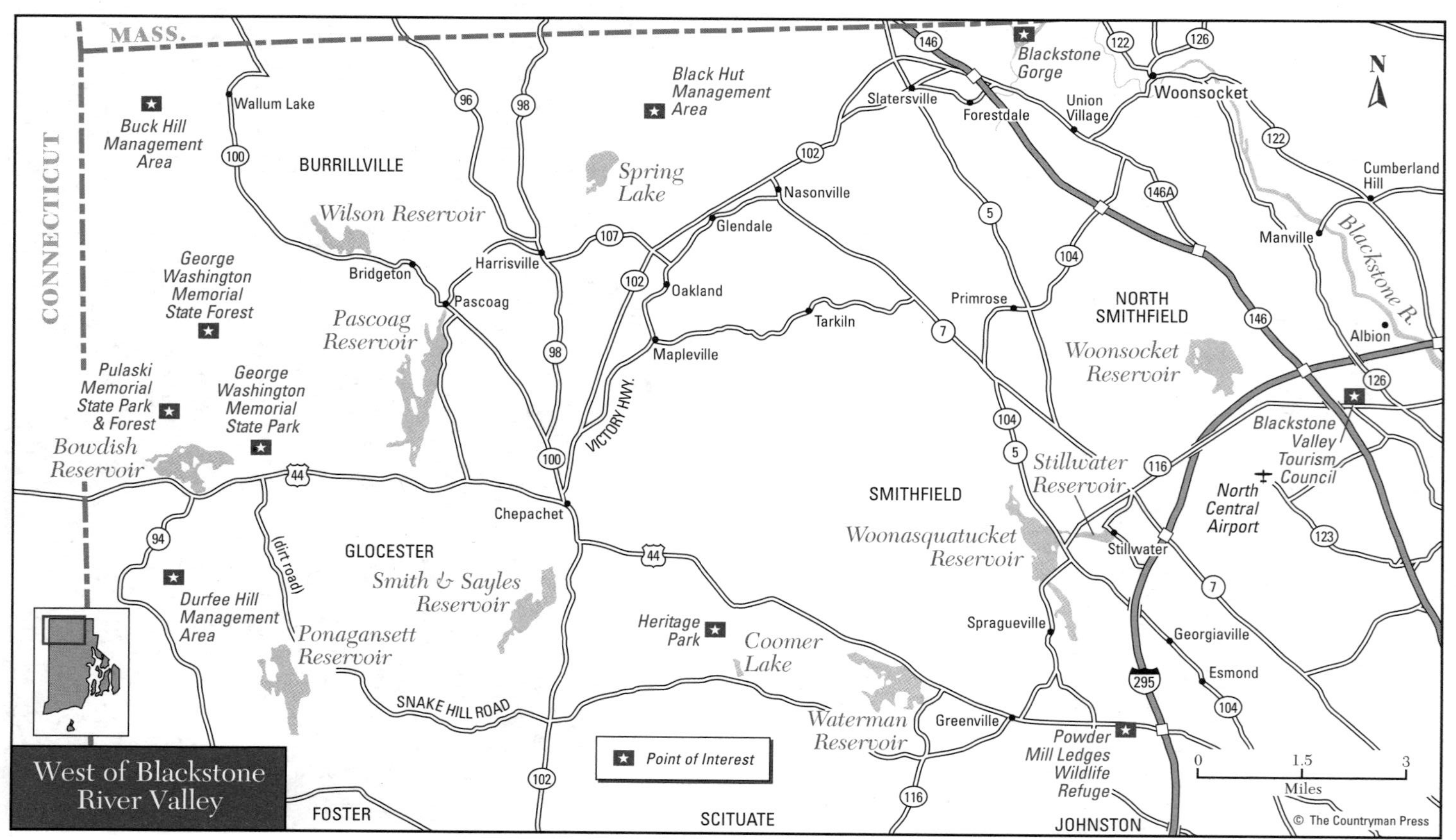
West of Blackstone River Valley
MASS.
CONNECTICUT
Buck Hill Management Area
Wallum Lake
BURRILLVILLE
Wilson Reservoir
George Washington Memorial State Forest
Pulaski Memorial State Park & Forest
George Washington Memorial State Park
Bowdish Reservoir
Bridgeton
Harrisville
Pascoag
Pascoag Reservoir
Black Hut Management Area
Spring Lake
Nasonville
Glendale
Oakland
Mapleville
Tarkiln
VICTORY HWY.
Chepachet
GLOCESTER
(dirt road)
Durfee Hill Management Area
Ponagansett Reservoir
Smith & Sayles Reservoir
SNAKE HILL ROAD
FOSTER
SCITUATE
Heritage Park
Coomer Lake
Waterman Reservoir
Greenville
Point of Interest
SMITHFIELD
Woonasquatucket Reservoir
Spragueville
Stillwater Reservoir
Stillwater
Primrose
Slatersville
Forestdale
Blackstone Gorge
Union Village
Woonsocket
NORTH SMITHFIELD
Woonsocket Reservoir
Manville
Cumberland Hill
Blackstone R.
Albion
Blackstone Valley Tourism Council
North Central Airport
Georgiaville
Esmond
Powder Mill Ledges Wildlife Refuge
JOHNSTON
N
0 1.5 3
Miles
© The Countryman Press

In Glocester: The **Chepachet River** is accessible from behind the Chepachet Fire Station on US 44. Trout fishing is most popular here. **Bowdish Reservoir** is full of panfish, largemouth bass, and pickerel. Access is through the George Washington Management Area off US 44, where there is a state boat ramp and parking. **Pascoag Reservoir** borders Burrillville as well as Glocester. It is accessible by the state boat ramp off Jackson Schoolhouse Road. Panfish, largemouth bass, and pickerel are likely catches. **Smith and Sayles Reservoir** access is by a state launching ramp and parking area off Sand Dam Road. There is a 10-horsepower limit on outboards. Fish for yellow perch, largemouth bass, and pickerel. Access **Waterman Reservoir** along US 44 for shore fishing of largemouth bass and northern pike.

In Lincoln: **Butterfly Pond** access is from Great Road. Fish for panfish and largemouth bass. **Olney Pond** offers a state boat ramp, a parking area, and shore-fishing facilities. Go for the trout and largemouth bass.

In North Smithfield: **Round Top Brook** is a good trout-fishing spot. Access to the Round Top Fishing Area is from RI 96. **Upper Slatersville Reservoir** is accessible from the state boat ramp and parking area off RI 102. Largemouth bass and panfish are found here. **Woonasquatucket Reservoir** (Stump Pond) is off RI 5 and RI 116. Fish for largemouth bass, northern pike, and pickerel.

In Pawtucket: **Slater Park Pond** is stocked with pickerel, trout, and sunfish.

GOLF **Country View Golf Club** (401-568-7157), 49 Club Lane, Burrillville. An 18-hole par-70 course with hilly terrain, two ponds, and a restaurant.

Crystal Lake Golf Course (401-567-4500), Steere Farm Road, Burrillville. There is an 18-hole golf course here, a clubhouse, tavern, and pro shop.

Foster Country Club (401-397-7750), 67 Johnson Road, Foster. The club offers an 18-hole course with a restaurant and golf shop.

HAYRIDES AND SLEIGH RIDES **Chepachet Farms** (401-568-9996), 226 Tourtellot Hill Road, Chepachet Village. Hayrides and sleigh rides, plus a petting corral.

HORSEBACK RIDING **Sunset Stables** (401-722-3033), 1 Twin River Road, Lincoln. Guided trail rides through Lincoln Woods Park.

Rhode Island Sports Center (401-767-2200), 1186 Eddie Dowling Highway, North Smithfield. Open to the public for ice-skating weekday mornings and Sunday afternoons.

SWIMMING **Frank Moody State Beach** (401-277-1415), Lincoln Woods State Park off RI 146, Lincoln. A pretty beach in a park setting, but on summer weekends it's wise to arrive early.

Casimir Pulaski Memorial State Park (401-277-1415), George Washington Management Area, Pulaski Road off US 44, Glocester. Swimming in Peck's Pond, Burrillville. Bathhouses and lifeguard.

Spring Lake, Spring Lake Road, Burrillville. There is a fee to swim in this pleasant lake, which is part of a town recreation area that also includes a collection of vintage arcade games. Lifeguard.

TENNIS Courts open to the public are available at the following locations:

In Burrillville: (401-548-9470), **Burrillville High School,** East Avenue, Harrisville; **Burrillville Middle School,** RI 102, Glendale.

In Cumberland: (401-728-2400), **Currier Play Area,** Broad Street; **Tucker Field Athletic Complex,** Mendon Road; **Windsor Park,** Snake Hill Road.

In Lincoln: (401-333-1100), **Lime Acres,** Jenckes Hill Road, Limerock.

In North Smithfield: (401-767-2200), **North Smithfield High School,** RI 104; **Pacheco Park,** off Main Street, Slatersville.

In Pawtucket: (401-728-0500), **Slater Park,** RI 1A.

In Smithfield: (401-233-1000), **Smithfield High School,** Pleasantview Avenue; **Willow Field,** Tucker Road.

✷ Green Space

Arboretum at Riverside (401-724-8733), 724 Pleasant Street, Pawtucket. Five miles of wooded trails and paths edge the Seekonk River and abut Riverside Cemetery. The arboretum was laid out in 1874 and inspired by the work of renowned landscape architect Frederick Law Olmsted. In May, Azalea Day celebrates these colorful flowers. At other times it's pleasant simply to stroll in the shade of the trees brought here from all parts of the world. There is a small admission fee.

Blackstone Gorge State Park, North Smithfield. This is an impressive wooded and rock-ledge park overlooking the Blackstone River Gorge, which is the only spot in Rhode Island for white-water canoeing. The park can be difficult to find because there is no marked access point. Take RI 146 north from North Smithfield to RI 146A north, turning right onto St. Paul's Street, then left onto RI 122. Continue to County Street, where you turn left and go to the dead end. It's then a short walk (don't be discouraged—it's through backyards, but access is allowed) to the woods above the river. Take any one of the three paths to the left (one is decorated with modern sculptures fashioned of wood and twigs). After about five minutes you'll arrive at the spectacular gorge overlook.

William Blackstone Park, Broad and Blackstone Streets (across from the Ann & Hope Specialty Shops), Cumberland. A granite monument to the first Blackstone River Valley settler, the Reverend William Blackstone, is the centerpiece of this 1-acre park.

Blackstone River State Park, Old Lower River Road, Lincoln. Off RI 146, take the RI 116 north exit to the second set of lights. Go right and immediately left onto River Road; then take the first left downhill. Go left again and park. Set beneath an underpass in urban Rhode Island, this little park between the Blackstone River and the Blackstone Canal is a peaceful retreat from the city bustle. Though the park is only a stone's throw from the highway, the rush of a waterfall masks vehicle sounds. The canal was constructed by Irish immigrants in the 1820s to transport manufactured products the 45 miles between Worcester, Massachusetts, and Providence. Although sections of the canal have washed away, it has been restored in this park, and you can amble the towpath between river and canal for about 2 miles, seeing the occasional blue heron. An extension of a bike path (see *To Do* in the "Providence" chapter) to the park is in the works.

Buck Hill Wildlife Management Area, Buck Hill Road, Burrillville. There are blazed trails past ponds and old stone walls, through woods rich in game and songbirds. During hunting season, fluorescent orange clothing is required.

Chase Farm (401-333-1100), Great Road, Lincoln. The 100 acres of this former dairy farm are open to the public for hiking, picnicking, kite flying, sledding, and horseshoe pitching. There's also a butterfly garden.

Chocolate Mill Overlook Park, Central Falls. This little park at the corner of Charles Street and Roosevelt Avenue on the bank of the Blackstone River is near the site of the 18th-century William Wheat Chocolate Mill.

Diamond Hill Park, Cumberland. This wooded, rocky park, which takes its name from the abundant quartz crystals found there, has unmarked trails and fields, a pond, and a picnic area.

Heritage Park, Glocester (Chestnut Oak Road between the villages of Harmony and Chepachet). There are rock ledges, skiing and hiking trails, picnic tables, brooks, and pine woods in this 127-acre town park that is ideal for Sunday-afternoon excursions with children.

Lincoln Woods State Park, RI 123, Lincoln (401-723-7892) You can idle away many a summer afternoon in this 627-acre park of woods, kettle holes, and rock outcroppings. There is a pond for fishing and swimming, and trails for walking and riding. This is also a great spot for cross-country skiing during winter.

The Monastery, Diamond Hill Road, Cumberland. In 1900 a Cistercian monastery was established on a 500-acre site here and was, at that time, one of only three Cistercian monasteries in the United States. Today the hilly, forested terrain is the property of the town of Cumberland, and a rugged walking trail winds through trees and fields, past a marsh and a monument called *Nine Men's Misery.* This marks the spot where the bodies of nine colonial soldiers killed in King Philip's War were found.

Powder Mill Ledges Wildlife Refuge, Putnam Pike (RI 44) and Cedar Swamp Road, Smithfield. Two miles of hiking trails thread through this area, the headquarters of the Audubon Society of Rhode Island.

Casimir Pulaski Memorial Recreation Area, Pulaski Road, Glocester. The attractions of this state management area include a beach, covered bridge, pond, picnic area, and four cross-country ski trails that, in the off-season, are fine for walking.

Slater Park, RI 1A, Pawtucket. This is a pretty, manicured park that has a particular appeal for children, with its Looff carousel, picnic sites, playground, barnyard, and duck-feeding pond. Adults will enjoy walks along the Ten Mile River Canal, lawn bowling, and tennis.

Valley Falls Heritage Park, Broad Street, Cumberland. A ruined mill stands on this 2-acre site beside a waterfall; interpretive signs explain how it once worked. There is a picnic area and historic footbridges over sluiceways.

George Washington Management Area, Burrillville and Glocester. Access is north of US 44 along a gravel roadway. This 3,489-acre area contains ponds and wetlands; evergreen, oak, and maple forests; many trails; and fine spots for winter birding. Among the evergreens there may be ovenbirds, northern waterthrushes and hermit thrushes, pine warblers, and occasionally tufted titmice. In the deciduous forest, many warblers pass through during spring and fall migrations. Animals of the area include white-tailed deer, cottontail rabbits and snowshoe hares, foxes, coyotes, and raccoons. During hunting season, which runs from October through March, all visitors and hunters must wear 200 square inches of fluorescent orange.

✷ Lodging

Since the Blackstone River Valley is largely a rural area, the number of accommodations is limited.

INNS **Grace Note Farm & Inn Trail Riding Center** (401-567-0354), 969 Jackson Schoolhouse Road, Pascoag. ($) Six rooms with shared bath on a 17th-century farm adjacent to the George Washington Management Area. Guests may help care for the horses. Those with riding experience may ride on more than 75 miles of trails. There is backpacking, mountain biking, hiking trails, and cross-country skiing. Three meals a day are included.

BED & BREAKFASTS **Pillsbury House** (401-766-7983; 1-800-205-4112), 341 Prospect Street, Woonsocket. ($) An 1875 mansard-roofed Victorian house with a wraparound porch in the city's tree-shaded North End. Four air-conditioned rooms, all with private bath, in a former mill superintendent's house. Apple pancakes are among the items on the breakfast menu.

CAMPGROUNDS **Bowdish Lake Camping Area** (401-568-8890), Bowdish Lake. Write: P.O. Box 25, Chepachet. Off US 44, 5 miles west of Chepachet Village. Open May 1 through October 15. The 450 sites near Lake Bowdish are suitable for tents or for RVs up to 35 feet in length. Water, electricity, dumping stations, toilets, hot showers, hiking trails, boat and canoe rentals, fishing, playgrounds, and recreation halls are available. Entertainment, sports, and crafts activities are offered in July and August.

Echo Lake Campground (401-568-7109), 180 Mononey Road, Burrillville. There are 150 trailer sites, 100 with full hookup. Hot showers, sewer hookup and sewage pump-out, water hookup, telephone, and camp store. Reservations required. Open May 1 through September 30.

George Washington Management Area (401-568-2013), 2185 Putnam Pike, Chepachet. This area is located off US 44, 2 miles east of the Connecticut line and 5 miles west of the junction of US 44 and RI 102. Open mid-April through mid-October. Overlooking Bowdish Reservoir in a wooded area, 45 primitive tent and trailer campsites plus two shelters provide splendid spots to spend the night after a day of swimming and hiking.

✷ Where to Eat

DINING OUT ✐ ♿ **Andrew's Bistro** (401-658-1515; www.andrewsbistro.com), 3755 Mendon Road, Cumberland. ($$–$$$) Open Monday through Thursday 11:30–9, Friday and Saturday 11:30–10. Tuesday's off-season, a three-course prix fixe dinner for two is $40.

✐ ♿ **Chan's Fine Oriental Dining** (401-765-1900; http://chanseggrollsandjazz.com), 267 Main

Street, Woonsocket. ($) Open daily for lunch and dinner. Live jazz and comedy shows are the highlights of Chan's weekends. As for the food, it's largely Cantonese and Mandarin, with an occasional Polynesian or spicy Szechuan dish.

♿ **Faial Restaurant** (401-231-1100; www.faialrestaurant.com), 970 Douglas Pike, Smithfield. ($–$$) Open Monday and Tuesday for lunch; all other days for lunch and dinner. Such Azorean specialties as pork and clams and beefsteak with an egg and hot peppers on top are menu highlights.

♿ **Fred & Steve's Steak House** (401-723-3200), 100 Twin River Road, Lincoln. ($$–$$$) Open Wednesday and Thursday 5–9, Friday and Saturday 5–11, Sunday 4–9. Steaks start at $32 and go to $72 (for two) at this upscale steakhouse that also offers prime rib, veal, and free-range chicken.

♿ **River Falls Restaurant** (401-235-9026), 74 South Main Street, Woonsocket. ($–$$) Open Tuesday 4–9, Wednesday 3–10, Thursday, Friday, Saturday, 4–10, Sunday 12–8; closed Monday. The Sunday chicken dinner for $10.99 is always a favorite, as are the fishcakes and crab cakes that are served in this refurbished 19th-century building.

♿ **Rasoi** (401-7285500; www.rasoi-restaurant.com), 727 East Avenue, Pawtucket ($$–$$$). This colorful Indian restaurant offering dishes characteristic of all parts of the country is open for lunch and dinner seven days a week.

♿ **Rosinha's Restaurant** (401-721-0770; www.rosinhasrestaurant.com), Hope Valley Artiste Village, 1045 Main Street, Pawtucket. ($$–$$$). Such dishes as pork and littlenecks; stewed and grilled octopus in a hot pepper and wine sauce; dried codfish with chickpeas, kale, and hard-boiled egg; and lobster, shrimp, littlenecks, mussels, squid, crab, and fin fish in a red sauce are highlights of the menu of this mainland Portugal, Azorean, and Cape Verdean restaurant.

♿ **The Tavern on Main** (401-710-9788; www.tavernonmainri.com), 1157 Putnam Pike, Chepachet Village. ($–$$) Open Wednesday and Thursday 3–9, Friday and Saturday 11:30–9:30, Sunday 11:30–8:30. It was in this tavern in 1842 that Thomas Wilson Dorr, instigator of the Dorr Rebellion, established his headquarters. He had been elected the People's Governor to seek universal white male suffrage in Rhode Island, rather than suffrage based on property rights. Troops of the governor elected by the property owners attacked him here with his supporters, and shots were fired through the tavern door. Today this is a tavern-restaurant, paneled and picturesque, with an extensive menu that includes such comfort foods as chicken potpie or pasta and meatballs for under $11 and a Colossal Cuisine Special of soup, salad, entrée, potato, and vegetable for less than $12.

♂ ♿ **Trattoria Romana** (401-333-6700; www.trattoria-romana.com), 3 Wake Robin Road, Lincoln. ($–$$) Open for lunch and dinner Sunday through Friday and Saturday for dinner. The fare here is sophisticated northern Italian.

Vintage (491-765-1234; www.vintageri.com), 2 South Main Street, Woonsocket. ($–$$) Open Monday through Thursday 11:30–10; Friday 11:30–midnight; Saturday 4–midnight, Sunday 4–9, Saturday 5–9. This stylish restaurant serves creative fusion cuisine in this workaday city. Appetizers include barbecued pulled-pork nachos; an entrée might be pistachio-encrusted tuna. Outdoor deck dining in-season.

EATING OUT ♿ **Bob and Timmy's Grilled Pizza** (401-768-3490; http://bobandtimmys.com), 621 Pound Hill Road, North Smithfield. Open Sunday through Thursday 11–10, Friday and Saturday 11–11. The pizza is wood-grilled, of course.

The Bocce Club (401-767-2000), 226 Saint Louis Avenue, Woonsocket. ($) Open for dinner Tuesday through Saturday 5–10, Sunday noon–9. The family-style chicken dinner includes an antipasto rather than a salad.

The Burrito Company (401-597-6400; www.theburritoco.com), 194 Cass Avenue, Woonsocket ($–$$). Closed Sunday and Monday, but open for lunch and dinner otherwise. Mexican food of all kinds and a children's menu of American food.

Doherty's East Avenue Irish Pub (401-725-9520), 342 East Avenue, Pawtucket. ($–$$) Open seven days a week 11–1 AM. Steak tips and barbecue are among the favorites at this sports bar popular with locals.

♿ **Davenport's Restaurant** (401-334-1017; www.davenportsri.com), 1070 Mendon Road, Cumberland. ($–$$). Open daily for lunch and dinner. A chicken Florentine pizza with chicken and spinach in an Alfredo sauce is ever popular in this family-oriented restaurant that serves children's meals and has specials that include a beverage and dessert on Monday and Tuesday.

♿ **Exchange Street Café** (401-722-5530), 49 Exchange Street, Pawtucket. ($) Open daily 7–10. There's no doubt about there being affordable meals at this popular local eatery where entrées can be had for between $5 and $6. Especially popular are the turkey dinners and the stuffed cabbage. There are also sandwiches.

♿ **Garden Grille** (401-726-2826; http://gardengrillecafe.com), 727 East Avenue, Pawtucket. ($–$$) Open Monday through Saturday for lunch and dinner, Sunday for brunch. An all-time favorite at this vegetarian restaurant is the butternut squash quesadilla, but the restaurant menu also features creative salads, wood-grilled vegetables and pizzas, and tofu specials.

♂ ♿ **Greenville Inn** (401-949-4020), 36 Smith Avenue, Greenville. ($) Open Monday through Thursday 4–10, Sunday noon–10. Prime rib on the bone is an inn specialty and all-time favorite is the Sunday family-style chicken, including soup, salad, chicken, and macaroni for $10.95

Kountry Kitchen (401-949-0840), 10 Smith Avenue, Greenville. ($) Open Sunday through Thursday 6:30 AM–2 PM, Friday 6:30-2 and 4–8 PM, Saturday 6:30 AM 2 PM. It's the weekday country breakfast of home fries, two eggs, and toast until 9 AM that makes this a favorite stopping place for locals.

♿ **LJ's BBQ** (401-395-5255; www.ljsbbq.com), 727 East Avenue, Pawtucket. ($–$$$) Open daily for breakfast, lunch, and dinner. Texas beef barbecue, barbecued ribs, pulled pork, fried catfish, Southern pecan pie, and sweet potato pie are all-time favorites,

♂ ♿ **Modern Diner** (401-726-8390), 364 East Avenue, Pawtucket. ($) Open Monday through Saturday 6–2, Sunday 7–2. This historic 1940s-style diner has old-time favorites like liver and onions daily, and fish-and-chips on Friday. A Pawtucket classic, especially popular for its weekend breakfasts.

♂ **Plouffe's Cup-N-Saucer** (401-722-0890). 267 Main Street, Pawtucket. ($) Open Monday through Wednesday 7–3, Thursday through Saturday 7–6, Sunday 7–2. There's a jukebox just inside the door that plays both World War II–era and 1980s musical hits. There are motorcycle and racing car pictures on the walls, and figures of Marilyn Monroe and Al Capone in the window of this period-piece eatery that specializes in French meat pies, but also offers fish-and-chips, clam cakes, and stuffies in the Rhode Island tradition.

♂ **Wright's Farm** (401-769-2856; www.wrightsfarm.com), 84 Inman Road, Harrisville. ($) Thursday and Friday 4–9, Saturday noon–9:30, Sunday noon–8. Chicken family-style is a northern Rhode Island tradition, and nowhere is it better presented than at this hillside chicken farm. You can get half a roast chicken, shell macaroni, salad, and rolls for under $12.

Ye Olde English Fish & Chips Shop (401-762-3637), 25 South Main Street, Market Square Plaza, Woonsocket. ($) Tuesday through Saturday 10–6. Aficionados say this little shop sells the best fish-and-chips in the state—crisp-fried and fresh.

CAFES **Wildflour Vegan Bakery and Juice Bar** (401-475-4718), 727 East Avenue, Pawtucket. ($–$$).There are vegan cupcakes and chocolate chip scones, cheesecake and cookies, coffee and juices in this restful, inviting café where guests always find bouquets of fresh flowers.

ICE CREAM AND SNACKS
Ice Cream Machine (401-333-5053), 4288 Diamond Hill Road, Cumberland. Open April into the fall, daily 11–8. There are 35 ice cream and three sherbet flavors to choose from at this ice cream stand opposite Diamond Hill Park. For the family pet, try the sugar-free, nondairy Frosty Paws ice cream.

✷ Entertainment

FILM/THEATER Blackstone River Theatre (401-725-9272; www.riverfolk.org), 549 Broad Street, Cumberland. The Pendragon Celtic Band offers its own weekend music and dance performances as well as sponsoring visits from leading musical groups from the United States, Canada, and Europe in this renovated former Masonic temple.

Community College of Rhode Island Theatre (401-333-7000), Flanagan Campus, 1762 Louisquisset Pike, Lincoln. Occasional performances.

The Community Players (401-726-6860; www.thecommunityplayers.org), Jenks Junior High School, Division Street, Pawtucket. This community theater group that has been in existence for more than 75 years performs comedies, mysteries, and Broadway musicals four times annually.

Sandra Feinstein-Gamm Theatre (401-723-4266), 172 Exchange Street, Pawtucket. Plays like William Shakespeare's *Hamlet* and David Mamet's *Glengarry Glen Ross* are the sort of serious theatrical fare this Trinity Repertory Company offshoot offers in a handsomely renovated space adjoining the historic Pawtucket Armory.

The Met Café (401-729-1005, 401-331-1005; www.themetri.com), Hope Artiste Village, 1005 Main Street, Pawtucket. Here there has been a rebirth of the longtime Providence rock 'n' roll club of the same name. Each night there's live music—jazz, blues, hip-hop, rock—and pub food.

Mixed Magic Theatre (401-305-7333; http://mmtri.com), Hope Artiste Village, 999 Main Street, Pawtucket. Some productions, like *Kwanzaa Song* in December, are given in the theater abutting the Blackstone Valley Tourism Council, but others are at Pawtucket's Veteran's Memorial Amphitheater. In summer, there are outdoor shows in Woonsocket's Riverside Park, in Narragansett at the Towers, in Pawtucket at the Town Landing, and in Bristol at Blithewold.

Rustic Drive-In (401-769-7601), RI 146, North Smithfield. This is the last drive-in movie theater still in operation in Rhode Island.

Stadium Theater (401-762-4545; www.stadiumtheatre.com), 28 Monument Square, Woonsocket. In this elaborate, restored 1920s theater, with its ceiling mural of muses and its fountains of cherubs, an impressive theater pipe organ and fine acoustics, touring companies offer concerts, dance, musicals, and drama.

Stone Soup Coffee House (401-921-5115; www.stonesoupcoffee house.com), 50 Park Place in St. Paul's Church, Pawtucket. For more than 20 years musicians have been entertaining the public here with folk music on Saturday nights.

GAMING **Twin River Casino** (401-723-3200), 100 Twin River Road, Lincoln. Open around the clock. There are 4,752 slot machines at this largest gaming facility in Rhode Island, restaurants, and the Catch a Rising Star Comedy Club, which offers performances Friday, Saturday, and Sunday, and Amateur Night open to everyone on Thursday.

SPECTATOR SPORTS **McCoy Stadium** (401-724-7300), 1 Columbus Avenue, Pawtucket. The Pawtucket Red Sox (PawSox), the Triple-A farm team of the Boston Red Sox, play here.

* Selective Shopping

ANTIQUES SHOPS **Brown & Hopkins Country Store** (401-568-4830; www.brownandhopkins .com), Main Street, Chepachet. Open Monday through Wednesday 10–5, Thursday 10–7, Friday and Saturday 10–5, Sunday noon–5. This is said to be America's longest-operating country store. It opened in 1809 and still sells sour lemon drops, black licorice, and root beer barrels in its penny-candy case by the potbelly stove on the ground floor. The two top floors, containing reproduction furniture and rugs, are for browsers.

Country Cupboards (401-568-0606), 1503 Putnam Pike (US 44), Chepachet. Open Thursday through Saturday 11–5, Sunday 1–5. Early-19th-century painted country furniture.

The Hope Chest (401-949-2333; www.thehopechest.com), 2953 Hartford Avenue, Johnston. Open daily 10–5. An antiques and collectibles store with thousands of items.

The Old Post Office (401-568-1795), 1178 Putnam Pike (US 44), Chepachet. Open Monday, Thursday, Friday, and Saturday 11–5, Sunday noon–5. Here some 10 to a dozen dealers offer collectible toys, books, glass, jewelry, china, furniture, and handcrafts.

Old Stone Mill Antiques and Treasures (401-710-7166), 1169 Putnam Pike, Chepachet. Call for hours. Early American antiques and collectibles.

Rhode Island Antiques Mall (401-475-3400; www.riantiques mall.com), 345 Fountain Street, Pawtucket. Open weekdays and Saturday 10–5 (until 7 Thursday); Sunday 11–5. Two floors of high-quality antique furniture and collectibles from more than 120 dealers.

Stillwater Antiques (401-949-4999; www.stillwaterantiques.net),

711 Putnam Pike, Greenville. Open 10–5 daily except Tuesday. In a 19th-century textile mill, 180 dealers display and sell antique and collectible items large and small, ranging from stick pins and coins to brass bedsteads.

The Town Trader (401-568-8800; www.thetowntrader.com), 1177 Putnam Pike (US 44), Chepachet. Open year-round, Wednesday through Saturday 11–5, Sunday noon–5.

The Village Barn and Country Store (401-568-4542), 963 Victory Highway, Mapleville. Open 10–5 Friday through Sunday. Bean pots and typewriters, rocking chairs and cedar chests are among the staggering number of antiques and collectibles that fill this old barn by the side of the road.

ART GALLERIES **Hope Artiste Village** (401-722-0752; www.hopeartistevillage.com), 1005 Main Street, Pawtucket. In a former webbing factory, there are now artists' studios and interior design studios open to the public, a restaurant, a nightclub, a violin maker, a jewelry shop, and, from time to time, a farmers' market.

Pawtucket Arts Collaborative Gallery (401-724-2200; www.pawtucketartscollaborative.org), Blackstone Valley Visitors' Center, 175 Main Street, Pawtucket. Call for hours. This is a small gallery of changing exhibits by local artists.

Rhode Island Watercolor Society (401-726-1876; www.riws.org), Slater Memorial Park Boathouse, off US 1A, Pawtucket. Open Tuesday through Saturday 10–4, Sunday 1–5. Exhibitions of watercolors by painters from Rhode Island and neighboring Massachusetts.

J. H. Rowbottom Fine Art (401-333-1109), 1590 Meadow Road, Cumberland. Call for hours. Exhibitions by Rhode Island artists.

BOOKSTORES **Bryant University Bookstore** (401-232-6240), 1150 Douglas Pike, Ste. 2, Smithfield. Open Monday through Thursday 8:30–6:30, Friday 8:30–4, Saturday noon–4 during the academic year; Monday through Friday 9–4 in summer. General titles.

FACTORY OUTLETS **Ann & Hope Outlet Shops** (401-722-1000; 401-722-1001), 1 Ann & Hope Way, off RI 122, Cumberland. Open Monday through Saturday 9:30–8, Sunday 11–6. There's a curtain and bath shop; a garden, pet, and patio shop; an eyewear outlet; and a shoe shop. Everything is a markdown from the original.

Colonial Mills Rug Factory Store (401-724-6279; www.colonialmills.com), 560 Mineral Spring Avenue, Pawtucket. Open Monday through Saturday 9–5. Colonial Mills not only supplies rugs for this outlet store but also for Old Sturbridge Village, but the prices are much lower here.

Lorraine Fabrics (401-722-9500), 593 Mineral Spring Avenue, Pawtucket. Open Monday through Saturday 10–6, Sunday noon–5. This is one of the largest fabric stores in the country, including bridal, fashion, and an extensive home decorating department—all with good savings. Rhode Island School of Design students buy here, so you'll find some interesting, even bizarre, fabrics. To get here from I-95 north, take exit 27. Turn right onto Pine Avenue, left onto Main Street, then right onto Mineral Spring Avenue. From I-95 south, take exit 25, turn right onto Smithfield Avenue, then right onto Mineral Spring Avenue.

Rhody Rug (401-728-5903; www.rhodyrug.com), 32 Meeting Street, Cumberland. Open daily 10–5, Saturday 10–4. High-quality braided rugs and rugs braided to order.

Ryco (401-725-1779; www.rycotrim.com), 25 Carrington Street, Lincoln. Open Monday through Wednesday 9:30–5:30, Thursday 10–7, Friday 10–8, Saturday 9:30–5:30, Sunday noon–4. Fabric, lace, ribbon, trims, and sewing notions.

SPECIAL SHOPS **Slater Mill Museum Store** (401-725-8638), 67 Roosevelt Avenue, Pawtucket. Open May through November daily except Monday 10–4. Closed December through February. March and April 11–3 daily except Monday. Jellies and jams and honey, books on weaving and spinning and the industrial revolution, replicas of children's toys of the past, and gift cards are among the offerings in this gift shop.

The Slater Mill Gallery Shop (401-725-8918; 401-725-8919), in the Blackstone Valley Visitors' Center, 175 Main Street, Pawtucket. Tuesday through Friday 10–4:30. This is an upscale gift shop carrying handmade hats, jewelry, metal sculpture, and glass items designed by Rhode Island artists.

See also *To Do* for apple-picking farms and farm stands.

✷ Special Events

April: **Pawtucket Red Sox Opening Day** (401-724-7300), McCoy Stadium, Pawtucket.

May: **May Breakfast** (401-949-4441), Smith-Appleby House, 220 Stillwater Road, Smithfield. Reservations must be made in advance for this festive salute to spring. The **Limerock Baptist Church May Breakfast** (401-334-2999), 1075 Great Road, Lincoln, also welcomes the month of May. A Cherry Blossom Festival (401-724-2200) is a spring highlight in Pawtucket and Central Falls.

May–October: Burrillville Farmers' Market, 135 Harrisville Main Street, Harrisville. Saturday 9–12.

June: **Strawberry Social** (401-949-4441), Smith-Appleby House, 220 Stillwater Road, Smithfield.

June–October: Slater Mill Farmers' Market, 67 Roosevelt Avenue, Pawtucket. Sunday, noon–3.

July: **Fourth of July Ancients and Horribles Parade,** Chepachet, brings marchers and bands together from all across the state for an "alternative" parade celebrating Rhode Island's quirks and peccadilloes. **Cumberland Fourth of July Parade,** Nate Whipple Highway, Cumberland. Road race, parade, band concert. **Annual chicken barbecue** at the Foster Center Volunteer Fire Department, RI 94. **Smithfield Independence Fireworks and Concert** (401-949-4590). **Arnold Mills July Fourth Parade** (401-334-9996).

July–August: **Jazz and Blues Concert** (401-765-1900), Chan's Fine Oriental Dining, Woonsocket.

July–October: Blackstone River State Park Farmers' Market, Route 295 Visitors Center, Lincoln (between exits 9 and 10 northbound). Tuesday 2–6,

August: **Cumberland Fest** (www.cumberlandfest.org), Diamond Hill State Park, Cumberland. Weekend-long event second weekend of the month. Booths, entertainment, and fireworks. **Blueberry Social** (401-949-4441), Smith-Appleby House, 220 Stillwater Road, Smithfield.

September: **Pawtucket Arts Festival** (401-724-2200; 1-800-454-2882; www.pawtucketartsfestival.org), Slater Mill and other locations, Pawtucket. Dragon boats race on the river, artists display their paintings and sculpture in Slater Park, and the Rhode Island Philharmonic plays outdoors to make it a grand time for all at this two-week-long event. **French Farmers' Market** and Heritage Days (401-769-9846), River Island Park, Market Square, Woonsocket. Open-air farmers' market, trolley tours of the city, arts and crafts, and an apple pie contest. **Manville Settlers Day Festival,** Manville Sportsmen's Rod and Gun Club, Manville. Costumed interpreters demonstrate colonial-era crafts and skills.

October: **Autumnfest** (401-762-8072; www.autumnfest.org), World War II Memorial Park, 40 Snow Street, Woonsocket. A three-day celebration featuring ethnic foods, parades, and fireworks. **Scituate Art Festival** (401-647-0057; www.scituateartfestival.org), Village Green, RI 116, North Scituate.

November: **Annual Harvest Supper** (401-949-4441), Smith-Appleby House, 220 Stillwater Road, Smithfield. Meals offered by servers in colonial costume. Reservations are required. **Christmas in the Village Bazaar** (401-333-0139), St. Joseph's Parish Center, 1303 Mendon Road, Cumberland. A seasonal highlight.

November–May: Wintertime Farmers' Market at Hope Artiste Village, 1005 Main Street, Pawtucket. Wednesday 4–7; Saturday 10–1.

December: **Pawtucket Winter Wonderland** (401-728-0500, ext.

251), Slater Memorial Park, 410 Newport Avenue, Pawtucket. The Looff Carousel whirls merrily to celebrate the season, and there are strolling clowns, hayrides, face painting, Christmas carols, and Santa the first two weekends in December. **Christmas Open House** at the Valentine Whitman House (401-333-1100, ext. 289), 1147 Great Road, Lincoln. **Christmas at Smith-Appleby House** (401-231-7363), 220 Stillwater Road, Smithfield. The 17th-century house and barn are gaily decorated to celebrate the season. Victorian Christmas at Hearthside (401-726-0597), 677 Great Road, Lincoln. The Federal-style Hearthside House gives visitors a taste of a turn-of-the-twentieth-century Christmas. **Foundry Artists' Holiday Show** (www.foundryshow.com), Pawtucket Armory, 172 Exchange Street, Pawtucket. **Candlelight Shopping** (401-568-5140; www.candlelightshopping.com), Historic Chepachet Village.

3

South of Providence

WARWICK, CRANSTON, AND SURROUNDING TOWNS

Kim Grant

WARWICK, CRANSTON, AND SURROUNDING TOWNS

South of Providence, edging Narragansett Bay, sprawl the bedroom communities of Cranston and Warwick. They are riddled with highways and speckled with malls and housing developments, but here and there a visitor will find sites and pockets of interest.

Indeed, early in Rhode Island's history these towns were supremely important. Gaspee Point in Warwick was the site of Rhode Island military defiance of the British in 1772, when Warwick men set fire to the grounded British revenue cutter *Gaspée.* Revolutionary War hero General Nathanael Greene lived just over the Warwick line in Coventry, in the village of Anthony, where his house still stands.

In Cranston the 19th-century mansion of two Rhode Island Governor Spragues—uncle and nephew—has recently been restored and may be seen by appointment.

Although urban sprawl has left little green space and often overwhelms historic and architectural attractions, the determined visitor can bypass the traffic jams and shopping malls to find good restaurants, special historic areas of interest, beaches for walking, and spectacular views over Narragansett Bay. On elegant Warwick Neck, hidden estates overlook the bay. Comfortable little Pawtuxet Cove showcases colonial and Victorian homes on tree-lined streets. To the south of Warwick and Cranston lies a gem of a Rhode Island town: East Greenwich. Many of its handsome houses were built during its heyday as an agricultural and seafaring community just before the Revolutionary War. Boats bob at anchor at the yacht club, and old-fashioned shops still edge the historic Main Street.

GUIDANCE Cranston Chamber of Commerce (401-785-3780; www.cranstonchamber.com), 48 Rolfe Square, Cranston.

Coventry Town Hall (401-821-6400; www.town.coventry.ri.us), 1670 Flat River Road, Coventry.

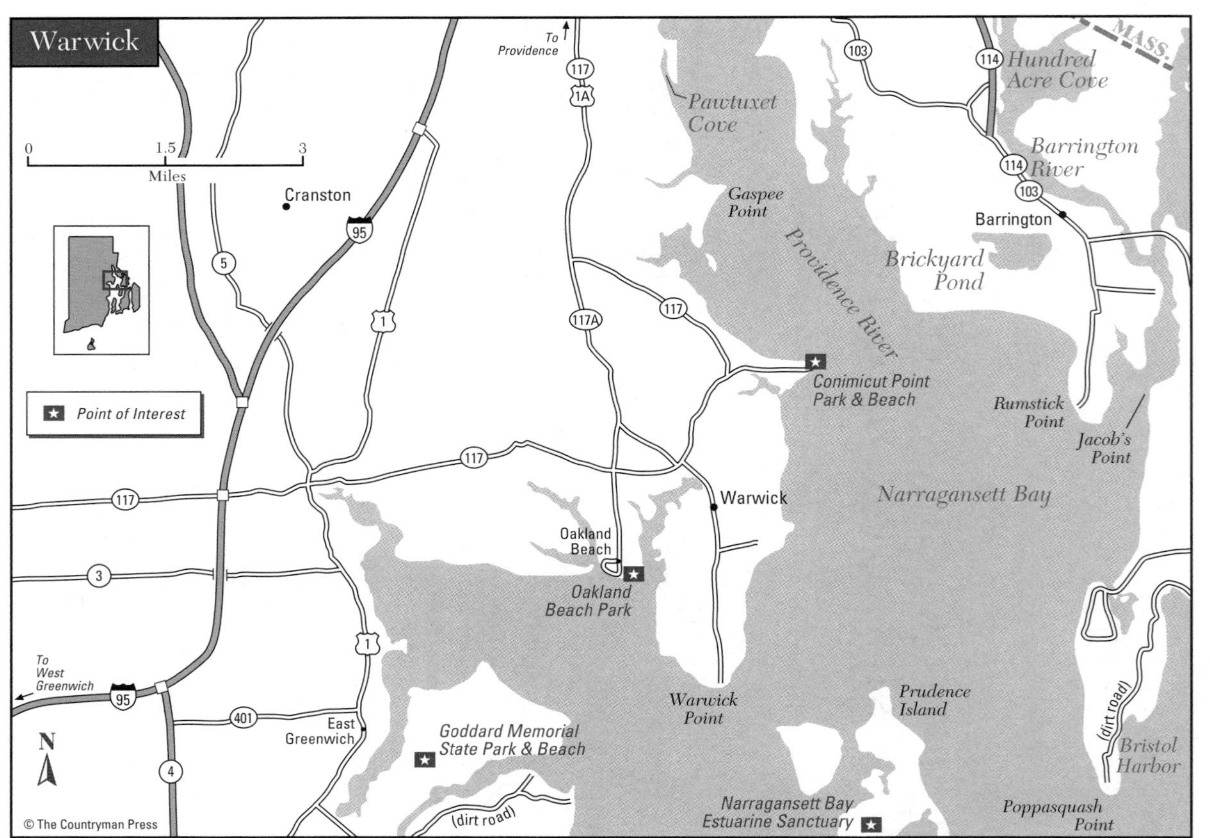
Warwick
0
1.5
3
Miles
Cranston
Point of Interest
To Providence
117
1A
117A
117
117
Pawtuxet Cove
Gaspee Point
Providence River
Conimicut Point Park & Beach
103
114
Hundred Acre Cove
MASS.
Barrington River
114
103
Barrington
Brickyard Pond
Rumstick Point
Jacob's Point
Narragansett Bay
Warwick
Oakland Beach
Oakland Beach Park
Warwick Point
Prudence Island
Bristol Harbor
(dirt road)
Poppasquash Point
Narragansett Bay Estuarine Sanctuary
Goddard Memorial State Park & Beach
(dirt road)
East Greenwich
401
4
95
95
5
1
1
3
To West Greenwich
N
© The Countryman Press

Michael Salerno

LIFE AS A DOG ON NARRAGANSETT BAY

East Greenwich Chamber of Commerce (401-885-0020; www.eastgreenwichchamber.com), 591 Main Street, East Greenwich.

Providence Warwick Convention and Visitors Bureau (401-274-1636; 1-800-233-1636; www.pwcvb.com), 1 Sabin Street, Providence.

Warwick Tourism Office (401-738-2000, ext. 6402; 1-800-4-WARWICK; www.warwickri.com), 3275 Post Road, Warwick.

GETTING THERE *By car:* From Providence, to avoid the traffic on I-95, take US 1 (sometimes Scenic RI 1A). From time to time this follows the shore of Narragansett Bay.

By bus: The **Rhode Island Public Transport Authority** (RIPTA; 401-781-9400) has frequent bus service throughout the day.

By air: Warwick is the site of Rhode Island's main airport, the **Theodore Francis Green State Airport** (401-737-4000). There are connections with various cities around the country from this spiffy, modernized airport that puts many a larger city's airport to shame. Modern artwork decorates it inside and out.

MEDICAL EMERGENCY The statewide emergency number is **911.**

Kent County Hospital (401-737-7000), 455 Tollgate Road, Warwick.

✷ To See

HISTORIC SITES John Waterman Arnold House (401-467-7647), 11 Roger Williams Avenue, off Warwick Avenue, Warwick. Open Wednesday 11–3 or by appointment. Headquarters of the Warwick Historical Society, this pleasant, late-1700s farmhouse is notable for its beehive oven, paneled dining room, and 18th-century furniture.

General Nathanael Greene Homestead (401-821-8630), 50 Taft Street, Anthony, Coventry. Open April through October. Call for hours. Small admission fee. This handsome gray-clapboard house on a cleared hill was the home of the Rhode Island–born general who was Washington's second-in-command during the Revolution. Its study is furnished with pieces that actually belonged to the general and his wife. The Victorian parlor contains items belonging to General Greene's grandson. Below the house, in a pretty country setting, the general's brother Jacob, his wife Margaret, and their children are buried. The general himself is buried in Savannah, where he died.

Kent County Courthouse/East Greenwich Town Hall (401-886-8607), 125 Main Street, East Greenwich. Open Monday through Friday 8:30–4:30. This square-towered, yellow-and-white-clapboard structure set back above Main Street was built in 1804 as the Kent County Courthouse and continued to serve in that capacity until 1978. Then, vacant and in disrepair, it was scheduled for demolition until concerned citizens saw to its preservation and restoration. The building was reopened as the town hall in 1996, and its handsome interior merits a visit. It was in the original courthouse on the site that, in 1775, the Rhode Island colony's General Assembly enacted a resolution that ultimately resulted in the creation of the U.S. Navy.

Paine House (401-397-5135), 7 Station Street, Coventry. Open June through September, Saturday 1–4 and by appointment. This 17th-century colonial home is attractively furnished with period pieces.

✐ **Governor Sprague Mansion** (401-944-9226), 1351 Cranston Street, Cranston. Open by appointment. Two Rhode Island governors lived in this recently restored, 28-room 1790s house with an 1864 addition. They were uncle and nephew, and both were named William Sprague. The Sprague family, originally farmers, acquired their wealth from nine textile mills. In addition to the house itself, there is a carriage house containing sleighs, carriages, a pony cart, a Conestoga wagon, and a gypsy wagon.

General James Mitchell Varnum House (401-884-1776), 57 Pierce Street, East Greenwich. Open weekends from Memorial Day through Labor Day; otherwise, by appointment. George Washington, the Marquis de Lafayette, and Thomas Paine were all guests in this handsome house that was started in 1773 by Continental army general Varnum. But it took seven years to finish because its owner was so eager to plan and construct it himself. Some of its walls are paneled, while others are covered with hand-painted 19th-century Chinese wallpaper. Period furnishings fill the house, and its unusual bric-a-brac includes Chinese temple vases from the sultan of Muscat, which were given to an East Greenwich sea captain as a reward for delivering Arabian vases to Queen Victoria. There is Sheffield silver, a Lowestoft tea set, and General Nathanael Greene memorabilia.

Varnum Memorial Armory (401-884-4110; www.varnumcontinentals.org), 6 Main Street, East Greenwich. Open the second Saturday of each month from 10–3 or by appointment. This little military museum displays everything from a 15th-century broadsword to World War I and II artifacts and a flag flown over the Baghdad Airport.

✷ To Do

BICYCLING **Coventry Greenway** (401-822-9174). A 5-mile trail through villages and greenery from Quidnick Village at the West Warwick town line to Coventry Center.

Cranston–Warwick Bike Path (401-222-4203, ext. 4042). Eleven miles of what will one day be a 25-mile bike path from Providence to Connecticut follow an abandoned rail line. You can get on at West Natick Road in Warwick below I-295.

Goddard Memorial State Park (401-884-2010). Eight miles of woodland trails wind through this pretty park.

FARM STANDS Morris Farm (401-738-1036), 2779 Warwick Avenue, Warwick. June–October, open daily 9–6.

Pippin Apple Orchard (401-943-7096), 751 Pippin Orchard Road, Cranston. Open July–December 9–5. Pick your own apples in season.

FOR FAMILIES ✐ **Impossible Dream Playground** (401-823-5566), 575 Centerville Road, Warwick. Open April to mid-October. A life-sized dollhouse, fort, garage, castle, and miniature golf are among the highlights of this playground, which—although created for physically challenged youngsters—is open to all.

East Greenwich Veteran Fireman's Association Fire Apparatus Museum (401-884-9817), 80 Queen Street, East Greenwich. Open May–September, first and third Saturdays of each month, 10–3. Antique firefighting equipment is on display.

New England Wireless and Steam Museum (1-401-665-0515; www.newsm.org), 1300 Frenchtown Road, East Greenwich. Open Thursday 9–2 or by appointment. This little museum showcases the history of steam engines and wireless technology and has, among its displays, a mid-19th-century George H. Corliss engine running under steam and the oldest surviving wireless station in the world.

GOLF **Coventry Pines Golf Course** (401-397-9482), 1065 Harkney Hill Road, Coventry. A nine-hole course in a wooded setting.

Cranston Country Club (401-826-1683), 69 Burlingame Road, Cranston. This 18-hole course offers both flat and hilly terrain plus several ponds. There is a bar and a place for snacks.

East Greenwich Golf and Country Club (401-884-5656), 1646 Division Road. A nine-hole golf course with a snack bar and lounge.

Goddard State Park Golf Course (401-884-9834), 345 Ives Road, Warwick. This is a nine-hole golf course with flat terrain. There is a snack bar in the clubhouse.

Midville Country Club (401-828-9215), 100 Lombardi Lane, West Warwick. Slightly hilly with a pond. In summer there is a hot dog concession stand and a bar.

Seaview Country Club (401-739-6311), 150 Gray Street, Warwick. A short, narrow, nine-hole course with two ponds overlooking Greenwich Bay.

CROSS-COUNTRY SKIING **Goddard Memorial State Park** (401-884-2010), Warwick. This 400-acre park is popular with cross-country skiers after snowstorms.

SPORTS CENTER **Mickey Stevens Sports Complex** (401-738-2000, ext. 6809 or 6811), 975 Sandy Lane, Warwick. Tennis courts, a swimming pool, and a winter ice rink are all operated by the city. Call for information on hours and fees.

SWIMMING **Briar Point Beach** (401-833-9170), Briar Point Avenue off Arnold Road, Coventry. At this little beach on 600-acre Lake Tiogue, there is supervised swimming from mid-June through Labor Day. You'll also find picnic facilities, a playground, and parking.

Warwick City Park/Buttonwoods (401-738-2000), Buttonwoods Avenue off West Shore Road, Warwick. This pretty little lifeguarded beach sits near a summer community of picturesque Carpenter Gothic cottages. In the 19th century, they were part of a Methodist camp meeting ground.

TENNIS **Tennis Rhode Island** (401-828-4450), 636 Centerville Road, Warwick. Six indoor courts open to the public.

✷ Green Space

BEACHES **Conimicut Point Park,** Point Avenue off RI 117, Warwick. There is a shallow-water beach and a playground for children and—in summer—a lemonade stand near the Conimicut Light. Water quality is questionable, and the beach is frequently closed to swimming. Most people go just for the view and the bay breeze.

Gaspee Point, Warwick. This is a quiet beach for youngsters to enjoy with their pails and shovels. To reach it from Pawtuxet Village, take the Narragansett Parkway south for 1 mile, then turn left onto Spring Green. At the first rotary, go left to the beach.

Oakland Beach Park, Oakland Beach Avenue, Warwick. This extensive beach on Greenwich Bay has a pleasant seafood restaurant. This is where, 60 years ago, the trolley from Providence brought daytrippers. In winter it's an ideal place for a waterfront stroll. Water quality is questionable for swimming.

Merrill S. Whipple Conservation Area, RI 117 and Sandy Bottom Road, Coventry. In this 57-acre wooded area along the south branch of the Pawtuxet River are hiking trails, vernal pools, waterfowl observation posts, and trout-fishing sites.

SETTLING IN FOR THE NIGHT

Michael Salerno

PARKS **Briggs Bosch Farm,** South Road, East Greenwich. This organic farm, the property of the East Greenwich Land Trust, is open to the public for walks.

Goddard Memorial State Park (401-884-2010), Warwick. This was an area of sand dunes along Greenwich Bay until the 1870s, when property owner Henry Russell began planting acorns. The oak and other tree varieties thrived. When Russell died, Colonel William Goddard continued his work, and the trees did so well that in the early 1900s the USDA Forest Service called it "the finest example of private forestry in America." The forest of some 400 acres was given to the state in 1927. Today the park offers bridle and walking paths, a sandy swimming beach (water quality often poor), outdoor concerts in summer, and cross-country skiing in winter.

Pawtuxet Park. The little bayfront park in Pawtuxet Village is a perfect place for a stroll along Pawtuxet Cove. To get here, drive south from Providence on Broad Street, through Cranston, into Pawtuxet Village.

Salter's Grove Park, Narragansett Parkway at Landon Road, Pawtuxet Cove. Wildflowers dot this small but pleasant wooded park on the waterfront. There is a marsh frequented by waterfowl, a boat ramp, a jetty for fishing and walking, and duck hunting for licensed hunters in-season.

Warwick City Park, Asylum Road, Warwick. A wooded park with a pretty beach, bicycle paths, and ball fields.

✷ Lodging

HOTELS AND MOTELS

♿ **Crowne Plaza Hotel at the Crossings** (401-732-6000; 1-800-2-CROWNE; www.crowneplaza.com), 801 Greenwich Avenue, Warwick. ($–$$) Warwick's largest and grandest hostelry, with 266 rooms, a pool, a restaurant, and an attractive garden.

🐾 ♿ **Motel 6** (401-467-9800; 1-800-4-MOTEL-6; www.motel6.com), 20 Jefferson Boulevard, Warwick. ($) This 123-room, two-building, three-story motel is 2 miles from T. F. Green Airport. It has no elevator. There is an outdoor pool and a restaurant next door.

♿ **Radisson Airport Hotel Providence** (401-739-3000; 1-800-333-3333; www.radisson.com), 2081 Post Road, Warwick. ($$$$) Operated in conjunction with Johnson & Wales University, this 111-room hotel is staffed by university students. Food is also prepared and served by students in its Libations Restaurant and Lounge.

Sheraton Providence Airport Hotel (401-738-4000; 1-800-325-3535; www.sheraton.com), 1850 Post Road, Warwick. ($–$$) The 207-room Sheraton is situated just beside T. F. Green Airport, and a shuttle bus links the two. A pool and workout facilities are available.

CAMPGROUNDS 🐾 ✐ **Colwell's Campground** (401-397-4614; 401-397-5818), Peckham Lane off RI 117, Coventry. Open May through September. Sites for 69 trailers and six tents. Electric hookups, telephone, pets allowed.

🐾 ✐ **Hickory Ridge Family Campground** (401-397-7474), Route 102, Greene. Open May through October 10. Sites for 200 trailers. Varying hookups and hot showers. Pets allowed.

✐ **Westwood Family Campground** (401-397-7779), 2093 Harkney Hill Road, Coventry. Open May 15 through October 15. Sites for 68 trailers and two tents. Varying hookups, a freshwater beach, hot showers, and a playground are among the amenities.

✳ Where to Eat

DINING OUT Café Fresco (401-398-0027; www.cafefrescori.com), 301 Main Street, East Greenwich. ($$–$$$) Open daily for dinner 5–11. This isn't a spot for intimate tête-à-têtes. It's brash and big and noisy, but the seafood and steaks and pasta in this Italian restaurant are well prepared and the service is friendly.

♿ **Elizabeth of Portofino** (401-461-8920; www.elizabethofportofino.com), 897 Post Road, Warwick. ($$) Open for dinner nightly. The strip-mall location leaves something to be desired, but the Italian fare is some of the best around. Once inside, you'll find a romantic setting. Portions are sizable, but try to leave room for the limoncello tiramisu.

✐ **Han Palace** (401-738-2238; www.hanpalacechineserestaurant.com), 2470 West Shore Road, Warwick. ($–$$) Open Sunday through Thursday 11:30–10, Friday and Saturday until 11. Chinese food, attractively presented.

♿ **Ichiban** (401-432-7220; www.ichibanri.com), 146 Gansett Avenue, Cranston. ($$–$$$) Open Tuesday through Sunday for lunch and dinner. Korean beef barbecue and sushi are among the specialties at this cozy Korean and Japanese restaurant.

♿ **L'attitude** (401-780-8700; www.l'attituderi.com), 2190 Broad Street, Pawtuxet Village, Cranston. ($$) Open daily for lunch and dinner. The specialty here is the bistro meal served family-style. It always includes a bowl of salad and might be followed by a whole roast chicken with potatoes and baby carrots, or a shellfish risotto with mussels and shrimp, calamari, scallops, chicken, and andouille sausage. It's enough for two or three, and the price is right—about $25. There is also always good fresh-grilled fish and, for the sweet-toothed, delectable bananas Foster with spiced rum and homemade vanilla ice cream. Live music on weekends.

🏵 ♿ **Legal Seafoods** (401-732-3663; www.legalseafoods.com), 2081 Post Road, Warwick. ($$) Open daily for lunch and dinner. A few university students from Johnson & Wales assist in serving at this restaurant next door to the Radisson Airport Hotel, where they also assist. As at all restaurants in the Boston-based Legal Seafoods chain, fresh fish has priority on the menu.

♿ **La Masseria** (401-398-0693, 401-39-0727; www.masseriari.com), 233 Main Street, East Greenwich. ($$-$$$) Open Monday through Thursday 12–10; Friday and Saturday 12–11, Sunday 12–9. This elegant (but noisy) southern Italian restaurant features, among other entrées, Schiaffoni rigatoni in a light tomato sauce with meatballs and short ribs and much more, and a carpaccio salad with Parmesan cheese.

♿ **Lucce Italian Bistro** (401-921-3300), 2317 West Shore Road, Warwick. ($$–$$$). Open nightly for dinner. Tuna puttanesca and baked pasta are all-time favorites, but there are many choices on this bistro's menu.

♿ **Siena Cucina** (401-885-8850; www.sienari.com), 5600 Post Road, East Greenwich. ($$–$$$) Open for dinner daily except Monday, with late-night bistro fare Friday and Saturday and dinner from 3 PM Sunday. The offerings are largely Tuscan in this trendy restaurant that bears the name of Tuscany's most famous city. There are filling entrées like Chilean sea bass and pasta Bolognese on the main menu, or light tapas such as calamari balsamico and eggplant with prosciutto and herbed ricotta cheese. Of course, there's pizza, too, in this restaurant with a counterpart on Providence's Federal Hill.

♿ **Spain** (401-946-8686; www.spainrestaurantri.com), 1073 Reservoir Avenue, Cranston. ($$–$$$) Open for dinner nightly. Paella for two, sirloin steak in roasted garlic and red wine sauce, a seafood combination in white wine, garlic, and parsley sauce—all are among the specialties at this Spanish restaurant.

♿ **Ted's Montana Grill** (401-275-5070; www.tedsmontanagrill.com), 2 Chapel View, Cranston. ($$$) Bison steaks, meatloaf, pot roast are the classics offered nightly at this Western grill, but for non-red-meat-eaters there's chicken cooked in beer with rosemary and garlic, or salmon or trout prepared in many ways. And there's plain old-fashioned beef as well.

♿ **Twin Oaks** (401-781-9693; http://twinoaksrest.com), 100 Sabra Street, Cranston. ($$–$$$) Open for lunch and dinner daily except Monday. This is a perennial Rhode Island family favorite, especially for its baked, stuffed shrimp, veal, and steaks.

EATING OUT Bistro 9 (401-398-1875; www.bistro9restaurant.com), 1646 Division Street, East Greenwich. $-$$ Open daily for lunch and dinner and serving Italian food with a contemporary twist. There are also such all-American favorites, however, as clam chowder, beef tenderloin, and sugar-glazed salmon.

Caffe Itri (401-942-1970; www.cafeitriri.com), 1686 Cranston Street, Cranston. ($–$$) Open for lunch and dinner Monday through Friday, for dinner only Saturday; closed Sunday. Homemade pasta is very popular here, but there is also a wide variety of Italian dishes at reasonable prices.

The Crow's Nest (401-732-6575; www.crowsnestri.com), 288 Arnold's Neck Drive, Apponaug, Warwick. ($) Open daily for lunch and dinner. The filling, inexpensive fare here includes chowder, fish-and-chips, clam cakes, and lobster rolls.

Efendi's Mediterranean Bar & Grill (401-943-8800; www.efendisbarandgrill.com), 1255 Reservoir Avenue, Cranston. ($$) Open Monday–Saturday 11:30–9:30 for lunch and dinner. Sunday 4–9 for dinner only. Greek, Turkish, Italian, and French dishes are all on the menu.

Greenwich Bay Gourmet (401-541-9190), 50 Cliff Street, East Greenwich. ($) Open Monday through Friday 10–6, Saturday 8–5. There are entrées like grilled chicken with artichokes and lemon-roasted vegetable wraps, and California turkey Cobb with avocado, pancetta, and cream cheese. It's bright and cheery, and the food is available to eat in or take out.

The Grille on Main (401-885-2200), 50 Main Street, East Greenwich. ($–$$) Open daily for lunch and dinner. Salads, burgers, grilled pizzas, fried calamari. Casual fare in a big, dark-walled setting with an upscale saloon look.

Haruki (401-463-8338; www.harukisushi.com), 1210 Oaklawn Avenue, Cranston. ($$) Open Monday through Friday for lunch and dinner, Saturday and Sunday for dinner. Authentic Japanese food—sushi, sashimi, teriyaki, tempura, maki (fish rolled up with rice in seaweed)—is on the menu of this simple, casual restaurant that the whole family can enjoy.

Kon Asian Bistro (401-886-9200; www.konasianbistro.com), 553 Main Street, East Greenwich. ($–$$) Japanese, Chinese, Cambodian, Thai meals are offered at this magical Asian-fusion restaurant.

Meritage (401-884-1255; www.meritageri.com), 5454 Post Road, East Greenwich. ($$–$$$) Open daily for dinner. Wood-grilled pizza is the specialty of this bistro. But seafood and pasta are also popular. Among the pastas, a particularly popular one is the pasta jambalaya: chicken and shrimp in a Cajun-spiced cream sauce.

Mike's Kitchen at Tabor-Franchi Post (401-946-5320), 170 Randall Street, Cranston. ($$) Open for lunch and dinner Monday and Wednesday through Friday, lunch only Tuesday and Saturday; closed Sunday. A Rhode

Island phenomenon: a casual, down-home Italian restaurant in a Veterans of Foreign Wars hall. The fried squid and snail salad are local favorites.

Nautika (401-398-7774; www.nautikari.com), 28 Water Street, East Greenwich. ($$–$$$) A lovely harbor-front setting with denizens of the deep popular on the menu. Open May to October. Call for hours.

O'Rourke's Bar and Grill (401-228-2444), 23 Peck Lane, Cranston. ($–$$) Open Monday–Saturday 11:30–1 AM; Sunday 12–1 AM. Fish-and-chips, burgers, corned beef, and beer, of course, are mainstays of this casual Irish pub with live music and outdoor tables in-season, with views of Pawtuxet Cove.

♿ **Papa Razzi** (401-942-2900; www.backbayrestaurantgroup.com), Garden City Center, Cranston. ($$–$$$) Open daily for lunch and dinner and especially popular for its pasta, pizzas, and calamari.

CAFÉS **The Cupcakerie** (401-467-2601), 1860 Broad Street, Cranston. Open Tuesday and Wednesday 10–6, Thursday through Saturday until 8. A creative bakery and coffee, tea, and chocolate house with outdoor seating in the warm weather.

Felicia's Coffee (401-886-4141; www.feliciascoffee.com), 5757 Post Road, East Greenwich. Open Monday through Saturday 6 AM–8 PM, Sunday 6:30 AM–5 PM. Although it's not a Viennese café, you can sit by the fireplace and browse among the newspapers while you enjoy pumpkin or pistachio or three-layer cheesecake, a German chocolate brownie, or cinnamon apple betty. Their made-on-the-premises, low-fat, high-fiber muffins are also popular.

Little Falls Bakery and Café (401-781-8010; www.littlefallscafe.com), 2166 Broad Street, Pawtuxet Village, Cranston. This warm, friendly little café with paintings by local artists on the walls is where Pawtuxet Villagers spend their spare time. They enjoy the art and conversation along with the muffins and scones.

♿ **Main Street Coffee** (401-885-8787), 137 Main Street, East Greenwich. This is where the locals go from 5:30 in the morning until 10 at night for lattes and smoothies, homemade biscotti, and scrumptious sandwiches. Occasionally, in summer, there's live music, too. There are tables outside in warm weather.

Water's Edge (401-941-9158), 2190 Broad Street, Pawtuxet Village, Cranston. Open Monday through Friday 6–4, Saturday 6–2, Sunday 7–2. Fresh-baked goods, soups, sandwiches, and coffee can be enjoyed over a magazine or newspaper in this bright and sunny café decorated with paintings by local artists.

✱ Selective Shopping

ANTIQUES AND COLLECTIBLES **Lost Treasures** (401-885-4500), 75 Main Street, East Greenwich. Antique jewelry and coins, crystal, silver, and silverplate in old-fashioned patterns, figurines, and other bric-a-brac.

BOOKSTORES **Heritage Book Store** (401-739-2356), T. F. Green State Airport. Paperbacks, hardcovers, and newspapers for travelers.

Symposium Books (401-886-1600), 247 Main Street, East Greenwich. Open Monday through Saturday 11–7. New and used books.

Twice Told Tales (401-785-9599), 2145 Broad Street, Pawtuxet Village, Cranston. Used paperbacks and some new books along with hand-knit baby sweaters, handmade jewelry, cards.

FARM STANDS **Briarbrook Farm** (401-884-2066), 2693 South County Trail, East Greenwich. Open daily 9–5 from Easter until the day before Christmas.

Confreda Greenhouses and Farms (401-827-5000), 2150 Scituate Avenue, Cranston. Open daily 8 or 9–6 April through December. Call for exact hours.

Pippin Apple Orchard (401-943-7096), 751 Pippin Orchard Road, Cranston. Open daily 10-4, August until Thanksgiving. Weekends Thanksgiving until Christmas. Pick-your-own apples in-season.

Russo's Vegetable Stand (401-828-3736), 1555 Pippin Orchard Road. Open mid-July through Columbus Day, 9–5.

SPECIAL SHOPS **Alex and Ani** (401-398-1023; alexandani.com), 232 Main Street, East Greenwich. Rhode Island's flagship Alex and Ani jewelry store is in Newport and there's another in Providence. Entirely made of recycled brass, each charm chosen for a bangle set is symbolic of positive energy.

Apponaug Color & Hobby Shop (401-737-5506; www.hobbyri.com), 1364 Greenwich Avenue, Apponaug, Warwick. Back in the 1950s this was a paint store (hence its name), but its owner, Charles Moore Sr., liked toy trains, so he added them to his stock. Now, a generation later, Charles Moore Jr. is selling electric trains and model boats, ships, and planes plus all the accessories.

The Chocolate Delicacy (401-884-4949), 219 Main Street, East Greenwich. Two Vassar graduates have gotten together to make chocolates at this tantalizing shop, where it's hard to choose among the truffles, the fudge, and the red lobster lollipops.

Clock Shop International (401-826-1212), 667 Bald Hill Road, Warwick. Grandfather and grandmother clocks, wall and mantel clocks—clocks of all eras for all tastes fill this shop.

The Green Door (401-885-0510), 130 Main Street, East

Greenwich. Hand-painted glass and wooden bowls, silk flower arrangements, miniature Chinese tea sets and Limoges boxes, Raku pottery from South Africa, and vintage linens and quilts are all among the offerings in this charming little gift shop.

Little Elegance (401-398-0755), 37 Main Street, East Greenwich. Jewelry and scarves, sandals and handbags at this eclectic gift shop.

Scrumptions (401-884-0844; www.scrumptions.com), 5600 Post Road (in Benny's Mall), East Greenwich. Scrumptious, indeed, are the scrumptions—handmade butter cookies, truffles, cakes, and the like—at this attractive little chocolate and pastry shop.

The Troll Shop (401-885-6066), 88 Main Street, East Greenwich. Trolls for a mantel, trolls for a living room, trolls for a garden—all hand-fashioned in wood by Norwegian or German troll carvers—are the principal stock in this store shared with the longtime East Greenwich rug company, Stevens Oriental Rugs.

Wild Birds Unlimited (401-826-0606; http://warwick.wbu.com), 1000 Bald Hill Road, Warwick. There's everything for the bird lover here: binoculars, birdhouses, bird feeders, birdseed, clocks that sing birdsongs, decorative ceramic birds, bird books, and bird-themed greeting cards.

✷ Special Events

May: **Memorial Day Parade,** East Greenwich.

Mid-May through June: **Gaspee Days** (http://gaspee.com; 401-781-1772). A crafts fair and other events at various points in Cranston and Warwick commemorate the June 9, 1772, burning of the British revenue schooner *Gaspee* by Rhode Island patriots.

May–September: **Main Street Stroll** (401-886-8662) in East Greenwich on selected evenings. Artists show their work, musicians play, shops are open.

May–November: **Pawtuxet Village Farmers' Market** (401-461-2618) Rhodes-on-the-Pawtuxet Parking Lot, 60 Rhodes Place, Cranston. Saturdays 9–noon.

June: **East Greenwich Chamber of Commerce Golf Classic** (401-885-0020). **Rhode Island Air Show** (401-885-0020; www.riairshow.org), Quonset State Airport, North Kingstown.

June–October: **East Greenwich Farmers' Market.** Academy Field, corner of Church and Rector Streets, East Greenwich. Mondays 3–6. Whole Foods Farmers' Market (401-621-5990), 151 Sockanosset Cross Road, Cranston, Tuesdays 3–dusk.

July: **4th of July Fireworks** (401-738-2000), Oakland Beach Seawall, Warwick.

July–August: Summer **Concert Series** (401-738-2000, ext. 6404), various Warwick parks.

August: **Oakland Beach Festival** (401-738-2000), Oakland Beach, Warwick. Crafts, music, and a flea market.

September: **Apponaug Village Festival** (401-738-2000), City Hall, Post Road, Warwick. Flea market, pony rides, crafts, and entertainment. **Rhode Island Philharmonic Orchestra Pops Concert** (401-248-7070), Eldridge Field, East Greenwich.

November: **Veterans Day Parade** (401-885-0020), East Greenwich.

December: **Holidays in East Greenwich** (401-885-0020) includes tree-lighting and carol ceremony, strolling carolers, hot chocolate with Santa, candlelight luminaria along Main Street, and candlelight tours of historic buildings and selected private homes. **Tree lighting** in Apponaug. **Carol singing** (401-738-2000, ext. 6404), Warwick Mall.

Year-round: **Kentish Guards Fife & Drum Corps rehearsals** Wednesdays 7–9 PM at the Kentish Guards Armory, 1774 Armory Street, East Greenwich.

East Bay

4

BARRINGTON, WARREN, AND BRISTOL

Kim Grant

BARRINGTON, WARREN, AND BRISTOL

Until the 17th century, Native Americans of the Wampanoag tribe happily inhabited what are now sites of the three towns of Bristol County: Barrington, Warren, and Bristol. They hunted on the wooded, abundant land and fished its rivers and Narragansett Bay. In 1621 two Pilgrim Fathers from the Plymouth Bay Colony approached the Wampanoag chief, Massasoit, to talk about buying land from him. They succeeded, and before long a trading post was established where Massasoit lived, in what is now Warren.

Relations were amicable between the white settlers and the Wampanoags during Massasoit's lifetime. Indeed, there was genuine respect and affection between the Pilgrim Fathers and the old sachem. But everything changed when he died in 1661. One of his sons, Wamsutta, died mysteriously when problems arose over hunting rights on lands the settlers claimed. His incensed brother, Metacom, also known as King Philip, vowed revenge and set out to get rid of the English. King Philip's War began in Bristol in 1675, uniting the Wampanoags from the east side of Narragansett Bay with the Narragansetts from the west side against the settlers. Before the war ended, tribes from central Massachusetts and Maine were also involved, and their joint determination to oust the settlers resulted in New England's bloodiest Indian war.

King Philip's War ended in 1676 with a massacre of the Narragansetts. King Philip was later killed at the hands of a fellow Wampanoag, and the lands he had sought to save for his people fell forever to the colonists.

As the Wampanoags had prospered on the fertile land and rich surrounding waters, so did the colonists. They farmed in Barrington, and they built boats and entered the shipping trade in Warren and Bristol. The captains' and shipowners' tall white houses still line the streets of these two communities—their prosperity born of the slave trade and whaling. In Warren, most of the old houses remain in private hands; in Bristol, the

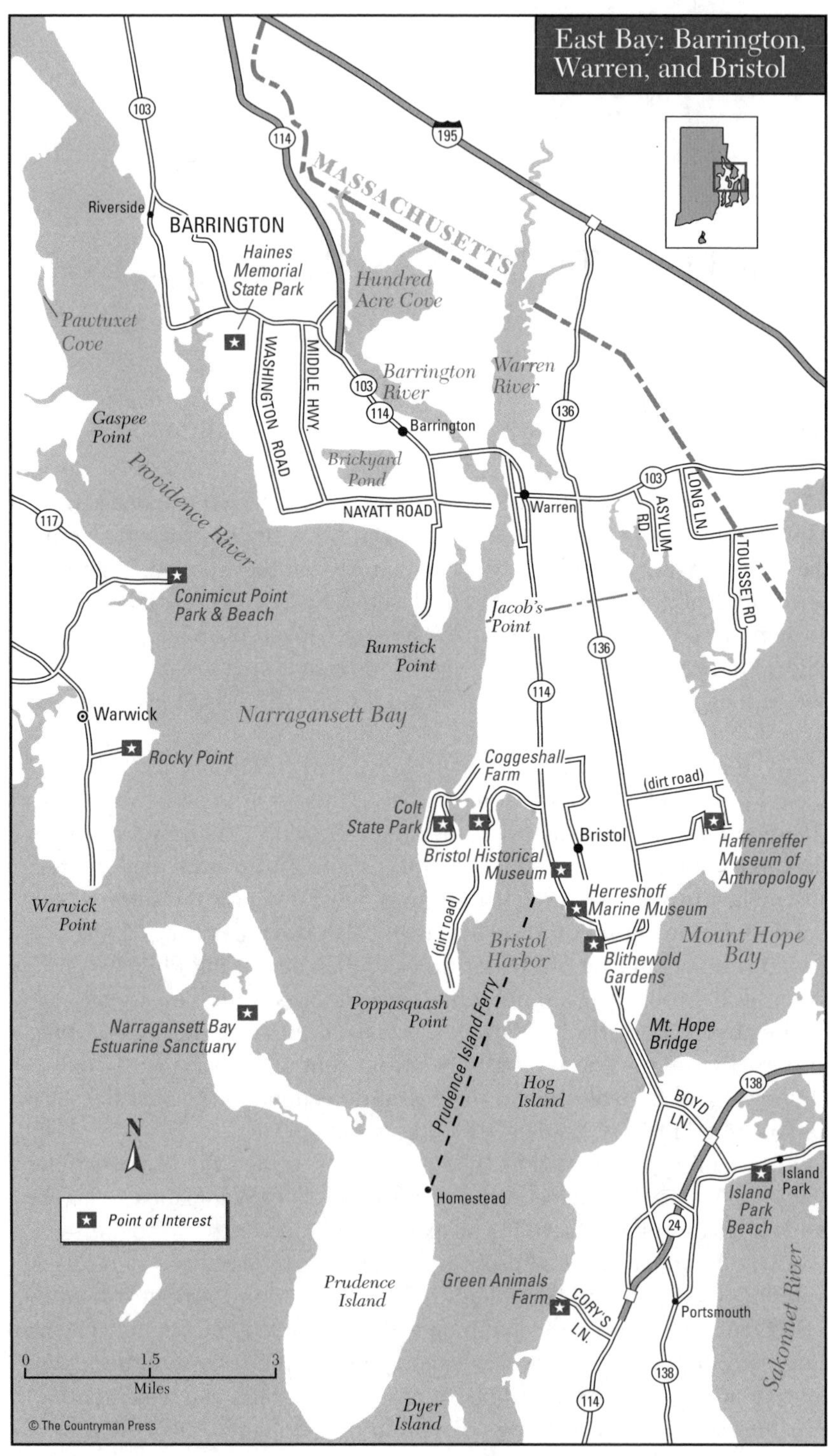
East Bay: Barrington, Warren, and Bristol
MASSACHUSETTS
Riverside
BARRINGTON
Haines Memorial State Park
Hundred Acre Cove
Pawtuxet Cove
WASHINGTON ROAD
MIDDLE HWY.
Barrington River
Warren River
Barrington
Gaspee Point
Brickyard Pond
Providence River
NAYATT ROAD
Warren
ASYLUM RD.
LONG LN.
TOUISSET RD.
Conimicut Point Park & Beach
Jacob's Point
Rumstick Point
Warwick
Narragansett Bay
Rocky Point
Coggeshall Farm
(dirt road)
Colt State Park
Bristol
Haffenreffer Museum of Anthropology
Bristol Historical Museum
Herreshoff Marine Museum
Warwick Point
(dirt road)
Bristol Harbor
Mount Hope Bay
Blithewold Gardens
Narragansett Bay Estuarine Sanctuary
Poppasquash Point
Prudence Island Ferry
Mt. Hope Bridge
Hog Island
BOYD LN.
N
Island Park
Island Park Beach
Homestead
Point of Interest
Prudence Island
Green Animals Farm
CORY'S LN.
Portsmouth
Sakonnet River
0
1.5
3
Miles
Dyer Island
© The Countryman Press

public is invited to visit Linden Place, one of the grandest of the shipowners' houses and a site with a most engaging history.

GUIDANCE **Bristol Visitor Center** (401-410-0040; http://gonewport.com), 400 Hope Street, Bristol. Open seasonally, 10–4.

East Bay Chamber of Commerce (401-245-0750; http://eastbaychamberri.org), 16 Cutler Street, Suite 102, Warren. Open Monday through Friday 9–4:30.

GETTING THERE *By train or bus:* Take **Amtrak** (1-800-USA-RAIL) to Providence and a **Rhode Island Public Transport Authority** (RIPTA; 401-781-9400; http://ripta.com) bus from Providence to any of the three Bristol County communities.

GETTING AROUND Local taxi service is provided by **A Taxi** (401-245-6684), Warren.

MEDICAL EMERGENCY The statewide emergency number is **911.**

Barrington Urgent Care (401-247-2870), 310 Maple Avenue, Barrington. Open Monday through Friday 8–8, Saturday and Sunday 9–5.

Bristol County Medical Center (401-253-8900), 1180 Hope Street, Bristol. Open Monday through Friday 8–8, Saturday 9–5, Sunday and holidays 10–4.

Metacom Medical Center (401-247-1500), 629 Metacom Avenue, Warren. Open Monday through Friday 8–5, Saturday and Sunday 9–1.

Warren Medical Center (401-247-1000), 851 Main Street, Warren. Open Monday through Friday 8–5, Saturday 8–noon.

✷ Villages

Barrington. Nowadays this pretty little area comprised of two large peninsulas on Narragansett Bay is largely a bedroom community for neighboring Providence only 12 miles away, but its waterfront setting is singularly attractive. Welcoming the visitor arriving from Providence is the white-steepled 1710 **Barrington Congregational Church** (401-246-0111) on County Road, which replaced a meetinghouse destroyed in King Philip's War. The nearby half-timbered and fieldstone English Tudor–style **town hall** was built in 1887–1888, largely of stones contributed by local farmers. **Tyler Point Cemetery,** between the Barrington and Warren Rivers, has picturesque gravestones, some dating back to 1702. During the Revolutionary War a Hessian soldier was killed by a farmer in Barrington—the only incident of that war that took place in this town.

Kim Grant

HARBOR VIEWS

Warren was once known as the Town of Ten Churches; three of historic importance still stand. The gray stone **Warren Baptist Church** (401-245-3669) on Main Street replaces a meetinghouse burned by the British in 1778; it was in its parsonage, also burned, that Rhode Island College (later renamed Brown University) was founded in 1764. The white-clapboard **St. Mark's Episcopal Church** (401-245-3161) on Lyndon and Broad Streets, with the lions of Saint Mark guarding the doors flanked by fluted columns, almost has the look of an Egyptian tomb. Both the 1844 Gothic-style Baptist church and the 1830 Greek Revival St. Mark's were designed by Russell Warren. Surely the most spectacular church in Warren is the enormous **First Methodist Church** (401-245-8474) on Church Street, whose tiered clock steeple rises 130 feet. Built in 1845 after a Christopher Wren design, it's one of the oldest Methodist churches in New England. Unfortunately, except for Sunday services and by appointment, these churches are all closed to the public.

Warren's other architectural attractions include the gray stone turn-of-the-20th-century **George Hail Free Library** (401-245-7686) on Main Street, with its stained-glass windows, sweeping staircase, and second-floor museum filled with memorabilia of both Native American times and Warren's seafaring days. The Federal-style **Masonic Temple** (401-245-3293) at Baker and Narragansett Way, built in 1796, has exterior carving and an interior made of timbers salvaged from sunken British ships. Handsome old houses line the streets of Warren, with some of the finest on Main,

Miller, Union, Liberty, and Water Streets. Only the red-clapboard 1753 Samuel Maxwell House on Church Street (see *Historic Homes*) is open to the public, however. Locals like to direct visitors to the tablet that marks the site of **Massasoit's Spring** and campsite and to the **Firemen's Museum** (see *Museums*).

Bristol. Of the three Bristol County communities, Bristol is the richest in attractions for the visitor, with museums, parks, gardens, grand mansions, and fine examples of New England architecture. Handsome Federal and Greek Revival houses feature columns and semicircular windows, doorway fanlights, and fine carving. There are Italianate houses with brackets under the roof, mansard-roofed Second Empire houses, and gingerbread-decorated Gothic Revival and shingle houses. Most of what stands in town today was built between 1825 and 1920. Some houses date from Bristol's prosperous years as a shipping port, when its families grew wealthy from privateering and the slave trade as well as through more legitimate businesses (one-fifth of all slaves coming to America were brought in Rhode Island ships, and most of these hailed from Bristol). Other elegant homes were built during Bristol's industrial and boatbuilding years. Imposing clapboard structures like the Russell Warren–designed Federal houses at 82, 86, and 92 State Street, his Greek Revival house at 647 Hope Street, and **Linden Place,** used in the filming of *The Great Gatsby,* are architectural highlights. At Hope and Court Streets the heavy stone Romanesque Revival **Burnside Memorial Building** honors General Ambrose Burnside, who commanded Union troops at the battle of Bull Run and returned from the Civil War to become Rhode Island's governor. At the corner of Walley and Hope Streets is **Seven Oaks,** which was designed by James Renwick, architect of St. Patrick's Cathedral in New York City.

Bristol's oldest house, and the oldest three-story wooden building in New England, is the 1698 **Joseph Reynolds House** at 956 Hope Street. The young marquis de Lafayette had his headquarters there in 1778. (According to local legend, Mrs. Reynolds did not recognize the marquis, who was one of the first in the French party to arrive, and took him to task for eating too much and not leaving enough for his commander.) Among civic buildings of architectural note is the **Bristol County Courthouse** on High Street, one of the five meeting places of the General Assembly until 1814. With its octagonal belfry, this structure is believed to be the work of either Russell Warren or John Holden Greene. The Bristol County Jail at 48 Court Street, now the **Bristol Historical and Preservation Society** (see *Museums*), was built in 1828 of ships' ballast. Bristol's 1814 **First Baptist Church,** also on High Street, bears a resemblance to the First Baptist Meeting House in Providence. **St. Michael's Episcopal Church** (401-253-7717), at 399 Hope Street, is a brownstone Gothic Revival church that replaces two earlier churches on the site. The first of these was burned by the British in 1778, when they mistook it for the Congregational church and thought its tombs were powder magazines.

✷ To See

MUSEUMS ✐ **Bristol Historical and Preservation Society Museum and Library** (401-253-7223), 48 Court Street, Bristol. Call for museum hours, as they change occasionally. Built in 1828 out of ballast from Bristol sailing ships, this museum and library is quite interesting. Originally the county jail, the building still contains a windowless cell. Also on exhibit are a writing desk and table that belonged to Benjamin Franklin, General Burnside's saddle and sword, a candlestand that Charles Dickens is said to have used on a visit to Newport, ship models and children's toys, and portraits by an early itinerant painter, Cephas Thompson.

✐ **Coggeshall Farm Museum** (401-253-9062; www.coggeshallfarm.org), Colt State Park, Route 114, Bristol. Open October through February, daily 10–5; March through September, daily 10–6. This little farm museum shows what agricultural life was like in Rhode Island in the late 18th century. Wiltshire sheep graze and Dominique chickens, the oldest strain in America, peck at their feed. Visitors may watch red Devon cattle being milked, as well as planting and lumbering operations. All farm animals are types known to have been on area farms in the late 1700s.

✐ **Firemen's Museum** (401-245-7600), 42 Baker Street, Warren. Open by appointment. This restored headquarters of the Narragansett Steam Fire Company Number 3 displays memorabilia of the early days of firefighting, such as Little Hero, the town's first fire engine, dating from 1802.

✐ **Herreshoff Marine Museum** (401-253-5000; www.herreshoff.org), 7 Burnside Street, Bristol. Open May through October, daily 10–4; ship model room open Friday 1–4. This museum is set on the site of the Herreshoff Manufacturing Company on Narragansett Bay. From 1863 to 1945 thousands of yachts and schooners and eight America's Cup defenders came off the ways there. Today the museum houses 46 Herreshoff boats as well as photographs, models, and building plans of many others. The company's founders, among the most notable of all American yacht builders, were John Brown Herreshoff, who went blind at the age of 18, and his brother, Captain Nathanael (Nat) Greene Herreshoff. Despite his blindness, John was able to dictate boat specifications to Nat, who would then make a model. John would judge the design by feeling the model and suggest alterations. Among the boats on display is the catboat *Sprite,* which the pair built as teenagers; it has been called "the first yacht in America."

✐ **Young Mariner's Discovery Center,** where youngsters can learn to hoist sails, crank winches, and steer boats, is also part of the museum, as is the America's Cup Hall of Fame, which recounts the history of that international sailing race.

HISTORIC HOMES AND SITES **Blithewold Mansion, Gardens & Arboretum** (401-253-2707; www.blithewold.org), 101 Ferry Road, Bristol. Grounds open year-round, daily 10–5 (mid-May through October, grounds close at 4 PM Saturday and Sunday); mansion open mid-April through October and the day after Thanksgiving through December 30, Wednesday through Sunday 10–4 (mid-May through October, mansion closes at 3 PM Sunday). Brown University graduate Augustus Van Wickle built the original Blithewold—"Happy Wood"—as a summer "trinket" for his wife, Bessie, in 1895. Earlier he had presented her with a 72-foot $100,000 Herreshoff yacht, which she adored, but it couldn't be moored where they lived in Hazelton, Pennsylvania. The Blithewold property, with 32 acres and possible moorings in either Bristol Harbor or Narragansett Bay, seemed the perfect place. A 45-room mansion was duly constructed with Van Wickle coal-mining money. Unfortunately Augustus had relatively little time to enjoy his mansion, for he was soon killed in a hunting accident. Bessie remarried, but tragedy struck again when the original Blithewold burned to the ground in 1907. The stone-and-stucco mansion that stands today was built a year later in the style of a 17th-century English manor house. Bessie, who enjoyed travel immensely, filled the house with mementos of her journeys. The grounds and gardens were laid out by New York City architect John DeWolf and contain unusual trees and

THE GARDENS AT BRISTOL'S BLITHEWOLD MANSION ARE SPECTACULAR YEAR-ROUND.
Kim Grant

plants, including a giant sequoia nearly a century old that is the largest of its kind east of the Rockies, and a chestnut rose that bears pink blossoms in June. Spring daffodil gardens and summer rose gardens are also especially noteworthy.

Linden Place (401-253-0390; www.lindenplace.org), 500 Hope Street, Bristol. Open May through September, Saturday and Sunday 1–4, Wednesday 2–4. This wedding-cake-like Federal mansion, notable in this century as the summer residence of actress Ethel Barrymore (Colt), was built in 1810 by shipowner and slave trader General George DeWolf to be "the most beautiful and the best" residence in Bristol. Russell Warren of Tiverton, who was to become known as one of Rhode Island's finest architects, designed the home. High-living General DeWolf spared no expense, either in the building of his house or in the entertaining of his guests. (He is said to have bought a solid silver pitcher and bowl for President James Monroe when he visited once.) Much of DeWolf's money, however, came from convincing others to invest in his schemes, and in 1825 they failed. His Caribbean sugar plantations didn't flourish, and he also lost shiploads of slaves. So on a snowy December night, he and his family slipped away by coach to flee to Cuba.

The day after his departure his Bristol creditors realized that their money would never be repaid, and they descended on his house to lay claim to the equivalent in goods. Emptied, the house fell first to DeWolf's brother and later to his nephew, William Henley. In 1840 Henley rehired the then-established Russell Warren to add onto the house. But Henley, too, had financial problems and went bankrupt. On his death his widow moved into a third-floor bedroom and turned the rest of the mansion into a boardinghouse. When she died in 1865, Linden Place went on the auction block. Edward Colt, a mysterious young man from Connecticut, bought it. All of Bristol was curious about the young stranger, until it was revealed that he was purchasing the house on behalf of his mother, Theodora DeWolf Colt, daughter of the original builder, General George DeWolf. Theodora was only five on the snowy December night when her family fled, but Linden Place had remained a beloved misty memory. By 1865 she was a wealthy widow (she married into the Colt firearms family) and was able, at last, to return to the house in which she had been born.

Maxwell House (401-245-0392), 59 Church Street, Warren. Open 10–2 Saturday and by appointment. This sparsely furnished 1755 brick house, the oldest house near the Warren waterfront, is of some interest. It is still being brought back to the look it had in its earliest days. Notable are its beehive oven, steep gable, and handsome old bricks of varying shades.

SCENIC DRIVES **Long Lane,** Warren. Few winding country roads remain in Warren, but Long Lane, turning into Touisset Road around

Touisset Point, has views of both Mount Hope Bay with Fall River across it and the Kickemuit River with Bristol on the other side.

Mathewson Road, Barrington. Elegant houses line this attractive road along the Warren and Barrington Rivers. In summer you'll see sailing yachts skimming the waters.

Nayatt Road, Barrington. There are beautiful homes along this road above Narragansett Bay.

Poppasquash Road, Bristol. This tree-shaded winding road edging Bristol Harbor in Colt State Park is a short but charming drive.

Rumstick Road, Barrington. Barrington thrived as a summer community at the turn of the 20th century, and many of the Tudor estates with river views are reminders of this period.

✷ To Do

BICYCLING Colt State Park Bike Trail. A 3-mile bike loop through the grounds of the former Colt estate offers views of Narragansett Bay, coves, and marshes, and is linked with the East Bay Bike Path.

East Bay Bike Path (401-245-0750). Beginning in Providence at India Point Park, 14.5 miles of paths for cyclists make their way along Narragansett Bay, over saltwater rivers, and through woods in Barrington,

THE EAST BAY BIKE PATH

Rhode Island Tourism Division

Warren, and Bristol. Maps are included in the *Rhode Island Visitor Guide,* which can be obtained by calling the above number.

BOAT LAUNCHES **Barrington Town Beach,** Bay Road, Barrington. **Bristol Narrows,** Narrows Road off RI 136, Bristol. Access to Mount Hope Bay. **Colt State Park,** Colt Drive, Bristol. Access to upper Narragansett Bay. **Haines Memorial State Park,** Metropolitan Park Drive, Barrington. Access to Bullocks Cove. **Independence Park,** Thames Street, Bristol. Access to Bristol Harbor. **Mount Hope Bay,** Annawamscott Drive off RI 136, Bristol. Access to Mount Hope Bay. **Striper Marina,** Tyler Point Road, Barrington. Access to the Warren River and upper Narragansett Bay. **Thames Street,** at the foot of State Street, Bristol. Access to Bristol Harbor. **Walker Farm,** County Road, Barrington. Access to Hundred Acre Cove.

DIVING **East Bay Dive Center** (401-247-2420), 8 Church Street, Warren. Diving instruction and rental of diving equipment.

FISHING **Brickyard Pond** (401-277-3576), Barrington, and the **Kickemuit River** (401-277-3576), Warren, offer good freshwater fishing. You must have a fishing license.

Narragansett Bay and **Mount Hope Bay** (401-277-3075). For blues, snappers, tautog, scup, and summer flounder. Fishing license required.

GOLF **Bristol Golf Club** (401-253-9844), 95 Tupelo Street, Bristol. Carts are available at this nine-hole par-71 course. Restaurant.

SAILING **Bayside YMCA** (401-245-2444), 70 West Street, Barrington. Summer sailing instruction for children and adults.

Bristol Yacht Club (401-253-2922), Poppasquash Road, Bristol. Summer instruction for children and adults.

SWIMMING **Barrington Town Beach,** Bay Road, Barrington. Open June through September, daily 9–6. Narragansett Bay swimming with lifeguards on duty but no parking for out-of-town cars.

Bristol Town Beach, Colt Drive off RI 114, Bristol. Open Memorial Day through Labor Day. The calmer waters of upper Narragansett Bay here are ideally suited for families with kids, and the beach fronts on 455 acres of Colt State Park land. Swimming; lifeguards. Parking fee for nonresidents.

TENNIS The following have outdoor courts open to the public: **Barrington High School,** 120 Lincoln Avenue, Barrington. **Barrington YMCA**

(401-245-2444), 70 West Street, Barrington. Two outdoor tennis courts. **Bristol Town Common,** Church and Wood Streets, Bristol. **Burr's Hill Park,** South Water Street, Warren. Parking is limited to town residents. **Jamiel's Park,** Market Street, Warren. **Kent Street Tennis Courts,** Kent Street, Barrington.

✷ Green Space

Audubon Society of Rhode Island Environmental Education Center (401-245-7500; http://asri.org), 1401 Hope Street (RI 114), Bristol. Open daily 9–5; admission $5 for adults, $3 for children. Walking trails wind through 28 acres of woodlands, and a boardwalk meanders over marshes to the edge of Narragansett Bay. The center is on the Warren–Bristol town line and is bisected by the East Bay Bike Path. The sleekly modern main building has exhibits of interest to both adults and children.

Hugh Cole Nature Trail and Park, Asylum Road, Warren. This town-maintained trail leads to the Hugh Cole Well and spring near the Kickemuit River.

Colt State Park (401-253-7482; http://riparks.com), RI 114, Bristol. Open dawn to dusk. Two bronze bulls mark the main entrance to the 455 acres of this state park that once was part of the Colt estate. Today azaleas brighten the grounds in spring, and roses perfume the air in summer. There are picnicking and fishing spots, boat-launching facilities, and hiking trails.

Haines Memorial State Park (401-253-7482; http://riparks.com), entrances on Washington Road and Metropolitan Park Drive, Barrington. Open dawn to dusk. This waterfront Rhode Island state park has 85 acres of open fields and woods laced with natural trails. Picnic tables are set in an oak tree grove overlooking Bullocks Cove, where a public boat ramp provides access to Narragansett Bay. The park was given to Rhode Island in 1911 in memory of Dr. George B. Haines, a physician who was an early advocate of protecting open natural areas as state parks. Haines State Park is at the midway point of the 14.5-mile East Bay Bike Path, making it a popular stop to rest, picnic, and view the bay. Restrooms. Farmers' market on summer Wednesdays.

Mount Hope Farm (401-254-1745; http://mounthopefarm.org), 250 Metacom Avenue (RI 136), Bristol. Two hundred acres of fields and woodlands laced with walking paths overlook Mount Hope Bay at this onetime gentleman's farm that has been preserved for the public to enjoy. The Governor Bradford House (see *Bed & Breakfasts*) is on the National Register of Historic Places and dates from the 1680s.

Osamequin River Nature Trail and Walker Farm, Hundred Acre Cove, RI 114, Barrington. There are 30 acres of field, farmland, and river-

Katherine Imbrie

SNOW BLANKETS HAINES MEMORIAL STATE PARK.

bank to explore here as well as boating and fishing. Winter presents fine opportunities to look for waterfowl; summer brings sharp-tailed and sea-side sparrows.

Touisset Marsh, Touisset Road, Warren. This 67-acre Rhode Island Audubon Society area offers walkways through fields and marshland where great blue herons, ospreys, snowy egrets, and even the occasional bald eagle may be seen.

✷ Lodging

BED & BREAKFASTS

Bradford-Dimond-Norris House (401-253-6338; http://bdnhouse.com), 474 Hope Street, Bristol. ($$) Familiarly known as the Wedding Cake House, this imposing white-clapboard mansion was built in 1792 by Rhode Island deputy governor William Bradford. It replaced his earlier home, which the British had destroyed in their raid on Bristol in 1778. In the 1840s Governor Francis Dimond was the owner, and when his daughter, Isabella, and her husband, Samuel Norris, moved in, they asked architect Russell Warren to add his touches to it. He contributed the north wing, an Ionic-style porch, and Chinese

Chippendale balustrades. Later the third story that gives it its wedding-cake aspect was added. Today there are four spacious antiques-furnished rooms for guests, all with private bath. Breakfast is served overlooking the garden. The house is on the Fourth of July parade route.

Governor Bradford House Country Inn at Mount Hope Farm (401-254-9300; 1-877-254-9300; http://mounthopefarm.com), 250 Metacom Avenue (RI 136), Bristol. ($$) Staying in one of the charming guest rooms in this colonial-era homestead that once belonged to the Haffenreffer family is like entering another era. The house sits on 200 acres of preserved waterfront land that had been part of a farm since the 1600s.

INNS **Bristol Harbor Inn** (401-254-1444; 1-866-254-1444; http://bristolharborinn.com), 259 Thames Street, Bristol. ($$$) This 40-room, boutique-style inn-hotel has a prime location on the waterfront at Thames Street Landing, an area that has in the past decade become an attractive harborfront destination with shops and restaurants.

Point Pleasant Inn (401-253-0627; 1-800-503-0627; http://pointpleasantinn.com), 333 Poppasquash Road, Bristol. ($$) Situated on 25 acres of land overlooking Bristol Harbor from the west, Point Pleasant is a once-private mansion that has been updated for guests with all the amenities, including an outdoor pool.

Rockwell House Inn (401-253-0040; 1-800-815-0040; http://rockwellhouseinn.com), 610 Hope Street, Bristol. ($$) A full, hearty breakfast that includes homemade granola and an afternoon spot of tea or sherry are among the attractions at this spacious four-bedroom, four-bath inn near the Bristol waterfront and on the Fourth of July parade route. Built in 1809 in the Federal style, the inn also reflects later architectural styles. A fieldstone "courting fireplace" can heat the porch, where breakfast is served in summer, spring, and fall. The courting fireplace was built in 1910 by then-owner Charles Rockwell to cheer up a jilted daughter who later became happily and firmly engaged beside it. In winter breakfast is served in the large candlelit dining room. Like the style of this enormous house, furnishings are eclectic.

William's Grant Inn (401-253-4222; http://wmgrantinn.com), 154 High Street, Bristol. ($$) An early-19th-century Federal house, this deep blue inn offers five rooms cooled by ceiling fans and with either private or shared baths. Family and friends have done much interior mural painting and decoration, and although the decor is a trifle heavy-handed, the William's Grant Inn is cozy and friendly. Breakfasts include egg dishes, Belgian waffles, and blueberry pancakes.

✷ Where to Eat

DINING OUT ♿ **Billy's** (401-289-2888; http://billysllc.com), 286 Maple Avenue, Barrington. ($$) Rather unprepossessing from the outside, as it is located in an off-street business plaza, Billy's is a real find in this bedroom community that is not particularly rich in restaurants. Pub-style atmosphere is cozy, both on the bar side and in the dining room. The menu varies, but offers a range of prices for well-prepared dishes such as seared salmon, pastas, steaks, salads, and burgers.

DeWolf Tavern (401-254-2005; http://dewolftavern.com), 267 Thames Street, Bristol. ($$$) One of Rhode Island's best restaurants is part of the Thames Street Landing harborfront complex, which also includes the Bristol Harbor Inn. The historic stone building right on the waterfront has been converted into a cozy pub downstairs and an elegant restaurant upstairs. Unusual dishes utilize Indian ingredients to put a fresh twist on traditional American fare.

Le Central (401-396-9965; http://lecentralbristol.net), 483 Hope Street, Bristol. ($$) Open daily, except Monday, for lunch and dinner, this authentic-looking French bistro includes the traditional as well as the nouveau on its menu. In an area where Italian and Portuguese food dominates the dining scene, it's a treat to find a place so Français.

♿ **The Lobster Pot** (401-253-9100; http://lobsterpotri.com), 121 Hope Street, Bristol. ($$$) Open daily, except Monday, for lunch and dinner. The view of Narragansett Bay is spectacular, and this seafood restaurant has been an area mainstay since the 1920s. The quality of its cooking tends to vary, but the outdoor patio is a fine spot for a sunset drink on summer evenings.

Persimmon (401-254-7474; http://persimmonbristol.com), 31 State Street, Bristol. ($$$) Open nightly, except Monday, for dinner. This much-celebrated chef-owned restaurant specializes in seasonal, local fare prepared with panache and served in a very small and sometimes noisy dining room.

♿ **Redlefsen's** (401-254-1188; http://redlefsens.com), 444 Thames Street, Bristol. ($$) Open daily from 5 PM for dinner only. One of very few German-style restaurants in Rhode Island, this casual eatery is especially noted for its Wiener schnitzel and its annual Oktoberfest specials.

♿ **S.S. Dion** (401-253-2884; http://ssdion.com), 520 Thames Street, Bristol. ($$) Open daily, except Sunday, for dinner. Arrive in time to see the sun set over Bristol Harbor if you can, and corner a table with a water view. There's nothing fancy, just straightforward fish dishes—devotees insist that the best-prepared swordfish in Rhode Island is served here.

Trafford (401-289-2265; http://traffordrestaurant.com), 285 Water Street, Warren. ($$) Open daily for lunch and dinner. Try to get a table on the porch, or inside with a harbor view. Opened in summer 2011, this is one of Warren's most attractive restaurants, with food to match. Dishes change with the seasons, but might include a seared duck breast with mango-pineapple salsa or a zippy stuffed quahog.

♿ **Tyler Point Grille** (401-247-0017; http:tylerpointgrille.com), 32 Barton Avenue, Barrington. ($$) Open nightly for dinner. Although it's close to the water, this local favorite doesn't offer much of a view. All diners see is the Barrington Yacht Club parking lot across the street and the stored boats of Stanley's Boatyard. However, the menu offers a wide assortment of Italian appetizers and pasta plus wood-grilled and oven-roasted meats and fish.

♿ **The Wharf Tavern** (401-289-2524; http://thewharftavernri.com), 215 Water Street, Warren. ($$) Reopened with new owners in 2011, the Wharf is a local legend whose quality has varied over the decades. Open daily for lunch

LOBSTER IS THE SPECIALTY AT WARREN'S WHARF TAVERN.

Kim Grant

and dinner. The specialty at this waterfront tavern is lobster, prepared in multitudinous ways: thermidor, Newburg, sautéed in sherry butter, in salad, stuffed with scallops and shrimp, or simply baked or boiled. There are other fine fish dishes at reasonable prices, too, as well as charcoal-broiled steak of many cuts and chicken and pasta dishes. In addition to the fish dishes, the lunch menu offers low-calorie salad plates, sandwiches, and soups.

EATING OUT

In Bristol

♿ **Aidan's Pub** (401-254-1940; http://aidanspub.com), 5 John Street. ($) Open daily, except Monday, for lunch and dinner. A good Irish pub serving such simple Irish fare as fish-and-chips, bangers and mash (sausages and mashed potatoes), and Irish breakfasts with Irish brown bread. It's set almost on the water, across from the Prudence Island ferry dock.

Bristol Bagel Works (401-254-1390), 420 Hope Street. ($–$$) Open daily 6:30 AM–3 PM (until 1 on Sunday). Made-on-the-premises coffee and bagels of all varieties are available here. In warm weather you can enjoy them outside. Soup and sandwiches are also on the menu.

♿ **Leo's** Ristorante (401-253-9300; http://leosristoranteri.com), 365 Hope Street, Bristol. ($$) Serving lunch and dinner daily, this classic Italian restaurant seems to have all the right ingredients. From the small tables outside on the sidewalk, to the window tables inside, the place is always packed. Traditional red-sauce Italian favorites are its specialty.

♿ **Quito's Seafood Restaurant** (401-253-9042; http://quitosrestaurant.com), 411 Thames Street. ($S) Open March through late November daily, except Tuesday, for lunch and dinner. Fresh fish fare is offered outdoors or indoors in a casual waterfront setting. The restaurant has upped its game in recent years, and the quality and sophistication is outstanding, making it one of this busy restaurant town's best dining options.

In Warren

♿ **Crossroads Restaurant** (401-245-9305; http://crossroadsrestaurantri.com), 133 Market Street. ($–$$) Open daily, except Monday, for lunch and dinner. Hearty sandwiches and chicken and lobster salads are favorites at this no-frills local pub. Dine in a garden room with plants and skylights or in a dark and cozy nook.

Sunnyside (401-247-1200; http://thesunnysideri.com), 267 Water Street. ($) Open Wednesday through Sunday for breakfast and lunch. Many people say that this is the loveliest breakfast setting in the state, and the food matches the view at this bright waterfront café on the Warren River. The freshest ingredients are used in abundant omelets, creative pancakes, and hearty roast turkey sandwiches.

Tuscan Tavern (401-247-9200; http://tuscantavern.net), 632 Metacom Avenue. ($$) Open daily, except Monday, for dinner. Here, from the largest wood-burning oven in the state, come crusty pizzas and bruschettas with a Tuscan flavor as well as plenty of pasta dishes, steaks, chicken, and fresh fish. Half and family-style portions are also offered.

SNACKS

In Warren

Coffee Depot (401-247-9890; http://coffeedepotonline.com), 501 Main Street. Great, fresh-roasted coffee drinks such as lattes and espressos are served from a copper-topped bar. Customers sip at their leisure while ensconced in deep leather chairs and surrounded by the work of local artists. Live folk-style music adds to the mix on Saturday. Sandwich wraps and pastries, too.

In Barrington and Bristol

Daily Scoop (401-245-0100 in Barrington; 401-254-2223 in Bristol; http://dailyscoopicecream.com), 230 County Road (RI 114), Barrington, and 446B Thames Street, Bristol. Both shops are open seasonally only, and they have some of the best and freshest ice cream you'll ever taste.

✷ Entertainment

2nd Story Theatre (401-247-4200; http://2ndstorytheatre.com), 28 Market Street, Warren. This highly regarded troupe puts on full-length plays with ticket costs of around $25—a real bargain for theater buffs.

✷ Selective Shopping

ANTIQUES AND COLLECTIBLES

Alfred's Antiques (401-245-3465), 331 Hope Street, Bristol. It's Christmas in Alfred's windows year-round. Inside, mahogany furniture, china, and crystal are charmingly displayed.

Alfred's of Barrington (401-245-3101), 18 Maple Avenue, Barrington. This location of Alfred's has some of the best consignment furniture around, nicely displayed on two floors.

Finders Keepers (401-247-7170), 147 Water Street, Warren. Consignment boutique has designer clothing as well as items for the home.

Jesse James Antiques (401-253-2240), 44 State Street, Bristol. Quality collectibles, 1920s furniture.

Robin Jenkins Antiques (401-254-8958; http://robinjenkinsantiques.com), 278 Hope Street, Bristol. A small shop with an eclectic assortment of collectibles and a few antiques.

Marie King Antiques (401-245-1020), 382 Main Street, Warren.

Furniture, art, and china are attractively arranged in a Colonial house in the heart of Warren.

The Meeting House (401-247-7043), 47 Water Street, Warren. Eighteenth-, 19th-, and 20th-century painted farmhouse furniture and reproductions of 18th-century tinware sconces, 19th-century chamber lights, and hogscraper candlesticks are on sale on the ground floor of the 1790 Jabez Bowen House.

Second Helpings (401-396-9600; http://secondhelpingsri.com), 32 Gooding Avenue, Bristol. A find for consignment lovers, this shop is crammed with great stuff of all kinds: furniture, textiles, kitchenware, books, and all sorts of interesting vintage items.

Thirds (401-253-1920; http://thirdsri.com), 34 Gooding Avenue, Bristol. Right next door to Second Helpings (above) is this consignment shop for women's clothing.

Wren & Thistle (401-247-0631), 19 Market Street, Warren. There's a nice selection of quality antiques in this small shop.

BOOKSTORES **Barrington Books** (401-245-7925), Barrington Shopping Center, 180 County Road, Barrington. Greeting cards, books, and book-related toys are sold in this customer-friendly independent bookstore.

A Novel Idea (401-396-9360), 54 State Street, Bristol. Good selection of new and used books in an attractive shop.

Roger Williams University Bookstore, Barnes & Noble (401-254-3036), 1 Old Ferry Road, Bristol. Books of general interest as well as textbooks are available in this on-campus store.

SPECIAL SHOPS **Blithewold Gift Shop** (401-253-4130), 101 Ferry Road, Bristol. In this gift store at the Blithewold Mansion and Gardens, the gifts reflect the environment. There are attractive garden decorations, cards designed with floral patterns, and garden books.

Bristol Art Gallery (401-396-9699; http://bristolartgallery.net), 423 Hope Street, Bristol. Attractive art shop has a range of paintings, prints, and photographs for sale.

Gallery 11 Fine Art (401-396-9311; http://galleryelevenfineart.com), 11 State Street, Bristol. Collection of works by a local collaborative of artists is well worth a look in this light-filled shop in the heart of Bristol.

Grasmere (401-247-2789; http://grasmeretheshop.com), 40 Maple Avenue, Barrington. Dried floral arrangements and prettily presented plants and fresh flowers are augmented by English country-style vases and garden accessories.

Herreshoff Marine Museum Nautical Shop (401-253-5000), 7

Burnside Street, Bristol. This gift shop in the Herreshoff Marine Museum has such items for the yachtsman or the want-to-be yachtsman as heavy-weather gear, compasses and ship's clocks, marine books, bookends, and paperweights with a nautical touch.

Hope Gallery (401-396-9117; http://hopegalleryfineartfinecraft.com), 435 Hope Street, Bristol. A collection of fine crafts and art pieces is in this pretty shop and gallery.

Jamiel's Shoe World (401-245-4389; www.jamiels.com), 471 Main Street, Warren. Family-run store is a local go-to for its great collection of first-rate shoes at bargain prices.

Imago (401-245-3348), 36 Market Street, Warren. Open Thursday through Sunday 11–5. A group of artists with studios nearby run this gallery for high-quality contemporary works including paintings, pottery, and sculpture.

Kate & Company (401-253-3117), 301 Hope Street, Bristol. There's a little bit of this and a little bit of that—baskets, gourmet foods, hand-painted furniture, decorative wooden boxes, dried wreaths, and picture frames—in this attractive gift shop.

Linden Place Gift Shop (401-253-0309), 500 Hope Street, Bristol. Well-selected gifts—pewter, crystal, paper, china—are in keeping with the tradition of historic Linden Place.

Summerwood (401-855-1751; http://summerwood.cc), 57 Water Street, Warren. Handcrafted teak furniture, art, and jewelry are imported directly from Indonesia to this family-owned shop in the heart of historic Warren.

FARM STANDS **Four Town Farm**, (508-336-5587; http://4townfarm.com), 90 George Street, Seekonk/Barrington. As its name suggests, this pick-your-own farm stretches into four towns, two of them (Barrington and East Providence) in Rhode Island. It's the best place around to pick strawberries, raspberries, peas, or anything else that's in-season, including your own bouquet of fresh flowers.

Frerich's Farm (401-245-8245; http://frerichsfarm.com), Kinnicutt Avenue, Warren. Open late April through December, Tuesday through Sunday 9–5. Famous for its family-fun events such as the annual Pumpkin Weigh-Off, Frerichs is a fun destination at other times of the year as well.

Johnson's Roadside Farm Market (508-379-0349), 445 Market Street, Warren/Swansea. Open year-round, this market right on the Massachusetts state line has an abundance of bakery goods and produce in a setting that's remarkably bucolic, given its proximity to the busy center of Warren.

✷ Special Events

March: **Maple Sugaring** (401-253-9062; http://coggeshallfarm.org), Coggeshall Farm Museum, Colt State Park, Bristol. Tree tapping, sugar on snow. First weekend in March.

April: **Daffodil Week** (401-253-2707; http://blithewold.org), Blithewold Gardens, Ferry Road, Bristol. First week in April.

Mid-April through mid-May: **Blithewold Mansion and Gardens Annual Spring Bulb Display** (401-253-2707), Blithewold Gardens, Ferry Road, Bristol. More than 50,000 flowering bulbs herald the arrival of spring.

Late April: **All Manner of Good Work Crafts and Skills Display** (401-253-9062), Coggeshall Farm Museum, Colt State Park, Bristol. Such traditional 18th-century crafts and skills as blacksmithing, coopering, and rake making are demonstrated.

May: **May Breakfasts** (401-222-2601). Churches, schools, and veterans posts serve up jonny cakes and other traditional breakfast dishes. **Sheepshearing** (401-253-9062), Coggeshall Farm Museum, Colt State Park, Bristol. Usually the third weekend of May.

Early June: **Bristol County Striped Bass Tournament** (401-245-6121), Striper Marina, Tyler Point Road, Barrington.

Late June: ✐ **Children's Day** (401-253-9062), Coggeshall Farm Museum, Colt State Park, Bristol. Such 18th-century children's games as ninepins, sticks and hoops, and top spinning. Usually the last Sunday in June.

June–August: **Concerts-by-the-Bay** (401-253-2707), Blithewold Gardens, Ferry Road, Bristol. Usually every other Sunday afternoon.

July: **Bristol Fourth of July Parade** (401-245-0750). The nation's oldest (1785) parade of civic, military, and firefighters' contingents marches through the streets of Bristol. **Firemen's Memorial Parade,** Barrington–Warren. **Barrington–Warren Rotary Club Quahog Festival** (401-245-3725), Burr's Hill Park, Warren. Live entertainment and clambake, open to the public.

July and August: **Fire Company Clambakes,** Warren. Individual fire companies have clambakes on weekends either at their fire stations or at the Rod and Gun Club in Warren. Individual town fire companies can provide information.

August: **Blessing of the Animals** (401-251-9062), Coggeshall Farm Museum, Colt State Park, Bristol. **Bristol Rotary Club Waterfront Festival** (401-254-0354), Guiteras Elementary School grounds. Two days of food, games, crafts, and music.

Late September: **Harvest Fair** (401-253-9062), Coggeshall Farm Museum, Colt State Park, Bristol. Music, pony rides, hayrides, jonny cakes and chowder, crafts, pumpkin painting.

November: **Warren Holiday Festival** (401-245-7340), Water and Main Streets, Warren. The day after Thanksgiving, holiday lights are lit along both streets. The festival continues through the post-Thanksgiving weekend with a visit from Santa Claus, gingerbread cookie workshops, hayrides, and music.

December: **Christmas Tree Sale and Father Christmas Visits** (401-253-9062), Coggeshall Farm Museum, Colt State Park, Bristol. **Christmas at Blithewold** (401-253-2707), Blithewold Mansion, Ferry Road, Bristol. Period decor, vignettes of Christmas past, and a 20-foot Christmas tree in the turn-of-the-20th-century mansion. **Bristol Festival of Lights** (401-245-0750). Downtown concert, lighting ceremony, refreshments.

Sakonnet 5

TIVERTON

LITTLE COMPTON

Kim Grant

TIVERTON

Sakonnet consists of two towns, Tiverton and Little Compton, which once were part of the Massachusetts Bay Colony and now make up the southeasternmost part of Rhode Island. Meaning "Place of the Black Geese" to members of the Wampanoag tribe, Sakonnet is the rural part of Newport County, lightly populated except for a few pockets, and filled with pastures and woods.

Once a popular waterfront resort centered on the area known as Stone Bridge, Tiverton is a sleepy rural community that has been around about as long as Plymouth Colony. The town was included within Rhode Island's borders by royal decree in 1746, although it took several skirmishes with Massachusetts to settle the issue. While officially part of Rhode Island, Tiverton nevertheless retains its Bay State mentality; its accents, culture, and most of its residents have roots in Massachusetts. Like its neighbor Little Compton, Tiverton was not occupied by the British during the Revolution (although it suffered periodic raids), and served as a haven for rebels and a staging point for sorties across the Sakonnet River.

GETTING THERE *By car:* From Aquidneck Island on RI 24, take the first or second exit off the Sakonnet River Bridge; from points north on RI 24 south, take the Tiverton exit and turn left onto Main Road (RI 77).

MEDICAL EMERGENCY The statewide emergency number is **911.**

Tiverton Rescue is 401-625-6744.

✷ To See

HISTORIC SITE **Fort Barton,** Highland Avenue, across from town hall. Highland Avenue can be reached from Main Road by taking any left up the hill before the remains of the Stone Bridge—Lawton Avenue in particular. Park your car (free) and walk up the blacktop path to the heights above. Fort Barton was hastily erected in 1777 in response to the British

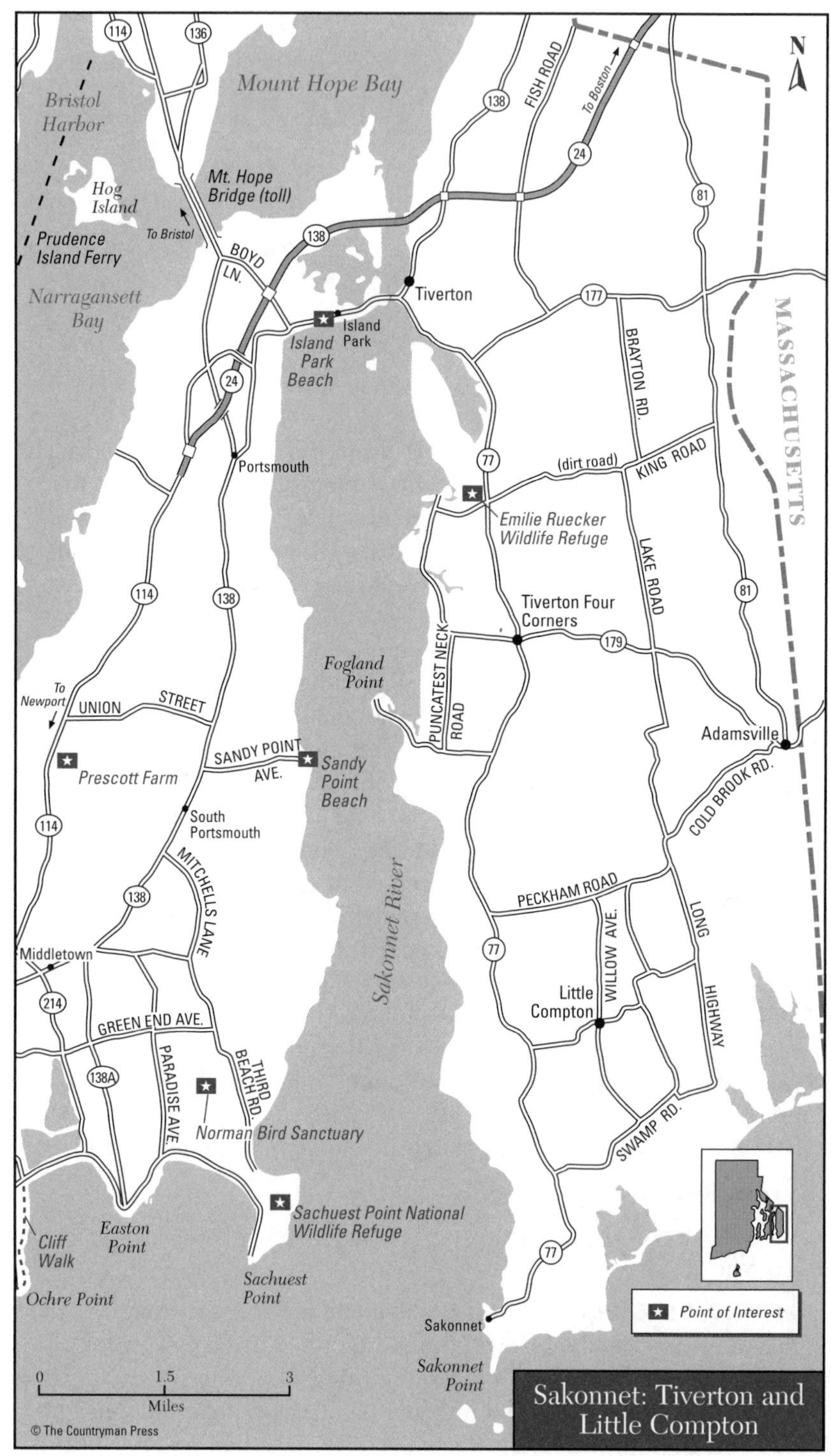
Mount Hope Bay
Bristol Harbor
Hog Island
Prudence Island Ferry
Narragansett Bay
Mt. Hope Bridge (toll)
To Bristol
BOYD LN.
To Boston
FISH ROAD
Tiverton
Island Park
Island Park Beach
MASSACHUSETTS
BRAYTON RD.
Portsmouth
(dirt road)
KING ROAD
Emilie Ruecker Wildlife Refuge
LAKE ROAD
Tiverton Four Corners
PUNCATEST NECK ROAD
Fogland Point
To Newport
UNION STREET
SANDY POINT AVE.
Sandy Point Beach
Prescott Farm
Adamsville
COLD BROOK RD.
South Portsmouth
MITCHELLS LANE
Sakonnet River
PECKHAM ROAD
WILLOW AVE.
LONG HIGHWAY
Middletown
Little Compton
GREEN END AVE.
PARADISE AVE.
THIRD BEACH RD.
Norman Bird Sanctuary
SWAMP RD.
Sachuest Point National Wildlife Refuge
Cliff Walk
Easton Point
Sachuest Point
Ochre Point
Sakonnet
Point of Interest
Sakonnet Point
0 1.5 3
Miles
© The Countryman Press
Sakonnet: Tiverton and Little Compton

capture of Newport. Named for Colonel William Barton, who kidnapped General Prescott, the fort was really an earthwork with some timber support. However, from its height 110 feet above the Sakonnet River, its guns held a sweeping command of the north end of Aquidneck. The fort was the jumping-off place for the attack on Aquidneck in 1778, a move that, but for the defection of the French fleet at a crucial moment, might have ended the war in its second year. Today the fort has been partially restored, and there are 3 miles of hiking trails and a lookout that will give you a good view of the northern end of Aquidneck Island and surrounding waters.

SCENIC DRIVES **Main Road** (RI 77) is a little-trafficked country road surrounded by pastures and running between inland woods and the Sakonnet River. It remains a favorite Sunday ride for area families. Driving south from Stone Bridge, you will pass Nanaquaket Pond and some farm stands and clam shacks before reaching a more rural setting. At 3119 Main Road, on the left, you'll notice a two-chimney house set back a bit. This is the **Abraham Brown House,** also known as the Adoniram Brown House. Lafayette stayed here during a stopover in Tiverton in 1778.

At 3622 West Main Road, on your right, is the **Captain Robert Gray House,** birthplace in 1755 of the man who skippered the first American ship to sail around the world (1780–1790). Captain Gray also discovered the entrance to the Columbia River, giving the United States a convincing claim to the Pacific Northwest. He died at sea of yellow fever in 1806.

VIEW OF AQUIDNECK ISLAND FROM SAKONNET

Kim Grant

The house is privately owned, but a small plaque near the street recalls its historical connection.

Half a mile up the road is Tiverton Four Corners, where there are several notable structures. The stately yellow house on the near left is the **Soule-Seabury House,** built in 1760 by Abner Soule, whaler, blacksmith, and soldier. His son, Cornelius Soule, enlarged the house in 1809 but in 1816 was forced to deed it to Cornelius Seabury, merchant and farmer, for payment of a debt. Once open as a museum, the building, unfortunately, was sold some years ago, along with all of its original furnishings. But don't be surprised if you see an ancient mariner comfortably seated on the stone wall outside—some local residents swear they've seen the spirit of Abner Soule return to his former homestead.

The building across the street, on the northwest corner of the intersection, was for years the **A. P. White Store,** built as a country general store in 1875. It now houses Provender, an upscale (and excellent) gourmet food store (see *Where to Eat—Snacks*). The late-Victorian structure has a high mansard roof and cupola. Original proprietor Andrew Peregrine White was postmaster, ice cutter, dry-goods supplier, and social director for this section of Tiverton for many years.

Also at Four Corners (next to Gray's Ice Cream) is the **Chase-Cory House,** a simple gambrel-roofed house that dates to at least 1730 and contains a 7-foot fireplace with beaded chimney. Owned by the Tiverton Historical Society, it is open to the public June through September, Sunday 2–4:30.

From Four Corners, you may continue straight on RI 77 to Little Compton, or take a left onto East Road (RI 179). Bear right at the fork onto Stone Church Road, pass the **Old Stone Church** (built back to front so the congregation could keep watch for hostile Native Americans), and continue down the long grade into the village of Adamsville, part of Little Compton. The large white private house across the street from Simmons' Variety was home to Rudolf, a son of the Von Trapp family who fled the Nazis in Austria. From Adamsville, you can wind your way via several routes to Little Compton center, or return to the Four Corners and turn left to continue on Main Road.

* To Do

FOR FAMILIES ✐ **Alpacas of Henseforth Farm** (401-624-4184), 460 East Road, about 1 mile east of Tiverton Four Corners. Call for an appointment. The Hensle family raises alpacas—gentle, fiber-bearing animals similar to llamas—on this private farm in south Tiverton. "We like to show our alpacas to people who are interested in alpacas," says Mrs. Hensle, adding that the animals are "friendly but shy." There also are

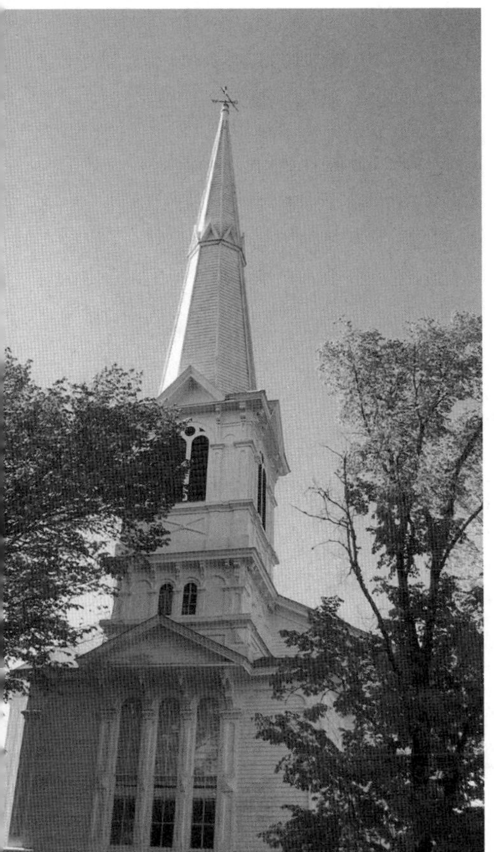

Katherine Imbrie

LITTLE COMPTON CHURCH

guinea hens, ducks, and a pack of enthusiastic but friendly dogs roaming the place.

HORSEBACK RIDING Roseland Acres (401-624-8866), 594 East Road (left at Tiverton Four Corners). Trail rides, indoor ring, and lessons in Western- and hunt-style riding.

SWIMMING Fogland Beach, Fogland Road, off Main Road (RI 77) via Neck Road. The drive to this rocky little beach takes you through some beautiful rural countryside. The half-mile beach itself is on a peninsula reaching into the Sakonnet River, whose calm, salty waters make for ideal family bathing. *Fogland* is not just a random name—this area frequently is wreathed in fog while the rest of the state basks in sunshine. The area is popular for windsurfing because of a reliable southwest breeze.

Grinnell's Beach, Main Road at Stone Bridge. A quarter-mile crescent of sand, framed by a seawall that's been a teen hangout for generations. Unfortunately, there's a gas station between the beach and the road. The small island you see just offshore is called Gould Island and is a private bird sanctuary, off-limits to human visitors.

✷ Green Space

Emilie Ruecker Wildlife Refuge (401-624-2759), 137 Sapowet Avenue, about a third of a mile from Main Road. Open year-round, daily dawn to dusk. Free entry and parking. Operated by the Audubon Society of Rhode Island, this 1.5-mile walk on the shores of the Sakonnet River is a bird lover's paradise. Once a farm, the property, which was donated to the Audubon Society in 1965, contains salt marshes, wooded areas, rocky outcroppings, and thick underbrush—a variety of terrain and foliage that attracts a variety of birds: herons, snowy egrets, pheasants, and sandpipers.

The refuge offers something during any season. Trails are marked by color and are easy to follow.

Weetamoo Woods, between East Road and Lafayette Road, both off Main Road (RI 77). Open all year and free. Lafayette Road is almost opposite the Sapowet Avenue route to the Ruecker refuge; the park entrance is less than half a mile up Lafayette. Four hundred acres of woods named for Weetamoo, or Weetamo, sachem of the Pocasset tribe of the Wampanoags, who wintered here until the time of King Philip's War. You can follow several trails—a walk around the perimeter is less than 5 miles—that are all easygoing. Sites include an abandoned sawmill and some impressive rock outcroppings.

✷ Where to Eat

DINING OUT **Boat House** (401-624-6300; http://boathousetiverton.com), 227 Schooner Drive (off Route 138 north of Sakonnet Bridge), Tiverton. ($$) Casually stylish waterfront dining in a building that evokes a real boathouse. Sunsets are spectacular; the food is creative modern, heavy on local seafood. Drinks on the patio sit nicely on the arm of an Adirondack chair. The only drawback here is the backdrop: A marching line of identically "upscale" condominiums look as if they're about to descend upon the little Boat House at the foot of the hill. (Diners can avoid the ghastly sight by keeping their eyes fixed to the west, where the water is.)

Evelyn's Drive-In (401-624-3100; http://evelynsdrivein.com), 2335 Main Road (RI 77), Nanaquaket. ($) Open daily in-season until 8 PM. Hamburger-and-clam stand overlooking peaceful Nanaquaket Pond. Order an overstuffed lobster roll with fries and take a seat at one of Evelyn's picnic tables.

♿ **Four Corners Grille** (401-624-1510), 3841 Main Road, just north of Tiverton Four Corners. ($) Open daily 7–9. Very nice country-pub atmosphere, with breakfast dishes, imaginative (and tasty) sandwiches—lemon tarragon chicken, the Wampanoag (smoked turkey and cucumbers)—and homey dinners, from fried clams or scallops to shepherd's pie or meat loaf. Try the lobster bisque and crabcakes. Outdoor court in summer.

Moulin Rouge (401-624-4320), 1403 Main Road, just south of Sakonnet River Bridge (second exit). ($$) Open Wednesday through Sunday for dinner. You've got to love a place in Tiverton, Rhode Island, that has a model of the Eiffel Tower in its front yard. Nothing especially fancy—steak, seafood, and French-inspired dishes with a variety of sauces.

SNACKS **Coastal Coffee Roasters** (401-624-2343; www.coastalroasters.com), 1791 Main Road at

Stone Bridge. This place roasts its own beans and serves espressos, lattes, and other coffee drinks, as well as snacks and pastries, in a pleasantly offbeat small café with outdoor seating overlooking the water in summer.

Gray's Ice Cream (401-624-4500; http://graysicecream.com), junction of RI 77 and 179 (Tiverton Four Corners). Open daily in summer 6:30 AM–10 PM. Gray's has been attracting hordes of summer weekend customers since 1922. Its central location still makes it perennially popular with summer visitors to Sakonnet.

Provender (401-624-8096), 3883 Main Road, at Tiverton Four Corners. Open daily except Tuesday 9–5. Housed in the former A. P. White Store, which also served as the local post office, this gourmet food shop and deli offers fancy sandwiches, picnics, and lots of homemade desserts.

✷ Selective Shopping

The Cottage at Four Corners (401-625-5814; www.thecottageri.com), 3847 Main Road, Tiverton. Upscale, country-style furniture, ceramics, glassware, cookbooks, and bath items are beautifully displayed on two floors.

Courtyards (401-624-8682; www.courtyardsltd.com), 3980 Main Road, Tiverton. Great place filled with chiseled stone birdbaths, concrete lawn and garden decorations, outdoor furniture, sundials, pottery, and a nice selection of jewelry. One of a number of interesting shops in the Mill Pond Shops complex, just past Four Corners.

Donovan Gallery (401-624-4000; www.donovangallery.com), Main Road, near Tiverton Four Corners. Mostly paintings, but also glassware, sculpture, and ceramics, much of it by local artists and quite good.

Milk and Honey Bazaar (401-624-1974; www.milkandhoneybazaar.com), 3838 Main Road, Tiverton. Find a sophisticated array of imported and domestic cheeses, as well as other gourmet goodies, year-round in this rustic barn. They specialize in party platters.

✷ Special Events

Fourth of July weekend: **Tiverton Waterfront Festival.** Games, crafts, music, pizza cook-off at Grinnell's Beach near Stone Bridge.

July and August: **Arts & Artisans Festival** (1-800-677-7150), Tiverton Four Corners. Nice weekend outdoor show of art and crafted items is one of a series of nearly weekly outdoor Four Corners shows in summer—some featuring, among other things, ethnic art from around the world and American antiques.

August: **Concert series** (401-624-2600), Tiverton Four Corners. Mostly folk music, every Sunday in August.

Tom Gannon

LITTLE COLONIALS AT THE INDEPENDENCE DAY PARADE

Early September: **Union Free Library Association book sale** (401-625-6799), 3832 Main Road, at Tiverton Four Corners. Annual book sale to benefit this one-room lending library, believed by some to be the second oldest in Rhode Island (after the Redwood in Newport).

LITTLE COMPTON

Little Compton, directly south of Tiverton, is a picture-perfect New England town, one of the few in Rhode Island to boast a classic village green anchored by church, municipal buildings, and commercial enterprises. The rarity of church-centered greens in Rhode Island lies in its roots as a renegade colony founded upon absolute separation of church and state (while still tolerating all forms of religious expression). Little Compton is an exception because it began its existence as a creature of Plymouth Colony. Covering 21.6 square miles and with a population of less than 4,000, this is one of the more rural towns in the state, with rolling farmlands and thick woods. To the west and south, it is bordered by the bright blue Atlantic Ocean; fishing, as well as farming, is a longtime occupation. Year-round and summer residents are proud of the town's character and setting (KEEP LITTLE COMPTON LITTLE was a popular bumper sticker some years ago), and so far they have succeeded in preserving things the way they've been for centuries.

GETTING THERE *By car:* RI 77 (Main Road) south from Tiverton.

MEDICAL EMERGENCY The statewide emergency number is **911.**
Little Compton Rescue is 401-635-2323.

✷ To See and Do

HISTORIC HOME Wilbor House (401-635-4035; www.littlecompton.org), West Main Road (RI 77). Open mid-June through mid-September, Tuesday through Saturday 2–4. Small admission charged. The original two-story, two-room section of this house dates from 1680. You can distinguish it from rooms added by succeeding generations of the Wilbors during the 18th and 19th centuries by its low ceilings and exposed beams. Restored in 1956 by the Little Compton Historical Society, the house contains furniture from the 17th and 18th centuries. There's also a display of

Katherine Imbrie

FISHING BOAT, SAKONNET HARBOR

antique farming and household equipment in the neighboring barn. Early settler Samuel Wilbor, who came over from Portsmouth in search of larger pastures, gave birth to the Wilbor clan that has split in several directions over the years and given rise to at least four spellings of the surname, including *Wilber, Wilbur,* and *Wilbour.* Adherents of the last were considered to be putting on airs by adding the *u* to the venerable name.

HISTORIC SITES **Commons Burial Ground,** Little Compton Commons, Meetinghouse Lane. This plot, extending down from behind the graceful United Congregational Church, was laid out in 1675. It is the final resting place for many early settlers, including Elizabeth Pabodie, who was the first infant of European descent born in New England, and the daughter of John and Priscilla Alden. Buried here also is Benjamin Church, the "Indian fighter" who in 1676 put an end to King Philip's War, which had ravaged the colony. Anyone familiar with colonial churchyards knows our ancestors' predilection for plain talk, even on their tombstones. Next to the grave of LYDIA, WIFE OF MR. SIMEON PALMER is another stone with the 1776 inscription ELIZABETH, WHO SHOULD HAVE BEEN THE WIFE OF MR. SIMEON PALMER. Now *that's* having the last word.

Gray's Grist Mill (508-636-6075; www.graysgristmill.com), Adamsville Road (RI 179). Open Tuesday through Sunday noon–4, but call ahead to be sure. The easiest way to get here is to take a left at Tiverton Four Corners on RI 179, bear right at Stone Church Road, and follow down the hill to Adamsville. The mill uses the engine from a 1946 Dodge truck instead of wind or water for power, but grinds out the real stuff our ancestors ate—corn, rye, and the special white flint cornmeal that's an essential ingredient in real jonny cakes.

SWIMMING **Goosewing Beach,** South Shore Road. This beautiful sand beach at the easternmost point of the Rhode Island coast is owned by The Nature Conservancy. The only parking area for Goosewing is in the South Shore Town Beach lot (see next listing). From there, you walk about a quarter mile to the east. The beach faces open water that sometimes kicks up strong surf.

Little Compton Town Beach (South Shore Beach), South Shore Road. More than 400 yards of rock-strewn sand is right in front of the parking lot (daily fee about $15). Despite the rocky aspect of the exposed sand here, the sand underneath the water is relatively rock-free, making this beach fine for swimming. If you want to leave the crowds, cars, and rocks behind, you need only walk a few hundred yards east to Goosewing Beach (see listing above).

WINERY **Sakonnet Vineyards** (401-635-8486; www.sakonnetwine.com), 162 West Main Road, 4 miles south of Tiverton Four Corners. Guided tours and wine tastings May through October, Wednesday through Sunday noon–4. Free. Built in the 1970s and cultivated on farmland that the original owners determined enjoys a climate similar to that of Burgundy, Sakonnet Vineyards is more than a local winery. Its vintages (vidal blanc, America's Cup White) have won national prizes. There's also a lovely seasonal café on the premises.

✷ Green Space

Wilbur Woods, Swamp Road, off West Main Road. A maze of paths and trails through natural woodlands. There's at least one brook flowing through the area (crossable by several wooden bridges and by stone steps), a pool, and a waterfall. Visitors will find tables and benches made from large stones as well as various inscriptions on rocks—all the work of 19th-century farmer Isaac Wilbour, who intended to fashion a memorial of sorts to the Native Americans who made Sakonnet their summer campground. This is a great natural habitat as well as a nice place to picnic. The woods are dotted with fireplaces for grilling.

See also *Swimming*.

✷ Lodging

The Stone House Club (401-635-2222; www.stonehouse1854.com), 122 Sakonnet Point Road. ($$$) This ultra-fancy boutique hotel is close to one of the best beaches in town. For decades, the Stone House was a private club that quietly rented simply furnished rooms in a big stone farmhouse (the granite walls are 2 feet thick) that dates from 1836. In 2007 it was sold to a partnership that extensively rehabbed it, adding a spa and two restaurants. The Stone House still offers a beautiful rural setting above a field overlooking the ocean.

✷ Where to Eat

DINING OUT The Stone House Club (401-635-2222; www.stonehouse1854.com), 122 Sakonnet Point Road. ($$$). This is undoubtedly the fanciest place to dine in Little Compton. New owners in 2008 added a fine-dining restaurant in the adjacent barn, as well as a cozy basement Tap Room. Several changes of management since then have made for hit-or-miss results, so it's a good idea to check the online foodie boards before going. (See *Lodging*.)

EATING OUT ♿ **The Barn** (401-635-2985), Adamsville Road (junction of RI 81 and RI 179), Little Compton. ($) Open year-round, daily 6:30 AM–noon, this place has been famous for decades for serving the best breakfasts for miles around. Pumpkin pancakes are a specialty, as are unique eggs Benedict combinations. Oh, and they have jonny cakes, Rhode

Kim Grant

Island's traditional fried cornmeal cake. Waitress Terry is locally famous for carrying a loaded tray on top of her head.

Commons Lunch (401-635-4388), south of Commons Road, Little Compton. ($) Open daily year-round for breakfast, lunch, and dinner, this comfortable little diner is always full of locals. The food is okay, but the main reason to come is that it's the hub of everything in this remarkably isolated and beautiful peninsula.

Crowther's (401-635-8367; www.crowthersrestaurant.com), 90 Pottersville Road, Little Compton. ($) Family favorite is open Wednesday through Sunday for lunch and dinner. Nothing fancy about this place. It's just home-style cooking in a simple country setting.

✷ Selective Shopping

C. R. Wilbur, General Merchandise (401-635-2356), the Commons. Next door to Commons Lunch, this meandering emporium is your classic general store, offering everything from nails to postcards, books to beach towels. It's a grocery store as well.

FARM STANDS The Last Stand, 374 West Main Road. This small farm stand sells fresh produce in-season, some organically grown, plus sandwiches and baked goods. Outdoor dining in the shade. Open summer only.

Delucia's Berry Farm (401-635-2698), 96 Willow Avenue. Fresh berries in-season, jams and jellies.

Walker's Farm Stand (401-635-4719), 261 West Main Road (Route 77), Little Compton. Open May through November, this farm stand has beautifully displayed produce, grown right there, as well as well-chosen grocery and pantry items that make it *the* place to shop for dinner in this bucolic region. A tiny bakery right next door completes the picture.

GARDEN CENTER Peckham's Greenhouse (401-635-4775; www.peckhamsgreenhouse.com), West Main Road. The Peckhams have a well-displayed array of perennials, annuals, and some shrubs. It's the place that everyone in town goes to when it's time to plant the seaside garden.

✷ Special Event

August: **Chicken barbecue and fair** on the town common.

Newport 6

Kim Grant

NEWPORT

Newport, sometimes called America's First Resort, owes its existence to the sea. Situated at the mouth of Narragansett Bay and blessed with a fine deepwater harbor, Newport quickly grew from a small settlement founded by Massachusetts refugees in 1639 to a bustling seaport. As early as 1646 residents were busy building ships, and by the middle of the next century the town was a major port in the New World, rivaling New York and Boston in size and importance. The local fleet was heavily involved in the slave trade, and the city was a haven for privateers—often indistinguishable from outright pirates—who'd as soon plunder a British ship as one flying the French or Dutch flag.

It was the sea and the natural beauty of the promontory on which the city stands that attracted wealthy visitors beginning in the early 18th century, culminating with the influx of wealthy New York society families toward the turn of the 19th century. Their presence helped make the city the country's "first" resort, and the extravagant mansions, or "summer cottages," as they were called, draw many of today's visitors.

Newport's nickname also can be traced to the impressive number of "firsts" it lays claim to. Among them: the first US post office and first free public school (1640); the first synagogue in the United States (1789); the first gaslit street (1803); the first open golf tournament (1895); the first national grass-court tennis championships (1881); and, in the field of vehicle control, the first traffic ordinance (1687) as well as the first motorized traffic arrest (1904—the offense: going 15 miles per hour).

Aside from its natural attributes, which include a mild summer climate softened by a prevailing southwest sea breeze, Newport is an important treasury of colonial homes—thanks in part to a three-year occupation by British and Hessian troops at the start of the Revolution. During the occupation, the city lost much of its population, all of its commerce, and many of its buildings. By war's end the city was deeply in debt and no longer a port of consequence. As a result, Newporters were too poor to tear down their humble (now prized) dwellings in the name of progress.

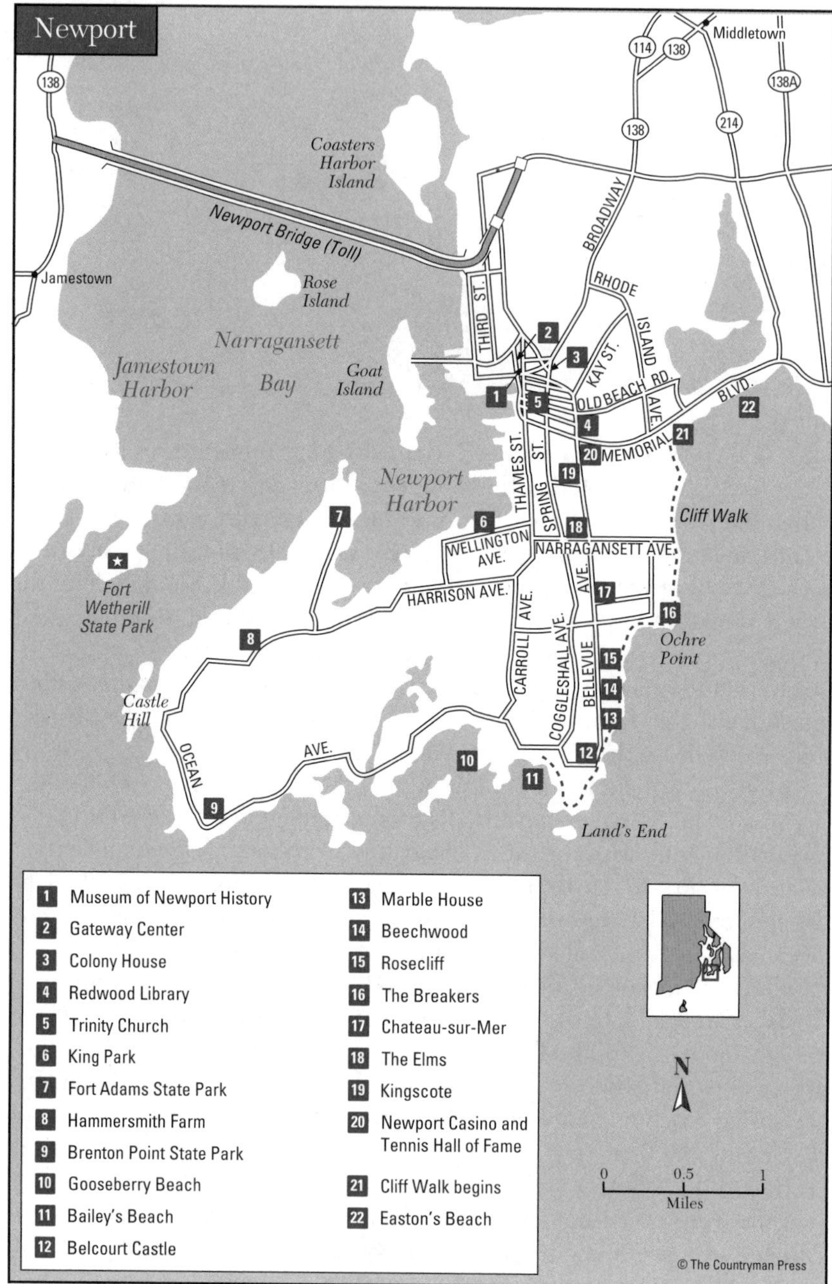
Newport
Middletown
114
138
138A
214
138
Coasters Harbor Island
Newport Bridge (Toll)
Jamestown
Rose Island
Narragansett Bay
Jamestown Harbor
Goat Island
THIRD ST.
BROADWAY
RHODE ISLAND AVE.
KAY ST.
OLD BEACH RD.
MEMORIAL BLVD.
THAMES ST.
SPRING ST.
Newport Harbor
Cliff Walk
WELLINGTON AVE.
NARRAGANSETT AVE.
HARRISON AVE.
CARROLL AVE.
COGGESHALL AVE.
BELLEVUE AVE.
Fort Wetherill State Park
Ochre Point
Castle Hill
OCEAN AVE.
Land's End
1 Museum of Newport History
2 Gateway Center
3 Colony House
4 Redwood Library
5 Trinity Church
6 King Park
7 Fort Adams State Park
8 Hammersmith Farm
9 Brenton Point State Park
10 Gooseberry Beach
11 Bailey's Beach
12 Belcourt Castle
13 Marble House
14 Beechwood
15 Rosecliff
16 The Breakers
17 Chateau-sur-Mer
18 The Elms
19 Kingscote
20 Newport Casino and Tennis Hall of Fame
21 Cliff Walk begins
22 Easton's Beach
N
0 0.5 1
Miles
© The Countryman Press

The city today retains traces of its past, with the commercial waterfront coexisting with the splendor of the Bellevue Avenue marble palaces and the timeless character of its many colonial buildings and cobbled byways. Newport, especially in summer, can be serene and raucous, often simultaneously. But it is never dull.

GUIDANCE The one-stop information center for Newport and its neighboring towns, Middletown and Portsmouth, is the **Gateway Visitor Center** (401-849-8098; 1-800-326-6030; http://gonewport.com), 23 America's Cup Avenue, run by the Newport County Convention & Visitors Bureau. Besides brochures and a helpful staff, the center offers room reservation services, tickets to many attractions, informational displays, and a narrated slide show. Visitors receive a free half hour of parking in the adjoining Gateway parking garage.

GETTING THERE *By car:* Newport is on the southern tip of an island, accessible from the south and west by US 95 (via RI 138) and the Newport (Claiborne Pell) Bridge; from the north, US 24 or US 195 lead to Newport, via either RI 138 or RI 114.

By bus: **Peter Pan Bus Lines** (401-846-1820), 23 America's Cup Avenue, at the Gateway Center, has direct connections from Boston and Providence. **Rhode Island Public Transportation Authority** (RIPTA; 401-781-9400) buses also provide direct service from Providence and the **Amtrak** (1-800-USA-RAIL) railroad station in South Kingstown, 19 miles away.

By shuttle: **Cozy Cab** (401-846-2500), 129 Connell Highway, provides shuttle service to and from T. F. Green Airport in Warwick.

GETTING AROUND *By car:* Most visitors to Newport arrive by car—and promptly get snagged in a summerlong traffic jam that virtually paralyzes the city's many colonial-era streets. When and if you find a place to park (more on that later), the best way to negotiate the city is on foot. This is a very walkable city, with most of the main attractions close together.

Parking is an ongoing problem in the City by the Sea, whose 300-year-old streets were designed for horse-powered transportation. Parking meters in the downtown area provide a stingy 15 minutes per quarter, and be warned: The city has a two-hour limit in any one space; beyond that, you may (and probably will) be ticketed whether there is money in the meter or not. Nor do the meters shut down at 6 PM—Newport meters run until 9 PM.

Other parking options include private and several (quickly filled) municipal parking lots, as well as rare on-street spaces in outlying neighborhoods.

Kim Grant

NEWPORT HARBOR AND BRIDGE AT DUSK

Once again, the visitor must be wary. Between Memorial Day and October 1, resident parking is in effect after 6 PM on many side streets, and cars without Newport stickers will be ticketed. Look for small RESIDENT PARKING signs on telephone poles, or ask a resident for guidance. Those staying at a neighborhood B&B or guest house can often obtain a temporary resident parking permit from the proprietor.

By public transportation: Newport has an excellent seasonal public transportation system of buses and trolleys that circulate frequently daily Memorial Day through Columbus Day. The routes are well planned to be easy to understand and get visitors quickly to all of the big attractions, including the mansions, beaches, Cliff Walk, and Bellevue Avenue. An all-day pass is $6, and you pay just $2 (when you buy the pass) to leave your car all day in the Gateway Visitor Center lot, making this the best way to experience the city without the hassle and expense of driving and parking a car at every place you want to visit. Many people combine a walk one way with a ride back to their starting point on the bus. The Yellow line, #67, is the big loop that covers almost everything you'll want to see.

By tour bus: **Viking Tours** (401-847-6921), 23 America's Cup Avenue, at the Gateway Center. Daily May through Columbus Day. Bus tours of varying length, including admission to one, two, or more mansions.

On foot: The **Newport Historical Society** and **Newport Restoration Foundation** (401-841-8770; http://newportrestoration.com) lead a variety of themed walking tours of the city, including "Working Waterfront" and "Rum and Rumrunners." Most begin from the Museum of Newport History at Brick Market, 127 Thames Street. The **Preservation Society of Newport County** (401-847-1000; http://newportmansions.org), which operates most of the mansions, also offers history tours of its neighborhood, Bellevue Avenue.

By rail: **Old Colony & Newport Railway** (401-849-0546), 19 America's Cup Avenue, beside the Gateway Center. Saturday, Sunday, and holidays from July 1 through early September. This 90-minute rail trip runs along the West Shore of Aquidneck to Portsmouth, where the train makes a stop at Green Animals, a topiary garden.

By taxi: **Cozy Cab** (401-846-2500), 129 Connell Highway; **Rainbow Cab** (401-839-1333), 326 Coddington Highway; **Yellow Cab** (401-846-1500), 129 Connell Highway. Good places to find taxicabs are in Washington Square or at the Gateway Center.

MEDICAL EMERGENCY The statewide number for emergencies is **911.**

Newport Hospital (401-846-6400) is located at Broadway and Friendship Street.

✷ To See

Much of what there is to see in Newport is connected with its history. If you want to see history in some cities, you have to go to a museum. In Newport you just take a right or left out of your hotel, and start walking. A handful of museums can be found in Newport, and the mansions technically could be considered museums. But most of the city's history has been incorporated into contemporary life—in the 18th-century dwellings that serve as homes, shops, or restaurants, and in the narrow, gaslit lanes.

Out in the open air you'll also have a chance to enjoy Newport's natural beauty—an attribute even the natives never seem to tire of. There's Ocean Avenue, the Cliff Walk, and several stunning seaside parks. Beyond it all is the sea; you can experience the magnificent waves breaking over the rocks at the southern tip, the vista of First Beach from the heights of Memorial Boulevard, or the quiet of the inner harbor. Be sure to catch as many sunsets as you can—Newport Harbor looks to the west.

HISTORIC HOMES **Hunter House** (401-847-1000; http://newportmansions.org), 54 Washington Street. The house and garden are open mid-June to mid-September, daily 10–5, with tours on the hour. Admission packages available with other Preservation Society mansions at varying prices. A National Historic Landmark, Hunter House is considered by architectural historians to be one of the finest examples of a

NEWPORT'S COLONIAL-ERA WASHINGTON STREET

Kim Grant

mid-18th-century dwelling in the country. Aside from its pure lines and stately proportions, the house is rich in history. More accurately called the Nichols-Wanton-Hunter House, it had its modest beginnings in 1748 when Jonathan Nichols bought the property on what was then called Water Street. Nichols was heavily engaged in the sea trade; he owned several ships, and there was probably a wharf and warehouse buildings on the site. According to a city map of 1758, a one-chimney dwelling also stood there.

Upon Nichols's death in 1757, the house was bought by Colonel Joseph Wanton Jr., a politically active merchant who added a south portion to the dwelling, giving it very much the appearance it has today. Both Wanton, a colonial deputy, and his father, governor of the colony, were staunch Tories and were forced into exile across the bay in 1775 as the rebellion heated up. With the arrival of British forces in 1776, Wanton came back to Newport, where he served as superintendent of police. But when the British withdrew three years later, the Wantons were again forced to flee. They died in exile, but Wanton Jr.'s Tory politics probably saved the house from destruction—an estimated 300 others on the Point and elsewhere in town were destroyed by the British.

When the French allies reached Newport in 1780, the house became headquarters for Admiral de Ternay, whose fleet delivered French commander Rochambeau and his troops to America. De Ternay's stay was brief; contracting a fever, he died on December 15, 1780, on his warship *Duc de Bourgogne,* anchored near the house. After several years of neglect, the house was purchased by William Hunter, a lawyer, US senator, and ambassador, who landscaped the grounds and, mainly through 44 years of ownership, gave the house its name.

Today the house has been meticulously restored by the Preservation Society of Newport County. Although many of the original furnishings were lost, the house has been refurnished with authentic Queen Anne, Chippendale, and Hepplewhite pieces made by the Townsend and Goddard families and other colonial craftsmen.

Wanton-Lyman-Hazard House (401-846-0813; http://newportrestoration.com), 17 Broadway, just up from Washington Square. Open Thursday through Saturday 10–4. Admission $4. Now situated somewhat incongruously in a commercial district, this restored house is one of the oldest in the city. Built between 1650 and 1700, its steeply pitched roof and central chimney are typical of the homes built by the early settlers. The interior walls are still covered with the original plaster—made, in some cases, from ground shells and molasses. There's also a fine early colonial fireplace.

A number of notable residents lived at this address, including Martin Howard Jr., a Tory who had to flee for his life during the Stamp Act riot of

August 26, 1765. During the French occupation, the house was frequented by French officers courting Polly Lawton, a Quaker teenager considered one of the most charming young women on either side of the Atlantic. "A nymph rather than a woman . . . so much beauty, so much modesty," a count confided to his diary. Their attentions were to no avail—Polly married an American soldier, Major Daniel Lyman. A National Historic Landmark, the house has been furnished by the Newport Historical Society. There is a restored colonial garden out back.

Samuel Whitehorne House (401-847-2448; 401-849-7300; http://newportrestoration.com), 416 Thames Street. Open May through October, Thursday through Monday. Adults $10, children $4; purchase tickets across the street at NRF Store. Now operated by Doris Duke's Newport Restoration Foundation, the Whitehorne House was built in 1811 and is a fine example of Federal-period architecture, when brick was being introduced into the construction of residences. Captain Samuel Whitehorne Jr., a prosperous merchant, was the original owner, but shipping losses bankrupted him, and he lost the home at auction in 1844. The house contains many fine period furniture pieces, including works by Goddard and Townsend, and silver and pewter made by Newport silversmiths between 1740 and 1840. Outside, there's a garden typical of the Federal period with early varieties of plants rarely seen now.

HISTORIC HOUSES OF WORSHIP **Channing Memorial Church** (401-846-0643; www.channingchurch.org), Pelham Street across from Touro Park. Open by appointment. Built in the mid–19th century, the church contains two beautiful stained-glass windows by John La Farge and a bronze plaque by Augustus Saint-Gaudens. The church is dedicated to William Ellery Channing, a Newporter credited with founding the Unitarian Church in America. Channing (his statue stands across the street in the park) was a philosopher, writer, and friend to many Newport literary figures. He did most of his preaching at the Union Church in Boston and in the Boston area but summered in Newport. Julia Ward Howe, early feminist and author of "Battle Hymn of the Republic," had a pew here.

Newport Congregational Church (401-849-2238; www.newportcongregationalchurch.org), Spring and Pelham Streets. Open Memorial Day through Labor Day, Tuesday and Thursday 10–noon, and by appointment. It has been called Church of the Patriots because its members refused to side with Mother England during the Revolution. As a result, the original church building on Mill Street was converted to a barracks for British troops and later a hospital for French forces. The church was heavily damaged; all that exists today is the cornerstone, bearing the legend FOR CHRIST AND PEACE, now at the parish house. The existing church, built in 1857, contains an interior designed by artist John La Farge and well worth seeing. The walls have a distinct Byzantine flavor, and the opalescent stained-glass windows were made using a technique devised by La Farge.

Quaker Meeting House (401-846-0813), Marlborough and Farewell Streets, one block north of Washington Square. Open by appointment. Recently restored, the Friends Great Meeting House was built in 1699 and is the oldest in the country. An outstanding example of 17th-century architecture, the meetinghouse contains models and architectural exhibits as well as changing exhibits on Quaker life and dress. The Quakers, persecuted in Massachusetts, found a welcome home in Newport. There they rose to political and commercial power, building many of the fine captains' homes in the neighboring Point section. (The Friends, however, did incur resentment on occasion, especially during the Revolution, for what was considered to be an overly pacifist attitude toward the British. In several instances windows in Quaker homes were broken by angry "patriots.")

St. Mary's Church (401-847-0475), Spring Street and Memorial Boulevard. Open Monday through Friday 7–11:30 AM, except holidays. Built between 1848 and 1852, this English Gothic church was designed by Patrick Keeley of New York. Jacqueline Bouvier and Senator John F. Kennedy, later the 34th president, were married here on September 12, 1953. St. Mary's is the seat of the oldest Catholic parish in the state and was designated a National Shrine in 1968.

Touro Synagogue (401-847-4794; www.nps.gov/tosy), 72 Touro Street. Open June through Labor Day, Sunday through Friday 10–5; spring and fall, Friday and Sunday 1–3. Saturday services at 9 AM, Friday services at 7:30 PM in summer, 6 PM the rest of the year. The oldest house of Jewish worship in North America and a National Historic Site, Touro Synagogue is one of the most handsome buildings in the city. Jews, like Quakers, were early settlers in the colony, which was noted for its religious tolerance. The synagogue was designed in 1759 by renowned colonial master builder Peter Harrison, who modeled it after Sephardic Jewish temples in Portugal and Holland. The result was a simple but elegant classical building whose lines may have influenced Thomas Jefferson's plans for Monticello.

Jefferson, George Washington, and other prominent men of the time were visitors to the synagogue, and it was to the Jewish community here that President Washington pledged religious freedom in the newly independent nation. His proclamation, containing the stirring words "To bigotry no sanction, to persecution no assistance," is read each year at Touro. After the Revolution, the building served as a temporary home for the General Assembly and the state Supreme Court while Colony House was repaired. The synagogue's interior, one of the most beautiful in any colonial house of worship, has been restored to its original glory.

At Bellevue Avenue and Kay Street, a short walk up the street, is Touro Cemetery, which is open daily. Here you will find headstones dating from the 1640s and inscribed in Hebrew, Spanish, Portuguese, and English.

Trinity Church (401-846-0660; www.trinitynewport.org), a National Historic Landmark at Church and Spring Streets at the head of Queen Anne Square. Open to visitors May through October: daily July 7 through September 1; Monday through Friday the rest of the time. Sunday services are at 8 and 10 AM. Considered by many the finest church building in Newport and possibly all of America, Trinity Church was built in 1725–1726 by Richard Munday after designs by Christopher Wren, the great 17th-century English architect. What's especially remarkable is that Munday chose to interpret English baroque principles using wood rather than masonry.

The church was spared British depredation during the Revolution because of its Church of England ties. Today it is notable for its tall, graceful spire, its Tiffany stained-glass windows (the first two on the left), and its triple-deck wineglass pulpit, the only one in America. Distinguished visitors have included George Washington (his pew was no. 81) and Dean George Berkeley, later bishop of Cloyne, who often preached here during his three-year stay. More recently the Archbishop of Canterbury and Queen Elizabeth II visited in 1976 as part of the Bicentennial celebration. The gallery holds the original organ case given to the church in 1733 by Berkeley; it was made by Richard Bridge of London, is believed to have been played by Handel, and is the second oldest organ in the country.

In the small graveyard beside the church lies Lucia, the infant daughter of Berkeley, as well as Admiral d'Arsac de Ternay, whose fleet arrived with Rochambeau during the Revolution and who died here of fever. A monument to de Ternay, given by King Louis XVI, is in the church vestibule.

United Baptist Church (401-847-3210), 30 Spring Street, behind Colony House. Open daily 9–4. Dr. John Clarke was the founder and first pastor (1638) of this church. In 1663 Clarke obtained a royal charter for Rhode Island from King Charles II, which set a precedent for the colonies by guaranteeing full freedom of religious pursuits. The church contains a room displaying items of historical interest.

HISTORIC SITES AND BUILDINGS **Colony House** (401-846-2980; http://newportrestoration.com), at the head of Washington Square. Free tours July through Labor Day, daily 9:30–4, and by appointment in the off-season. This handsome building, designed by Richard Munday and built in 1739–1741, is the second oldest capitol in the United States. It served as the seat of government for both the colony and the state of Rhode Island when Newport was the capital city. Colony House once was the site of public whippings and pillorying of colonial lawbreakers. (Law in

Kim Grant

MANY CONSIDER NEWPORT'S TRINITY CHURCH THE FINEST CHURCH BUILDING IN THE NATION.

the colonies was harsh; for example, children who struck their parents could be put to death.) It also played a central role in the Revolution. It was from here that Governor Stephen Hopkins issued the order in July 1764 to open fire on the British warship *St. John*—possibly the first shots fired in what was to become the Revolutionary War. And it was from here that Rhode Island declared its independence from Britain on May 4, 1776, anticipating the Declaration of Independence by two months. During the war George Washington met here with French general Rochambeau to plan the final defeat of Cornwallis at Yorktown. (Other notables who have been entertained at Colony House include Lafayette and Presidents Jefferson, Jackson, and Eisenhower.) Upstairs, in the Governor's Council Chamber, hangs a full-length portrait of Washington by Gilbert Stuart.

Common Burial Ground, Farewell Street. Once well beyond the city limits, the burial ground started as several distinct cemeteries, the south side for freemen, the north for slaves. Of the 3,000 or so stones here, about 800 date from the 1600s to before 1800. Among them are some excellent examples of colonial gravestone carving. The adjacent Island Cemetery, with an entrance on Warner Street, is notable for its monuments to the Perry brothers and *Standing Angel,* by Augustus Saint-Gaudens, a major sculptor of the late 19th century.

NO ONE REALLY KNOWS WHO BUILT THE OLD STONE MILL IN TOURO PARK—OR WHY.

Tom Gannon

The Old Stone Mill, Touro Park at Mill Street and Bellevue Avenue. One of the real architectural oddities in America, the stone mill has been attributed to Vikings, Native Americans, and Portuguese or English colonists, which would mean it dates from somewhere between 1100 and 1650. Recent thinking holds it was built as a windmill by Governor Benedict Arnold, fifth great-grandfather of the notorious Arnold. But the peculiar architecture, along with the suit of armor found farther up the coast and immortalized in Longfellow's "The Skeleton in Armor," has convinced many locals that the Vikings were responsible. Some say it may have served as a lighthouse, while others maintain it was simply Arnold's mill-granary, fortified because of the ongoing Indian wars. At any rate, situated as it is in one of Newport's prettiest parks, it is well worth a visit. If you hang around long enough, you'll probably hear a new theory about it.

Redwood Library (401-847-0292), 50 Bellevue Avenue, at Redwood Street. Open Monday through Saturday 10–5. Built in 1748, this National Historic Landmark was designed by Peter Harrison and is the oldest library building in America in continuous service. The structure, which has been enlarged four times, is Palladian in style. Although built of wood like most early buildings in Newport, the siding has been blasted to resemble stone. The library's lending service is private, but the building is open to the public. Writers Henry James and Edith Wharton visited often, and it's easy to see why: Inside and out on the grounds, the library is one of the most pleasant and peaceful sites in the city. The Redwood also has an excellent collection of early American paintings and rare books.

THE MANSIONS AND THE GILDED AGE Henry James called them "white elephants" and "grotesque." A former French ambassador, perhaps forgetting Versailles, once referred to them as "horrors." Others have described them as the perfect symbols of the Gilded Age, a time when America's newly rich sought ways to flaunt their tax-free wealth. Architectural monstrosities or gracious reminders of a past glory, the mansions that line Bellevue Avenue and Ocean Avenue are without a doubt the single most popular attraction in the City by the Sea. They are visited by more than 1 million people each year, and to come to Newport without seeing at least one would be like missing the ocean.

Newport was always a favorite summer place for the wealthy, beginning well before the Revolution, but it wasn't until the 1880s, when New York society began arriving in force, that the city entered its heyday. Much of the opulence—some would say extravagance—of the time was due to a new definition of *wealth*. Where once the accumulation of a million dollars defined wealth, the new fortunes, built on coal, railroads, oil, and finance, were measured in tens and hundreds of millions. Lacking hereditary titles or long family tradition, the members of this new elite attempted to create an instant American aristocracy by doing what they did best: spending money.

The Golden Era was ushered in with lavish balls and dinners set in equally lavish surroundings. No matter that a family might spend no more than a month here in summer—each "summer cottage" had to be more opulent than the one next door. And opulent they were. The Marble House, including furnishings, cost a total of $11 million when it was built in 1892, about a tenth of what it would cost today. Not so much, really, when you consider that families spent as much as $200,000 for a single party. For her Fête des Roses in 1902, Grace Vanderbilt provided $10,000 worth of "favors" for her guests and brought in the entire company of the hit play *The Wild Rose,* a feat that involved closing the theater in New York for two days.

The summer colonists spent so much and so freely that a newspaper correspondent was prompted to report that Newport's rich "devoted themselves to pleasure regardless of expense." Not so, corrected Colonel George Waring, a prominent resident, who explained that the rich were actually devoting themselves to expense regardless of pleasure. A disapproving Henry James wrote that the summer visitors "danced and they drove and they rode, they dined and wined and dressed and flirted and yachted and Casino'd." It couldn't last, of course, and the advent of the income tax and, finally, the Depression put an end to these excesses of America's richest families. For most, the great summer homes became too expensive to own, and by 1950 only a handful were left in private hands.

Fortunately for posterity, the Preservation Society of Newport County—formed in 1945 to preserve the historic, colonial-era Hunter House—began acquiring the mansions as they closed up. It now owns the best, including Rosecliff, the Elms, and the Breakers.

A word about the architecture of the mansions and Richard Morris Hunt, who designed some of them: Most of the architecture is derivative, modeled after the great houses and palaces of Europe. The European tradition came naturally to Hunt, who was the first American to receive a degree from the École des Beaux-Arts in Paris, where he became familiar with the neoclassical and neobaroque design elements regarded as the height of artistic expression. His training came in handy for an America that after the Civil War had no defined style of its own and was compelled to look back to Europe for direction.

All the mansions open to the public are either on or directly off Bellevue Avenue between Bowery Street and the beginning of Ocean Avenue. The Preservation Society houses are well marked with green-and-white signs, and free parking is provided at each estate. Tours generally last about 45 minutes. Admission varies: $19.50 for the Breakers, $14.50 for the other houses, $5.50 for children; combination tickets for two or more mansions are available at discounts. The best web site for all Preservation Society mansions is newportmansions.org.

Belcourt Castle (401-846-0669; http://belcourtcastle.org), 657 Bellevue Avenue. Open March through December. Summer hours between late May and November 1 are 9–5; winter hours are 10–4. Most tours $18. Belcourt was designed by Richard Hunt for Oliver Hazard Perry Belmont in 1891. The medieval-style museum-castle, based on plans for a Louis XIII hunting lodge that Hunt saw in France, is a departure from Hunt's usual grandiose palaces.

The castle contains 60 rooms, each done in a different period of French, Italian, or English design. Notable features include the hand-carved Grand Stair—a reproduction of the Francis I stair in the Musée de Cluny in Paris—and the elegant Versailles dining room. Within the many rooms is the family collection of antiques and art treasures from 32 countries. The castle contains many fine Oriental rugs and what is said to be the largest collection of stained glass in the country. Also on display is a 23-karat-gold Royal Coronation coach decorated with oil paintings and gold lead and weighing 4 tons.

One of the nicest features of the castle is the center courtyard, where Mr. Belmont had his horses exercised daily (the stables are built into the house). Belmont was kind to his horses: They slept in a Hunt-designed stable on white linen sheets embroidered with the Belmont crest. After a tour, visitors are invited to have tea or coffee. Besides the regular tour, Belcourt hosts a weekly Thursday "ghost tour" at 5 PM (reservations required), which consists of a slide show, a tour of the castle, and a chance to meet Belcourt's own ghost, believed to be a monk who hangs out in the medieval chapel.

The Breakers (401-847-1000; http://newportmansions.org), 44 Ochre Point Avenue. Open April through October, daily 10–5, and for special hours during the Christmas season. The Breakers is the largest, most opulent, and best known of the Newport mansions and a National Historic Landmark owned and operated by the Preservation Society of Newport County. To reach it, turn off Bellevue Avenue at either Victoria, Shepard, or Ruggles Avenue. The estate is enclosed by a beautiful, ornamental wrought-iron fence. From the back, the grounds command an awe-inspiring view of the Atlantic Ocean. The grounds also feature an original parterre garden and many unusual imported trees and shrubs.

Covering nearly an acre of Cornelius Vanderbilt's 11-acre oceanfront property, the four-story limestone palace contains 70 rooms, including a two-story ballroom that epitomizes the Gilded Age. It took a force of hundreds of workers just two years to complete the building. Entire rooms were built overseas by European craftsmen and shipped to Newport. Crystal chandeliers were equipped for gas as well as electricity in case the power failed. Bathroom taps supplied either fresh rainwater or salt water, hot and cold. The house contains all the original furnishings.

The Breakers was opened with a coming-out party for 20-year-old Gertrude Vanderbilt on an August evening in 1895. Missing was architect Richard Hunt, who had died on July 31. Cornelius Vanderbilt, who inherited $70 million of the Vanderbilt family's railroad empire fortune, was not able to enjoy his summer home for long: He suffered a stroke in 1896 and died three years later at the age of 56. The Countess Laszlo Scechenyi (née Gladys Vanderbilt) sold the house to the Preservation Society in 1972. Countess Szapary, her daughter, resided in the family quarters on the third floor until her death in 1998.

The tour includes admission to The Breakers' Stable and Carriage House on nearby Coggeshall Avenue. Built in 1895, the stable contains a central carriage room on the ground floor and 28 stalls at the rear. The horses are gone, but some period carriages and coaches are on display.

Chateau-sur-Mer (401-847-1000; http://newportmansions.org), Bellevue Avenue, corner of Shepard Avenue. Open April through October, daily 10–5. Another of the Preservation Society's houses and one of the older mansions in Newport, this fine example of mid-Victorian architecture is actually a blending of two structures. The first was built in 1852 by a local contractor for William Shepard Wetmore, another China trader who settled in Newport. Twenty years later it was enlarged by Richard Morris Hunt, who added a French ballroom and so altered the house that what you see today is largely his design. Some critics felt that he converted a charming Victorian villa into a somewhat severe pile of granite, but the imposing result was a hint of grander summer palaces to come.

The neighborhood surrounding Chateau-sur-Mer is built up now, but once the 35-acre estate offered a clear view of the sea, hence its name. Note the many exotic plants on the grounds and the Chinese moon gate on the south side, which once framed an ocean vista.

The first room on the tour is the elegantly paneled library, originally the kitchen. For a time it served as a billiard parlor for the second owner, George Peabody Wetmore, governor and senator; but when he died, his spinster daughters had the pool table removed and the cue racks converted to coatracks. The whole house is notable for its extensive wood paneling done in the "honest" style—all the mistakes were left to be seen—and large ornate mirrors. Many of the original furnishings are displayed, including a fine collection of Rose Medallion and Rose Mandarin china sets acquired by Wetmore. On the second floor is a special treat for children: a charming collection of Victorian toys and dollhouses. Each

Christmas the Preservation Society decorates the house in Victorian holiday style and opens it to the public.

The Elms (401-847-1000; http://newportmansions.org), Bellevue Avenue, corner of Dixon Street. Open April through October, daily 10–5. Built in 1901 for Philadelphia coal baron Edward J. Berwind, the French-style château is the best furnished of the Preservation Society's houses. As striking as the house is—in a coolly classical manner—the biggest attraction is the 14 acres of grounds and sunken French gardens complete with terraces, fountains, statues, and teahouses. There's a wide variety of exotic trees and shrubs, all labeled. This is a perfect place to stroll on a sunny afternoon.

Designed by Horace Trumbauer of Philadelphia after the 18th-century Château d'Asnières near Paris, the Elms offers more than meets the eye. Although from the ground it appears to be a two-story structure topped with a sculpture-bearing parapet, in reality there is a hidden third story that contains the servants' quarters—16 rooms and three baths. In the same way, kitchen and laundry facilities are discreetly concealed in the basement. A secret underground railroad, which surfaced a block away on Dixon Street, transported the coal to fuel the huge burners that kept the house and furnishings warm during winter.

Kingscote (401-847-1000; http://newportmansions.org), Bellevue Avenue, corner of Bowery Street. Open April through October, daily 10–5. Heading south down the avenue, this is the first mansion you come to, but perhaps it should be saved until after you've viewed several of the other Preservation Society mansions. With its wooden exterior and charming early-Victorian design, Kingscote comes as a welcome change of pace after you've viewed the huge granite and marble structures farther along. Among the oldest summer residences in the city, Kingscote was built in 1839 by Richard Upjohn for George Noble Jones of Savannah, Georgia, who continued the tradition of southern families summering in Newport. On what was, at the time, 2 acres surrounded mostly by farmland, Upjohn designed a Gothic Revival house that was picturesque without being overly quaint. A dining room was added in 1881 by Stanford White of McKim, Mead, and White, who later designed Rosecliff.

The least well known of the society's houses, Kingscote is well worth a visit to see its early Rhode Island furniture and art. There is also a priceless collection of porcelain and paintings courtesy of later owner William Henry King, who made his fortune in the China trade. The interior of the house is rich with parquet floors, a Tiffany glass wall in the dining room, and mahogany paneling.

Marble House (401-847-1000; http://newportmansions.org), Bellevue Avenue, just south of Beechwood. Open April through October, daily

10–5. Another Preservation Society house, this one was designed by Richard Hunt for William K. Vanderbilt in 1892. Marble House looks like a mansion should, with a white marble driveway curving up to an arch under a porte cochere, pilasters and capitals, and 10 tons of bronzed entrance grille. Hunt's model was the Petit Trianon at Versailles, Marie Antoinette's private hideaway, and the result epitomizes the architect's notion of the Beaux-Arts neoclassical style. Like The Breakers, the house retains its original furnishings, which cost $9 million in early-1900s dollars. Out on the grounds, near the Cliff Walk, Alva Vanderbilt oversaw construction of a red-and-gold-lacquered teahouse; when she realized there was no means of making tea in it, she ordered a tiny railroad to be built from the main house to carry her footmen back and forth with a silver tea service.

MARBLE HOUSE WAS MODELED AFTER THE PETIT TRIANON AT VERSAILLES.
Kim Grant

The Gold Ballroom—the gold is real—was the scene of many extravagant entertainments. It was here that Alva (as Mrs. Oliver Hazard Belmont—she had divorced William Vanderbilt and married her cross-avenue neighbor) held one of her most famous dinners, 10 courses at which her 100 "guests" were dogs in various forms of fancy dress. The newly divorced Alva had given a more serious party earlier, in 1895, to present her (reluctant) daughter Consuelo to the titled but poor duke of Marlborough, who dutifully proposed. After an unhappy marriage, Consuelo divorced the duke in 1921 to marry again—for love.

Ochre Court (401-847-6650), 100 Ochre Point Avenue, off Narragansett Avenue. Open daily 9–4. Admission is free, although donations are welcome. Now the administration building for Salve Regina University, Ochre Court is a 50-room medieval-style mansion designed in 1891 by Richard Hunt for Ogden Goelet, a wealthy New York real estate developer.

Kim Grant

ROSECLIFF HAS SEEN ITS SHARE OF TRAGEDY.

Although much of the building is taken up by college offices, visitors can see the great hall, which rises three stories. In keeping with the medieval atmosphere, the walls are finished with heraldic designs carved in Caen stone. Many of the original furnishings have been removed, but the hall still has its huge marble Atlas table, so called because of the carved Atlas figures that support it. Other rooms open to the public contain many fine period paintings, and there is a stained-glass window dating from the Middle Ages above the landing on the grand staircase. Outside, the grounds sweep down to the Cliff Walk and an unobstructed view of the Atlantic Ocean.

Rosecliff (401-847-1000; http://newportmansions.org), Bellevue Avenue. Open April through October, daily 10–5. With its white terra-cotta finish, heart-shaped grand staircase, and beautiful rose garden, Rosecliff is the most romantic of the Newport mansions. Designed in 1900 by Stanford White for the Hermann Oelrichses, the house boasted the largest ballroom in the summer colony and was the scene of many notable entertainments during the Gilded Age. For one of these, the White Ball, Tessie Oelrichs decreed that all the women guests wear white and powder their hair. The men, for contrast, dressed in black. The ballroom was filled with white roses, orchids, and lilies of the valley, and Mrs. Oelrichs even had a fleet of full-sized white artificial ships constructed, which was anchored out in the Atlantic and illuminated for full effect.

Like many romantic settings, Rosecliff saw its share of tragedy. A later owner had the mansion renovated for his family without ever being able to see it. While on his way to view the finished work, he was killed in a car accident. The family immediately sold the house. Its flower gardens and decorative pools make strolling the grounds a must.

Rough Point (401-849-7300; http://newportrestoration.com), 680 Bellevue Avenue. Open for tours mid-April through early November, Thursday

Katherine Imbrie

DORIS DUKE'S ROUGH POINT MANSION

through Saturday in spring, Tuesday through Saturday in summer and fall. Admission: adults $25, children under 12 free. The last house on the left before Bellevue makes a sharp right and becomes Ocean Avenue, Rough Point is concealed from street view by a high gate, but is visible from the ocean side from the Cliff Walk. The gates are testimony to the desire for privacy by the late owner, tobacco heiress Doris Duke, who founded the Newport Restoration Foundation, the organization responsible for restoring many of Newport's finer colonial homes. The house, built in 1888–1891 for Frederick Vanderbilt, remains just as Duke left it before her death in 1993. It is filled with her personal effects, furnishings, and an impressive collection of museum-quality artwork. Despite its undeniable grandeur, this is one mansion that also looks like a home. And the setting, right on the wild Atlantic, is spectacular. If you were to choose just two mansions to visit in Newport, this should be one, and the other, The Breakers.

MUSEUMS The Artillery Company of Newport (401-846-8488; http://newportartillery.org), 23 Clarke Street, just off Washington Square. Open May through October, Saturday 10–4. Small admission fee. Chartered in 1741 by King George, the company is the oldest militia in continuous service in America. Its headquarters, built in 1836 in solid Greek Revival style, houses military uniforms and weapons from colonial times to the present as well as artifacts from more than 100 countries.

International Tennis Hall of Fame (401-849-3990; www.tennisfame.com), in the Newport Casino, 194 Bellevue Avenue. Open daily 9–5. Adults $11, seniors $9, children age 16 and under, free. Newport has good reason to call itself the home of American tennis: One year after the Newport Casino was built in 1880, it became the site of the first National Men's Championship and all subsequent lawn tennis nationals until 1915. The National Grass Court Championships are held here each year, as are professional men's and women's tournaments.

Designed by Stanford White, the casino complex is a wonderful example of period architecture surrounding green grass courts that predate those at Wimbledon. The stately atmosphere belies the fact that the casino was founded by two Newport society delinquents. Visiting British polo player Captain Henry Candy, acting on a dare from publisher and yachtsman James Gordon Bennett, rode his horse onto the front porch of the ultra-staid Newport Reading Room club on Bellevue Avenue. The members were not amused; Candy was barred from the club, and Bennett was reprimanded. Bennett's response was to build his own club, which soon became a gathering spot for Newport's best, especially during Tennis Week each August. The casino was designated a National Historic Landmark in 1987.

Today the front portion of the complex houses the Hall of Fame and museum, billed as the largest tennis museum in the world. Filling two

THE INTERNATIONAL TENNIS HALL OF FAME

Kim Grant

floors, the museum contains at least a dozen rooms housing every kind of tennis memorabilia, including equipment, trophies, period costumes, paintings, and photographs. There is a Davis Cup Room and Davis Cup Theater, where old tennis films are shown.

International Yacht Restoration School (401-848-5777; http://iyrs.org), 449 Thames Street. Open daily 10–5; closed January through March. Free admission. Visitors can watch shipwrights and students restore classic wooden vessels and take a tour of the 1885 schooner *Coronet.*

The Museum of Newport History (401-841-8770; http://newport historical.org), Brick Market at the foot of Washington Square. Open daily. Suggested donation: adults $4, children $2. Validated free parking at Long Wharf Mall North and the Gateway Center. If you've never been to Newport before, this is a good place to start. The museum is a quick means of getting acquainted with 300 years of local history in as little as half an hour. Lots of interactive exhibits and interesting artifacts, photographs, and oral histories await visitors. The building itself, designed by Peter Harrison and completed in 1762, is of historical importance and has been designated a National Historical Landmark. Built as a market and warehouse by Long Wharf merchants, Brick Market anchored the west end of busy Washington Square, the center of early Newport civic and commercial activity. Also offered are walking tours of Newport historical areas ($7, including admission to the museum) and/or a tour of Colony House ($6) on Thursday, Friday, and Saturday.

Museum of Yachting (401-847-1018; http://moy.org), Fort Adams State Park, off Ocean Avenue. Open June through October, daily 10–5. Adults $5, seniors and children $4. Housed in a 19th-century brick building that looks out over the waterfront, this museum offers a tour of the history of yachting through its displays of photos, paintings, boating gear, and various kinds of vessels. The America's Cup Gallery traces the history of this prestigious event, which took place off Newport from the glorious J-boat days of the 1930s, when Harold S. Vanderbilt manned the helm, to the era of the 12-meter boats, when the Cup was lost to Australia in 1983. The 12-meter *Courageous,* two-time Cup defender, is part of the museum collection. There is also a Single-Handed Sailors' Hall of Fame that honors intrepid sailors from around the world who have taken to sea alone, many of whom have Newport ties. Outside, you may see the museum's own J-class sloop, *Shamrock,* or its sister ship, *Endeavour,* lying at anchor nearby.

Looming beside the museum is Fort Adams, a sturdy granite structure that is one of the largest seacoast fortifications built in the United States. During the Revolution, patriots began fortifying this strategic point overlooking the entrance to Narragansett Bay, but the occupying British destroyed their work. In 1799 the fort was rededicated and named for President John Adams. It fell into disrepair until the War of 1812 put a

THE MUSEUM OF YACHTING IN NEWPORT'S FORT ADAMS STATE PARK

scare into Congress, and work began in earnest to build a fort that could withstand attack from land or sea. Begun in 1824, the fort took 33 years to complete and, in fact, never was attacked. It served briefly as the U.S. Naval Academy during the early years of the Civil War when Annapolis was threatened. An ongoing restoration effort has opened parts of the fort to the public for the first time in decades; call 401-841-0707 for current hours. The surrounding park, which offers a superb spot to fish, swim, or watch yachts come and go, is open daily 6 AM–11 PM.

Naval War College Museum (401-841-4052; www.nwc.navy.mil), Coasters Harbor Island, through Gate 1 at the southern end of the Naval Education and Training Center. Open year-round, Monday through Friday 10–4:30; June through September, also open weekends noon–4:30. Call in advance to register. Free admission. The War College is where navy officers get their advanced training. The museum, located in Founders Hall, offers exhibits on the history of the "art and science" of naval warfare as well as local seafaring history.

The Newport Art Museum (401-848-8200; http://newportartmuseum.org), 76 Bellevue Avenue. Open daily 10–5 Memorial Day through Labor Day; 10–4 Tuesday through Saturday and noon–4 Sunday the rest of the year. Adults $10, seniors and students $8, children under 5 free. Designed by Richard Morris Hunt, the John N. A. Griswold House that now serves as the art museum's main building is a prime example of mid-Victorian stick-style architecture, in which vertical and diagonal "sticks" on the exterior suggest the underlying structure. The museum has regular exhibits by internationally known artists in four galleries, including the adjacent Cushing Gallery. There's also a permanent collection of 19th- and 20th-century American artwork.

Newport Historical Society (401-846-0813; http://newporthistorical.org), 82 Touro Street, just up from Washington Square. Open Tuesday through Friday 9:30–4:30, Saturday 9:30–noon. Free admission. The historical society building incorporates the Sabbatarian Meeting House built in 1729. The meetinghouse is the oldest of its faith in the United States and contains a beautiful wineglass pulpit. The society's collection contains rare and valuable paintings and fine period furniture, especially that made by the local Goddard and Townsend families.

The reference collection contains many manuscripts and historical documents that recall the flavor and tempo of early colonial life in Newport, back when the city was an active center of trade, politics, and intrigue. The first floor has changing exhibits. Upstairs, the library contains the second-largest genealogical collection in Rhode Island and will conduct research for a small fee. The society also conducts walking tours of colonial Newport from June 15 through September on Friday and Saturday mornings at 10. Cost for the two-hour tour is $12 for adults, $5 for children.

SCENIC DRIVE **Ocean Avenue** is one of the great coastal drives in the country, taking you past the mansions of the Gilded Age and some breathtaking vistas of sea and breaking waves. The road, which skirts the southern rim of Aquidneck, can be approached from two directions: From the east it begins where Bellevue Avenue ends; from the west you can pick it up at the end of Wellington Avenue, which runs along the south end of the harbor.

Most of the large houses along Bellevue and Ocean Avenue have their stories. One is **Clarendon Court,** on the east side of Bellevue a few houses beyond Marble House, opposite Rovensky Park. This is where Claus von Bülow either did (first trial) or did not (second trial) attempt to murder his wife, heiress Sunny von Bülow, with a lethal injection of insulin. The house was designed in 1904 by Horace Trumbauer, architect of the Elms, and is patterned after an 18th-century English house. The quiet park across the street was given to the city by John Rovensky, who owned Clarendon Court at one time.

Crossways, on Ocean Avenue, straight ahead after you make the turn past Bailey's Beach, was built by McKim, Mead, and White, and is notable for its four-column Colonial-style portico. During the heyday of Newport society, it was noted more for being the summer residence of the imposing Mrs. Stuyvesant Fish, who reigned over Newport with the Vanderbilts and Astors. Mrs. Fish was known for abruptly cutting short her dinner parties and insulting her guests, who couldn't wait to be asked back for more abuse. "Make yourself at home," she told one group. "Certainly there is no one who wishes you were there more than I." Crossways is now condominiums.

✷ To Do

BICYCLE/SCOOTER RENTALS **Scooters of Newport** (401-619-0573; http://scootersofnewport.com), 476 Thames Street, has motorized scooters to rent by the day or hour.

Ten Speed Spokes (401-847-5609; http://tenspeedspokes.com), 18 Elm Street. You can rent a bicycle at this shop located within an easy walk of the Gateway Visitor Center.

BOAT EXCURSIONS Several operators offer one- or two-hour narrated tours of Newport Harbor and Narragansett Bay. These are a bargain and a great way to get out on the water. ***Amazing Grace*** (401-849-9019; http://oldportmarine.com) departs Sayer's Wharf, next to the Mooring restaurant. ***Spirit of Newport*** (401-849-3579; http://spiritofnewport.com) departs Newport Harbor Motel & Marina, America's Cup Avenue. ***Viking Queen*** (401-847-6921; www.vikingtoursnewport.com), Goat Island, offers one- and two-and-a-half-hour cruises of Newport Harbor and Narragansett Bay. ***Rumrunner II*** (401-847-3033; http://cruisenewport.com), Bannister's Wharf, offers high-speed bay and harbor tours.

You can sail out of Newport on anything from a 20-foot sloop to 80-foot (and longer) schooners. Among the sailing vessels giving tours: ***Adirondack II*** (401-846-0000; http://sail-newport.com), Bowen's Wharf. This 78-foot schooner makes day and evening trips around the harbor. ***Madeleine*** (401-849-3033; 1-800-395-1343; http://cruisenewport.com), a 70-foot schooner departing Bannister's Wharf four times daily. ***Flyer*** (401-848-2100; 1-800-863-5937; http://flyercatamaran.com), a 57-foot catamaran sailing from Long Wharf. ***Aurora*** (401-849-6683; http://newportexperience.com) is the harbor's largest charter schooner at 101 feet. **Sightsailing of Newport** (401-849-3333; 1-800-709-7245; http://sightsailing.com) runs ***Sightsailer,*** a 50-foot daysailer that accommodates 18 passengers, as well as smaller boats for groups of two to six. (See also *Sailing/Rentals.*)

FISHING There's some good saltwater fishing in the Newport area. Bass, bluefish, and blackfish all run fairly steadily from spring to late fall. Try Ocean Avenue—at Agassiz Beach near Castle Hill, off the rocks at Brenton Point, or at state-run King Beach fishing area near Price's Cove. Beavertail on the southern tip of Jamestown is also good. Good sources of information are **Edwards Fishing Tackle** (401-846-4521), Middletown, and in Jamestown, Gregory Zeek of **Zeek's Creek Bait & Tackle** (401-423-1170), 194 North Road. If you're in town on a Friday, check the weekly fishing report in the free weekly *Newport This Week* or in *The Newport Daily News*, the city's daily newspaper.

Charter fishing is surprisingly limited in Newport, given its ocean location, but several boats offer inshore and offshore trips. (See also *Fishing* in "Narragansett" for more charter boats.) For information about area charters, write to the RI Party and Charter Boat Association, P.O. Box 3198, Narragansett 02882. The cost for adults is usually $30–40 per person, or $300 and up for a half-day charter, $700 and up for a full day.

Flaherty Charters (401-848-5554; http://flahertycharters.com) offers a full range of charter packages at varying prices.

Fishin' Off (401-683-5557; http://fishinoff.com). Full- or half-day charters for up to six people aboard a 36-foot Trojan sportfisherman. Mostly inshore fishing for striped bass or bluefish, but also the occasional offshore jaunt for tuna.

The Saltwater Edge (401-842-0062; http://saltwateredge.com), 561 Thames Street, supplies guides to take you fly-fishing in the surf or out on a boat. Hour lessons in fly-fishing. Outings include gear and flies.

FOR FAMILIES **Ryan Family Amusement Center** (401-846-5774), 266 Thames Street. Video games galore—a virtual arcade—in a Victorian-style building downtown. Great break from all the historical and cultural activities in Newport.

KAYAK RENTALS **Adventure Sports** (401-849-4820; http://newportriwatersports.com), Long Wharf, or **Kayak Newport** (401-848-9249; http://newportkayak.com), 365 Thames Street.

SAILING/RENTALS Sailing instruction is offered in sessions of several days up to a week, and generally costs a minimum of $300–500 per person. Call around to see what a particular school specializes in (racing or cruising skills, small or larger boats).

J World Sailing School (401-849-5492; http://jworldschool.com), 1 Commercial Wharf. Hands-on instruction in sailing and/or racing by certified instructors.

Newport Sailing School (401-848-2266; www.newportsailing.com), Goat Island Marina, Dock A5. Provides instruction for beginning and intermediate sailors.

Sail Newport (401-846-1983; http://sailnewport.org), Fort Adams State Park. Offers sailing instruction as well as half-day and full-day charters. Those renting boats are asked to demonstrate competency.

♿ **Shake-A-Leg Sailing Center** (401-847-3630; www.shakealeg.org), Fort Adams, has specially equipped 20-foot sloops for the physically challenged.

Sightsailing of Newport (401-849-3333), Bowen's Wharf, offers small-boat sailing tours for two to six people as well as rentals and instruction.

See also *Boat Excursions*.

SWIMMING See *Green Space—Beaches*.

TENNIS There are free City of Newport courts at five locations in the city. **Pop Flack,** behind the Bellevue Gardens shopping center on Bellevue, has four courts with lights. **Hunter Park,** off Third Street in the north end of the city, has two courts. **Vernon,** on Caswell Avenue off Vernon Avenue in the north end, near the Middletown line, has four courts. In the south end there are the three courts at **Murphy Field** on Carroll Avenue. Nearby at **Rogers High School** on Old Fort Road there are six courts.

Indoor Tennis (401-849-4777; www.tennisfame.com), 194 Bellevue Avenue. Open daily 6 AM–11 PM. The fee for these indoor courts is $30–40 per hour.

Newport Casino (401-846-4567; www.tennisfame.com), 194 Bellevue Avenue. The same grass courts that Ashe, Evert, McEnroe, and Navratilova have played on are open to the public from May through October except during tournaments. Open daily 10–7. The fee is $70 per hour for two players.

✷ Green Space

BEACHES Newport and its neighboring towns are blessed with a plentiful supply of good bathing beaches. And because the Gulf Stream lies relatively close offshore, the waters are warm by New England standards—certainly warmer than on much of Cape Cod, for example. Although some of the better spots along the southern tip of the island belong to private clubs, most of the sandy stretches remain in the public domain. On the hottest summer days, especially on weekends, parking can be a problem. To be assured of a spot, arrive well before noon or wait until 4 or 5 PM, when the crowds have gone and the water and air are still warm from the day's sun.

Easton's Beach (401-845-5800), 175 Memorial Boulevard. Also known as First Beach or Newport Beach, this popular bathing spot is a 0.75-mile stretch from the northern end of the Cliff Walk in Newport to the Middletown line. Access is easy—just follow Memorial Boulevard down the hill to the entrance. During Victorian times the water at Easton's was considered an elixir, and the infirm were carted down for a dip. Bathing was a much more modest activity at that time; the sexes were strictly segregated, women getting the first turn at 10 AM. "At noon all this changed," recalled George C. Mason in his chronicle *Newport and Its Cottages.* "The white flag is hauled down; a red bunting takes its place; the ladies retire, and for a few hours the beach is given up exclusively to gentlemen." Newport's largest public beach, Easton's has three parking lots accommodating about 700 cars. Daily parking fees are $10 weekdays, $20 weekends. There's limited on-street parking, but don't park in a restricted zone—you'll be ticketed and towed. A well-used recreation area at the beach includes a carousel, playground, skateboard park, and small aquarium. Surfing is permitted in a restricted area at the west end of the beach. Be warned: A clingy type of red seaweed (not red tide) often afflicts Easton's in August. When it does, head instead to Sachuest (Second) Beach, just over the town line in Middletown.

Fort Adams State Park (401-847-2400), off Harrison Avenue on the way to Ocean Avenue. The park includes a modest beach on Brenton Cove that is the perfect place for family swimming. There's a roped-off area for budding swimmers and plenty of picnic tables and charcoal grills. Coin-operated hot showers are available. Lifeguards are on duty 10 AM–6 PM between Memorial Day and Labor Day.

Gooseberry Beach (401-847-3958), on Ocean Avenue, shares a cove with private Hazard's Beach to the west and is one cove over from exclusive Bailey's Beach to the east. As well as an attractive setting, Gooseberry offers safe ocean bathing for families. The parking lot has room for 150 cars; daily parking is $20. Restrooms and a concession stand are available.

King Park, on Wellington Avenue in Newport, is close to town, facing north across the harbor. Parking along Wellington is free. Lifeguards are on duty Memorial Day through Labor Day 9–6, and on most hot days the beach is crowded with families. Charcoal grills and picnic tables are available, and you can sit on the grass under the trees or down on the sand. The shallow portion of the water is marked off with buoys for kids; there's a raft with a slide for the more daring swimmers. On land, there are free bathhouses, swings, and slides. Because of its proximity to the city, the water quality here is questionable following heavy rains, and swimming is sometimes banned for short periods.

People's Beach, on Ocean Avenue at the junction of Bellevue Avenue. This is a short stretch of fine sand located right beside Bailey's Beach, a private club, making People's a best-kept secret for some of the best swimming and people-watching in Newport. And it's free. The catch is, there's no parking, except for motorcycles and bicycles. The best way to get there is by bus or trolley from the Gateway Visitor Center; the Yellow Line, #67, will drop you off right there.

Kim Grant

GOOSEBERRY BEACH

PARK Brenton Point State Park (401-847-2400; http://riparks.com), Ocean Drive. Free parking. This 89-acre park on the site of a former estate offers broad lawns for lounging or kite flying, picnic tables, toilets, and scenic overlooks, including an observation tower. This is a great place for viewing the waves or parking for a stroll along the seawall. Kite fliers from all over New England congregate on Sundays.

WALK ♿ **Cliff Walk** (http://cliffwalk.com) is a 3.5-mile path that offers spectacular views as it runs from Easton's (or First) Beach off Memorial Boulevard on the north to Bailey's Beach on Ocean Avenue. It's free and, along with the mansions, it's the city's top tourist attraction, popular with locals, too. You can enter the walk at various points, but a good starting point is at the end of Narragansett Avenue, where you can scramble down the Forty Steps for a look at the crashing surf. From there, the path twists, winds, and even tunnels between the ocean many feet below and the Bellevue Avenue mansions, allowing walkers a glimpse of their expensively manicured backyards. A recent extensive restoration financed by a coalition of state, federal, and city agencies has solved erosion problems and made the path better than ever. It's now safe to walk from end to end for anyone of reasonable fitness. The northern end close to Memorial Boulevard is paved and is suitable for wheelchairs; the southern end is much more of a footpath, requiring some scrambling over rocks. The best way to walk the whole path is to take the #67 bus (see *Getting Around*) to

Katherine Imbrie

NEWPORT'S CLIFF WALK

the Memorial Boulevard entrance, walk the path to its end at Ocean Avenue, and there catch the same bus back to the beginning.

✷ Lodging

HOTELS ♿ **Best Western Mainstay Inn** (401-849-9880; 1-800-528-1234), 151 Admiral Kalbfus Road, at the exit ramp of Newport Bridge. ($$–$$$) Rates vary almost weekly at this inn, which has 165 rooms and a full-service restaurant, although it remains a bargain by Newport standards.

Hotel Viking (401-847-3300; 1-800-556-7126), 1 Bellevue Avenue, at the top of Touro Street and Historic Hill. ($$$–$$$$) Slightly outside the city's center, in one of the best sections of town, the Viking is within reasonable walking distance of downtown and the waterfront. Built in 1926, it was the queen of Newport hotels, the largest in the city until the newer buildings on the waterfront were built. The Colonial-style building is on the National Historic Register. Some of the waterside rooms have spectacular harbor panoramas. There's an outside patio and a small jazz bar where Ella Fitzgerald once sang. Thornton Wilder stayed here while he wrote his Newport book, *Theophilus North*.

♿ **Hyatt Regency Hotel** (401-851-1234; http://newporthyatt.com), 1 Goat Island. ($$$$) The second-largest of Newport's hotels, with 253 rooms, the Hyatt is a bit removed from the hustle of the city, which is the way many guests prefer it. With excellent views of the harbor and bay, the Hyatt is a short, pleasant walk across the causeway from the Point section, or you can make use of the hotel's shuttle van. But perhaps the best thing about being at the hotel is that you don't have to look at it: The hulking brick structure is considered by many to be an eyesore on an island in the middle of an otherwise beautiful harbor. Several restaurants and lounges.

The Newport Harbor Hotel & Marina (401-847-9000; 1-800-955-2558; www.newporthotel.com), 49 America's Cup Avenue. ($$$–$$$$) In a city where names can sometimes be deceptive, the Harbor Hotel is indeed right on the harbor. It's also downtown and close to the wharf action. Restaurant and nightclub offering live entertainment.

♿ **Newport Marriott** (401-849-1000; 1-800-228-9290), Long Wharf, America's Cup Avenue, adjacent to the Gateway Center. ($$$$) The Marriott, opened in 1988, is the city's largest hotel, with more than 300 rooms. The hotel has an impressive five-story atrium as you enter, two restaurants, several lounges with live entertainment or DJ, an indoor pool, and a health club with sauna for guests' use. Racquetball courts are available for a small fee, and in summer there is an oyster bar. The Marriott also has a good central location on the harbor, close to downtown and the wharf areas.

Vanderbilt Grace Hotel (401-846-6200; 1-888-826-4255; http://vanderbiltgrace.com), 41 Mary Street, off Spring Street. ($$$$) A 1909 men's club has been converted into a luxury hotel that includes an excellent restaurant, Muse. The location of this hotel is perfect: It's close to the heart of the city but situated on a quiet side street.

INNS Admiral Farragut Inn (401-848-8015; www.innsofnewport.com), 31 Clarke Street. ($$$–$$$$) Clarke Street, just off Washington Square and one block up from Thames Street, is one of the oldest byways in the city, with lots of history contained in its short length. For several years now it's been the "street of B&Bs and inns," with many of the colonial homes converted to guest houses. Admiral Farragut is in the circa-1750 Robert Stevens House, which served as quarters for several of General Rochambeau's aides during the Revolution. The three-story building has been restored to reflect colonial authenticity, with 12-over-12-paned windows, hardwood floors, and exposed ceiling beams. You can have breakfast seated at a long pine table or in one of several high-backed booths. The 10 rooms all have private bath but no television (there's a TV in the common room).

Admiral Fitzroy Inn (401-848-8000; 1-866-848-8780; www.admiralfitzroy.com), 398 Thames Street. ($$$) The Fitzroy, in a former convent on Thames Street, is more a small hotel than an inn. The 17 rooms on five floors (there is an elevator) are individually decorated and feature brass or European-style sleigh beds. Two have outside decks, and all have a private bath, cable TV, and telephone. A full breakfast is served in a cheery room downstairs. Despite its location in the thick of things, this is a remarkably quiet retreat. It's unlikely that the inn's namesake ever tied up in Newport (he was best known as skipper of the *Beagle,* the ship that transported Charles Darwin to new discoveries), but models of a barometer of his invention are on display (and also for sale) in the lobby.

🐾 **Bannister's Wharf Guest Rooms** (401-846-4500; www .bannistersnewport.com), Bannister's Wharf. ($$$–$$$$) One of the few places in town that accepts pets. Part of the Clarke Cooke House complex, this inn has five rooms on a deck overlooking the harbor and a suite overlooking Bowen's Wharf, as well as two suites on the second and third floors of a building adjacent to the Clarke Cooke House restaurant (see *Dining Out*); all have a private bath. For those who really want to be in the middle of summer wharf life.

Brinley Victorian Inn (401-849-7645; 1-800-999-8523; www.brinley victorian.com), 23 Brinley Street, off Kay Street. ($$$) Tucked away on a side street but still close to Bellevue Avenue and downtown, the Brinley contains 16 rooms in two 19th-century buildings. There are porches to relax on and a great courtyard, where you can have a full breakfast in warm weather. Owners John and Jennifer Sweetman have redone the rooms to brighten what was a slightly worn, if still charming, milieu.

Castle Hill Inn & Resort (401-849-3800; 1-888-466-1355; www .castlehillinn.com), 590 Ocean Avenue. ($$$$) This shingle-style mansion—small only by Newport standards—was built in 1877 for Professor Alexander Agassiz, naturalist and geologist, who chose the castle-shaped point of land as the ideal place for his marine laboratory. He sited his house on the crest of a hill with a sweeping view of the ocean and his laboratory at the foot, facing the harbor. There are nine rooms in the main house, including the dramatic Turret Room, all recently renovated and with private bath and ocean view. The six Harbor House rooms are close by, all with private bath, but for the ultimate in luxury there's nothing in Newport to rival the beach cottages, which are a short walk from the main inn and right on a private ocean beach. The inn also operates an excellent restaurant, serving a sophisticated menu that changes with the seasons but is always one of the best in the city. This is a special place in an incomparable setting, a longtime favorite of its many returning guests. In 2007 the inn was named a member of the Relais &

Katherine Imbrie

THE CASTLE HILL INN LAWN IS A SUMMERTIME FAVORITE.

Châteaux group of international luxury hotels and restaurants, the only member in Rhode Island.

The Chanler (401-847-1300; 1-866-478-8491; www.thechanler.com), 117 Memorial Boulevard. ($$$$) A recent addition to Newport's increasingly crowded field of luxury-level accommodations, the Chanler has a spectacular setting overlooking Easton's Beach at the beginning of the famously scenic Cliff Walk. The French Empire mansion was built in 1873 by New York congressman John Chanler as his summer home. The building subsequently became a hotel, one that had seen some less-than-glorious seasons before being sold in 2000 to new owners who spent millions rehabbing it as a no-holds-barred luxury palace. There are 20 rooms—each decorated in a distinctive theme such as Gothic or Mediterranean—including six villas outside the main building. A restaurant, the **Spiced Pear,** is over-the-top elegant, one of the most expensive in an expensive town.

Cliffside Inn (401-847-1811; 1-800-845-1811; www.cliffsideinn.com), 2 Seaview Avenue. ($$$$) Seaview, off Cliff Avenue, is just a few steps from the start of the Cliff Walk above First Beach. A former summer cottage for Governor Thomas Swann of Maryland, this 1880s Victorian contains seven antiques-furnished guest rooms and 10 suites, all with a fireplace and whirlpool bath. A later resident was Newport artist Beatrice Turner, whose lifework consisted of more than 1,000 self-portraits, several of which hang in the inn.

Katherine Imbrie

THE CHANLER HOTEL IS A RENOVATED FRENCH EMPIRE MANSION OVERLOOKING CLIFF WALK.

Sanford Covell Villa Marina (401-847-0206; www.sanford-covell.com), 72 Washington Street. ($$$–$$$$) This inn is a wonderful bright blue Victorian house in a great spot: right on the shore of the upper harbor in the Point section. There is a heated backyard saltwater pool, a Jacuzzi, and a long porch perfect for catching the sunset. Five Victorian-appointed rooms are furnished with original artifacts. All have private bath and include a continental breakfast served downstairs.

Hilltop Inn (1-800-846-0392; www.hilltopnewport.com), 2 Kay Street. ($$$–$$$$) This boutique inn in a turn-of-the-20th-century doctor's house is a new venture by the innkeepers of the equally elegant Francis Malbone House. Craftsman-period details, an on-site spa, and a host of other luxurious appointments characterize this inn, which is conveniently located to both Bellevue Avenue and Washington Square.

Hydrangea House (401-846-4435; www.hydrangeahouse.com), 16 Bellevue Avenue. ($$$$) One of the prettier inns in the city, this is a quiet haven in a busy part of town, across from the Hotel Viking at the head of Bellevue Avenue. Eight nicely done rooms, all with original art and each with private bath. The owners recently, and somewhat reluctantly, added televisions and phones to the rooms, responding to the modern taste for remaining hooked up even while trying to get away.

From the back porch guests can enjoy the inn's garden, which features, of course, lots of hydrangea shrubs.

Ivy Lodge (401-849-6865; www.ivylodge.com), 12 Clay Street, off Bellevue Avenue. ($$$$) This large Victorian—or "small mansion," as the owners describe it—is located on a quiet side street in the heart of the mansion district. Designed by Stanford White and built as a summer house in 1886, Ivy Lodge has a wraparound veranda—the perfect spot to catch a cool summer breeze. The central architectural attraction of the inn, though, is its oak-paneled entryway that rises 33 feet. The regal staircase, with hand-turned balusters, was crafted of English oak by local ships' carpenters. There are eight guest rooms on three floors, all with a private bath. A full breakfast, prepared by the host-chef, is served at a long dining room table or out back on the veranda.

Jailhouse Inn (401-847-4638; www.jailhouse.com), 13 Marlborough Street, one block from Washington Square. ($$–$$$) Housed in the former county jail (circa 1772) and Newport police station, this unique inn now serves voluntary inmates. Just the same, the front desk and breakfast room retain their cell bars, and the jailhouse motif is carried out in the black-and-white-striped bed linen. The inn has 24 rooms, all with a private bath, cable TV, and telephone. Continental breakfast.

Sarah Kendall House (401-846-7976; 1-800-758-9578; www.sarahkendallhouse.com), 47 Washington Street. ($$$–$$$$) Built by merchant Isaac Choate Kendall, a Rockefeller partner, in 1871 for his second wife, Sarah, this National Historic Register Victorian structure is one of the more impressive houses on the Point. The front porch overlooks historic Hunter House across the street and, beyond that, the harbor. Inside, there are lofty ceilings and fine wood floors in the sizable parlor and dining room, where a full breakfast is served each morning. The four guest rooms on the second floor and one on the third all have private bath. The largest, fronting Washington Street, is the former master bedroom and enjoys a sweeping harbor view. Despite the tranquility, it's just a two-minute walk to Long Wharf and downtown Newport.

THE SARAH KENDALL HOUSE IS ON THE NATIONAL HISTORIC REGISTER.

Kim Grant

La Farge Perry House (1-877-736-1100; www.lafargeperry.com), 24 Kay Street. ($$$) Painter and stained-glass artist John La Farge lived here with his wife in the mid-1800s. The six comfortable and well-appointed rooms in this period inn—part of Newport's Hill neighborhood—put guests within an easy walk of Washington Square and Bellevue Avenue. A full breakfast is served in a lovely dining room that features an original mural of Newport painted around 1900.

Francis Malbone House (401-846-0392; 1-800-846-0392; www.malbone.com), 392 Thames Street. ($$$$) This beautifully restored and elegantly furnished Georgian colonial house (circa 1760) is in the heart of busy Thames Street, yet manages to be an oasis of peace. Eighteen rooms in two wings, including an adjoining suite that once served as a countinghouse, are furnished with Queen Anne reproductions and queen-size four-poster beds. All have private bath, and nine have a working fireplace. There is a lovely garden out back and a terrace where breakfast is served in good weather. Three elegant sitting rooms on the first floor provide lots of room to relax or socialize. The Malbone is consistently ranked one of the top inn properties in Newport.

Melville House (401-847-0640; 1-800-711-7184; www.melvillehouse.com), 39 Clarke Street. ($$–$$$) The seven guest rooms (five with private bath) in this 1750s house are small but comfortable; for those who want more space, a fireplace suite is available November through April. One of the inn's best features is its location on a relatively peaceful byway that is close to Historic Hill and downtown. The street itself is resonant with history: The Vernon House at Clarke and Mary Streets was home to the comte de Rochambeau during the Revolution, and the French general met there with George Washington and Lafayette to plan the final victory at Yorktown; the Reverend Ezra Stiles, historian, scientist, and friend to Benjamin Franklin, lived at no. 14, where he planted mulberry bushes in an attempt to introduce silkworms to the colony.

Mill Street Inn (401-849-9500; 1-800-392-1316; www.millstreetinn.com), 75 Mill Street. ($$$$) Halfway between the waterfront and Bellevue Avenue, this inn features sleek, loft-style, contemporary rooms, all suites, in a restored sawmill built in 1815. There are also eight townhouse suites, which are more expensive. Parking is available in an underground garage. Buffet-style breakfast is served, weather permitting, on the rooftop deck. A good, central location close to Thames Street.

Newport Blues Inn (401-847-4400; www.newportbluesinn.com), 96 Pelham Street. ($$$–$$$$) The former La Forge Cottage Inn is now a property of the nearby

Newport Blues Café. The inn has always had a great location: close to the action, but in a relatively quiet neighborhood bordering Touro Park. Newly renovated, the inn has eight guest rooms, each with a private bath.

Old Beach Inn (401-849-3479; www.oldbeachinn.com), 19 Old Beach Road, near Bellevue Avenue. ($$$$) This Gothic Revival "cottage" is a comfortable, thoughtfully appointed guest house. Built in 1879 for retired China trader Stephen Powell and his wife, the main house features five rooms, all with private bath, three with working fireplace. Each room has a flower theme and is decorated appropriately (the Ivy Room has a more masculine, hunt-club motif). A carved oak staircase leads to the four second-floor rooms; a beautiful stained-glass panel depicting the four seasons highlights the first landing. The inn's only television is in one of two downstairs parlors. A "continental-plus" breakfast is served at separate tables in the dining room or outdoors on the porch or patio. For those who prefer extra privacy, an 1850s carriage house contains two more rooms. The grounds are exceptional, with plantings, benches, a lily pond, and a gazebo. There are nice architectural touches throughout the house and thoughtful touches by the innkeepers as well, including a second-floor pantry with an ironing board and umbrellas for each room.

The Pilgrim House Inn (401-846-0040; 1-800-525-8373; www.pilgrimhouseinn.com), 123 Spring Street. ($$–$$$) By Newport standards, this is a modestly priced inn in a great location within easy walking distance of Thames Street. Nothing fancy, but comfortable, with a rooftop deck that provides a view of the harbor. Ten rooms, each with a private bath. Continental breakfast.

Stella Maris Inn (401-849-2862; www.stellamarisinn.com), 91 Washington Street. ($$$–$$$$) Built as a summer house in 1861 and named Blue Rocks by a New York businessman, this three-story mansion was renamed Stella Maris ("Star of the Sea") by the Sisters of Cluny, who made it their convent until 1989, when the current owners converted it to an inn. Situated near the north end of Washington Street, across from Battery Park, Stella Maris commands excellent views of the harbor and Newport Bridge from its several porches and waterside rooms. There are good-sized rooms on the second and third floors, the former with working fireplaces, the latter with window seat, and all with private bath. There's also a single cottage out on the grounds that's ideal for a couple with children. Breakfast of granola, homemade breads, cereal, and yogurt is served buffet-style and taken in a sunroom or outside on the patio.

Adele Turner Inn (401-847-1811; www.adeleturnerinn.com), 93 Pelham Street. ($$$–$$$$) Just up the hill from downtown and around the corner from Bellevue Avenue, the Adele Turner offers a measure of tranquility but is still close to the heart of things. Built not for an admiral but a sea captain (Augustus Littlefield) in 1855, the inn contains 15 nicely done rooms in Victorian style. Pineboard floors, four-poster beds, and lofty arched windows reminiscent of Touro Synagogue add to the effect. A continental breakfast is served in the brick-walled common room warmed by a big cast-iron stove.

Victorian Ladies Inn (1-888-849-9960; www.victorianladies.com), 63 Memorial Boulevard. ($$$–$$$$) Don't let the frilly name put you off: Many people call this their favorite inn in a city full of inns. Eleven rooms are split among the main house—an 1841 Victorian—and two outbuildings. The rooms are done in "subtle Victorian" style, and all come with private bath and air-conditioning. Despite its location on a busy thoroughfare—en route to the beaches—the inn is sufficiently insulated from traffic noises. You won't have much driving to do if you stay here—the Cliff Walk and Easton's Beach are just steps away.

Wayside Guest House (401-847-0302; 1-800-847-0302; www.waysidenewport.com), 406 Bellevue Avenue. ($$$) This handsome, Georgian-style brick building was added to an existing Victorian structure in 1896 to serve as a home for Elisha Dyer, dance master for society cotillions from Palm Beach to Maine. Dorothy Post rents out 7 of the 22 rooms in what is one of the oldest continuously run inns in the city. Most of the rooms are large and airy—the "library" guest room on the first floor has a 15-foot ceiling. Many are furnished with four-poster canopy beds, and all come with a ceiling fan and private bath. Continental breakfast is served in the large family dining room. Guests get to use the 18-by-36-foot in-ground swimming pool—a rarity for guest houses. Directly across from the Elms, in the heart of the avenue district.

Yankee Peddler Inn (401-846-1323; 1-800-427-9444; www.yankeepeddlerinn.com), 113 Touro Street. ($$$$) One of the Historic Inns of Newport group, the Peddler has a central location close to downtown on Touro Street. A garden and deck provide a private oasis. Nineteen rooms come with continental breakfast and afternoon tea.

BED & BREAKFASTS Don't expect bargain prices from Newport bed & breakfast operations: Rooms average $150 and up—way up—per night. Rates quoted are for peak season, between April and October; prices drop anywhere from 10 to 30 percent off-season. In most cases it is still cheaper to stay at a B&B than at one of the name-brand hotels, and the atmosphere is almost always cheerier and more personable. By law, a place that calls itself a B&B is required to serve breakfast. Competition has spurred owners to provide ever-more-sumptuous spreads, and even so-called continental breakfasts should provide more than enough fuel to start the day.

Reservations are recommended during the busy season and on weekends during spring and fall. Some B&Bs require a minimum stay of two nights—three on holiday weekends or during special events—so it's wise to check ahead. Most don't permit smoking on the premises. Reservation services are free and provide the only access to a considerable number of smaller guest houses that don't advertise. Among the services are **Newport County Bed & Breakfast Association** (www.newportribedandbreakfast.com); **Bed & Breakfast Newport** (401-846-5408; 1-800-800-8765; www.bbnewport.com); **Taylor-Made Reservations** (401-848-0300; 1-800-848-8848; www.citybythesea.com); **Newport County Inns and Bed & Breakfasts Association** (www.newportinns.com); and **14 Best BnBs of Newport** (www.14bestbnbsofnewport.com).

Almondy Inn (401-848-7202; 1-800-478-6155; www.almondyinn.com), 25 Pelham Street. ($$$) Five rooms and suites occupy this elegantly appointed 1890s bed & breakfast inn located in the Historic Hill district. All have private bath and Jacuzzi; some have views of the harbor.

Architect's Inn (401-847-7081; 1-888-834-7081; www.architectsinn.com), 31 Old Beach Road. ($$–$$$) This beautiful 1873 Swiss-chalet-style Victorian was the home of famed Newport architectural historian George Champlin Mason (he designed it himself). Now it's a B&B with five rooms, all with private bath, three with working fireplace. The inn is located a few blocks from Bellevue Avenue at Touro Park.

Elliott Boss House (401-849-9425; http://elliottboss.com), 20 Second Street. ($$$) Two upstairs antiques-furnished rooms can be found in this quiet 1820s house on the Point with a beautifully landscaped garden, a regular on Newport's annual Secret Garden Tours. In summer, a full breakfast is served on the back patio.

The Clarkeston (401-848-5300; 1-800-524-1386; www.innsofnewport.com), 28 Clarke Street. ($$–$$$$) Colonial-style inn on historic Clarke Street near downtown. Nine guest rooms, five with working fireplace, four with Jacuzzi, and all with private bath. The front portion of the house dates from 1705, when it was the home of Joseph Burrill. The house has been nicely restored, and you can see evidence of the original flooring and doors in two third-story rooms. The rooms, furnished with four-posters and thick mattresses, are named for well-known Newporters—Doris Duke, Alva Vanderbilt, and Harry Belmont among them—and come with appropriate reading material. Rooms include full breakfast.

Rose Island Lighthouse (401-847-4242; roseislandlighthouse.org), offices at 365 Thames Street. ($$$) For those who like to combine romance with roughing it, an overnight stay on 16-acre Rose Island, 1 mile offshore in Newport Harbor, might be the ticket. Here, guests get to play lighthouse keeper and weather-station manager while doing regular chores to help keep the place up. There's no running water or electricity, and no maid service. The light was first lit in 1870, then relit and restored in 1993 with the help of the nonprofit Rose Island Lighthouse Foundation. You get to Rose Island via boat if the weather is right—otherwise the foundation arranges for you to stay in town. It's a fun experience, but not for everyone.

Marshall Slocum Guest House (401-841-5120; 1-800-372-5120; www.marshallslocuminn.com), 29 Kay Street. ($$–$$$) Just a block and a half from Bellevue Avenue, this pleasant, airy guest house is within reasonable walking distance of Historic Hill and downtown. The Slocum is a friendly, unpretentious B&B. Five guest rooms, all with private bath, are on the second and third floors of this former parsonage. Full breakfast is served from 8 to 10 in the dining room or, weather permitting, on the back porch. This is a pleasant neighborhood, with stately houses lining Kay Street, once home to writers and artists (Henry James spent summers farther down the street). A shady front porch with a porch swing and rockers is the place to take it all in.

* Where to Eat

You can dine very well in Newport, thanks to *Homarus americanus* and the French—which shows you how far the tastes of local residents have evolved in the past 200 years.

At one time, difficult as it is to believe, *H. americanus*, the lobster, was shunned by educated palates and considered throwaway food, fit only for bait or for the tables of the poor. Happily, it was discovered somewhere along the line that the lobster ranks with any other food known to humans, and fortunately Rhode Island and nearby ocean waters abound with the creatures.

As for the French, they've made quite an inroad since the days of the British occupation. The British may have been the enemy, but they shared the same language, religion, and culture as the majority of Americans. Before they retreated, they solemnly warned the colonists that the French not only worshipped the pope, but also ate—can you imagine?—such things as frogs' legs and snails. Well, Newporters were famous for their religious tolerance (although the General Assembly had to hastily okay the presence of Roman Catholics in the colony for the arrival of General Rochambeau and his troops), and the first French Masses in America were celebrated in 1780–1781 at Colony House in Washington Square. It did not take long for French cooking to catch on, and today the best restaurants in the city celebrate French cuisine.

You can eat well here for moderate amounts, or you can spend a lot. Lobster is, of course, the great equalizer, although you will find differences of $10–20 among restaurants. Because lobster prices are in constant flux, many restaurants don't post a fixed price; ask your waiter or waitress for the daily quote. And watch the extras—an appetizer and dessert can double the cost of dinner. Most Newport restaurants post their menu outside the door, so you can compare prices without entering. But don't be fooled by a full house, especially in the waterfront area—the food might be great or the place may simply be packed with unsuspecting tourists.

DINING OUT **At the Deck** (800-960-4573; http://waiteswharf.com), 1 Waites Wharf. ($$–$$$) Open daily for lunch and dinner; closed January and February. Right on the water toward the south end of the harbor, this restaurant has a small indoor dining room and bar where those who can't get a table are welcome to dine while watching the chefs at work on the line. The menu changes with the season, but always features fresh, inventive fare that's far more sophisticated than the sometimes boisterous outdoor bar-and-grill scene would indicate.

Black Pearl (401-846-5264; http://blackpearlnewport.com), Bannister's Wharf. ($$–$$$$) Open daily for lunch and dinner. Located in a former sail loft and named for the original owner's brig, the Pearl is two restaurants in one. On one side is an informal tavern, serving sandwiches, light dinners, and excellent chowder and French onion soup. The other side, the Commodore's Room, is one of Newport's more formal restaurants, with fine cuisine inventively prepared and served in a Colonial-style setting. You can take home the Pearl chowder, hot or frozen, by the quart and half gallon.

Café Zelda (401-849-4002; http://cafezelda.com), 528 Thames Street. ($$–$$$) Open daily for lunch and dinner. The bar at this comfortable spot is a long-popular hangout of the local yachting crowd. The dining room is no slouch, either. French-inspired dishes and a menu that includes steak as well as local seafood make Zelda a reliable favorite for many.

Canfield House (401-847-0416; http://canfieldhousenewport.com), 5 Memorial Boulevard. ($$$–$$$$) Open daily for dinner. Baked stuffed lobster and chateaubriand are the house specialties (and two of the more expensive menu items) in this elegant 1897 building that once hosted a gambling casino. This is a dressy, another-era place; the fireplace lounge is a great spot for a hot toddy on a cool day.

Castle Hill Inn (401-849-3800; http://castlehillinn.com), 590 Ocean Avenue. ($$$$) Open daily for breakfast, lunch, and dinner. The view from the dining room of the top resort hotel in the city is simply stunning, taking in the entrance to Newport Harbor, the cliffs of Jamestown, and the graceful arch of the Newport Bridge. Always one of the best (and most expensive) places to dine in Newport, Castle Hill's menu and service justify the splurge.

Clarke Cooke House (401-849-2900; http://clarkecooke.com), Bannister's Wharf. ($$$–$$$$) Open daily for lunch and dinner. This ever-changing restaurant (there's currently a bistro, a regular restaurant, and a formal, high-priced dining room as well as a sushi bar) is housed in a 1790s building moved here from Thames Street in 1973. The Cooke House is a landmark on the waterfront that enjoys a long-standing status as a favorite of celebrity sailors and just plain celebrities. The top-floor restaurant displays fancy French ways with lamb, beef, and seafood. A must-visit for those who enjoy an elegant meal and a taste of ultra-Newport waterfront nightlife.

Cliff Walk Terrace at the Chanler (401-847-2244; http://thechanler.com), in The Chanler Hotel, 117 Memorial Boulevard. ($$$$) For a super-elegant experience of outdoor dining in summer, the Terrace is hard to beat. The view is of Easton's Beach sweeping east to Middletown. The food is expensive but generally worth the price, especially a creative twist on a lobster roll that tops $30 all by itself. (For indoor dining year-round, try the Veranda in the same hotel.)

♿ **La Forge Casino** (401-847-0418; http://laforgenewport.com), 186 Bellevue Avenue. ($$–$$$) Open daily for lunch and dinner. A Newport institution, with mainstream meat and seafood dishes (the baked shrimp stuffed with lobster is a house favorite). The Porch dining room overlooks the greens of the adjoining Newport Casino, offering a breath of spring even in cold weather. The Casino Room, open for lunch and dinner, is an early-1900s restaurant-cum-Irish-pub with lots of salads, sandwiches, and moderately priced pub dinners such as Dublin Shrimp. A small but strategically located sidewalk café overlooks the broad Bellevue sidewalk, a perfect spot, the owners point out, for observing the daily parade of "cabbages and kings." Diners can get a discount to visit the adjoining Tennis Hall of Fame.

Mamma Luisa (401-848-5257; http://mammaluisa.com), 673 Thames Street. ($$–$$$) Open Tuesday through Sunday for dinner. Authentic northern Italian cooking (Mamma was a chef in Bologna) can be found in this lower Thames ristorante. A sampler plate of two or three kinds of pasta (under $20) is an excellent way to start. Spinach-stuffed gnocchi, veal scaloppine in balsamic sauce, and lots of pasta fill out the menu.

The Mooring (401-846-2260; http://mooringrestaurant.com), Sayer's Wharf, off America's Cup Avenue. ($$–$$$) Open daily for lunch and dinner. Seafood and meat dishes are done up in straightforward style in a waterfront building that once served as a summer outpost of the New York Yacht Club. If the weather is pleasant, the deck out back offers one of the best views of busy Newport Harbor; if there's a chill, try a table near the great fireplace inside.

Newport Dinner Train (401-841-8700; http://newportdinner train.com), 19 America's Cup Avenue, next to the Gateway Center. ($$$$) Full-course meals served as you proceed slowly (about 10 miles per hour) aboard the Old Colony railroad train along the west side of Aquidneck Island. Usually several choices of entrée, such as shrimp, prime rib, and the chef's choice of chicken, veal, or lamb. This is a dress-up affair—jackets required—and while it may not be the Orient Express, it's as close as you'll get in these parts.

The Place at Yesterday's (401-847-0116; http://yesterdaysand theplace.com), 38 Washington Square. ($$$–$$$$) Open daily for dinner. While the original Yesterday's (see *Eating Out*) next door serves up burgers, nachos, and light dinners, the Place, alternatively known as the Wine Bar, turns out some of the finest and most imaginative dishes in town. Portobello mushrooms are a fad, but here they are done right—close your eyes and it could be tenderloin you're tasting. Whether you choose crabcakes or soft-shell crabs with garlic mayonnaise, everything here is prepared just right and beautifully presented. In fact, the food is so delicious, you may be tempted to avoid taking off on their multivintage "wine flight" sampler.

Puerini's (401-847-5506; http://puerinisrestaurant.com), 24 Memorial Boulevard. ($$–$$$) Open daily for dinner. Very popular with the locals, the dining rooms here (all smoke-free) fill up quickly on summer nights as long lines gather outside. Homemade pasta (the spinach pasta is excellent) in lots of varieties at reasonable prices account for the family-run restaurant's popularity. Have some gelato for dessert.

The Red Parrot (401-847-3140; http://redparrotrestaurant.com), 348 Thames Street. ($$–$$$) Open daily for lunch and dinner. Caribbean-influenced dishes (Cayman Cajun shrimp, Jamaican jerk) and, of course, seafood on two floors of dining. The large bar is a popular hangout for racers during the sailing season. At the junction of America's Cup Avenue and Thames Street, this place is as central as it gets.

Restaurant Bouchard (401-846-0123; http://restaurantbouchard.com), 505 Thames Street. ($$–$$$) Open Wednesday through Monday for dinner. Bouchard offers traditional bistro fare—sautéed veal sweetbreads and breast of duck, along with Dover sole and restuffed lobster. Validated parking on adjacent Waites Wharf.

The Rhumbline (401-849-3999), 62 Bridge Street. ($$–$$$) Open daily for lunch and dinner. Set in the Colonial Point neighborhood, a block and a half from the Gateway Center, the Rhumbline (a nautical term for a direct line between two points) is a quiet haven away from the commercial area. It has a warm, inviting atmosphere, and is known among locals for its mussels, fish, and veal dishes as well as sandwiches and daily specials.

Salvation Café (401-847-2620; http://salvationcafe.com), 140 Broadway. ($) Open for dinner Tuesday through Sunday 5–10. This recently expanded café is a little off the beaten path, several blocks north of Washington Square in a block that has recently become home to a number of good, moderately priced restaurants. It's well worth a visit for its inventive fusion cuisine and vegetarian fare. The common denominator here among the specials each evening is spicy: Jamaican jerk shrimp, chicken, and beef; pad Thai with shrimp; scallion and caper tempura. The decor is camp (busts of JFK and Elvis, potted palms), the atmosphere relaxed, and the food, well, spicy.

Sardella's (401-849-6312; http://sardellas.com), 30 Memorial Boulevard, next door to Puerini's. ($$–$$$) Open daily for dinner. Italian food with more of a gourmet touch and a slightly more formal atmosphere than its neighbor. Extensive menu of northern and southern specialties—Sogliole alla Fiorentina, Cotolette al Griglia. Excellent antipasti, including snail salad (a Rhode Island favorite) and fried mozzarella.

Scales and Shells (401-846-3474; http://scalesandshells.com), 527 Thames Street. ($$–$$$) Open daily for dinner. For seafood lovers only, but you'll probably love the seafood you get in this bustling informal restaurant on lower Thames. Seating is in one big room with the kitchen grills open for all to see. The daily menu is posted on a large blackboard on one wall. Mesquite-grilled shrimp, grilled clam pizza, and fresh fish of all kinds are all good bets. Pasta with red or white sauce and vegetable kebabs are served with meals or available as main courses. Terms are cash only; no credit cards.

Tallulah on Thames (401-849-2433; http://tallulahonthames.com), 464 Thames Street. ($$–$$$) Chef Jake Rojas creates sophisticated magic using locally sourced ingredients. The atmosphere is intimate, the location ideal on trendy Lower Thames. Opened in 2010, Tallulah's has already become a foodie favorite.

Tucker's Bistro (401-846-3449; http://tuckersbistro.com), 150 Broadway. ($$) Open daily for dinner. Tucker's brings a touch of class to Newport's north end, serving a mix of nouveau California/New York cuisine in comfortable surroundings. Appetizers include that Ocean State standby, calamari; entrées range from red meat to vegetarian lasagna; and desserts are chocolatey and imaginative.

♿ **Twenty-Two Bowens Wine Bar & Grille** (401-841-8884; http://22bowens.com), 22 Bowen's Wharf. ($$–$$$) Open daily for lunch and dinner. A great setting right on cobblestoned Bowen's Wharf and the inner harbor makes this upscale restaurant popular with both tourists and locals. Steaks are a good bet.

The Pier (401-847-3645; http://pierrestaurantnewportri.com), 10 Howard Wharf, on the harbor. ($$–$$$) Open daily for lunch and dinner. The Pier doesn't have to be as good as it is. (It was bound to be a tourist favorite because of its location right on the water.) But Chef Kevin Gaudreau brings finesse and style to what might have been just another harborfront seafood joint. Some of Newport's most sophisticated diners consider The Pier the best restaurant in the city.

White Horse Tavern (401-849-3600; http://whitehorsetavern.us), Marlborough and Farewell Streets. ($$$$) Dinner daily, lunch daily except Tuesday. The White Horse is arguably the most formal, and one of the most expensive, restaurants in town. The setting, in the oldest still-operating tavern in America, is Colonial, with candlelit atmosphere. Before, after, or in lieu of dinner, you can relax in the comfortable fireplace bar where patriots once conspired to rebellion (and probably a little piracy) while quaffing tankards of cider.

EATING OUT ♿ **Brick Alley Pub** (401-849-6334; http://brickalley.com), 140 Thames Street. ($–$$) Open daily for lunch and dinner. Always crowded, this pub, just around the corner from Washington Square, has its own "ultimate nacho" fans, but you'll also find burgers, fresh fish, homemade pasta, and a big salad bar. The drinks are sizable as well. In warm weather enjoy the outdoor patio at the rear, where you can forget for a time that you're in the middle of a city.

Fastnet Pub (401-845-9311; http://thefastnetpub.com), 1 Broadway, across from the Colony House. ($) Open daily for lunch and dinner. Fairly authentic Irish pub is one of the city's most popular bar hangouts. Named for a lighthouse off the coast of Cork, Ireland, the Fastnet serves Irish-American pub fare such as bangers and mash, fish-and-chips, and shepherd's pie.

Fourth Street Diner (401-847-2069), 184 Admiral Kalbfus Road. ($) Open for breakfast, lunch, and dinner. Classic diner food in a classic diner: cheeseburgers, open-faced prime rib sandwiches, Portuguese soup. Desserts—lemon meringue pie, tapioca pudding—fit the setting and the bill.

Franklin Spa (401-847-3540), Spring and Thames Streets. ($) Breakfast and lunch are served at this combination soda fountain/variety store. This is no deli—the hot turkey sandwiches are made from real turkeys. One of the best (and busiest) spots for cheap eats in the heart of downtown.

Handy Lunch (401-847-9480), 462 Thames Street. ($) One of the last of Newport's lunch counters, the Handy serves breakfast and lunch—meat loaf, American chop suey—in an atmosphere that is loud, friendly, and decidedly local. And cheap, of course. Popular with both the New York Yacht Club types and commercial fishermen, the Handy is a Newport institution.

Marina Café and Pub (401-841-0999; http://marinacafepub.com), Goat Island. ($–$$) Open daily for lunch and dinner. Sailors off the yachts docked nearby rub elbows with landlubber Newporters at this best-kept-secret kind of place that's just a little bit out of the way from the busier side of the harbor. The pub serves sandwiches and soups in an airy setting all day, along with some lighter meals. Steak and seafood dinners in the evening. Outside, there's a great view of Newport across the water.

Mudville Pub (401-619-4680), 8 West Marlborough Street. ($–$$) Open daily for lunch and dinner. A genuine sports bar, Mudville is also a great place to grab a sandwich or a light meal. The burgers are among the best in town. A bullpen outdoor area overlooks the action at Cardines Field from a right-centerfield perspective. Lively, noisy atmosphere and some interesting sports memorabilia: The dude with the wild hair and mustache battling Stacom for the ball in one photo is coach Pat Riley, in his pre-gel days.

Newport Creamery (401-846-6332; http://newportcreamery.com), Bellevue Gardens shopping center. ($) Open daily for breakfast, lunch, and dinner. Rhode Island's equivalent of Friendly's serves much the same fare: sandwiches and ice cream desserts at reasonable prices in an air-conditioned setting. Jackie Kennedy Onassis was a customer when visiting her hometown, and you're liable to spot a celebrity or two in town for a shoot or a vacation.

Wharf Deli & Pub (401-846-9233; http://thewharfpub.com), 37 Bowen's Wharf. ($) Open daily for lunch and dinner. Reasonably priced sandwiches and salads in the heart of the high-rent wharf district. The back porch is a great place to people-watch, and there's always plenty of Bass Ale and other brews on tap.

Yesterday's (401-847-0125; http://yesterdaysandtheplace.com), 28 Washington Square. ($–$$) Open daily for lunch and dinner. Big menu, strong on sandwiches, burgers, and the locally famous Yesterday's Nachos. Full meals served as well, many with a Mexican flair, in early-1900s saloon decor. In all a good, centrally located place to enjoy a casual meal.

✷ Entertainment

If you can't find entertainment in Newport, you're not looking or listening. The city's reputation as a rowdy party town has been a matter of much civic debate for years and has been the object of an ever-tightening string of regulations and ordinances aimed at quieting down the nightlife and allowing residents and visitors the chance for at least a few hours' sleep at night. There is something going on every night in summer in virtually every restaurant, hotel, and bar in the city, especially along the waterfront. Entertainment ranges from easy jazz and rollicking blues to DJs to out-and-out rock-and-roll. Crowds of young and old fill the streets each summer night, and people-watching (and interacting) could be considered a major source of entertainment.

CASINO Newport Grand (401-849-5000; http://newportgrand.com), Admiral Kalbfus Road. The only slots casino in the area is just off the second exit ramp from the Newport Bridge.

MUSIC Newport Blues Cafe (401-841-5110; http://newportblues.com), 286 Thames Street. Dinner with a New Orleans flavor downstairs; live music in the upstairs lounge.

One Pelham East (401-847-9640; http://thepelham.com), Thames and Pelham Streets. This oldie but goodie has been showcasing live bands since the 1970s. A popular midtown spot.

SPECTATOR SPORTS
Sunset League Baseball, Cardines Field, America's Cup Avenue and Marlborough Street, across from the Gateway Center. For just $4 for adults, $2 for kids, you can take in a Newport Gulls (http://newportgulls.com) collegiate or Sunset League baseball game at historic Cardines Field, one of the oldest (1908) ballparks in the country. The Sunset League is reputed to be the oldest surviving amateur circuit, dating to 1919. Cardines Field is even older than Boston's Fenway Park. Where else can you watch a baseball game with Colonial houses crowding the outfield fence? Games begin at 7 PM weekdays, 1 or 3 PM on Saturday.

THEATER/FILM Firehouse Theater (401-849-3473; http://firehousetheater.org), 4 Equality Park Place, just off Broadway. Live, improvisational comedy shows by the Bit Players are performed in a former firehouse. All seats $20. Weekend evening shows year-round.

Newport Playhouse & Cabaret (401-848-7529; http://newport playhouse.com), 102 Connell Highway. Broadway comedies and musicals. Dinner and a play, or just the play.

Jane Pickens Theater and Event Center (401-846-5252; http: //janepickens.com), 49 Touro Street, on Washington Square. Last of the big-screen movie palaces in town, the Pickens presents quality first-run and offbeat flicks.

✷ Selective Shopping

Newport has its share of tourist-trap T-shirt and trinket shops as well as the usual scattering of national outlets—Banana Republic, Chico's, Rockport Company Store, and so on. It also has locally owned stores, some long in business, some with the paint still drying. It's up to the customer to discern the difference, but that, after all, is part of the fun of shopping.

ANTIQUES SHOPS The best place to begin antiques hunting in Newport is on Spring Street, which runs one-way north, parallel to Thames Street. A dozen shops here and along adjacent Franklin Street cater to just about any taste or budget.

A&A Gaines (401-849-6844; http://aagaines.com), 40 Franklin Street. Upscale emporium selling period furniture, clocks, and China trade wares.

Armory Antiques (401-848-2398), 365 Thames Street. This is a must-stop for those who love browsing around old things. The 125-dealer group shop fills the floor of a vast, castle-like former armory and is full of the kind of vintage items, artwork, and furniture that have character but are perhaps not of museum quality. The Armory is a great place to spend a rainy afternoon, and its location close to the Memorial Boulevard intersection puts it right in the center of things. Plus, in an area of precious few public restrooms, it's an insider's secret that you can duck in here when nature calls when you've been too long engrosssed in shopping Thames Street. Open daily except holidays, year-round.

The Drawing Room of Newport (401-841-5060), 152–154 Spring Street. Authentic furnishings from Newport's Gilded Age, with a sideline of Zsolnay Hungarian art pottery and fine European porcelains.

JB Antiques (401-849-0450), 33 Franklin Street. Porcelain, silver, paintings, and furniture.

Newport China Trade Co.(401-841-5267), 8 Franklin Street. Domestic antiques and 18th-through 20th-century export china and porcelain: Rose Medallion plates, temple jars, therapeutic porcelain pillows.

ART STORES AND GALLERIES **Gallery Night** (401-848-8200, http://newport galleries.org), held on the second Thursday of each month (except January and February), is the best way to experience a wide array of Newport art galleries and shops. From 5 to 8 PM on Gallery Nights, more than two dozen art venues open their doors and invite visitors to see newly opened exhibits along with ongoing ones. You can shop if you like, or just look and listen. Frequently, the artists themselves are on hand to introduce their work.

Arnold Art (401-847-2273; http://arnoldart.com), 210 Thames Street. Arnold's began life as an art supply store, then blossomed into a full gallery that specializes in marine painting but also shows other local and regional art.

Blink Gallery (401-847-4255; http://blinkgalleryusa.com), 89 Thames Street. Contemporary gallery has edgy works by local artists working in a variety of media. Wooden bowls and other pieces by Jeff Soderbergh and art photographs of Newport by Alexander Nesbitt are on view, along with changing exhibits of paintings and other art. Open daily in-season.

DeBlois Gallery (401-847-9977; http://debloisgallery.com), 138 Bellevue Avenue. Created by a coalition of local artists, DeBlois has regular shows exhibiting the best work of member and guest artists.

Roger King Fine Arts (401-847-4359; http://rkingfinearts.com), 21 Bowen's Wharf. Roger King buys and sells fine art by American and European painters of the 18th, 19th, and 20th centuries. King is also an expert in early African American art.

Spring Bull Studio (401-849-9166; http://springbullgallery.com), 55 Bellevue Avenue. Part of this shop is a permanent collection of works by local artists, including Richard Grosvenor. The other section presents shows that change monthly. Mostly representation work, including seascapes, landscapes, and portraits. This is also a working studio, so you might see Grosvenor and other artists at work when you stop in. *Spring Bull* refers to the studio's original location at Spring and Bull Streets.

William Vareika Fine Arts (401-849-6149; http://vareikafinearts.com), 212 Bellevue Avenue. One of the larger galleries in New England dealing in museum-quality American art of the 18th, 19th, and early 20th centuries. Vareika's specialty is artists who have some Newport connection, including works by John La Farge, William Trost Richards, John F. Kensett, Childe Hassam, and Edward M. Bannister.

SPECIAL SHOPS **Army & Navy Surplus** (401-847-3073), 262 Thames Street. This crowded shop—part museum, part army-navy store that's gotten way out of hand—has been written up in, of all places, *Vogue* magazine. Besides the usual trenching tools, peacoats, and marine knives, you can buy diving helmets, field radios, gas masks, and regular camping equipment. Also a good place to shop for Levi's, flannel shirts, and some of the cheapest Newport T-shirts in town.

Ball & Claw (401-848-5600; http://theballandclaw.com), 29 America's Cup Avenue. Jeffrey Greene's fine handcrafted furniture in period styles recalls the era when Newport's cabinetmakers were among the best in the world. The shop also sells accessories for the home, including paintings, quilts, porcelain, and lamps.

Cadeaux du Monde (401-848-0550; http://cadeauxdumonde.com), 26 Mary Street. Fine crafts and folk art from around the world—clothing, bags, jewelry, and handwoven rugs are sold in what the owners describe as an "alternative trading organization." The owners are happy to give you the story behind each of the items for sale and expound a little on the culture that produced it.

Down Under Jewelry (401-849-1078; http://downunderjewelry.com), 479 Thames Street. An unusually fine collection of handcrafted jewelry in this unpretentious shop at the artsy end of Thames.

Ebenezer Flagg Co. (401-846-1891), 65 Touro Street, corner of Spring Street. Custom and production flags, pennants, yacht ensigns, and wind socks. Ebenezer Flagg was a patriot who died during the Revolution. Company founder Leo Waring, who set his store near the (now underground) spring where Newport's founders first settled, found Flagg's name on a headstone in the Common Burial Ground. Leo, who died in the late 1980s, was a Massachusetts native who passionately believed that Newport was one of the last bastions of democracy in the world.

Michael Hayes (401-846-3090; http://michaelhayesnewport.com), 204 Bellevue Avenue, and (401-849-1888), 19 Bowen's Wharf. Designer clothing for men, women, and children tops the charts for style (and price), even in fashion-savvy Newport.

Helly Hansen (401-849-6666; http://hellynewengland.com), 154 Thames Street. The H/H brand is nationally known for the quality of its outdoor and adventure clothing, including specialty items for sailing.

The Narragansett (401-847-0303), 3 Bowen's Wharf. Classic sportswear for men and women, along with well-chosen contemporary pieces, can be found in this comfortable shop. You'll find Polo Ralph Lauren, Max Mara, Three Dots, Geiger, and others.

Papers (401-847-1777; http://papersnewport.com), 178 Bellevue Avenue. Cards, stationery, and gifts combine elegance with utility at this small shop in the carriage trade block of tony Bellevue.

Potter & Co. (401-847-0392; http://potterandcompanynewport.com), 172 Thames Street. The oldest still-operating shop in Newport is this 100-year-old emporium whose wooden cabinets and shelves are filled with practical clothing, coats, hats, and gloves for men, women, and children. North Face, Columbia, Woolrich, Levi's, and Pendleton are among the manufacturers you'll find here, but the real reason to go is to soak up the authentic old-time atmosphere of the place.

Karol Richardson (401-849-6612; http://karolrichardson.com), 24 Washington Square. Natasha, daughter of designer Karol, has her mother's eye for easy, sophisticated styles for women.

Scrimshanders (401-849-5680; 1-800-635-5234; http://scrimshanders.com), 14 Bowen's Wharf. "Two hundred years behind the times" is the way this small shop advertises itself. Inside can be found all manner of antique and modern scrimshaw pieces. It's as much a museum as a gallery, with information on the history of the art of etching black designs on ivory, a practice begun by sailors centuries ago to pass the time at sea. Modern pieces use alternatives to the whale's teeth and elephant tusks that it is no longer legal to obtain.

Sole Desire (401-846-0067), 171 Thames Street. If you're doing a lot of walking in Newport, you'll want to visit this shop that specializes in shoes and boots that are both comfortable and stylish. A large selection of Dansko, Merrell, Puma, Steve Madden, Rocket Dog, Uggs, and more.

Didi Suydam (401-848-9414; http://didisuydam.com), 25 Mill Street. Contemporary art jewelry by Suydam and other artists is lushly displayed along with some contemporary wall pieces in this light-filled gallery.

Team One (401-848-0884; http://team1newport.com), 561 Thames Street. Located way down at the southern end of Thames, near where it turns the corner of the harbor to Wellington, this store is worth finding if you're looking for high-end authentic sailing gear. Names include Henri Lloyd, Patagonia, and Douglas Gill.

Thames Glass (401-846-0576; http://thamesglass.com), 688 Thames Street. Glassblower Matthew Buechner creates beautiful objects—vases, bowls, perfume bottles—in his studio adjacent to a small retail space on lower Thames. His work has been collected by the Corning Museum of Glass in Corning, New York (where his father served as president of Steuben Glass), and the Frauenau Museum of Glass in Germany. Visitors can watch Buechner fire and blow glass at the shop; any object with the slightest of flaws goes onto the seconds table at a bargain price.

Third & Elm Press (401-846-0228; http://thirdandelm.com), 29 Elm Street, corner of Third Street. Open Wednesday through Saturday 9–5. Ilse Buchert Nesbitt makes and sells her own woodblock prints, notepaper, small books, and Christmas cards—many with a Newport theme—in this old-fashioned print shop on the Point.

Onne van der Wal Photography (401-849-5556; http://vanderwal.com), Bannister's Wharf. Lushly displayed framed photographs capture the nautical spirit of Newport.

✷ Special Events

Newport has a full calendar of special events, from its jazz and folk festivals to regattas to the Black Ships Festival that celebrates the city's historic ties to Japan. For a listing of events, contact the **Gateway Center** (401-849-8098; 1-800-326-6030).

January 1: **Polar Bear Plunge,** Easton's Beach at noon. Polar Bear members swim throughout the year; each New Year's Day, they are joined by scores of amateurs and hundreds of spectators.

Late January, early February: **Newport Winter Festival**. Ten days of activities to brighten up the winter—fireworks, concerts, dogsled races, snow/sand sculpture contest, carriage rides.

March: **Irish Heritage Month** is a monthlong program of Irish drama, music, culture, and cuisine at various venues throughout the city.

June: The **Secret Garden Tour,** usually held the second weekend of the month, gets you behind the garden gates of more than a dozen homes in Newport's Colonial Point section. **Benefactors of the Arts** (401-847-0514), 33 Washington Street, Newport 02840.

July: The **Newport Music Festival** offers two weeks of great classical music in and around the mansions. Morning, afternoon, and evening concerts. Information: 401-846-1133; http://newportmusic.org. Tickets: 401-849-0700. **International Tennis Hall of Fame** (401-849-3990), professional tennis tournaments at the Newport Casino and Tennis Hall of Fame. For tickets or information: 401-849-3990; www.tennisfame.com. **Black Ships Festival** (401-846-2720; www.newportevents.com/Blackships) salutes Newport's historic ties to Japan, dating from 1853, when Newport native son Commodore Matthew Perry, acting at the behest of President Millard Fillmore, pressured the Japanese to open their shores to foreign trade. There are no ships at this festival (*Black Ships* is how the Japanese described Perry's fleet), but there are plenty of events celebrating Japanese culture, including tea ceremonies, origami, sumo wrestling, and dancing.

August: **Newport Folk Festival** (401-847-3700; newportfolk.com) presents two afternoons of top-flight folk music. This is the place where Bob Dylan shocked the audience by plugging in his guitar. Generally the first weekend of the month at Fort Adams State Park, Fort Adams Road. **The Newport Jazz Festival** (401-847-3700; www.festivalproductions.net), held the second weekend in August, continues to bring the best of the old(er) performers as well as the latest in fusion and modern jazz. Also held at Fort Adams State Park, Fort Adams Road. **Weekend of Coaching** (401-847-1000; http://newportmansions.com), usually the third weekend of the month. Newport returns to its Gilded Age as society returns to its favorite 19th-century pastime: clopping about in horse-drawn coaches.

Labor Day weekend: The annual **Classic Yacht Regatta** (http://moy.org), hosted by the Museum of Yachting at Fort Adams, brings together some of the finest old sailing vessels afloat. Much of the racing and the Parade of Sail is visible from various points around the harbor.

Mid-September: The **Newport International Boat Show** (401-846-1600; http://newportboatshow.com), held at the Newport Yachting Center, is one of the largest in-water sail- and powerboat shows in the country.

Late September: **Taste of Newport** (401-846-1600; www.tasteofnewport.com), Newport Yachting Center. Newporters love this weekend event, in which area restaurants serve up samples of their trademark dishes. A great way to check out a lot of chefs in an afternoon.

November: Newport Restaurant Week (http://gonewportrestaurantweek.com) allows diners to sample meals at dozens of participating restaurants at bargain prices.

December: **Christmas in Newport** (http://christmasinnewport.org) is a monthlong series of events: religious services, madrigals, colonial masques, a reading of "A Visit from St. Nicholas," written by Newport summer resident Clement C. Moore, and a crafts fair.

Aquidneck and Conanicut

7

MIDDLETOWN

PORTSMOUTH

JAMESTOWN

Tom Gannon

MIDDLETOWN

Middletown and Portsmouth are the two towns that share Aquidneck Island with their more glamorous sister, Newport. (Southern Middletown's beaches, Second and Third, are often mistakenly assumed to be part of Newport.) Jamestown, occupying Conanicut Island to the west of Newport and linked to it by the Newport Bridge, might be described as Newport's quieter, yachtier sister.

Middletown derives its name from its location between the first Aquidneck Island settlement, Portsmouth, and Newport to the south. Separated from Newport in 1743, the town was heavily garrisoned by British and Hessian troops during the Revolution and was the site of the British Green End Fort, now reduced to a plaque on Vernon Avenue. The great valley that bisects Middletown was the final barrier to American troops, who invaded the island from Tiverton in 1778 and almost succeeded in trapping upward of 7,000 royalist troops between them and the French fleet. Alas, the French sailed off, and the Americans were forced to withdraw. Middletown for years boasted many of the remaining working farms in this once agricultural state. The farms are now mostly gone, though nurseries and vineyards remain, but the town still seems like "country" to folks leaving the urban center of Newport.

Meanwhile, Jamestown has taken flight in the past decade as the wealthy increasingly choose the island for its relaxed, village pace and beautiful views of the entrance of Narragansett Bay from atop rocky bluffs, especially those within its two state parks: Fort Wetherill and Beavertail.

Long popular with coastal-cruising yachters, Conanicut Island's shoreline has tight harbors, but no sandy beaches to attract day-trippers, as Newport does. With only one main street and just a few restaurants and shops concentrated along it, Jamestown may be said to enjoy the best of both worlds: The commerce and activity of Newport just a bridge away, and the peace and tranquility of small-town life in an unspoiled natural area.

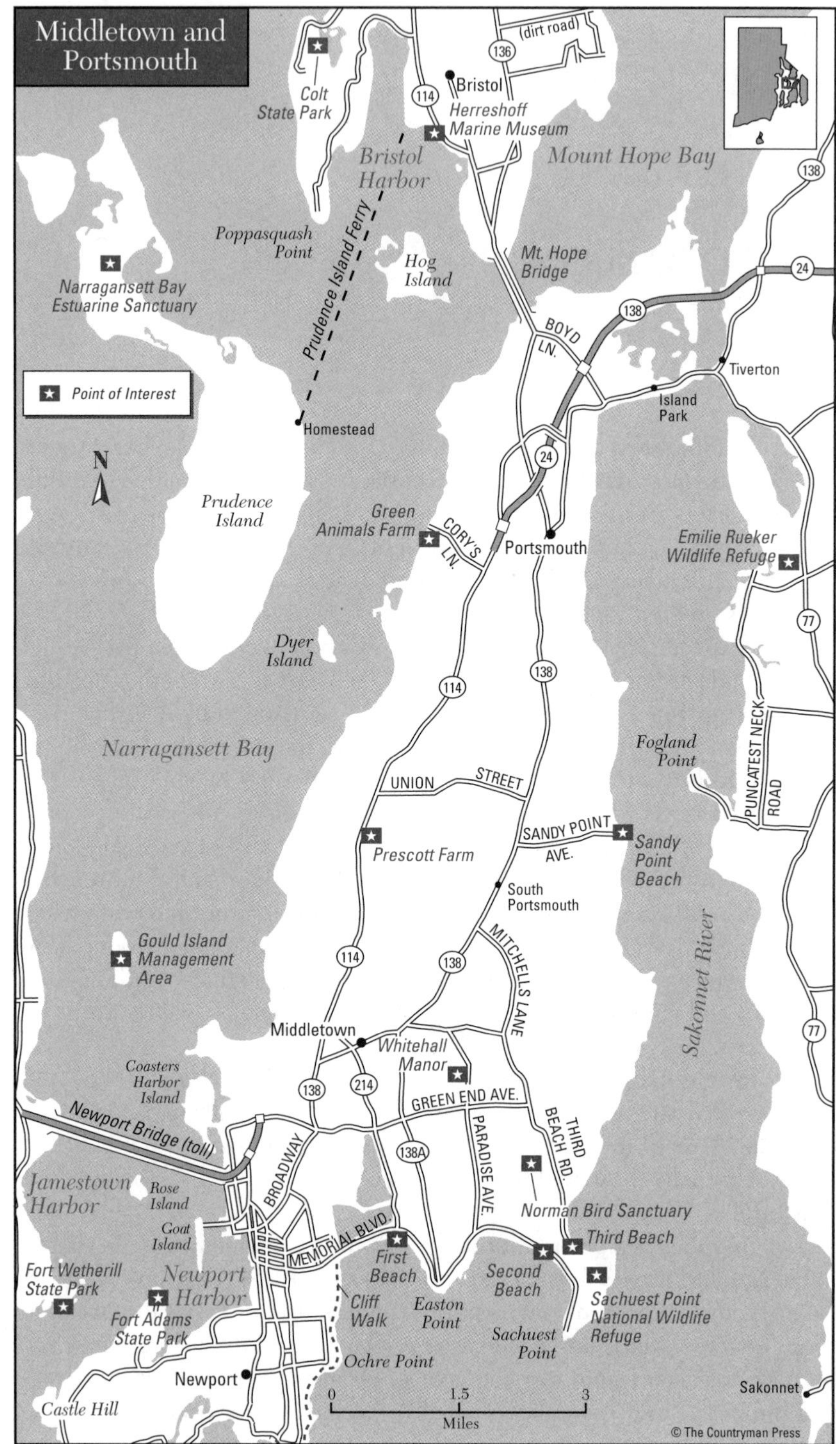
Middletown and Portsmouth
Point of Interest
Colt State Park
Bristol
Herreshoff Marine Museum
Bristol Harbor
Mount Hope Bay
Poppasquash Point
Prudence Island Ferry
Hog Island
Mt. Hope Bridge
Narragansett Bay Estuarine Sanctuary
Boyd Ln.
Tiverton
Island Park
Homestead
Prudence Island
Green Animals Farm
Cory's Ln.
Portsmouth
Emilie Rueker Wildlife Refuge
Dyer Island
Narragansett Bay
Fogland Point
Union Street
Puncatest Neck Road
Sandy Point Ave.
Sandy Point Beach
Prescott Farm
South Portsmouth
Mitchells Lane
Sakonnet River
Gould Island Management Area
Middletown
Whitehall Manor
Coasters Harbor Island
Green End Ave.
Newport Bridge (toll)
Broadway
Paradise Ave.
Third Beach Rd.
Jamestown Harbor
Rose Island
Goat Island
Memorial Blvd.
Norman Bird Sanctuary
Third Beach
First Beach
Second Beach
Fort Wetherill State Park
Newport Harbor
Fort Adams State Park
Cliff Walk
Easton Point
Sachuest Point
Sachuest Point National Wildlife Refuge
Ochre Point
Newport
Castle Hill
Sakonnet
0 1.5 3 Miles
© The Countryman Press

GUIDANCE Information about Middletown (and all Aquidneck) is available at the Newport **Gateway Center** (401-849-8098; 1-800-326-6030; http://gonewport.com), 23 America's Cup Avenue, Newport.

GETTING THERE *By car:* Directly to the north and east of Newport, Middletown is accessible via half a dozen or more routes. From Newport, follow Broadway north to One Mile Corner, which becomes Middletown's West Main Road. Or you can follow Memorial Boulevard east, past Easton's (First) Beach, and cross the line at the bottom of the long hill. From the north (Portsmouth), RI 114 and 138 (West Main and East Main Roads, respectively) lead to the town border.

MEDICAL EMERGENCY The statewide emergency number is **911.**

Newport County Medical Treatment Office (401-847-4950), 67 Valley Road, is a walk-in clinic for minor emergencies and medical complaints. Open Monday through Friday 8–8, Saturday and Sunday 9–5.

✷ To See

HISTORIC HOMES **Prescott Farm** (401-849-7300; www.newportrestoration.org), 2009 West Main Road (RI 114). Open May through October, daily 10–4. Small fee. Shortly before midnight on July 9, 1777, a band of 40 raiding colonists led by Colonel William Barton landed their rowboats on the west shore of British-controlled Aquidneck Island. Splitting into five groups, they sneaked up to a farmhouse owned by Mrs. John Overing, captured the guard, and burst inside. When they left minutes later, they took with them (still in his nightclothes) General William Prescott, commander of the British occupying troops and the highest-ranking prisoner taken during the Revolution. Prescott was later exchanged for a captured American general. Barton was awarded a sword by Congress, and the house in Middletown has been known as Prescott Farm ever since. In addition to the house itself, the farm complex (owned by Doris Duke's Restoration Foundation) includes a late-18th-century grain mill moved to the site several years ago. There's also a guardhouse and a country store that offers cornmeal ground at the mill.

Whitehall (401-846-3116; http://whitehallmuseumhouse.org), 311 Berkeley Avenue, off Green End Avenue. Open July 1 through Labor Day, daily except Monday, 10–5; other times by appointment. Admission: adults $5, children free. This is a fine Colonial farmhouse built in 1729 by the British philosopher and cleric Dean George Berkeley (pronounced *Barkley*). Berkeley, later to become bishop of Cloyne, Ireland, arrived in Newport that year accompanied by his bride and with a scheme to open up commerce and bring religion to the "savages" of Bermuda. "The town of Newport," he wrote home, "contains six thousand souls, and is the most thriving place in all America for bigness." While waiting for the king to grant him £20,000 for his mission, Berkeley preached at Trinity Church, helped found the Redwood Library, and made Whitehall a center for religious and philosophical discussion. The dean gave up his dream after three years and returned to Ireland; his house was taken over by a succession of tavernkeepers, served as quarters for British troops during the Revolution, and eventually fell into disrepair. It is now owned by the Rhode Island chapter of the National Society of Colonial Dames of America.

✷ To Do

GOLF **Newport National Golf Course** (401-848-9690; www.newportnational.com), 324 Mitchell's Lane. Newest 18-hole course on Aquidneck Island.

HELICOPTER RIDES **Bird's Eye View** (401-843-8687; 1-877-914-8687; www.riaerial.com), 211 Airport Access Road. Jeff Codman takes up to two people on scenic rides starting at about $59 per person.

HORSEBACK RIDING **Newport Equestrian Center** (401-848-5440; http://newportequestrian.com), 287 Third Beach Road. Trail rides.

SAILBOARDING **Island Sports** (401-846-4421; http://islandsports.com), 86 Aquidneck Avenue. Located near the beaches, just down the hill from Newport, Island Sports rents rigs and also offers two levels of lessons: a two-hour introductory session and an advanced course, six hours over two days. Lessons are given either at Third Beach in Middletown or at Fort Adams State Park in Newport.

SWIMMING **Sachuest Beach** (Second Beach) in Middletown is the most popular beach in the area, with a long expanse of dunes and sand running between Hanging Rock and a nature preserve on Sachuest Point. To get there, follow Memorial Boulevard or Aquidneck Avenue to Purgatory Road. In-season parking fees are $10 weekdays, $20 weekends.

Third Beach, off Third Beach Road in Middletown. Smaller but less crowded than Second Beach, this beach is ideal for younger swimmers, with little or no surf and warmer waters from the mouth of the Sakonnet River. Parking is $10 to $20 in-season.

✷ Green Space

Norman Bird Sanctuary (401-846-2577; www.normanbirdsanctuary.org), 583 Third Beach Road. Open daily 9–5; no dogs. Admission: adults $6, children $3. The sanctuary is a 450-acre bird and wildlife habitat with 7 miles of nature trails open to the public. There are usually a few local species in captivity (while on the mend), but everything else you're lucky enough to see will be in the wild. There are regular Sunday-morning bird walks and guided tours by appointment for groups of 10 or more. One of the big attractions here is Hanging Rock, a striking mass of rock 50 feet high that overlooks the Atlantic. Dean Berkeley is said to have written part of his anti-freethinker treatise *Alciphron* here, in a recess now called Bishop Berkeley's Chair.

Purgatory Chasm, Purgatory Road, on the cliff overlooking Second Beach. The chasm is a narrow but deep cleft in the rocky cliff that was created by thousands of years of erosion by the sea below. Or was it? A Narragansett legend says it came about when the devil repeatedly chopped away at the head of an uncooperative Native American maiden. There are countless other stories about lovers who dared each other to hop across the fissure. Don't try it—it's more than 160 feet straight down.

Sachuest Point National Wildlife Refuge (401-364-9124; www.fws.gov/sachuestpoint), 769 Sachuest Point Road, past Second Beach. Open daily dawn to dusk. This 242-acre refuge offers a little of everything—salt marsh, beach, grassy woodlands—with 3 miles of hiking trails, some bordering dramatic surf-splashed rocks. Good place for viewing migratory shorebirds. As in any coastal grassy area, dress sensibly to discourage Lyme-disease-bearing deer ticks, which are prevalent here. Dogs must be leashed.

✷ Lodging

HOTELS AND MOTELS 🐾 **Bay Willows Inn** (401-847-8400; 1-800-838-5642; www.baywillowsinn.com), 1225 Aquidneck Avenue. ($–$$) Twenty-one motel-style rooms, including some that are pet-friendly.

♿ **Courtyard by Marriott** (401-849-8000; reservations: 1-800-321-2211), 9 Commerce Drive, off West Main Road. ($$–$$$) The Courtyard chain is a no-frills Marriott operation, originally designed to attract the business crowd. The Middletown facility, with 148 rooms, gets its share of families as well. The restaurant serves breakfast only.

🐾 **Econo Lodge** (401-849-2718) 1359 West Main Road (RI 114). ($$) This budget hotel offers 55 rooms on the outskirts of town, less than 3 miles from downtown Newport.

Hampton Inn & Suites (401-848-6555; 1-800-426-7866), 317 West Main Road (RI 114). ($$–$$$) Hamptons are midpriced hotels of the Hilton chain that cater to businesspeople and any traveler who likes a brand-name property. Indoor pool, convenient to Newport.

🐾 ♿ **Howard Johnson's** (401-849-2000; 1-800-446-4656), 351 West Main Road, near Two Mile Corner. ($$–$$$) Standard HoJo, with indoor pool and sauna, tennis courts, and an adjoining restaurant. Breakfast is included with your room Monday through Friday.

Inn at Newport Beach (401-846-0310; 1-800-655-1778), Memorial Boulevard (east end at junction of Aquidneck Avenue and Purgatory Road, on Easton's Beach). ($$–$$$) Expansive inn right on the beach is a member of the Historic Inns of America group. It's an unbeatable location for those who want to be able to walk to the beach and still stay no more than a mile or so from downtown Newport. Room includes continental breakfast.

🐾 **Knights Inn** (401-324-6200; 1-888-534-9698; www.knightsinn.com), 240 Aquidneck Avenue. ($$) Forty rooms (some pet-friendly), all with an ocean view; continental breakfast. Convenient to the beach.

♿ **Newport Inn & Spa** (401-846-7600; www.newportspa.com), 936 West Main Road. ($$–$$$) Just a few minutes north of the Newport city line, the remodeled motor inn has 40 rooms, a heated indoor pool, exercise room, restaurant, and lounge. In-season shuttle into Newport.

♿ **Royal Plaza Hotel** (401-846-3555; 1-800-825-7072; www.royalplazahotel.net), 425 East Main Road (RI 138). ($$–$$$) The 117-room Royal Plaza caters to vacationers as well as business travelers.

Sandpiper Cottages (401-847-9726; 401-862-9874), 985 East Main Road. ($) Open April 15 through November 15. Old-fashioned motor court with individual cabins.

Sea Whale Motel (401-846-7071; 1-888-257-4096; www.seawhale.com), 150 Aquidneck Avenue. ($$) There are just 16 rooms in this motel, but all overlook Easton's Pond. The motel itself is within walking distance of First Beach.

🐾 **Travelodge** (401-849-4700; 1-800-862-2006; www.travelodge.com), 1185 West Main Road (RI 114). ($$–$$$) Several miles north of Newport on RI 114, with 70-plus rooms. Outdoor pool; some rooms pet-friendly.

CAMPGROUNDS **Meadowlark Recreational Vehicle Park** (401-846-9455), 132 Prospect Avenue, off RI 138A. Hookups and picnic tables provided on 40 trailer sites.

Middletown Campground (401-846-6273), Second Beach. Write: Town Hall, 350 East Main Road, Middletown. This popular town-run spot right across from the beach offers 36 trailer sites with toilets, hot showers, and sewer hookups.

Paradise Mobile Home Park (401-847-1500; www.newportcamping.com), 459 Aquidneck

Avenue (RI 138A). Write: 265 Prospect Avenue, Middletown. Trailer sites for 16 self-contained units. Full hookups.

✷ Where to Eat

DINING OUT ♿ **Atlantic Beach Club** (401-847-2750; www.atlanticbeachclub.com), 55 Purgatory Road, at the far end of First Beach. ($$) Open daily for lunch and dinner. A popular beach hangout in summer, the Atlantic also has gained many fans for its fare, emphasizing pasta dishes and fresh seafood (stuffed sole, shrimp scampi, broiled scallops), but with some meat entrées as well. Try one of the big salads, filling enough to suffice for lunch. Excellent desserts are made fresh daily.

♿ **Coddington Brewing Company** (401-847-6690; www.coddbrew.com), 210 Coddington Highway. ($–$$) Open daily for lunch and dinner. A brewpub, this joint offers a menu of beer-compatible food and lots of freshly brewed beer.

Gold's Wood-Fired Grill & Café (401-849-3377; www.goldsgrill.com), 21 Valley Road. ($$) The stylish but casual atmosphere here draws both locals and tourists for excellent wood-grilled pizzas as well as sophisticated entrées and salads. Lunch and dinner daily except Monday; breakfast on weekends from 7.

♿ **Sea Shai** (401-849-5180; www.seashai.com), 747 Aquidneck Avenue. ($$) Open daily for lunch and dinner. Pleasant restaurant with a varied Japanese and Korean menu. Popular with local diners for its sushi bar.

EATING OUT ♿ **Anthony's Seafood Restaurant** (401-848-5058; www.anthonysseafood.net), 963 Aquidneck Avenue. ($) Open 11–8 weekdays, until 8:30 on weekends. Formerly located on the Newport waterfront, this is casual shore dining-hall seafood fare minus the shore. Small outside dining area, too. You know the food's fresh here—the restaurant adjoins Anthony's seafood market.

Atlantic Grille (401-849-4440; www.atlanticgrille.com), 91 Aquidneck Avenue. ($) Open daily for breakfast, lunch, and dinner, with great lobster deals Monday to Wednesday. Recently renovated and expanded, this is a popular spot with locals and is situated close to Easton's (First) Beach.

Flo's (401-847-8141; www.flosclamshack.net), 4 Wave Avenue, at the base of Memorial Boulevard across from Newport's Easton's (First) Beach. ($) The original Flo's Clam Shack is up in Portsmouth. This one is the more expansive of the two, offering indoor seating and full seafood dinners. Very popular; consistently ranked one of the best places around for fried clams and lobster rolls.

Rhea's Family Restaurant (401-841-5560; www.rheasinn.com), 120 West Main Road, between

One and Two Mile Corners. ($–$$) Open daily for lunch and dinner. Rhea's delivers just what its name suggests—simple, uncomplicated family seafood and meat dishes. The menu may state "pasta and meatballs," but it's really just good old spaghetti and meatballs.

🏵 ✐ ♿ **Tito's Cantina** (401-849-4222; www.titos.com), 651 West Main Road. ($) Good selection of traditional Tex-Mex favorites and a special "Little Amigos" menu. Tito sells his own brand of tortilla chips and salsa, which are worth taking home.

✷ Selective Shopping

🏵 **Christmas Tree Shop** (401-841-5100; www.christmastreeshops.com), Aquidneck Shopping Center, just past Two Mile Corner. One of a chain of wildly popular discount stores that began on Cape Cod some years back. The shop gets its merchandise from surplus, discontinued lines, and distress sales. Some surprisingly good stuff, including brand names, at very good prices.

Newport Vineyards and Winery (401-848-5161; www.newportvineyards.com), 909 East Main Road (RI 138). Open daily. Formerly Vinland, which began with plantings in 1977, the vineyard offers local wines, which include a vidal blanc, Seyval blanc, Viking red, and other varieties. Visitors can sample the wines at this retail store and also arrange for a tour of the winery. You can even buy wine here on Sundays, because it falls under the category of "farm produce."

BOOKSTORE **Island Books** (401-849-2665; www.islandbooksri.wordpress.com), 575 East Main Road (RI 138). One of the better new-book shops for browsing on the island. Hard-to-find literature as well as good sections of art, cooking, and children's books, both fiction and nonfiction.

FARM STANDS **Aquidneck Growers' Market** (401-848-0099; www.aquidneckgrowersmarket.org), 909 East Main Road (RI 138). Open June through mid-October, Saturday 9–1. Located at Newport Vineyards, this popular market has dozens of vendors selling everything from artisan breads and pastries to organically grown vegetables and fruits.

Simmons Farm Stand (401-848-9910), 91 Greene Lane. Farm produce, fresh eggs, and flowers at this family-run operation.

Sweet Berry Farm (401-847-3912; www.sweetberryfarmri.com), 19 Third Beach Road. Breezy, hilltop location overlooks fields where you can pick your own strawberries, raspberries, and more in-season. Fresh herbs and baked goods, too.

GARDEN CENTER **Chaves Gardens** (401-846-9623), 935 East Main Road (at the traffic sig-

Kim Grant

NEWPORT VINEYARDS AND WINERY HAS BEEN IN BUSINESS SINCE 1977.

nal). Flowers, plants, and garden tools and accessories.

✷ Special Events

Early October: **Harvest Fair** (401-846-2577), Norman Bird Sanctuary, 583 Third Beach Road. This annual event is designed to resemble a country fair, with hayrides, sack races, a rope walk, and greased-pole climbing (or slipping). There are baked goods and vegetable competitions and lots of locally made crafts and produce for sale. Continuous entertainment from a slew of fine local performers adds to the fun. You can tour the grounds while at the fair; proceeds help support this important bird and wildlife sanctuary.

PORTSMOUTH

Oldest (1638) and largest (23.3 square miles) of the Aquidneck communities, Portsmouth at one time was the most populated of Rhode Island's towns. Called Pocasset by the Narragansetts, its current name was proposed by residents a year after their arrival and approved by the General Court at Newport in 1640. Now a suburban bedroom community, Portsmouth once relied on agriculture, and to a lesser extent fishing, for its existence. Portsmouth also operated some coal mines in the north part of town during the 19th and early 20th centuries, but the coal was extremely hard and difficult to ignite, and it became an early casualty as the demand for the fossil fuel waned.

GETTING THERE *By car:* From Providence take either RI 114 or RI 138 to the Mount Hope Bridge in Bristol. Also accessible from the north via RI 24, which connects with a second bridge leading onto the island at its northern end. From Newport and points south, both RI 114 and 138 (West and East Main Roads) are the paths to, and through, Portsmouth.

MEDICAL EMERGENCY The statewide emergency number is **911.**

✷ To See

HISTORIC BUILDING **Portsmouth Historical Society** (401-683-9178), in the Old Union Church, East Main Road and Union Street. Open Memorial Day through Columbus Day, Sunday 2–4. Free. There are several interesting historical buildings on this site, including what may be one of the oldest one-room schoolhouses in the country, the original Portsmouth Town Hall, and the Old Union Church, home to a 19th-century fundamentalist sect whose church provided a forum for such abolitionists as Julia Ward Howe and William Ellery Channing. The original church was built in 1821, burned, and was rebuilt during the 1860s. Recently restored, it also houses an eclectic array of Portsmouth artifacts, including coal fossils from the town's once-operating coal mines, stone tools and arrowheads from area Native American tribes, and a large collection of possessions from Julia Howe's Union Street house, including her writing desk and one of her lace caps. The former town hall contains a carriage collection and old farm implements, including an apple press. The schoolhouse was started in 1716 and completed in 1723.

HISTORIC SITES **Black Regiment Memorial,** at the junction of RI 114 and RI 24. During the battle of Rhode Island, in which Continental troops were attempting to retreat after an unsuccessful siege of Newport, the Americans had to hold off several attacks by the British while awaiting boats to remove them from Aquidneck. It was here on August 29, 1778, that the First Rhode Island Regiment, composed entirely of slaves earning their freedom through military service, whipped the Hessian allies of the British. Lafayette later called the battle "the best-fought action of the war" and wept because he had missed most of it. The retreating regiment inflicted heavy casualties on the enemy in rearguard fighting without losing a single soldier. A flagpole and a stone monument now mark the spot where America's first black troops earned their glory.

Hessian Hole, Cory's Lane, on the grounds of Portsmouth Abbey. After the battle of Rhode Island, according to legend, 30 dead Hessian soldiers (Germans fighting as mercenaries for the British) were buried in a pit just west of where the abbey now stands. Nearby flows Bloody Run Brook, so named because it supposedly ran red for days after the burial. There's some doubt about where the actual burial site is, but you may want to follow the brook and look for a noticeable depression in the land.

Portsmouth Abbey Chapel (401-683-2000), Cory's Lane. Open to the public daily 8–4:30; call ahead for a tour. The Chapel of St. Gregory at this Benedictine abbey and prep school is beautifully contemporary. Designed by Pietro Belluschi, it contains a wire sculpture by Richard Lippold.

WINERY **Greenvale Vineyards** (401-847-3777; www.greenvale.com), 582 Wapping Road. Open Thursday through Sunday noon–5 for free tours and tastings.

✱ To Do

FOR FAMILIES ✐ **Green Animals** (401-683-1267; http://newportmansions.org), 380 Cory's Lane, off RI 114. Open daily April through October. Admission: adults $11, children to age 17 $4. This splendid topiary garden, started by Thomas Brayton about 1880, contains some 80 sculpted trees and shrubs, formal flower beds, and fruit and vegetable patches. The animal figures—carved from California privet—are the best

Tom Gannon

GREEN ANIMALS TOPIARY GARDEN

part. There's a camel, a giraffe, a bear, and many others to pick out as you wander down intricate pathways. A garden shop sells various herbs, plants, and flowers. The adjacent Brayton House overlooking Narragansett Bay contains a child's Victorian toy museum. Green Animals is a property of the Preservation Society of Newport County.

GOLF **Green Valley Country Club** (401-847-9543; www.greenvalleyccofri.com), 371 Union Street, between RI 138 and RI 114. Eighteen holes, public driving range.

Montaup Country Club (401-683-0955), Anthony Road, Portsmouth, at the northern end of Aquidneck Island and adjacent to Sakonnet River Bridge on RI 24. Eighteen holes.

HORSEBACK RIDING **Glen Farm** (401-846-5321; www.glenfarmstables.com), 163 Glen Farm Road, off East Main Road. Indoor/outdoor riding; jumping and riding lessons.

Sandy Point Stables (401-849-3958; www.sandypointstables.com), Sandy Point Lane, off East Main Road. Indoor and outdoor rings; hunt-seat instruction.

SWIMMING ✐ **Sandy Point Beach,** Sandy Point Avenue, off RI 138, about 15 minutes from Newport. This is a pleasant family beach with no surf and warm Sakonnet River water. Sandy Point opens Memorial Day weekend and closes Labor Day, with lifeguards on duty 9–6 daily. Parking fees are $7 weekdays, $12 weekends. There are restrooms with an outside shower, picnic benches, and charcoal grills. No concession stand, but a snack truck stops by regularly.

✷ Green Space

Narragansett Bay National Estuarine Research Reserve (401-789-3094; www.nbnerr.org), Prudence Island. North and South Prudence Islands, in upper Narragansett Bay, are part of a three-island research preserve. About 60 percent of Prudence, some 2,100 acres, is part of the reserve, which offers hiking and naturalist programs to the public in summer. You can get to Prudence by private boat (some public moorings are available in Potter's Cove on the northeast side) or by ferry from Bristol (401-245-8303). However, Prudence Island, which has a large deer population, is prime deer tick territory, and visitors should dress accordingly to avoid the possibility of contracting Lyme disease.

✷ Lodging

MOTEL **Founder's Brook Motel** (401-683-1244; www.foundersbrookmotelandsuites.com), 314 Boyd's Lane, at the junction of RI 138 and 24. ($$ rooms; $$–$$$ suites with kitchenette) Good location at the north end of Aquidneck, near the Sakonnet River Bridge. The suites, which have a foldout bed in the living room, are handy for couples traveling with children.

CAMPGROUND **Melville Ponds Campground** (401-682-2424; www.portsmouthri.com), 181 Bradford Avenue, off RI 114. Town-run campground has spots for 66 trailers, 57 tents; full hookups and facilities.

✷ Where to Eat

DINING OUT ♿ **Fifteen Point Road** (401-683-3138; www.15pointroad.com), 15 Point Road, Island Park. ($$$) Open Tuesday through Sunday for dinner. Locally popular restaurant overlooks the Sakonnet River. The cuisine is classic American; seafood dishes, especially the lobster casserole, are the way to go.

Melville Grille (401-683-4400; www.melvillegrille.com), 1 Lagoon Road, at Bend Boat Basin. ($$) Open daily except Sunday for lunch and dinner. Situated as it is between two of the largest marinas in Rhode Island, Melville Grille attracts a diverse clientele, from former navy personnel (this area of Portsmouth was home to a torpedo station in World War II) to international sailboat racers. Hamburgers and sandwiches to full dinners.

EATING OUT **Cindy's Country Cafe** (401-683-5134; www.cindys

countrycafe.com), 1324 West Main Road, just past Melville. ($) Breakfast and lunch daily. Hearty home cooking/diner fare at very reasonable prices. Breakfast runs from 6 to about 11:30 and involves the usual egg and pancake dishes as well as combination plates such as the The Portuguese, which consists of chourico (a Portuguese sausage), eggs, and cheese, with beans and home fries. Lunch plates include great soups and such sandwiches as tuna melts and The Popeye—a cheeseburger with spinach.

♿ **Flo's** (401-847-8141; www.flosclamshack.net), Park Avenue, Island Park. ($) Open Thursday through Sunday in summer. CLOSED HURRICANES, according to its sign. A classic clam shack by the shore that draws huge crowds in-season. You place your order, receive a stone with your number on it, and wait as impatiently as a child for your clams, stuffies, or fish-and-chips. You can eat them in the car or take them across the street to the seawall overlooking Sakonnet River.

♿ **Food Works** (401-683-4664), 2461 East Main Road. ($) Open daily for breakfast and lunch. Sandwiches, salads, light lunches. Outdoor patio.

♿ **North End Pizzeria** (401-683-6633), 3030 East Main Road. ($) This former pizza joint has an expanded Italian menu in cozy quarters in Portsmouth Village.

♿ **Reidy's Family Restaurant** (401-683-9802), 3351 East Main Road, RI 138, just before Island Park. ($) Open daily from breakfast until 8 PM. Club sandwiches, meat loaf dinners, fish-and-chips, all done in good diner style and served at the counter or booths. This is the kind of place where you find yourself ordering a slice of chocolate cream pie for dessert. Raucous and informal, as the waitstaff and regulars engage in friendly banter.

Steve's Famous Pizza (401-683-1505), 2460 East Main Road, on Quaker Hill. ($) Pizza, subs, and sandwiches as well as a good feta-covered Greek salad that serves two.

✷ Selective Shopping

Corner Consignment (401-683-1771), 980 East Main Road. Rated highly by thrift-shop devotees, Corner Consignment carries men's, women's, and children's clothing and also jewelry.

Eagles Nest (401-683-3500), 3101 East Main Road, just north of Portsmouth Village. Open daily. Several floors of antique furniture, jewelry, knickknacks, and that stuff from the 1950s they like to call "collectibles."

Ma Goetzinger's (401-683-9400), 2918 East Main Road. Comfortable, stylish women's clothing and Dansko shoes are attractively displayed in an antique farmhouse in Portsmouth Village. A destination shop for its devotees.

FARM STANDS The following roadside farm stands offer fresh produce in-season: **W. De Castro & Sons Farm** (401-683-4688), 1780 East Main Road; **Mello's Flower Center** (401-683-6262), 444 Boyd's Lane, between East and West Main Roads at the Sakonnet Bridge; **Stone Wall Stand,** Quaker Hill, East Main Road (look for its sign on a tree); and **Quonset View Farm** (401-683-1254), 895 Middle Road, a pick-your-own berry farm, in-season.

GARDEN CENTERS **Island Garden Shop** (401-683-2231; www.igsinc.com), 54 Bristol Ferry Road, off West Main Road near the Mount Hope Bridge. Perennials, annuals, shrubs—this is one of the largest and best garden centers in the region.

Mello's Flower Center (401-683-6262), 444 Boyd's Lane. Nice selection of annuals and perennials, plus garden gizmos and adornments.

✷ Special Events

End of June: **Annual Church Fair** (401-849-4332), St. Barnabas Church, 1697 East Main Road.

July: **Glen Farm Polo Productions** (401-847-7090; www.nptpolo.com), 163 Glen Farm Road, off East Main Road. Weekend polo matches between international teams. **4-H Country Fair** (401-847-0287), Glen Road, off RI 138.

August: **Annual Lawn Party** (401-846-9700), St. Mary's Episcopal Church, 324 East Main Road.

JAMESTOWN

Jamestown (Conanicut) is Newport's neighbor island to the west, connected to Aquidneck Island by the Newport (or Pell) Bridge and to South County by the Jamestown-Verrazzano Bridge. The island was bought in 1656 by William Coddington, Benedict Arnold, and other Newport settlers, incorporated as a town in 1678, and named in honor of King James II. Among the early residents were Quaker farmers and shepherds, and the island also had its share of shipwrights, sailors, and privateers. Captain Kidd spent much time here visiting with fellow pirate Thomas Paine and supposedly buried some of his loot in the area. He was lured to Boston in 1699, where he was arrested, taken to England, tried, and hanged. His treasure has never been found.

The island's strategic importance, at the mouth of Narragansett Bay, was recognized early, and it was fortified by the colonists in 1776. British troops invaded the island in December 1776, burned many of the buildings, and held possession until the French allies of the colonists arrived in 1778. The British continued to bombard Jamestown periodically, and the colonists, in turn, sniped at passing British ships. During the Gilded Age, Jamestown, like the shoreside communities of South County, became something of a secondary resort, playing host to summer visitors who were either unable or unwilling to make their way in Newport society. Many of these families were from Philadelphia, and their descendants still summer on the island. Until 1969 Conanicut was connected to Newport only by ferry service, and the island retains its sense of separateness, of being its own community.

Jamestown is one of the few Rhode Island communities that hasn't blocked off its waterfront with development. Conanicus Avenue, which leads into town from the Newport Bridge, brings you to the East Ferry Landing, where the harbor is in full view. You can walk the docks, take a bench by the seaside, and enjoy an ice cream from a nearby shop. On a summer afternoon or evening, it's hard to do better than this.

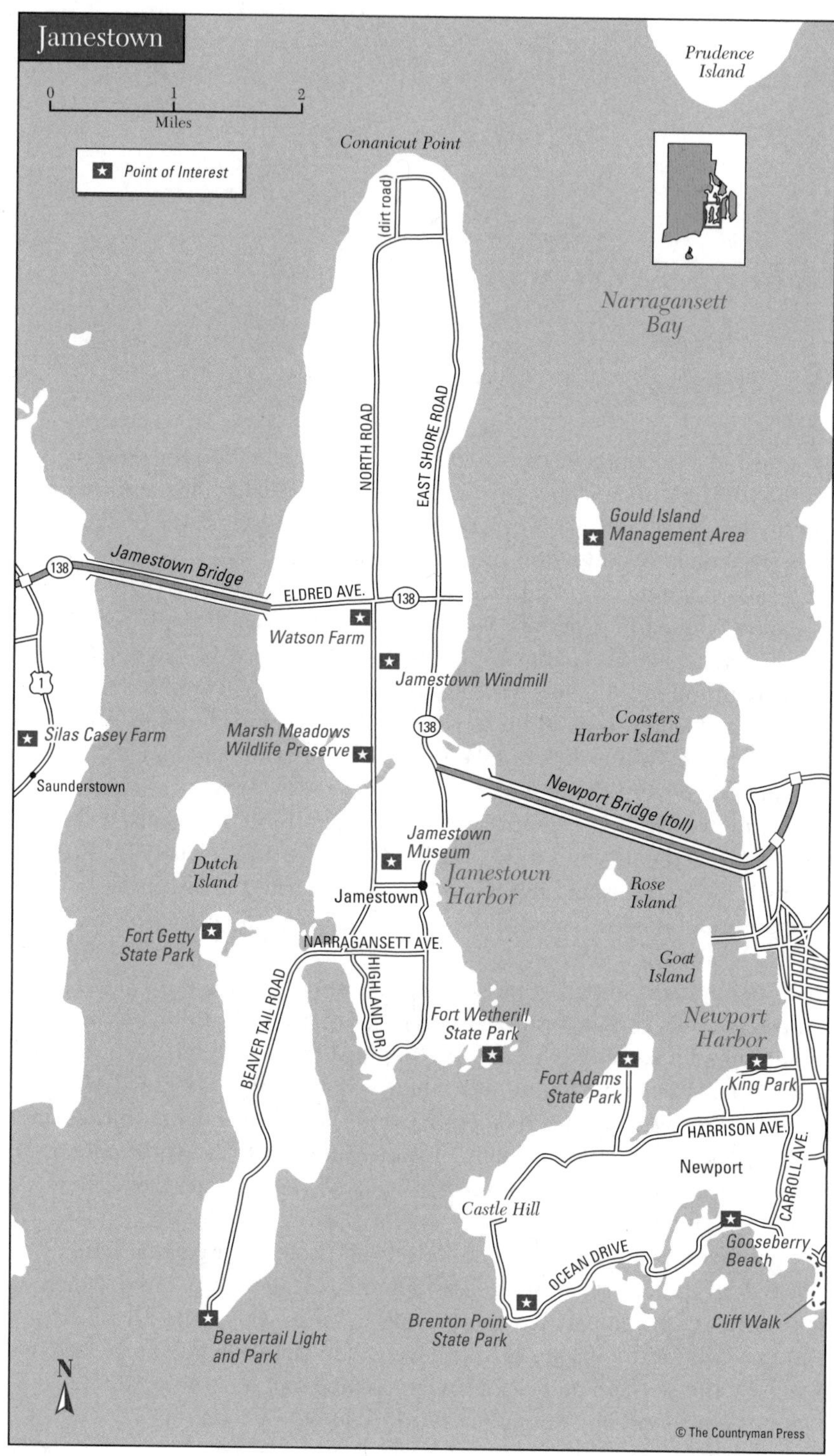
Jamestown
0
1
2
Miles
Point of Interest
Prudence Island
Conanicut Point
(dirt road)
Narragansett Bay
NORTH ROAD
EAST SHORE ROAD
Gould Island Management Area
138
Jamestown Bridge
ELDRED AVE.
138
Watson Farm
Jamestown Windmill
1
Silas Casey Farm
Saunderstown
Marsh Meadows Wildlife Preserve
138
Coasters Harbor Island
Newport Bridge (toll)
Jamestown Museum
Jamestown Harbor
Dutch Island
Jamestown
Rose Island
Fort Getty State Park
NARRAGANSETT AVE.
Goat Island
BEAVER TAIL ROAD
HIGHLAND DR.
Fort Wetherill State Park
Newport Harbor
Fort Adams State Park
King Park
HARRISON AVE.
CARROLL AVE.
Newport
Castle Hill
OCEAN DRIVE
Gooseberry Beach
Brenton Point State Park
Cliff Walk
Beavertail Light and Park
N
© The Countryman Press

Katherine Imbrie

A WEATHERED SHACK AT QUIET DUTCH HARBOR IN JAMESTOWN

GETTING THERE *By car:* Jamestown is reached via RI 138 from east and west. From the west, the new Jamestown-Verrazzano Bridge links the island to mainland North Kingstown. To the east, the Newport Bridge (officially the Claiborne Pell Bridge, for the state's venerable former senator) connects the town to Newport. The toll is $4 per car (accepts EZ Pass), and the view of Narragansett Bay is spectacular.

By ferry: The 45-passenger, open-deck **Jamestown Ferry** (401-423-9900; http://conanicutmarina.com) is a great way to get over to the island from Newport, or vice versa. The short, scenic trip, with stops at Fort Adams and Rose Island, doubles as the best deal going for a harbor tour. An all-day pass is $18. The ferry travels between Ferry Wharf, right in the heart of Jamestown Village, and Bowen's Landing in Market Square, Newport, Memorial Day through mid-September.

MEDICAL EMERGENCY The statewide emergency number is **911.** **Jamestown Rescue** is 401-423-0062.

✷ To See

Beavertail Lighthouse Museum (401-423-3270; http://beavertaillight.org), Beavertail Road, at the southern tip of Conanicut. Donations accepted. Open mid-June through Labor Day, daily 10–4; weekends spring and fall. One of the oldest lighthouses on the Atlantic Coast (the original was built in 1749), this still-active beacon that marks the way into Narragansett Bay has spawned its own museum, with displays and artifacts depicting the history of lighthouses in the region. Exhibits include models of 33 Rhode Island lighthouses and various artifacts, including the lens used at Beavertail from 1897 to 1991 and a vent ball used to divert heat and fumes from the lantern room in the days when beacons were fired with whale oil and kerosene. The museum is housed in the former assistant lighthouse keeper's cottage (you can't ascend the existing granite tower, built in 1856), and the view from Beavertail Point—considered one of the best ocean vistas in the state—alone is worth the trip.

Jamestown Fire Memorial (401-423-0062; http://jamestownfd.com), next to the fire department, 50 Narragansett Avenue. Open Monday through Friday 8–3 (check with the fire department to see who has the key). Interesting display of the town's early firefighting equipment, including a horse-drawn pumper.

Jamestown Museum (401-423-7280), 92 Narragansett. Open early June through Labor Day, Tuesday through Saturday 1–4. Free. This tiny museum contains memorabilia from the 300-year-old Jamestown ferry system, the island's only link to Newport until the Newport Bridge opened in 1969 (still a traumatic event for islanders on both sides). There are also other Jamestown historical items.

VIEW OF NEWPORT BRIDGE FROM A JAMESTOWN FARM

Katherine Imbrie

Katherine Imbrie

THE JAMESTOWN WINDMILL

Jamestown Windmill (401-423-0784), North Road. Open mid-June through mid-September, Wednesday through Sunday 1–4. Free, but donations welcome. The mill, which operated between 1789 and 1896, was called a smock mill for its appearance, based on a popular English design of the 16th and 17th centuries. Rhode Island once was dotted with these mills, but this is the last in working condition. Inside, you can view the gears, the stone for grinding corn, and the granary.

Sydney L. Wright Museum (401-423-7281; http://jamestownri.com), 26 North Road, in the Jamestown Philomenian Library. Open Monday through Saturday during library hours. Native American artifacts from prehistoric to colonial times are on display. When the Europeans arrived, Jamestown was inhabited by the Narragansett tribe, who used the island as a summer camp. Archaeologists are still researching the many centuries of Narragansett life on the island.

✱ To Do

FOR FAMILIES ✐ **Jamestown Playground,** North Road, near the public library. Imaginative and award-winning playground made from recycled materials. An environmentally friendly place that is also a lot of fun for kids.

Katherine Imbrie

FARMHOUSE AT WATSON FARM

Watson Farm (401-423-0005; http://historicnewengland.org), 455 North Road. Open June through October, Tuesday, Thursday, and Sunday 1–5. Admission: adults $4, children $2. Run by the Society for the Preservation of New England Antiquities, this is a working farm complete with sheep, cows, and agricultural equipment. A mid-1800s farmhouse was relocated here, and the farm, 280 acres of rural haven, offers views of the sea in several directions.

HAPPY DENIZENS OF WATSON FARM

Katherine Imbrie

GOLF Jamestown Country Club (401-423-9930; www.jamestowngolf.com), 245 Conanicus Avenue, near the Newport Bridge. Public course offers nine holes in a nice island setting. One of the best golf bargains in the area.

SWIMMING Mackerel Cove, Beavertail Road. Conanicut's only town-run beach is a family beach at the tip of a cove and fairly well protected from waves. Parking and entrance fee for nonresidents.

✷ Green Space

Beavertail State Park (http://riparks.com), Beavertail Road. Lots of places to hike, picnic, and just enjoy the scenery in this 153-acre park at the southern tip of Conanicut. Great spot to watch a sunset (or sunrise), and one of the best ocean views you'll find in the Ocean State. Many people pack lawn chairs and picnic food and sit for hours watching the surf on the rocks, a quintessentially Rhode Island experience.

Fort Wetherill State Park (401-423-1771; http://riparks.com), Ocean Street, off East Shore Road. The fort, set on the highest point of the island, overlooks the East Passage of Narragansett Bay (some feel the Sakonnet River is the true East Passage and not a river at all). The first fortification here was Fort Dumpling, built in 1776. The federal government later built Fort Wetherill, parts of which remain. Now run as a state park, the area is in the wild, and it's a good place for hiking, picnicking, and just plain viewing. You can pick out Newport's Trinity Church to the east, Point Judith and the outline of Block Island to the south. Somewhere down along the shore is where Captain Kidd, who stayed here with friend and fellow pirate Thomas Paine in 1699, supposedly buried some of his treasure. Again, beware of deer ticks.

✷ Lodging

INNS **Bay Voyage Inn** (401-423-2100; 1-800-225-3522; www.bayvoyageinn.com), 150 Conanicus Avenue. ($$$–$$$$) Formerly a country house in Newport, this Victorian structure, once called Rhoda-Ridge, was transported across the bay by barge to Conanicut Island in 1899 and renamed Bay Voyage. There are 31 one-bedroom suites, some with a balcony overlooking the harbor, with Pullman kitchen and private bath. Outdoor pool.

East Bay Bed & Breakfast (401-423-0330; 1-800-243-1107; http://eastbaybnb.com), 14 Union Street. ($$) Four comfortable, bright rooms, each with queen-sized bed and private bath, occupy this attractive bed & breakfast inn. Home-cooked breakfast.

CAMPGROUND **Fort Getty Recreation Area** (401-423-7211; www.jamestownri.net), Fort Getty Road. Open Memorial Day through Columbus Day. Good location toward the south end of the island. Sites for 100 trailers, 25 tents; boat ramp.

✷ Where to Eat

DINING OUT **Bay Voyage Inn** (401-423-2100; 1-800-347-8182; www.bayvoyageinn.com), 150 Conanicus Avenue. ($$–$$$) Open daily for dinner. Best known for its bountiful Sunday brunch, which is consistently voted the best in Rhode Island in local polls. The inn's dining room, overlooking the harbor, also dishes out such standbys as filet mignon, rack of lamb, lobster thermidor, and scallops.

Jamestown Fish (401-423-3474; www.jamestownfishri.com), 14 Narragansett Avenue. ($$) New in 2012, this gleaming addition to the island's "restaurant row" along Narragansett Avenue looks promising. Owned by experienced locals, Fish will of course spotlight local seafood, but it will also have a variety of meats on the menu. Open for dinner (perhaps also for lunch during the summer), Fish has an upstairs deck and bar that affords views of the Pell Bridge and Newport, as well as a patio for al fresco dining.

♿ **Jamestown Oyster Bar** (401-423-3380), 22 Narragansett Avenue. ($$) Open daily for lunch and dinner. Probably the most popular dining-out spot in town for local residents, the Oyster Bar serves mostly fresh fish—swordfish, tautog, flounder, tuna—often blackened, always a treat. Burgers, soups, sandwiches, fried calamari, and stuffed quahogs are also available.

♿ **Trattoria Simpatico** (401-423-3731; www.trattoriasimpatico.com), 13 Narragansett Avenue. ($$–$$$) Open daily for lunch and dinner. Classy Italian restaurant that has gained a reputation for consistently excellent food beyond Jamestown. Antipasti include miniature flat-bread pizzas, grilled portobello mushrooms, mussels steamed in tomato broth with wine and olive oil, and duck and radicchio salad. Main dishes include grilled Atlantic salmon, oregano-marinated shrimp, and various pasta/seafood combinations. In warmer weather you can dine out in the yard, on weekends to the accompaniment of soft jazz.

EATING OUT ♿ **Chopmist Charlie's** (401-423-1020; www.chopmistcharlies.com), 40 Narragansett Avenue. ($) Open daily for lunch and dinner. Chowder, seafood in an informal setting.

East Ferry Market & Deli (401-423-1592), 47 Conanicus Avenue. ($) Open daily 6 AM–5 PM. Sandwiches, soups, and snacks. The outside patio, across the street from the old ferry landing and harbor, is the best spot in town to people-watch.

BAKERIES **Slice of Heaven** (401-423-9866; www.sliceofheavenri.com), 32 Narragansett Avenue. Breads, pastries, and cookies round out the deli selections at this pleasant café with outdoor seating.

Village Hearth Artisan Bakery (401-423-9282; www.villagehearthbakerycafe.com), 2 Watson Avenue. Just a block north of Jamestown village, this homey place makes excellent country-style loaves and baguettes, as well as pastries and (on Sundays only) wood-grilled thin-crust pizzas to take out. A special spot, beloved by both locals and the lucky travelers who find it.

✷ Entertainment

Narragansett Cafe (401-423-2150; www.narragansettcafe.com),

25 Narragansett Avenue. The Narragansett may look like a dive, but it's really a friendly neighborhood bar whose summer patrons include local residents, area fishermen, and bluebloods from out of state. The draw for all is the same: cheap drinks and lively rock-and-roll bands. The crowd is of all ages, and it's an active one: "Narry" customers come to dance.

✷ Selective Shopping

Conanicut Marina Ship Store (401-423-7158), 20 Narragansett Avenue. A well-stocked ship's store and chandlery is conveniently located for boaters on Jamestown's main street. Marine hardware and gear, too.

Jamestown Designs (401-423-0344; www.jamestowndesigns.com), 17 Narragansett Avenue. Frame store and upscale gift shop. There are also paintings and prints of local scenes by area artists for sale, including Jamestowner John Mecray, whose marine paintings enjoy a national reputation.

The Secret Garden (401-423-0050; www.thesecretgardenjamestown.com), 12 Southwest Avenue, just around the corner from Narragansett Avenue at the flashing light. This pleasant shop sells flowers and plants as well as dried flowers, wreaths, candles and candlesticks, and other little odds and ends. It also offers its own brand of scent oils and, of course, *Secret Gardens*, the locally published book about the gardens in Newport's historic Point section.

✷ Special Events

Early August: **Swim the Bay** (401-272-3540; www.savebay.org). Potter's Cove, near Newport Bridge, is the finish point for this cross-bay swim of about 2 miles. Swimmers of all ages compete for the benefit of Save the Bay, a statewide environmental watchdog group, and there is usually a big crowd on shore to cheer them on.

Mid-August: **Fools Rules Regatta** (401-423-1492), Jamestown Harbor. Fun race for charity in which contestants build their own boats on the beach (no marine gear allowed) and attempt to race them across a short course just offshore. The result is sort of a floating (sometimes) Mardi Gras parade.

Mid-October: **'Round the Island Bike Race** (401-423-7260). Okay, so it's only 18 miles around the circumference of Conanicut, but it's still a fun race for young and old, as well as a chance for participants to raise money for island charities.

Southern Rhode Island

8

NARRAGANSETT

NORTH KINGSTOWN AREA

SOUTH KINGSTOWN AREA

CHARLESTOWN AND RICHMOND AREA

WESTERLY AND WATCH HILL

Katherine Imbrie

NARRAGANSETT

With its miles of beautiful beaches and rocky cliffs overlooking the ocean, this town is the essence of Rhode Island. Narragansett Bay, as lovely as it is, does not project the awesome power of the open sea. Here it's the ocean that you see, and the ocean that imparts its unique light to the lower sky. While Narragansett was settled early, it gained its own identity relatively late by Rhode Island standards, separating from sprawling South Kingstown only in 1888. A popular beach resort area near the end of the 19th century, with many large oceanfront hotels, the town reached its peak with the construction of the Narragansett Pier and the Stanford White–designed Towers Casino in 1883. Then a devastating fire in 1900 wiped out much of the ocean district; the big stone towers and arch were saved, but the town returned to a fairly small (less than 13,000 people in 14 square miles), rural, and sleepy state, except when summer crowds from upstate filled the beaches. Extensive urban renewal in the 1970s rebuilt a major portion of the Narragansett Pier area, and what the downtown lost in character, it gained in an influx of new shops and a resurgence of tourism. Today Narragansett offers resort-like atmosphere along its east coast, and on the west, where Point Judith Pond slices inland, the salty aspect of Galilee, the state's major fishing port. *Spartina,* the excellent novel by John Casey, who spent time here working the fishing boats, evokes the spirit of this special place.

GUIDANCE Narragansett Tourist Information Center (401-783-7121; www.narragansettri.com/chamber), Ocean Road, at the Towers, Narragansett Pier. This office dispenses information and brochures about Narragansett and all of South County.

South County Tourism Council (401-789-4422; 1-800-548-4662; www.southcountyri.com), 4808 Tower Hill Road (US 1), Wakefield.

Two local biweekly newspapers, the *South County Independent* and *The Narragansett Times,* provide listings of events and entertainment.

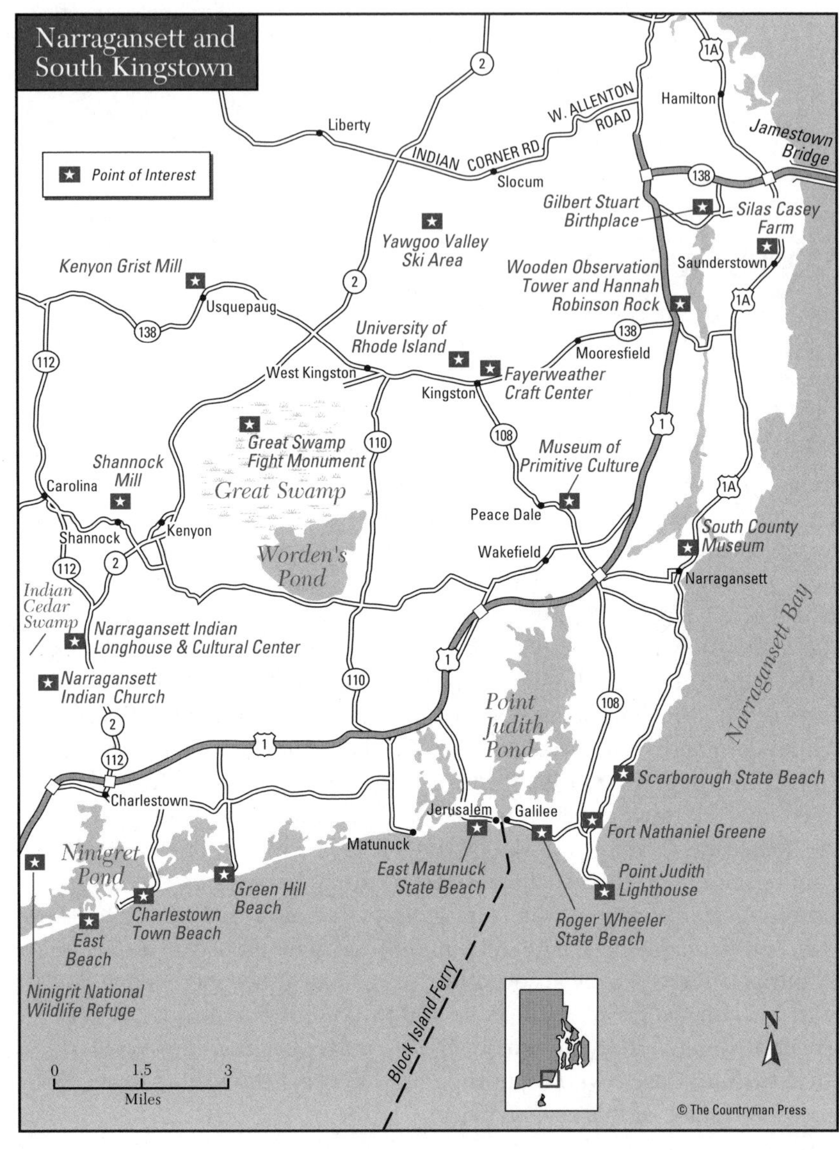
Narragansett and South Kingstown
Point of Interest
Liberty
INDIAN CORNER RD
W. ALLENTON ROAD
Slocum
Hamilton
Jamestown Bridge
Gilbert Stuart Birthplace
Silas Casey Farm
Yawgoo Valley Ski Area
Kenyon Grist Mill
Usquepaug
Wooden Observation Tower and Hannah Robinson Rock
Saunderstown
University of Rhode Island
Mooresfield
West Kingston
Kingston
Fayerweather Craft Center
Great Swamp Fight Monument
Great Swamp
Museum of Primitive Culture
Shannock Mill
Carolina
Shannock
Kenyon
Peace Dale
Wakefield
Worden's Pond
South County Museum
Narragansett
Indian Cedar Swamp
Narragansett Indian Longhouse & Cultural Center
Narragansett Indian Church
Narragansett Bay
Point Judith Pond
Scarborough State Beach
Charlestown
Jerusalem
Galilee
Fort Nathaniel Greene
Matunuck
Ninigret Pond
East Matunuck State Beach
Point Judith Lighthouse
Green Hill Beach
Charlestown Town Beach
East Beach
Roger Wheeler State Beach
Ninigrit National Wildlife Refuge
Block Island Ferry
0
1.5
3
Miles
N
© The Countryman Press

GETTING THERE *By car:* From points south, take I-95 to RI 138 east to US 1—then follow the signs to Narragansett. If you prefer the scenic route, take exit 92 in Connecticut, and follow CT 2 to CT 78 until you reach US 1 north in Westerly, Rhode Island. It's about 20 miles to the first Narragansett exit. From points north, take I-95 south to RI 4 east to US 1 south. It's about 8 miles to the first exit.

GETTING AROUND Local taxi service is provided by **Eagle Cab** (401-783-2970) or Wright's Taxi (401-769-0400). The free Southern Rhode Island Trolley (www.southernritrolley.com) goes to Narragansett restaurants, shops, and beaches approximately every two hours between Memorial Day and Labor Day.

MEDICAL EMERGENCY The statewide emergency number is **911.**

✷ To See

South County Museum (401-783-5400; www.southcountymuseum.org), Strathmore Street off RI 108, Narragansett. Open Wednesday through Saturday 10-4 in July and August; Friday and Saturday, 10–4 May, June, and September. Small admission fee. The museum houses almost 10,000 items relating to rural life in Rhode Island from 1800 to 1930—everything

NARRAGANSETT COASTLINE

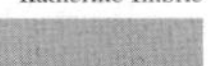

from a general store and cobbler shop to antique carriages, a blacksmith's forge, and a country kitchen sink. The museum holds a quilting festival each August and a harvest festival at the end of September.

✷ To Do

BOAT EXCURSIONS **Block Island Ferry** (401-783-4613; www.blockislandferry.com), State Pier, Galilee. Departs hourly 8–7; call or check website for current schedule and prices. Carries cars. The trip to "the Block" takes about 55 minutes. From May through October, a high-speed ferry, taking only about 30 minutes, carries passengers, but not cars, five times a day.

The Frances Fleet (401-783-4988; www.francesfleet.com), 33 State Street, Galilee. Whale-watching cruises and half-day fishing trips on one of the fleet's three large motor vessels.

Seven B's V (401-789-9250; www.sevenbs.com), Periwinkle Road, Narragansett. This 80-foot motor vessel is available for fishing, whale-watching, and special events.

CANOEING/KAYAKING **Narrow River Kayaks** (401-789-0334), 94 Middlebridge Road, Narragansett. Kayak instruction and rentals.

FISHING There's great blue-water fishing in these parts—blues, cod, and pogies—and plenty of charter fishing (party) boats operating out of Galilee. Some are individually chartered with a crew by groups of six or eight splitting expenses, while others make regular trips for a set fee. Most depart from Galilee's charter boat dock. For information about area fish-

NARRAGANSETT TOWERS

Katherine Imbrie

Kim Grant

AT REST IN GALILEE

ing charters, visit the website of the Rhode Island Party & Charter Boat Association at www.rifishing.com.

Misty (401-789-6057), 102 Kimberly Drive, Wakefield. Captain Andy Ambrosia.

Old Salt Charters (401-783-4805), 12 Amancio Street, Wakefield. Captain Bill Della Valle.

Persuader (401-783-5644), 110 Avice Avenue, Narragansett. Captain Dennis Dillon.

Sakarak Sport Fishing Charters (401-783-9015), 42 Exeter Boulevard, Narragansett. Captain Mitch Chagnon.

FOR FAMILIES **Adventureland** (401-789-0084; www.adventureland ri.com), Point Judith Road. Open 10–10 daily Memorial Day through Labor Day. Weekends from April 15 to Memorial Day and Labor Day to Oct. 13. Miniature golf, bumper boats, go-carts, carousel, and batting cages.

Narragansett Ocean Club (401-783-1711), 360 South Pier Road. Call for hours. Indoor roller skating—loud and lots of fun.

SURFING It's not exactly California, but Narragansett offers tolerable East Coast–style surfing. **Narragansett Surf and Skate Shop** (401-789-7890), 74 Narragansett Avenue, and **Warm Winds** (401-789-9040), 26 Kingstown Road, offer rentals and give lessons.

Katherine Imbrie

FRESH FARE IN JERUSALEM

SWIMMING Narragansett boasts some of the state's best beaches, ranging from the jam-packed, surf-heavy sands of Scarborough to the quiet waters of Roger Wheeler and Salty Brine State Beaches. For information about state beaches, call 401-222-2632 or visit www.riparks.com.

Narragansett Town Beach (401-785-6430). Parking, walk-on fees. Half a mile of beach right at the Pier. Good wave action makes this one of the best surfing spots in the state. Best of all, you're right downtown.

SOUTH COUNTY SWIMMING HOLE

Katherine Imbrie

Salty Brine State Beach (401-789-8374). Named for a legendary Rhode Island radio personality, the former Galilee State Beach is a short stretch of sand to the west of Roger Wheeler.

Scarborough State Beach (401-783-1010), Ocean Road. This stretch of 300-plus yards of sand and dunes is a major summer attraction, especially for young adults and teens, who spend equal time checking out one another and

Kim Grant

NARRAGANSETT BEACH

Katherine Imbrie

SAILING OFF NEWPORT

the surf. Busy, busy, busy. The lot holds almost 3,000 cars and still fills up quickly on weekends.

Roger Wheeler State Beach (401-789-3563), Sand Hill Cove Road, near Galilee. Families with children will like the calm, protected waters of this beach. There are also cabanas and playground equipment.

✱ Green Space

Black Point, Ocean Road, near Scarborough State Beach. Environmentalists and state officials fought hard to keep this cliffside pathway a public right-of-way. Park your car in the adjoining beach lot and walk back a few yards to the walkway entrance. The path is less than half a mile long, but the view to the horizon across Rhode Island Sound is spectacular. To the northeast you can see the outlines of Beavertail in Jamestown and Brenton Point in Newport. Well worth the trip.

✱ Lodging

HOTELS AND MOTELS Lighthouse Inn of Galilee (401-789-9341; 1-877-789-9341; www.lighthouse-inn-ri.com), 307 Great Island Road, Galilee. ($$–$$$) This is a full-service hotel with 100 rooms right across from the docks and ferry landing on the waterfront. Indoor pool.

Ocean Rose Inn (401-783-4704; www.oceanroseinn.com), 113 Ocean Road, Narragansett. ($$$–$$$$) Restored not long ago, this is one of the surviving structures from Narragansett's glory days as a beach resort. The inn consists of a 1900s three-story house (which served as a speakeasy and gambling house in its time) with nine rooms, and an adjacent, motel-like structure of 20 rooms. All rooms have a private bath and many, especially those in the main house, enjoy an ocean view. Restaurant and lounge on the premises serving lunch and dinner.

BED & BREAKFASTS While you won't find as many inns and bed & breakfasts in South County as on Aquidneck, the number is growing. South County B&Bs, whether on the sea or in the country, have a quiet, calming charm of their own. About two dozen are members of a reservation service, **Bed & Breakfast Referrals of South Coast Rhode Island** (1-800-853-7479), which will help you find a room if the inns are full.

The 1900 House (401-789-7971; www.1900houseri.com), 59 Kingston Road, Narragansett. ($$$) There are two bedrooms and one suite in this restored Victorian. It is furnished with Victorian-era antiques but brought up-to-date with air-conditioning and cable TV. Screened-in porch. No children under 10. Gourmet breakfasts. A block and a half from the ocean.

The Richards (401-789-7746; www.therichardsbnb.com), 144 Gibson Avenue, Narragansett. ($$) Located in a quiet area about a mile from the Pier, this 1884 guest house is surrounded by English gardens. Each of the four spacious rooms has a private bath. Nicely furnished with antiques and Oriental rugs, this is one of the oldest B&Bs in town.

Sheppard's Place (401-742-5903), 172 Boon Street, Narragansett. ($$) Guests can enjoy breakfast above a woodsy private garden with a fishpond when the weather is fair, and, after breakfast, take a five-minute walk to Narragansett Beach. There are three spacious double rooms with air-conditioning or a two-bedroom suite at this inviting B&B.

CAMPGROUNDS **Fishermen's Memorial State Park** (401-789-8374), 1011 Point Judith Road, near Galilee. Reservations: www.riparks.com; 1-877-RICAMP5. Season runs from April 15 through October. Sites for 147 trailers, 35 tents, with varying hookups. Pets accepted. Recreational facilities include tennis and basketball courts as well as playground equipment.

Long Cove Marina Family Campsites (401-783-4902), Long Cove Marina, RR 9, off Point Judith Road. Write: Point Judith Road, #325, Narragansett. Open May through mid-October. Spaces for 150 trailers. Because this is a marina, you also get the benefit of a boat ramp, plus shower and head (toilet) facilities.

✶ Where to Eat

DINING OUT ♿ **Basil's** (401-789-3743; www.basilsri.com), 22 Kingstown Road, at Narragansett Pier. ($$$–$$$$) Open Wednesday through Sunday for dinner. As the French Provincial decor suggests, this small but elegant restaurant specializes in fine French cuisine: steak Diane, rack of lamb Dijonnaise, and the chef's choice, Veal à la Basil's. Lots of spicy cream sauces and fresh and flavorful herbs. Chocolate mousse makes an excellent finale. Basil's also has a comprehensive wine list.

♿ **Coast Guard House** (401-789-0700; www.thecoastguardhouse.com), 40 Ocean Road, at Narragansett Pier. ($$$) Open daily for lunch and dinner (except for a brief midwinter closing). Perched on the edge of the Atlantic, this former Coast Guard station serves up lobster ravioli and pan-fried scallops, meat dishes, and one of the best (and closest) ocean views in the state. Busy at dinner, but perhaps best known for its Sunday brunch. The upstairs bar and deck are popular in summer.

Maharajah Indian Restaurant and Lounge (401-792-7999; www.maharajari.com), 1 Beach Street, Narragansett. ($-$$) Open daily year-round for lunch and dinner. Serving a wide variety of vegetarian dishes and seafood curries as well as Tandoori dishes.

Spain of Narragansett (401-783-9770; www.spainri.com), 1144 Ocean Road. ($$–$$$) Open Tuesday through Saturday 4–10, Sunday 1–9. Heaps of Iberian-inspired food—shrimp, swordfish, snapper, and paella—draw summer crowds to this large, Mediterranean-themed dining spot about 3 miles south of Narragansett Pier on the coast road. The prices are reasonable; the portions, enormous.

♿ **Trio** (401-792-4333; www.trio-ri.com), 15 Kingstown Road, Narragansett, ($$-$$$). Crab cakes, calamari, vegetable spring rolls, clams casino pizza, tortellini with lobster are all among the offerings at this Italian American and American fusion restaurant.

♿ **Turtle Soup** (401-792-8683; www.turtlesouprestaurant.com), 113 Ocean Road, Narragansett. ($$–$$$) Call for hours; no reservations taken. Even though there's no turtle soup on the menu, there are plenty of fin and shellfish dishes like Mussels Zuppa, Prince Edward Island mussels simmered in a piquant wine and tomato sauce, or salmon with walnuts and a balsamic raspberry glaze. Lighter fare might be a pesto pizza. In warm weather, dining out on the shady porch with a view of the ocean is especially pleasant. There are French as well as Italian touches in the kitchen.

EATING OUT ✐ ♿ **Aunt Carrie's** (401-783-7930; www.auntcarriesri.com), 1240 Ocean Road, near the tip of Point Judith. ($) Open June through Labor Day, daily except Tuesday for lunch and dinner. Quintessential clam shack by the sea. Fried clams, clam cakes, french fries, and other seafood dinners (plus kids' dinners) eaten the old-fashioned way—outside at picnic tables; in a semi-enclosed, porchlike area; or in your car. Eating here is a summer ritual for many Rhode Islanders.

Champlin's Seafood (401-783-3152; http://champlins.com), 256 Great Island Road. ($–$$) Open daily for lunch and dinner. You have your choice of seafood operations in Galilee, but you won't go wrong with Champlin's, overlooking Point Judith Pond. Your basic Rhode Island menu of fried clams, stuffed clams ("stuffies" to natives), and lobster rolls enjoyed indoors or out. Good for take-out, too.

♿ **Crazy Burger** (401-783-1810; www.crazyburger.com), 144 Boon Street, one street up from Ocean Road. ($–$$) Open daily for breakfast, lunch, and dinner from early morning to 9 or 10 PM. A fun place that serves excellent food—real burgers along with turkey, chicken, and salmon burger concoctions. Plenty of vegan dishes, too, as well as Rhode Island standards like fried calamari. There's a nice patio (partly covered with a canopy) out back for fresh-air dining.

Jim's Dock (401-783-2050; www.jims-dock.com), 1175 Succotash Road, Jerusalem, across the harbor from Galilee. ($) Open daily for breakfast, lunch, and dinner until Labor Day. Chowder, clam cakes, and local fish dishes. Very casual; bring your own liquor.

Marco's Kabob and More (401-783-9083). 126 Boon Street. ($) Open Tuesday through Sunday 11–5. Such Near Eastern fare as falafel, kebabs, and stuffed grape leaves make up the menu here.

FRIED CLAMS AT CHAMPLIN'S

Katherine Imbrie

The Picnic Basket (401-782-2284), 20 Kingstown Road, Narragansett. ($) Open daily except Monday 10–5. Sandwiches, soups, salads, pizza, and chili—and the sandwiches range from a simple turkey club to an extravagant honey-maple turkey, roasted peppers, lettuce, tomato, and melted mozzarella combination put together on basil focaccia.

♿ **Twin Willows** (401-789-8153), 865 Boston Neck Road (RI 1A), Narragansett. ($–$$) Open daily for lunch and dinner. The willows are long gone, but this bar and restaurant seems to have been around forever. Chowder, stuffies, sandwiches, and seafood dinners at reasonable prices. Extensive beer menu and an outside deck with great views of the ocean at Bonnet Shores.

CAFES **Cool Beans Café** (401-789-9500), 18 Kingston Road, Narragansett. Daily 7–6. The homemade cinnamon buns and muffins are a particular attraction.

✷ Entertainment

As in many beach communities, there's a variety of entertainment—from jazz to dancing—in Narragansett's restaurants and hotels.

Charlie O's Tavern (401-782-2002; www.charlieosri.net), 2 Sand Hill Cove Road, just off Point Judith Road. Restaurant, sports bar, pool tables, and a juke box. Simon's Martini Lounge is upstairs.

Coast Guard House (401-789-0700), 40 Ocean Road. Piano bar offering everything from TV theme songs to dance music.

The Towers (401-782-2597), 35 Ocean Road. Dancing Thursday night from Memorial Day to Labor Day.

✷ Selective Shopping

Most Naturally (401-789-9077; www.mostnaturally.com), 24A Pier Marketplace, Narragansett. Open in summer 10–10 daily. Off-season 10–5. Handmade South American scarves and South African jewelry. Glassware and some jewelry made from recycled materials. Cotton and bamboo clothing, locally made organic skin care items. Everything's green in this attractive little marketplace store.

Sweet Twist (401-782-1006), 12A Pier Marketplace. Open daily in summer, weekends year-round. Summer, of course, is the season for this little candy shop that, in another era, would have been a penny-candy store. The candies cost more than pennies nowadays, but there is a wonderland of choices for children—miniature Tootsie Rolls, gummy bears, Squirrel Nut Zippers, Bazooka bubblegum. And there are more sophisticated candies for their parents, too.

✷ Special Events

End of June: **Narragansett Art Festival** (401-789-4422), Veterans Memorial Park.

Mid-July: **Concert on the Beach at Narragansett Town Beach.** Bring a blanket and a picnic for this annual evening of classical pops.

End of July: **Blessing of the Fleet** (401-789-9491), Galilee.

Mid-September: **Summer's End Festival,** Narragansett Town Beach. Rides and evening band music.

December: **Narragansett Festival of Lights,** The Towers, 35 Ocean Road, early December. Jingle Bell Run on the Beach. A 5K run on Narragansett Beach.

NORTH KINGSTOWN AREA

North Kingstown, on the west side of Narragansett Bay, has a most happy situation, stretching as it does along the Narragansett Bay shore. Woodsy roads wind inland past amber ponds. In North Kingstown's principal village of Wickford, yellow- and white-clapboard 18th-century houses line Main Street and the narrow waterfront lanes. Its cozy harbor of working quahog boats still looks much as it did in the late 1800s. Indeed, much of Wickford remains as it was then, making it a prime tourist attraction.

A mile and a half north of Wickford at Cocumscussoc—"Marked Rock"—Rhode Island founder Roger Williams built a trading post on a tract of land given to him by the Narragansett sachem Canonicus. It was in a garrison near the trading post that, after Williams's return to England and the souring of relations with the Native Americans, soldiers of the Massachusetts and Plymouth Bay Colonies and of Connecticut, with a handful of Rhode Islanders, laid plans for the Great Swamp Fight.

The abutting rural townships of Exeter and West Greenwich hold three-quarters of the Arcadia Wildlife Management Area. With 13,817 acres of woods, ponds, rivers, and streams, crisscrossed by dirt roads, it is the state's largest area of its kind and one of the most attractive to hunters, trout fishermen, and birders.

GUIDANCE **North Kingstown Chamber of Commerce** (401-295-5566), 245 Tower Hill Road, Wickford. Open Monday through Friday 9–5.

South County Tourism Council (401-789-4422; 1-800-548-4662), 4808 Tower Hill Road (US 1), Wakefield. Situated in the Oliver Stedman Government Center building on the right side of US 1 heading north. Open weekdays 9–5, as well as Saturday and Sunday 9–3 in summer.

GETTING THERE *By train or bus:* You can take **Amtrak** (1-800-USA-RAIL) to Providence and a **Rhode Island Public Transport Authority** (RIPTA; 401-781-9400) bus from Providence to Wickford. Exeter and

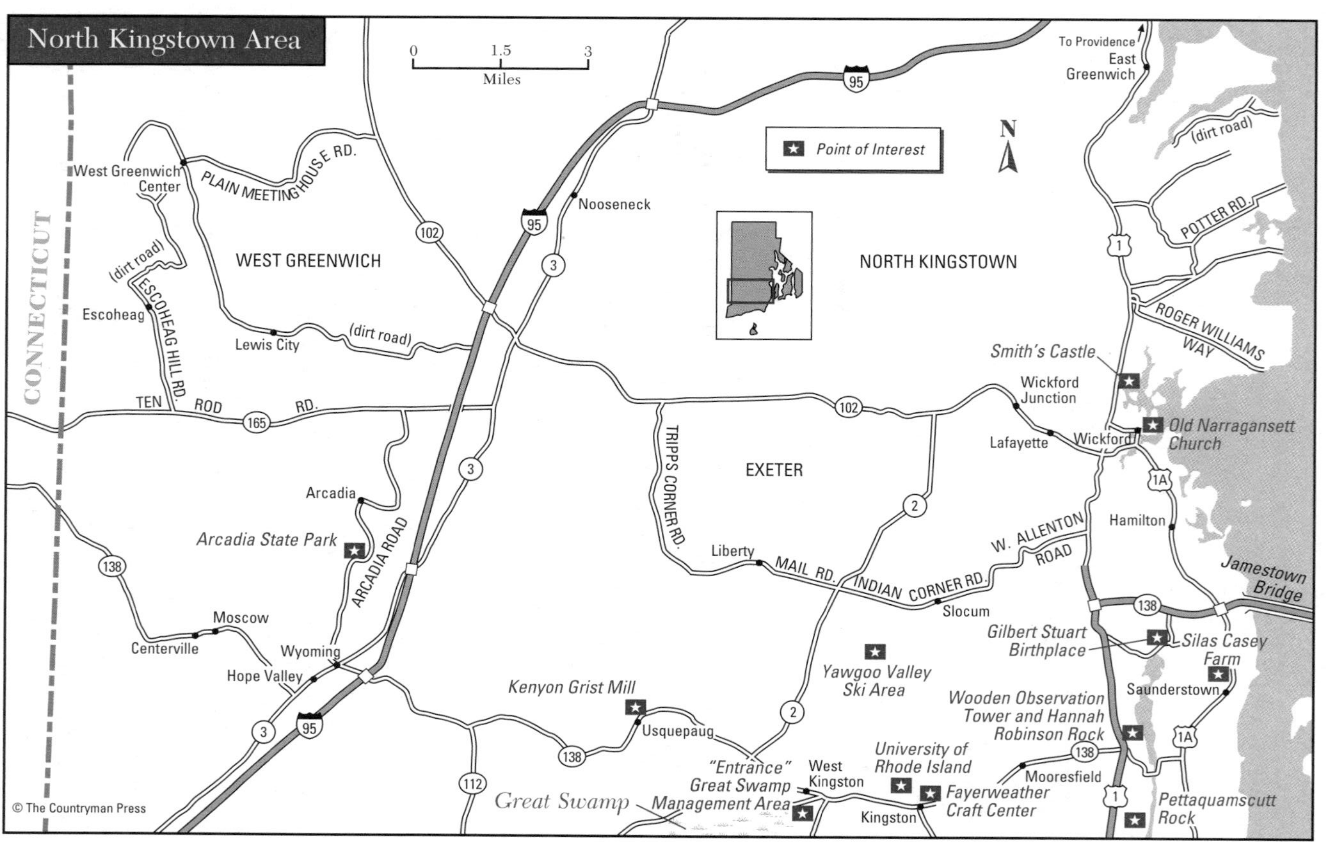
North Kingstown Area
0 1.5 3
Miles
Point of Interest
N
To Providence
East Greenwich
(dirt road)
POTTER RD.
ROGER WILLIAMS WAY
NORTH KINGSTOWN
WEST GREENWICH
EXETER
CONNECTICUT
West Greenwich Center
PLAIN MEETINGHOUSE RD.
Nooseneck
(dirt road)
Escoheag
ESCOHEAG HILL RD.
Lewis City
(dirt road)
TEN ROD RD.
Smith's Castle
Wickford Junction
Old Narragansett Church
Lafayette
Wickford
Hamilton
W. ALLENTON ROAD
Jamestown Bridge
TRIPPS CORNER RD.
Arcadia
Arcadia State Park
ARCADIA ROAD
Liberty
MAIL RD.
INDIAN CORNER RD.
Slocum
Gilbert Stuart Birthplace
Silas Casey Farm
Saunderstown
Moscow
Centerville
Wyoming
Hope Valley
Kenyon Grist Mill
Yawgoo Valley Ski Area
Wooden Observation Tower and Hannah Robinson Rock
Usquepaug
"Entrance" Great Swamp Management Area
West Kingston
University of Rhode Island
Kingston
Fayerweather Craft Center
Mooresfield
Pettaquamscutt Rock
Great Swamp
© The Countryman Press

West Greenwich, however, are accessible only by car. Even to Wickford, bus service is infrequent, and there is no local taxi company. Automobile is distinctly the best way to see this southern part of the state.

MEDICAL EMERGENCY The statewide emergency number is **911.**

South County Hospital (401-762-8000), 100 Kenyon Avenue, Wakefield. Emergency room as well as regular hospital care serving the entire southern portion of the state.

✷ Village

Wickford. In this pretty, 1-by-1.5-mile village, there are believed to be more fine examples of 18th-century architecture than in any other community of its size in New England. Colonial and Federal houses with fanlights over the doors, shiny black shutters, and gleaming brass doorknockers line Main Street. More of the same is found on streets and lanes with names like *Washington, Fountain, Friend, Gold, Bay,* and *Church.* Tree-lined Pleasant Street, bordering the harbor, offers a blend of the village's earliest homes and 1890s shingle-style summer "cottages" from the days when Wickford was a summer resort. Where West Main Street meets Brown Street—today's commercial center—rise two 19th-century business blocks: the redbrick **Avis Block,** with its elaborate facade, and the brick, stone, and terra-cotta 1890s **Gregory Block.**

Wickford has largely been spared the encroachment of development over the centuries, though the village has not always been so happy about it. In pre–Revolutionary War days, when it thrived on trade with the West Indies, it was a bustling place. But when the Revolution closed down the bay to commercial traffic, it languished gloomily. After the war, a revival of trade lasted until 1825. Then came the era of steam vessels and trains, and Wickford was bypassed by both. Nowadays residents recognize that it was this very stagnation that preserved the old-fashioned streets and lanes that visitors so enjoy.

✷ To See

HISTORIC SITES **Silas Casey Farm** (401-295-1030), Scenic RI 1A, north of Ferry Road, Saunderstown. Open June through October 15, Saturday 11–5. Chickens (and sometimes cows) enjoy the barns and the 300 acres that surround this early-18th-century farm. There are also 9 acres of vegetables, fruits, and flowers. The farmhouse has one room open to the public. In Revolutionary days, when a few colonial militias spent nights here, the British learned of their presence and fired on the house. A musket-ball hole can still be seen in the parlor door.

Kim Grant

A REVOLUTIONARY-ERA MUSKET-BALL HOLE IS STILL VISIBLE INSIDE THE SILAS CASEY FARM.

Old Narragansett Church (Old St. Paul's; 401-294-4357), 60 Church Lane, Wickford. Open for tours in summer, Thursday through Monday 11–4; off-season by appointment. Constructed in 1707, this simple white structure with gracefully arched windows flanking its double doors is the oldest Episcopal church north of Virginia. Its restored 1680 organ is the oldest church organ in use in North America today.

The approach to Old Narragansett Church is down the Greenway from May Street, a flagstone walk into which the names of many past church pastors and benefactors have been cut. The church is noted for its box pews, an upstairs gallery for slaves from the plantations, the silver communion service and baptismal font presented to St. Paul's by Queen Anne, and its wineglass pulpit, which was enlarged by pre-Revolutionary wardens to accommodate the girth of one of its preachers.

It was in the silver baptismal font that the infant Gilbert Stuart, the renowned painter famous for his portraits of George Washington, was christened. Originally the church stood about 7 miles south of town on Shermantown Road. In 1800 it was moved to its current site so that its parishioners would not have to travel so far. Since this was a controversial idea in those days and many were in opposition, 24 yoke of cattle hauled it into the village on a dark January night when the snow was crusted with ice and when, it was hoped, parishioners opposed to the move were unlikely to be out. Today **New St. Paul's,** built in 1847 in Romanesque Revival style at 76 Main Street, is used primarily for winter services.

Smith's Castle (401-294-3521), US 1 (Post Road), Wickford. Open June, July, and August, Thursday through Sunday noon–4; May, September, and October, Friday through Sunday noon–4. Small admission fee. On spacious grounds above Mill Pond stands the red-clapboard plantation house called Smith's Castle. This impressive house replaced a garrison trading post that Richard Smith had built about 1640 on land sold to him by Roger Williams. It was in the original structure that in December 1675 the colonists planned their attack against King Philip of the Wampanoags, who was seeking to drive settlers out of the area. After the bloody battle, the weary soldiers returned to Smith's Castle carrying their dead and dying. A tablet at the site marks the common grave of the men who were killed.

Within a few months of the battle, the Native Americans set fire to the hated garrison, damaging it severely. The base of the current structure was erected two years later, using materials from the damaged building. Smith's great-great-grandnephew, Daniel Updike, eventually inherited the three-room house. A lawyer and a socialite, he needed more room for entertaining and built on extensively.

Smith's Castle is the only surviving example of the plantation houses that once existed all across the southern part of the state.

Gilbert Stuart Birthplace and Museum (401-294-3001; www.gilbertstuartmuseum.org), 815 Gilbert Stuart Road, Saunderstown. Open May through September. Call for hours. Small admission fee. Until he was seven, painter Gilbert Stuart lived in this barn-red, hip-roofed building

THE PAINTER GILBERT STUART LIVED IN THIS FARMSTEAD UNTIL HE WAS SEVEN YEARS OLD.

Kim Grant

constructed by Gilbert Stuart Sr. to be a snuff mill. The elder Stuart, an able millwright, had come to Rhode Island at the urging of a Scots-born Newport physician, James Moffat. Tobacco was growing well in the area in those days, and Moffat and Stuart hoped that construction of a snuff mill would make them wealthy. Unfortunately, the enterprise was not a success, and the Stuarts left Saunderstown for Newport.

Though furnishings in the house are of the Stuart period, they were not there during the painter's lifetime, and the house contains only a reproduction of one of the 111 portraits that Stuart painted of the first president. A genuine childhood drawing of a dog may be seen in Newport, however.

Wickford Town Dock, foot of Main Street. Broad-beamed Rhode Island quahog skiffs vie for attention with sleek sailing yachts off this dock, where small boys fish and seagulls wheel. Nowadays this is a tranquil spot for watching small boats come and go, but both before and after the Revolution, Wickford Harbor was a bustling waterfront. The village thrived on trade with the West Indies, sending cargoes of grain, pork, beef, geese, turkeys, horses, and renowned Rhode Island cheese from the plantations of South County to the Caribbean, returning with sugar and spices, molasses, and tobacco.

MUSEUMS **Quonset Aviation Museum** (401-294-9540; www.theqam.org), 488 Eccleston Avenue, Quonset Point. Open April through September, daily 10–3; October through March, Saturday and Sunday 10–3. Small admission fee. A MiG-15, a TBM Avenger, an A-4 Skyhawk, and an F6F-5 Hellcat are among the airplanes and airplane memorabilia housed and displayed here.

Tomaquag Indian Memorial Museum (401-539-7213; www.tomaquagmuseum.com), 390 Summit Road, at Dovecrest Cultural Center, Exeter. Open Monday through Friday 11–4 or by appointment. Small admission fee. Pottery, beadwork, and baskets of northeastern Native Americans are on display in this little museum.

SCENIC DRIVES An interesting excursion off Scenic RI 1A in Saunderstown is down **Ferry** and **South Ferry Roads,** affording an attractive view of Narragansett Bay, then along Old Boston Neck Road, site of several plantation houses, including the 18th-century Hannah Robinson House.

Annaquatucket Road off Scenic RI 1A in Saunderstown edges pretty Annaquatucket Pond, with its swans and wild ducks.

Gilbert Stuart Road between Scenic RI 1A and US 1 in Saunderstown dips down through deciduous and piney woods. It passes ponds and the

Gilbert Stuart Birthplace, then crosses streams and climbs hills before reaching US 1.

Both **Mail Road** and **Liberty Road** off RI 2 in Exeter are routes through the typical rural Rhode Island countryside of woods, streams, and ponds.

Shermantown Road, an extension of Gilbert Stuart Road, is, similarly, a winding, wooded country road, though houses are springing up along it. It was on Shermantown Road that Old St. Paul's stood before it was spirited away (see *Historic Sites,* Old Narragansett Church).

South County Trail (RI 2) begins in Exeter and continues through Charlestown to Route 1, passing through woods and nurseries and crossing farmland.

Ten Rod Road (RI 165) meanders from RI 3 to the Connecticut border through the Arcadia Wildlife Management Area's deciduous and white pine woods. Many dirt side roads penetrate deeper into the woodland, past the rivers, ponds, scrub, wetlands, and swamps that are part of the preserve.

Waldron Avenue off Scenic RI 1A in Hamilton offers a panoramic view of the bay, including Fox Island and several rocks to its south that are visited by harbor seals in winter.

A GIANT SCARECROW OFF RI 2

Kim Grant

✻ To Do

BICYCLING **Wilson Park,** West Main Street, Wickford. This short but pleasant bike path winds along Wickford Harbor.

CANOEING AND KAYAKING **Kayak Centre** (401-295-4400), 9 Phillips Street, Wickford. Canoe and kayak rentals and guided trips.

Quaker Lane Bait & Tackle (401-294-9642), 4019 Quaker Lane, North Kingstown. Canoe and kayak rentals. Fresh and saltwater fishing licenses.

FISHING **Beach Pond,** Exeter. Boat launching is possible on the Connecticut side of the pond. Fish for yellow perch, pumpkinseed sunfish, black crappies, largemouth and smallmouth bass, and brook, brown, and rainbow trout, among others.

Breakheart Pond, Arcadia Management Area, Exeter. Brook, brown, and rainbow trout, chain pickerel, largemouth bass, yellow perch, bluegill sunfish, and more.

FOR FAMILIES ✐ **Yawgoo Valley Water Park** (401-295-5366; www.yawgoo.com), Yawgoo Valley Road, Exeter. Open June through Labor Day, with a swimming pool, kiddie pool, and waterslides.

GOLF **Exeter Country Club** (401-295-1178), Victory Highway, Exeter. This is a public 18-hole course with flat terrain, ponds, and a covered bridge, plus breakfast and luncheon facilities and golf carts.

North Kingstown Municipal Golf Course (401-294-4051), Callahan Road, Quonset, on the former naval air base. Eighteen holes, flat terrain. Golf carts, handcarts, and golf supplies are available. There is a restaurant at the 19th hole.

Rolling Greens Golf Course (401-294-9859), 1625 Ten Rod Road, North Kingstown. Nine holes, well-maintained hilly terrain, a pond, and a clubhouse serving mostly sandwiches and drinks. Golf carts and handcarts.

Woodland Greens Golf Course (401-294-2872), 655 Old Baptist Road, North Kingstown. Nine holes, mixed terrain. Golf carts, handcarts, and a bar and grill.

HIKING **Arcadia Wildlife Management Area,** West Greenwich and Exeter. There are innumerable hiking trails and gravel roads through woods and scrub, past ponds, marshes, and wetlands, and along the Wood River. Among the most popular is the 3.5-mile **Arcadia Trail,** which is maintained by the Appalachian Mountain Club (AMC) and links Dawley State Park in Exeter to the John B. Hudson Trail.

The **Mount Tom Trail,** also cared for by the AMC, passes through the Arcadia Management Area in West Greenwich. It is reached from RI 165 via the **John B. Hudson Trail.** More than 5 miles long, the Mount Tom Trail travels through a pine forest and along the banks of the Wood River, climbing ridges and overlooking cliffs. The **Breakheart Trail** is another 5-mile-long AMC trail beginning off RI 165, with the entrance into Arcadia on Bliven Road. Here and there stone walls rest among the pine and oak, maple, and birch.

The **Tippecansett Trail** links Beach Pond State Park with Yawgoo Pond in Exeter. This AMC-maintained trail begins off RI 138 about 5 miles west of exit 3 from I-95. The trail runs back and forth across the Connecticut line through farmland and forest.

HORSEBACK RIDING **Legrand G. Reynolds Horsemen's Camping Area** (401-539-2356;), Escoheag Hill Road, Exeter. Open May through September. This campground for horseback riders is equipped with picnic tables, fireplaces, a horse-show ring, a corral, water, pit toilets, and riding trails.

Stepping Stone Ranch (401-397-3725; www.steppingstoneranch.com), 201 Escoheag Hill Road, Exeter. Riding lessons, trail rides, horsemen's camping, overnights at the ranch bunk house

SKIING ✐ **Yawgoo Valley Ski Area** (401-295-5366; www.yawgoo.com), 160 Yawgoo Valley Road, Exeter. Open December through March 15, weekdays 10–10, Saturday 8:30–10, Sunday 8:30–5. This is Rhode Island's only ski area. The longest of the 12 ski trails is 2,300 feet; the greatest vertical drop is 245 feet. Two double chairlifts and a surface tow serve the trails; half-day, full-day, and evening tickets are sold; and skis may be rented. Tubing down a slope on the ice is also offered for those age 4 and older.

TENNIS **Wilson Park,** West Main Street, Wickford. Two outdoor courts available on a first-come, first-served basis.

✷ Green Space

Both West Greenwich and Exeter are largely rural, with endless expanses of green space. Listed below is only a sampling of the most frequented. Information about other areas available for public enjoyment may be obtained from the state's **Department of Environmental Management, Division of Fish and Wildlife** (401-789-0281; www.dem.ri.gov).

Arcadia Wildlife Management Area (401-789-3094; 401-539-7117). The main entrance to this 13,817-acre wildlife preserve—the state's largest—is off RI 165 in Exeter. It offers endless opportunities to the outdoor enthusiast, birder, hunter, angler, hiker, and bicyclist. Its many trails (see *Hiking*) and gravel roads crisscross the preserve, providing access to the woods and scrub growth, ponds, marshes, wetlands, and the trout-filled Wood River. Pheasants and bobwhites are stocked by the state for hunting, and there are also ruffed grouse and wild turkeys, white-tailed deer, cottontail rabbits, and snowshoe hares. Frosty Hollow Pond is stocked with trout for youngsters under 14.

Big River Wildlife Management Area, West Greenwich. This wildlife refuge protects 8,319 acres of forest, wetlands, and agricultural lands. There is access from Division Street and RI 3 (Nooseneck Hill Road), principally for hikers, cyclists, hunters, birders, and anglers, with many roads closed to vehicles. Both stocked and native trout abound in the Big River, and in addition to ruffed grouse and wild turkeys, there is a variety of waterfowl.

Wickaboxet Wildlife Management Area, Plain Meeting House Road, West Greenwich. Songbirds and birds of prey populate this woodland area, which is rich in upland game such as deer and rabbits as well as other wildlife such as coyotes, foxes, and raccoons.

Wilson Park, West Shore Road, Wickford. This park offers both bicycle and walking trails, a boat ramp, picnic tables, outdoor tennis courts, and a playground.

✷ Lodging

BED & BREAKFASTS

The Haddie Pierce House (401-294-7674; www.haddiepierce.com), 146 Boston Neck Road, Wickford. ($–$$) This spacious Victorian house sits virtually in the heart of Wickford village. It has five rooms with private bath. The first-floor double parlor is furnished with period antiques, and there's a front porch for rocking on warm summer days.

MOTEL

♿ **Hamilton Village Inn** (401-295-0700; www.hamiltonvillageinn.com), 642 Boston Neck Road, North Kingstown. ($–$$) This 60-room motel, open year-round, has its own restaurant serving breakfast and lunch daily.

CAMPGROUNDS

Oak Embers Campground (401-397-4042: www.oakembers.com), 219 Escoheag Hill Road, West Greenwich. Open May to November. There are 60 sites at this privately owned campground, with freshwater fishing, swimming, boating, and horseback riding nearby. Facilities include water and electric hookups, hot showers, a swimming pool, picnic tables, a game room, restrooms, a dumping station, a laundry, and a grocery store.

See also **Legrand G. Reynolds Horsemen's Camping Area** under *To Do—Horseback Riding.*

✷ Where to Eat

DINING OUT ♿ **Beach Rose Café** (401-295-2800; www.beachrosecafe.com), 85 Brown Street, Wickford. ($–$$) Open for breakfast and lunch weekdays, dinner Friday and Saturday in summer; call for hours. Lobster salad rolls, clam or scallop rolls, clam cakes, chowder, and paninis are favorites at this café with a deck overlooking Wickford Harbor.

♿ **Seven Moons** (401-885-8383; www.7-moons.com), 6900 Post Road, North Kingstown. ($–$$) Open Monday through Thursday 11:30–9:30, Friday and Saturday 11:30–10:30, Sunday 4–9:30. *Seven Moons* refers to the seven national cuisines the restaurant offers—Chinese, Vietnamese, Thai, Cambodian, Laotian, Malaysian, and Japanese.

♿ **Tavern by the Sea** (401-294-5771; www.tavernbytheseari.com), 16 West Main Street, Wickford. ($–$$) Open daily in summer for lunch and dinner; in winter, closed on Monday. There's a Mediterranean emphasis at this casual restaurant with a waterfront deck for summer dining, but New England clam chowder, crab cakes, a hummus platter, calamari, lobster rolls, and a lobster salad plate are also on the menu.

SNACKS Allie's Doughnuts (401-295-8036), 3661 Quaker Lane (RI 2), North Kingstown. Open Monday through Friday 5–3, Saturday and Sunday 6–1. Rhode Islanders from all across the state make expeditions here for the fresh, old-fashioned, homemade doughnuts ($7.20 a dozen), which are a far cry from ordinary chain-store doughnuts. There's take-out coffee, too, but no place to sit down.

The Inside Scoop (401-294-0091; www.insidescoopri.com), 30 Ten Rod Road, Wickford. Open March to November, noon–9. Homemade ice cream in such offbeat flavors as pumpkin, apple and blueberry pie, and ginger—along with all the old favorites, of course.

ENTERTAINMENT Courthouse Center for the Arts (401-782-1018; http://courthousearts.org), 3481 Kingstown Road, West Kingston. In summer, in this 1835 Richardson Romanesque former Washington County Courthouse, theater, dance programs, films and art exhibits invite visitors.

✷ Selective Shopping

ANTIQUES SHOPS Once in a Blue Moon (401-295-9085), 7535 Post Road, North Kingstown. European antiques and accessories.

Wickford Village Antiques & Collectibles (401-294-1117), 93

Brown Street, Wickford. Furniture, paintings, and bric-a-brac.

SPECIAL SHOPS **Allie's** (401-294-9121; www.alliesstore.com), 3700 Quaker Lane (RI 2), North Kingstown. This tack shop has a top-notch supply of boots, jeans, and horseback-riding gear, as well as general pet supplies.

Canvasworks (401-295-8080; www.canvasri.com), 10 Main Street, Wickford. Canvas bags of all sizes and shapes printed with designs in a variety of colors.

JW Graham / Yes! Gallery (401-295-0757; 401-295-5525), 17 and 26 Brown Street, Wickford. Pottery, glass, and handmade jewelry are among the items in these upscale gift shops.

The Grateful Heart (401-294-3981; www.gratefulheart.com), 17 West Main Street, Wickford. This New Age store specializes in spiritual and environmental books, crystals, New Age jewelry, tarot cards, greeting cards, and candles. You can have a photograph taken of your "aura" and learn the colors of your spiritual energy.

Green Ink (401-294-6266; www.greeninkboutique.com), 89 Brown Street, Wickford. Style is important in this women's clothing and accessories boutique, and the South County woman with Fifth Avenue tastes might well shop here.

Green River Silver Company (401-295-0086; http://greenriversilver.com), 24 Brown Street, Wickford. There are Mexican and Native American silver items, amber, freshwater pearls, semiprecious stones, and jewelry from Bali and Thailand in this pleasant little shop where the prices start at $9 and go to thousands of dollars.

Kitchen & Table of Wickford (401-295-1105; www.kitchenandtableofwickford.com), 68 Brown Street, Wickford. Anything and everything for the kitchen is for sale in this attractive shop.

Lulabells (401-667-7676; www.lulabellsgifts.com), 12 Main Street and 35 Brown Street (in the back of Wilson's of Wickford), Wickford. Jewelry and accessories, bowls and rugs and pillows and other gift items with a summery, marine theme.

The Mermaid's Purl (401-268-3899; www.themermaidspurl.com), 1 Main Street, North Kingstown. Everything for the knitter, crocheter, felter and beader—specialty yarns, buttons, beads, books, and patterns.

Narragansett Bay Olive Oil (401-295-2500; www.nboliveoil.com) 4 Brown Street, Wickford. Organic olive oil, extra virgin olive oil from Italy and California and such vinegars as pomegranate or raspberry balsamic.

Nautical Impressions (401-295-5303), 16 West Main Street, Wickford. Find gifts aplenty for the yachtsman and the wannabe sailor—anchor andirons and bookends, globes and telescopes, galley signs and books on sailing—in this second-floor shop that is an adjunct to the World Store.

Scrimshanders (401-294-2262; www.scrimshanders.com) 35 Brown Street (in the rear of Wilson's of Wickford). Hand-carved scrimshaw carved from woolly mammoth ivory, ancient walrus ivory, shed antler bone, and Tagua nuts from Ecuador, and sailors' shell valentines.

Village Reflections (401-295-7802), 5 West Main Street, Wickford. Women's clothing that ranges from casual to office-appropriate.

Wickford Gourmet Factory Outlet (401-294-8430), 656 Ten Rod Road, North Kingstown. In the gatehouse of the former Lafayette Textile Mill, seconds and discontinued china, glassware, cutlery, and kitchenware are offered at reasonable prices.

The World Store (401-295-0081), 16 West Main Street, Wickford. The merchandise in this shop emphasizes a better environment and appreciation of the world around us. There are stained-glass window decorations, balloon globes, fossils, and bird- and bat houses.

ART GALLERIES **Bailey Art Gallery** (401-284-2919; www.baileyfineart.com) 11 Brown Street, Wickford. Pen-and-ink art, pastels, watercolors and oils, postcards, and bookmarks by Jane and Mike Bailey.

Voila (401-667-5911; www.voila-art.com), 31 West Main Street, Wickford. A showplace for the work of Wickford and other Rhode Island artists.

FARM STANDS **Hensley's Farm** (401-294-4336), 1100 Lafayette Road, North Kingstown. Open November and December to sell Christmas trees and wreaths.

The Little Tree Farm (401-295-8733), 7470 Post Road, North Kingstown. Trees, wreaths, garlands, vegetables in-season. Open year-round, daily 8–5, Sunday 8–3.

Schartner Farms (401-294-2044; www.schartnerfarms.com), 1 Arnold Place, Exeter. Open March through December, daily 8–dusk. This is the area's premier farm market, one of the largest and best in the state, a vast rustic emporium that functions as a combination of produce stand, market, nursery, gift shop, and pick-your-own farm fields. A must-stop for both locals and visitors en route to South County beaches. (Try the farm's own red fries, potatoes fried outdoors in aromatic batches and sold to-travel in cardboard containers.)

✷ Special Events

May: **Smith's Castle Bridge to the Past,** Smith's Castle, off US 1 in Wickford. Celebration of the 17th century, with reenactments, children's activities, talks, vendors, often a puppet show.

June: **Rhode Island Air Show (www.riairshow.org),** Quonset

Katherine Imbrie

DAN MORETTI BAND PERFORMS AT WESTERLY BEACH.

State Airport, North Kingstown. **Lafayette Band Concerts** (401-295-0072), Band Shell, Town Beach, Wickford. **Strawberry Festival and Crafts Fair** (401-294-3521), Smith's Castle, off US 1, Wickford.

June–August: **Summer Concert Series** (401-294-3331), behind the Town Hall Annex, 55 Brown Street, Wickford.

June–October: **Coastal Growers' Market** (401-295-1030; http://coastalmarket.org), Saturday morning market at Casey Farm, 2325 Boston Neck Road, Saunderstown.

July: **Wickford Art Festival** (401-294-6840). Paintings, photographs, sculptures, and food on the sidewalks of Wickford. **Lafayette Band Concerts** (401-295-0072), Band Shell, Town Beach, Wickford, and Chapel of St. John the Divine, Church Way at Willett Road, Saunderstown. Thursday-night Children's Concerts at the North Kingstown Town Beach (401-295-0072).

July–October: **North Kingstown Farmers' Market,** Smith's Castle parking lot, 55 Richard Smith Drive, North Kingstown, 1–5.

August: **Lafayette Band Concerts** (401-884-8579), North Kingstown Free Library, 100 Boone Street, Wickford.

September: **Annual Dahlia Show** (401-294-3486), Cold Spring Community Center, 30 Beach Street, Wickford.

October: **Colonial Harvest Festival** (401-294-3521), Smith's Castle, 55 Richard Smith Drive,

North Kingstown. Old-fashioned games, musicians, vendors, castle tour.

November: **North Kingstown Veterans Day Parade,** Wickford.

November–April: **Coastal Growers' Winter Market** (401-285-1030; http://coastalmarket.org/Winter_Market) Lafayette Mill, 650 Ten Rod Road, North Kingstown, Saturdays 10–1.

December: **Festival of Lights** (401-295-5666), Wickford Village, North Kingstown. Bell ringers, children's activities, Father Christmas, and hot cider. **Christmas at the Castle** (401-294-3521), Smith's Castle, off Route 1 in Wickford. First weekend of the month. An old-fashioned Christmas celebration with storytelling, caroling, tours of the castle, hot apple cider, and baked goods.

SOUTH KINGSTOWN AREA

South Kingstown, the Ocean State's largest town, occupies roughly 62 square miles in its southwest corner. Surrounding South Kingstown are some of the state's most inviting beaches—East Matunuck, Roy Carpenter's Green Hill, and more sheltered spots like Sand Hill Cove and Galilee State Beach.

Roads wind inland past woods and ponds, and through villages of virtually untouched 18th- and 19th-century houses and gray stone mills. There are turf and potato farms, pick-your-own strawberry patches, a wildlife refuge rich in bird and animal life, and a picturesque 1875 railroad station. Here you'll find 1,075-acre Worden's Pond, the largest body of fresh water in the state, and, abutting it, the historic Great Swamp, the site of the colonists' 1675 attack on King Philip.

Oliver Hazard Perry and his brother Matthew were born in South Kingstown. The former was a naval hero in the War of 1812's battle of Lake Erie; the latter, also a navy man, negotiated the first modern commercial treaty with Japan in 1854, opening that nation to the world.

The principal villages in the town are Kingston, Wakefield, and Peace Dale. Except for its beaches and University of Rhode Island campus, South Kingstown is a quiet, slow-moving part of the state, well worth exploring on a sunny summer or fresh spring day, or when the Great Swamp's maple, sumac, and oak have turned crimson and gold.

Although Kingston today is the site of most of the University of Rhode Island campus, it remains a quiet, tucked-away place untouched by commercialism. Along RI 138, its main street, green- and black-shuttered clapboard houses stand just as they did in the 19th century. Then known as Little Rest, the village was one of the seats of the Rhode Island General Assembly. That, some say, was the reason for its original name, for when the assembly was in session it was, indeed, a place of little rest. Another story, however, attributes the name to a brief stop that soldiers made in the village on their way to the Great Swamp battle.

Wakefield, the administrative center of South Kingstown, grew up around the Narragansett Mills, a textile manufacturing company established in 1800. Later known as the Wakefield Mill, it is long since defunct. There are some fine old houses along US 1 plus a main street of 19th-century commercial storefronts, art galleries, and a fish ladder below the Main Street bridge. In spring you can watch the alewives climbing upstream. A pedestrian bridge across the Saugatucket River affords a pretty view downstream.

Peace Dale owes its beginning to the Peace Dale Manufacturing Company, a woolen mill founded in 1800 by Isaac and Rowland Hazard. In its heyday it was known for its shawls and worsted. The mill is still operating, although the gray granite buildings are of later-19th-century construction, the name has changed to Palisades, Ltd., and it does finishing and dyeing.

GUIDANCE **South County Tourism Council** (401-789-4422; 1-800-548-4662), 4808 Tower Hill Road (US 1), Wakefield. Open Monday through Friday 9–5. Situated in the Government Center building on the right side of US 1 heading north.

GETTING THERE *By train or bus:* You can take **Amtrak** (1-800-USA-RAIL) to Kingston or a **Rhode Island Public Transport Authority** (RIPTA; 401-781-9400; www.ripta.com) bus from Providence to Kingston. RIPTA's Flex Service (401-784-9500, ext. 220), for which reservations must be made in advance, will connect with the beaches. All public transportation, however, is infrequent, and by far the best way to explore this part of the state is by car.

GETTING AROUND Local taxi service is provided by **Wright's Taxi** (401-789-0400) and **Eagle Cab** (401-783-2970, 401-783-0007), both in Narragansett. The Southern Rhode Island Trolley (southernritrolley.com) also links accommodations with beaches, restaurants, and shops from Memorial Day to Labor Day.

MEDICAL EMERGENCY The statewide emergency number is **911.**

South County Hospital (401-782-8000), 100 Kenyon Avenue, Wakefield. Emergency room and regular hospital care serving the entire southern portion of the state.

* To See

HISTORIC SITES **Peace Dale Congregational Church** (401-789-7313), 261 Columbia Street, Peace Dale. Open for tours in summer, Monday through Thursday 9:30–11:30, Sunday 8–1. The stained-glass windows in this impressive granite building are the work of John La Farge, designer of the stained glass in New York City's Cathedral of St. John the Divine.

George Fayerweather House (401-789-9072), RI 138, Kingston. Open mid-May through mid-December, Tuesday through Saturday 10–4 and in November and December also on Sunday from 10-4. This little white Cape was built in 1820 by George Fayerweather, the son of a slave from one of the plantations that stretched along the Rhode Island shore in the 17th century. It now houses the Fayerweather Craft Guild, which displays crafting techniques and sells the finished products.

Great Swamp Fight Monument, RI 2 (South County Trail), 1 mile south of the junction with RI 138 in West Kingston. Unfortunately, the historic marker designating the road to the Great Swamp Fight Monument is old and weathered, so travelers seeking this memorial of the bloodiest battle ever fought on Rhode Island soil must keep a keen eye out for it. Reaching the monument requires a quarter-mile trail walk through the swamp maple and oak to the obelisk. It's surrounded by stone markers that commemorate the troops of the Massachusetts, Plymouth Bay, and Connecticut Colonies, who fought in the December 19, 1675, battle of King Philip's War.

Colonial forces attacked the winter camp that the Narragansetts had built here in the center of the swamp. The targets were the warriors of the Wampanoag chief King Philip, who was seeking to oust the settlers from Native American lands. Ordinarily the fort would have been inaccessible because of the swampy lands around it, but December 1675 was unusually cold, and the swamp had frozen. So despite a blizzard and relentless Native American arrows, the colonists managed to set fire to the fort. It turned out that it sheltered not only Wampanoag warriors, but also their wives and children. Mercilessly, the colonists slaughtered all who escaped the fire, and by nightfall virtually all the Native Americans within the fortification had been wiped out. The colonists' losses numbered 70 men dead and 150 wounded.

Hazard Memorial Hall (401-789-1555), Kingstown Road, Peace Dale. Call for hours. This gray granite 1891 Richardson Romanesque structure now houses the town library. It was built by the Hazards to be a community cultural center, and inside there are still reminders—like the plaster casts of Florentine singing boys—of when part of the structure was a music hall. Richly polished cypress, oak, and ash wainscoting are other highlights of the interior. On the lawn outside, the bronze relief *The Weaver* is the work of Daniel Chester French, whose *Abraham Lincoln* sits in the Lincoln Memorial. This is the only sculpture by French in Rhode Island.

Helme House (401-783-2195), 2587 Kingstown Road (RI 138), Kingston. Open during shows, Wednesday through Sunday 1–5. Now a gallery for the South County Art Association (see *Selective Shopping*), this inviting yellow-clapboard structure was a center of village activity in the 18th century, when it was two separate buildings housing a saddler's shop and a lodging house.

Kingston Congregational Church (401-783-5330), Kingstown Road (RI 138), Kingston. This simple, 1820 Federal-style church with a three-story clock tower and steeple is open on Sunday for a 9:30 AM service.

Kingston Free Library (401-783-8254), 2605 Kingstown Road (RI 138), Kingston. Open Monday and Tuesday 10–6, Wednesday 10–8, Thursday noon–8, and Friday and Saturday 10–5. Tan and gray and imposing with its cupola, this building served as the Kings County Courthouse when Rhode Island was a colony. Later, from 1776 until 1853, it was one of the five statehouses of Rhode Island. (The other communities where the legislators met, in addition to Providence and Newport, were East Greenwich and Bristol.) Since 1890 the courthouse, now completely renovated, has been a library.

In the small stone building beside it, Kingston's most notorious criminal, 18th-century silversmith Samuel Casey, was imprisoned for a time. After suffering severe financial losses, Casey tried to recoup by melting down his wife's spoons and making counterfeit money. He was tried and sentenced to be hanged. While he awaited execution in the little jailhouse, his friends managed to engineer his escape.

Kingston Inn, Kingstown Road (RI 138), Kingston. This white-clapboard former inn, which stands on the same side of the street as the church and diagonally across from the Kingston Free Library, now houses university students. But when it was constructed in the 18th century, the General Assembly was sometimes gathering in Kingston, and it was a center of public activity. Legislators, travelers, and tradesmen all stopped to wet their whistles there in those tavern days. Later, after the railroad was built in 1837, it became a mail and stagecoach stop, and after that, when the citizen-soldiers of the militia held training exercises in Kingston, it was from its porch that the crowds viewed them. One day, when too many viewers were assembled there in high hilarity, the porch collapsed. The inn was reconstructed without a porch.

Kingston Railroad Station, Railroad Avenue, West Kingston. This picturesque, old-time railroad station—a famous Kingston landmark—has been restored and moved back to make way for high-speed Boston–New York trains. There is a small museum of railroad memorabilia open Saturday and Sunday 3–6, and a bicycle path to Wakefield starts here.

Kim Grant

THE HISTORIC KINGSTON RAILROAD STATION

Pettaquamscutt Rock, Middlebridge Road, off Bridgetown Road near Tower Hill Road, South Kingstown. A bronze plaque marks the way to this rock that juts from the eastern slope of Tower Hill. This is where, in 1658, Native American sachems agreed to sell the land that today is South Kingstown, Narragansett, part of North Kingstown, and Exeter. From the top of the rock there are views out across the Narrow River to Jamestown, Newport, and lower Narragansett Bay.

Joe Reynolds' Tavern, Kingstown Road (RI 138), Kingston. Built in the mid-18th century, this was the principal village hostelry in the first half of the 19th century. Both Benjamin Franklin and George Washington are said to have been guests here, and a famous local story recounts how Franklin, arriving on a particularly cold night and not offered a seat by the fire, asked one of the servants to take some oysters to his weary, hungry horse for dinner. The whole assemblage in the tavern followed the houseboy to see the oyster-eating horse, giving Franklin plenty of room by the fire. The tavern is now a private residence.

The University of Rhode Island (401-874-1000), North Road, Kingston. At the corner by the Kingston Free Library, a sign points the way to the leafy campus of the state university. Founded in 1887 as a state agricultural school, the university still owns an extensive agricultural tract and the 1790 **Oliver Watson Farmhouse** (401-792-8296), which contains furnishings from 1790 to 1840. Located on Watson Road, it is open by appointment. On the edge of the campus is the **International Athlete-Scholar Hall of Fame** (401-874-5088), with Olympic flags, pictures, and memorabilia housed in the impressive new Feinstein Building. Open 9–5 weekdays, by appointment weekends. The Botanical Garden at 9 East Alumni Avenue (401-874-2999) is open to the public daily and its Chet Clayton Rose Garden is particularly inviting in June.

MUSEUMS **Kenyon Grist Mill** (401-783-4054), Glenrock Road, Usquepaugh, South Kingstown. Corn, wheat, rye, oats, and assorted other grains are ground here Monday through Friday 9–4. The mill is open to the public then, and the ground grains are for sale, but guided tours are only by appointment. Though a variety of grains is produced at the mill, it's the white cornmeal used to make Rhode Island jonny cakes that brings it fame. These thin, flat, crisp, dollar-sized cornmeal cakes made of Rhode Island–grown hard native flint corn were called journey cakes in colonial days. Rhode Island travelers always packed them in their saddlebags for on-the-road eating. Today native flint corn is usually unavailable, and white dent corn from the Midwest is generally substituted.

The Museum of Primitive Art and Culture (401-783-5711), 1058 Kingstown Road (RI 108), Peace Dale. Open Wednesday 10–2 or by appointment. This is a small collection of tools belonging to New England Native Americans; baskets, pottery, bows and arrows, and weaving from other native North American cultures; boomerangs from Australia; an Inuit kayak; East African lion-hunting spears; and South Sea Island head-hunter shields, among others. The museum was opened in 1892 by Rowland G. Hazard II, who urged local residents to donate the objects that are the basis of the current collection.

Pettaquamscutt Historical Society (401-783-1328), RI 138, Kingston. Open year-round Tuesday, Thursday, and Saturday 1–4. This gray granite building beside the Kingston Congregational Church served as the Washington County Jail from 1858 to 1956. A guide shows visitors the downstairs convicts' cells with their cast-iron doors. The debtors' cells on the second floor are now filled with a fine collection of quilts and costumes and a re-creation of a 19th-century Wakefield women's finery and millinery shop. There are also re-creations of a one-room schoolhouse and 18th- and 19th-century rooms, as well as a collection of local toys from 1800 to the 1950s. Among the particularly interesting exhibits are a mural, formerly in the Wakefield post office, of 18th-century South County planters, and the Civil War Room, which contains the desk of Julius Booth. He was the actor-brother of Abraham Lincoln's assassin, John Wilkes Booth, and a onetime South Kingstown summer dweller. Nominal admission fee.

University of Rhode Island Rock, Mineral, and Fossil Collection (401-874-2265), Woodward Hall, Kingston campus. Open year-round, Monday through Friday 8–4.

SCENIC DRIVES **Curtis Corner Road.** Although development is beginning to scar this laurel-edged road from RI 108 in Peace Dale to Ministerial Road, it still retains considerable sylvan charm.

Middlebridge Road. From Tower Hill head east to reach this road, which crosses the Narrow River and wends its way through marshland rich in birds.

Ministerial Road. Controversy has been considerable about keeping this narrow, winding road—where rhododendron bloom in spring and native laurel in summer—from being widened. Local residents have won the battle, but the result is a road that, though lovely, is bumpy and must be traveled with care. All the same, it's worth it. The road begins at RI 138 in Kingston and ends at US 1 in Matunuck.

Saugutucket Road. This woodsy road, crossing rivers and streams, joins US 1 in Wakefield to RI 108.

Shannock Road. This winding country road passes an attractive horse farm; it starts at US 1 in South Kingstown and ends at RI 2 in Charlestown.

STONE BREAKWATERS OPEN SOUTH COUNTY'S SALT PONDS TO THE SEA.

Kim Grant

South Road. Stone walls edge this tranquil road from Scenic RI 1A in Wakefield to RI 138 in Kingston. It is, however, beginning to fall to developers.

✷ To Do

BICYCLING William C. O'Neill Bike Path. Familiarly known as the South County Bike Path, it is 7 miles in length but when completed will be an 8-mile path around the Great Swamp and the village of Peace Dale to Narragansett. Starts at the Kingston Railroad Station or from RI 108 in Wakefield.

CANOEING AND KAYAKING In early spring, before the insect pests arrive, and again in late summer and fall after they have left, the Great Swamp is an inviting area for canoeists. The Rhode Island State **Division of Parks and Recreation** (401-222-2632; www.riparks.com) in Johnston can provide information.

FISHING, FRESHWATER Largemouth bass, northern pike, catfish, and yellow perch swim in the freshwater ponds and rivers of the state; trout and salmon are stocked. For complete information, call the Great Swamp Management Area in West Kingston (401-789-7481, 401-789-0261).

Barber's Pond, RI 2. The pond is stocked with trout annually on March 1 and cannot be fished until the second week in April. There is a gravel boat ramp.

Tucker's Pond, on Tuckertown Road off Ministerial Road, is equipped with a flat stone-and-gravel boat ramp; there is a 10-horsepower limit. Trout are stocked here in spring, so there is no fishing from March 1 until the second week in April.

Worden's Pond, Tuckertown Road off Ministerial Road. Fish for pickerel, bluegills, catfish, yellow perch, and bullheads. There is a flat stone-and-gravel boat ramp.

FISHING, SALTWATER **C-Devil II Sportfishing** (401-364-9774), Point Judith Marina, Snug Harbor. Tuna, shark, stripers, blues, and sea bass are the fish usually sought.

L'il Toot Charters (401-783-0883), Galilee. Fishing for shark, tuna, codfish, stripers, blues, fluke.

Old Salt Sport Fishing Charters (401-783-4805), 10 Amanco Street, Wakefield. Cod fishing in spring, summer, and fall off Cox Ridge, Block Island.

FOR FAMILIES ✐ **Old Mountain Lanes** (401-783-5511), 756 Kingstown Road, Wakefield. Bumper bowling.

Kim Grant

THE TOWER NEAR HANNAH ROBINSON'S ROCK.

GOLF Laurel Lane Golf Course (401-783-3844), Laurel Lane, West Kingston. This is an 18-hole, par-71 course with a snack bar and lounge.

Rose Hill Golf Club (401-788-1088), 222 Rose Hill Road, South Kingstown. This rolling nine-hole, par-3 course is made prettier with a little pond. Restaurant and snack bar.

SWIMMING East Matunuck State Beach (401-222-2632), Succotash Road, South Kingstown. Matunuck, as it's known, is one of the state's finer beaches.

TENNIS Brusseau Park, Succotash Road south of US 1, Wakefield. **Old Mountain Field Courts,** Kingstown Road, Wakefield (lit courts at night). **Tuckertown Park Courts,** Tuckertown Road, Wakefield. **Village Green Courts,** Kingstown Road, Peace Dale (lit at night). **West Kingston Park Courts,** Route 138 between the University of Rhode Island and RI 2.

The **South Kingstown Recreation Department** (401-789-9031) reserves all tennis courts, with preference given to local children.

✷ Green Space

Great Swamp Management Area (401-789-0281), off Liberty Lane, West Kingston. This is a 2,895-acre swampland of holly and rhododendron, white oak, red maple, tupelo, and pin oak. There are berries of all sorts and more than 5 miles of walking trails. Mink, raccoon, deer, foxes, ospreys, owls, black and wood ducks, pheasants, woodchucks, and grouse are among the swamp inhabitants, and there are both hunting and trout fishing in-season. A canoe is a good way to explore the area.

Observation Tower and **Hannah Robinson's Rock,** intersection of RI 138 and US 1. From the top of this 100-foot wooden observation tower, there is a view of the waters of lower Narragansett Bay and its surrounding countryside. One of South Kingstown's favorite legends concerns

Hannah Robinson's Rock, which rises just adjacent. Rowland Robinson was a prospering 18th-century Narragansett planter whose lovely daughter fell in love with her French music teacher. When her father frowned on the romance, she eloped but was soon left high and dry by her husband. Her father refused to look after her in any way until she became seriously ill. Finally relenting, he agreed that she could come home to the family house just south of Saunderstown to die. On her way there, she asked the bearers carrying her litter to bring her to this site for a last look at her beloved Narragansett Bay.

Trustom Pond National Wildlife Refuge, off Matunuck Schoolhouse Road. The refuge protects more than 640 acres of fields, shrubs, and woods. In May the white blossoms of the shadbush and the beach plum are everywhere; least terns come to nest, and the songs of prairie warblers and bobolinks are in the air. Summer brings the fragrance of honeysuckle and sweet pepperbush and shorebird migration in August. In September the eyes can feast on the velvet orange and black of migrating monarch butterflies. From mid-September into early October the hawk migration dominates, and ruddy ducks and scup begin to raft on the pond. Even in winter there is much for the visitor to see—gray foxes, river otters, raccoons, and here and there the nests of great horned owls. Observation platforms along the 3 miles of trails allow viewing without disturbing the birds.

✷ Lodging

INNS AND BED & BREAKFASTS While you won't find as many inns and bed & breakfasts in South County as on Aquidneck, the number is growing. South County B&Bs, whether on the sea or in the country, have a quiet, calming charm of their own. About two dozen are members of a reservation service, **Bed & Breakfast Referrals of South Coast Rhode Island** (1-800-853-7479), which will help you find a room if the inns are full.

The Admiral Dewey Inn (401-783-2090; www.admiraldeweyinn.com), 668 Matunuck Beach Road, South Kingstown. ($$–$$$) Nicely restored early-1900s beach boardinghouse; 10 rooms with private bath. When the inn was first opened, rooms cost 50¢ a night; another 50¢ bought three meals per day. Classic laid-back South County living.

🐾 🖍 **The King's Rose** (401-783-5222), 1747 Mooresfield Road (RI 138), South Kingstown. ($–$$) The King's Rose is a large, old-fashioned house in a lovely garden. It offers a welcoming host and hostess, five rooms, tennis courts, a willingness to take children and pets. Full breakfast. All baths are private.

CAMPGROUNDS **Long Cove Marina Family Campsites** (401-783-4902), off Point Judith Road (RI 108), 1 mile south of the intersection of US 1 and RI 128, Narragansett. Open May through October 15. Water, electricity, a dumping station, hot showers, flush toilets, picnic tables, and a boat ramp serve 150 trailer sites.

Worden's Pond Family Campground (401-789-9113), 416A Worden's Pond Road, Wakefield. Open May through October 15. This campground has 250 trailer sites, but only 20 for transients. Water, electric hookups (but not at campsites), toilets, showers, a dumping station, and play area and equipment.

✷ Where to Eat

DINING OUT ♿ **Hanson's Pub** (401-782-0210; www.hansonspub.com), 210 Salt Pond Road, Wakefield. ($–$$) Open Wednesday through Sunday 11:30–10 PM. The view of Salt Pond and the Wakefield Marina from this restaurant couldn't be better. A good-sized bar looks out over the pond and has a pubby atmosphere. Fish, hamburgers, pizza, and clam chowder are staples on the menu. Outside, there's a splendid deck for casual dining. In summer, there is sometimes live entertainment.

Matunuck Oyster Bar (401-783-4202; www.rhodyoysters.com), 629 Succotash Road, East Matunuck. ($$) Lunch and dinner daily 11:30 A.M.–9 P.M. Native farmed oysters out of Potter Pond are the star attraction at this relatively new addition to the South County dining scene. Dine indoors or on the attractive deck overlooking the pond. The menu features local seafood, prepared simply but with panache.

♿ **The Pump House** (401-789-4944), 1464 Kingstown Road (RI 108), Peace Dale. ($$–$$$) Call for hours. In 1888 this stone structure was built as a pumping station for the water system of Peace Dale, Narragansett, and Wakefield. Today it's a friendly dining place where baked stuffed shrimp and the catch of the day are highlighted on the menu. There are also several steak and chicken dishes and a fine salad bar.

EATING OUT **Camden's Restaurant and Pub** and The Coffee Shop (401-782-2328), 756 Kingstown Road (RI 108), Wakefield. ($–$$) Open daily for breakfast, lunch, and dinner. Here you're dining right at Old Mountain Lanes Bowling Alley, where you can work up an appetite rolling a string or two before ordering clam cakes, chowder, fried calamari, prime rib, or steak. The dining is more formal in the restaurant than in the coffee shop, and prices are only a dollar or so more.

Cap'n Jack's (401-789-4556; www.capnjacksrestaurant.com), 708 Succotash Road, Wakefield. ($$) Open daily, except Monday and Tuesday, for lunch and dinner. The denizens of the deep are the specialty of this waterfront restaurant overlooking Point Judith Pond. For homespun American tastes there are fisherman's and seafood platters, and for the more adventuresome such Italian seafood specialties as squid, snails, and mussels in marinara sauce. Clam or lobster rolls and fried clam strips are on the menu, too. For those who don't like fish, veal, chicken, beef, and pasta entrées are offered.

♿ **Fat Belly's Irish Pub and Grille** (401-284-4540; www.fatbellyspub.com), 333 Main Street, Wakefield, Open 11–1 AM daily. ($) There are five of these across the state—two in Warwick, one in East Greeenwich, one in Providence—but this is a particularly inviting one. Burgers come in a basket with sweet potato fries, truffle fries, or bacon-cheese fries, and the price for most is under $10. Then, of course, there's plenty of beer for washing them down.

♿ **Rhody Joe's** (401-783-0008; www.rhodyjoes.com), 515 Kingstown Road (RI 108), Wakefield. ($) Open Monday through Thursday 4–1, Friday and Saturday noon–1. This isn't the place to go for quiet dining. It's a busy and noisy sports bar, but the prices are right for such Rhode Island favorites as fish-and-chips, clam cakes, and chowder. Burgers, chicken any way you like it.

International Pocket Cafe (401-782-2720), 99 Fortin Road, University of Rhode Island campus, Kingston. ($–$$) Open Sunday through Wednesday 10–12, Thursday through Saturday 10–2, and holidays 10–10. An energetic young Syrian American and an equally energetic Lebanese American teamed up to start this fast-food operation that serves such dishes as hummus, gyros, falafel, stuffed grape leaves, tabbouleh, and beef kebabs. The ingredients couldn't be fresher. The paper-thin-crusted baklava—four different kinds—comes from the oven of one of the owners' mothers. Unpretentious but with delicious food.

Italian Village Restaurant (401-783-3777), 195 Main Street, Wakefield. ($–$$) Open Tuesday through Sunday for lunch and dinner. Plentiful portions of American-style Italian food and the best pizza around, all at reasonable prices, make this an attractive family restaurant.

The Mews Tavern (401-783-9370; www.mewstavern.com), 456 Main Street, Wakefield. ($–$$) Open daily 11 AM–1 AM. There's never a dull moment in this sprawling tavern-restaurant where mixed drinks, wine, and appetizers are served in a sophisticated setting upstairs; there are 69 draft beers on tap in the tavern and wood-fired pizza in the Pizza Bar. In the center of the spacious Tree Room, a giant light-festooned beech tree spreads its limbs. The burgers and fried squid are some of the best around if you're not watching your waistline. For those who want to eat in relative quiet, the hours between 11 AM and 2 PM are best.

♿ **Trattoria Romana** (401-792-4933; www.trattoria-romana.com), 71 South County Commons Way, Wakefield. Open daily except Monday from 4:30–9 or until 10 on Friday and Saturday. ($–$$) Macaroni and cheese with fresh Maine lobster is an all-time favorite at this spacious Italian restaurant, or there's pasta with calamari, jumbo shrimp, sea scallops, and littlenecks.

✷ Entertainment

Theatre by the Sea (401-782-8587; www.theaterbythesea.com), 364 Cards Pond Road, Matunuck. For more than 60 years (though with a brief hiatus a few years ago), this theater through which sea breezes blow has been offering the best of Broadway to vacation audiences from the end of May through Labor Day. The old weathered-shingled theater building itself is on the National Register of Historic Places.

University of Rhode Island (401-874-2431), South Kingstown. The university offers frequent concerts (see *Special Events*).

✷ Selective Shopping

ANTIQUES SHOPS Cheshire Cats Antiques & Consignments (401-792-0035; www.cheshirecats antiques.com), 333 Main Street, Wakefield. In summer 11–5 Tuesday through Saturday, 12–4 Sunday. Call for other hours. Antique porcelain, kitchenware, rugs, clocks, lighting fixtures, furniture and much more.

Verdigris (401-783-3700), 335 Main Street, Wakefield. Antique jewelry, nautical items, garden decorations, and collectibles.

ART GALLERIES Courthouse Center for the Arts (401-782-1018; www.courthousearts.org), 3481 Kingston Road (RI 138), West Kingston. Open 10–4 Monday through Friday. At this gray granite, early-20th-century former courthouse, the South County Center for the Arts offers art exhibits, community theater, and concerts. Handicrafts and art are sold at an artisan's shop.

Hera Gallery (401-789-1488), 327 Main Street, Wakefield. Open year-round, Wednesday through Friday 1–5, Sunday 10–4. This lively, modern art gallery displays the work of Rhode Island—and other—artists.

South County Art Association (401-783-2195), 2587 Kingstown Road (RI 138), Kingston. Located in the historic Helme House (see *To See—Historic Sites*) and open occasionally for exhibitions by area artists.

ARTISANS Thomas Ladd Pottery (401-782-0050), 352 High Street, Wakefield. Salt-glazed stoneware and Raku. Open Tuesday through Saturday 9–6 or by appointment.

Peter Pots Pottery (401-783-2350; www.peterpotspottery

.com), off RI 138, down Dugway Bridge Road, Usquepaugh, South Kingstown. Open Monday through Saturday 10–4, Sunday 1–4. Since 1948 Peter Pots Pottery has created dishes in muted tones with subtle designs, making it a popular spot for gift buying in Rhode Island. It's worth the trouble to find this hidden spot, down a road that is exceptionally lovely in fall.

BOOKSTORES **Kingston Hill Store** (401-792-8662), 2528 Kingstown Road (RI 138), Kingston. Antique prints, old postcards, and used and rare books, including many of local interest, are displayed in an atmospheric old bookshop.

Rhode Island Book Co. (401-789-8530), 99 Fortin Road, Kingston. Reference and instructional books, including a wide selection of computer manuals.

University of Rhode Island Bookstore (401-874-2721), Memorial Union Building, URI campus, Kingston. Textbooks and general books.

Wakefield Books (401-792-0000), 160 Old Tower Hill Road (in the Wakefield Mall), Wakefield. Open daily.

SPECIAL SHOPS **BasketCase** (401-284-1551), 212 Main Street, Wakefield. Open 10–6 Monday through Saturday, 12–5 Sunday. Rhode Island–made seashell and sea glass jewelry, rugs, bedding, scarves. Hats. Many items with a coastal look.

Birdwatchers Nature View (401-789-8020; 1-800-270-8020; www.e-natureview.com), 484 Main Street, Wakefield. Open daily, though the hours vary. There's everything from binoculars, birdseed, bird and guidebooks, and bird feeders to singing toy bluebirds and cardinals in this charming little shop for ornithologists.

Folk Art Quilts (401-789-5985), 344 Main Street, Wakefield. Open Tuesday through Saturday 10–5. Everything the quilter needs—fabric, patterns, thread, lessons, and expert advice.

The Glass Station (401-788-2500), 318 Main Street, Wakefield. Open every day except Wednesday, with glassblowing on the premises. It may be vases or bowls or drinking glasses, jewelry or Christmas tree ornaments being created. It's wise, however, to call ahead to find out what time the glassblowing is being done.

Jennifer's Chocolates (401-783-1673, 401-783-8423), 254 Robinson Street, Wakefield, and 160 Tower Hill Road in the Wakefield Mall. Old-fashioned, scrumptious handmade chocolates and brownies and hot chocolate mix are made in the sweet-smelling Robinson Street shop where there is also a mini-café. Mall store hours are 10–9 daily and 11–5 Sunday. Robinson Street hours are 10–6 Monday through Friday, 8–5 Saturday, closed Sunday.

Kenyon's Grist Mill (401-783-4054; www.kenyonsgristmill.com), off RI 138, Usquepaugh, South Kingstown. Open weekdays 9–4, Saturday and Sunday 11–4, weekdays only 11–4 January through April. Flour and grain of all sorts along with mixes for Rhode Island clam cakes are all sold here.

Knit One, Purl Two (401-783-8883), 406 Main Street, Wakefield. Yarn and more yarn for dedicated knitters, patterns and knitting accessories. Open Monday through Saturday.

The Purple Cow (401-789-2389; http://thepurplecow.net), 205 Main Street. Wakefield. Handmade jewelry, pottery, and whimsical gift items.

Store Four (401-783-7388; www.storefour.net), 673 Kingstown Road, Wakefield. Open daily. This is a store that sells the perfect wedding gift—elegant kitchenware and tableware, tablecloths and napkins and flatware.

Sweenor's Chocolates (401-783-4433; 1-800-834-3123; www.sweenorschocolates.com), 21 Charles Street, Wakefield. Three generations of Sweenors have been making delectable chocolates, almond brittle, and fudge here for more than 50 years. The shop is open 9:30–5:30 Monday through Saturday and Sunday from noon to 5. Candy making—in particular candy cane making—can be seen in the kitchen. Other outlets are in Charlestown and Cranston.

Zero Wampum (401-789-7172), 161 Old Tower Road, Wakefield. Open weekdays 10–8, Saturday until 6, Sunday noon–5. There's a little bit of everything in this cheerful gift shop—colorful ceramics and glass, Japanese paper lanterns, handcrafted Rhode Island jewelry, note cards.

FARM STANDS **John and Cindy's Harvest Acres Farm** (401-789-8752), 425 Kingstown Road, West Kingston. Open May through Christmas Eve, daily 10–6.

✷ Special Events

For up-to-date Special Events visit the website of the South County Tourism Council at www.southcountyri.com.

January–May: **Concerts and recitals** (401-874-2431), Fine Arts Center Concert Hall, University of Rhode Island, Kingston.

April: **Easter Egg Hunts** the Saturday before Easter in Wakefield.

May: **Spring concerts** (401-874-2431), URI Symphony Orchestra, Fine Arts Center, URI. **Arbutus Garden Club Annual Plant Sale,** South Kingstown American Legion Hall, Wakefield. **Kingston Village Fair,** Kingston Congregational Church and Fayerweather Craft Center, Kingston. **Memorial Day Parade,** Wakefield.

May–October: South Kingstown/URI **Farmers' Market** (401-789-1388), URI East Farm, 2095 Kingstown Road (off Route 108), South Kingstown. Saturday 9–noon. Wakefield/Marina

Park **Farmers' Market** (401-789-1388), Marina Park,South County Hospital exit off Route 1, 2 Salt Pond Road, Wakefield, Tuesday 3–6.

June: **Summer Chamber Music Festival** (401-789-0665), Fine Arts Recital Hall, URI, Kingston. **Laurel Day Festival,** Ministerial Road, Kingston.

July: **Fourth of July Parade and Fireworks,** Wakefield. **Kingston Chamber Music Festival** (401-789-0665), Fine Arts Recital Hall, URI. **Hot Air Balloon Festival,** Athletic Field, URI, Kingston. **Snug Harbor Shark Tournament and Fluke Tournament** (401-783-7766), Snug Harbor Marina, Wakefield.

July and August: **Neighborhood Guild Concerts** (401-789-9301), village green, Peace Dale. Kingston Chamber Music Festival. **Washington County Fair** (401-539-2497), Route 112, Richmond, usually held in August.

September: **Narragansett Great Swamp Fight memorial service** (401-364-1100), at the Great Swamp Fight Memorial, 1 mile south of RI 138 in West Kingston.

December: Annual Village Green **Tree Lighting,** Peace Dale.

CHARLESTOWN AND RICHMOND AREA

The tribal lands of the Narragansett Nation extend over 1,800 acres of woods and fields in rural Charlestown, which was named for Charles II, who gave Rhode Island its charter in 1663. Each summer and fall Native American musicians and dancers perform in celebrations open to all. Here are the Cup and Saucer Rocks—huge boulders, balanced on a ledge, that the Narragansetts rolled together centuries ago so that the rumbling would send messages. This area also holds the Narragansett Coronation Rock, church, and royal burying ground.

The level land here was once dominated by potato farming. That gave way to turf farming in the 1970s after a potato bug infestation caused crop failures at the same time that housing developments and businesses multiplied, which increased the demand for ready-made patches of lawn.

Along the ocean, Charlestown is edged with long barrier beaches, ever-popular with neighboring Connecticut residents, and windswept salt ponds rich in crabs, quahogs, and steamers. In the Charlestown woods, freshwater ponds sparkle, and its swamps are rich in bird life. Charlestown is one of the Ocean State's most laid-back areas, and its appeal is largely to visitors who are laid back, too.

In the town of Richmond to the north, white-clapboard mill villages like Carolina, Kenyon, Shannock, Woodville, and Wyoming suddenly appear at the end of long, bosky roads, and the Wood River, Rhode Island's best trout stream, winds among maple and oak, laurel and birch.

GUIDANCE **Charlestown Chamber of Commerce** (401-364-3878), Ninigret Park exit off US 1 and Scenic RI 1A northbound. Open limited hours mid-June through September. Sells tickets to such events as the Big Apple Circus, as well as providing travel information.

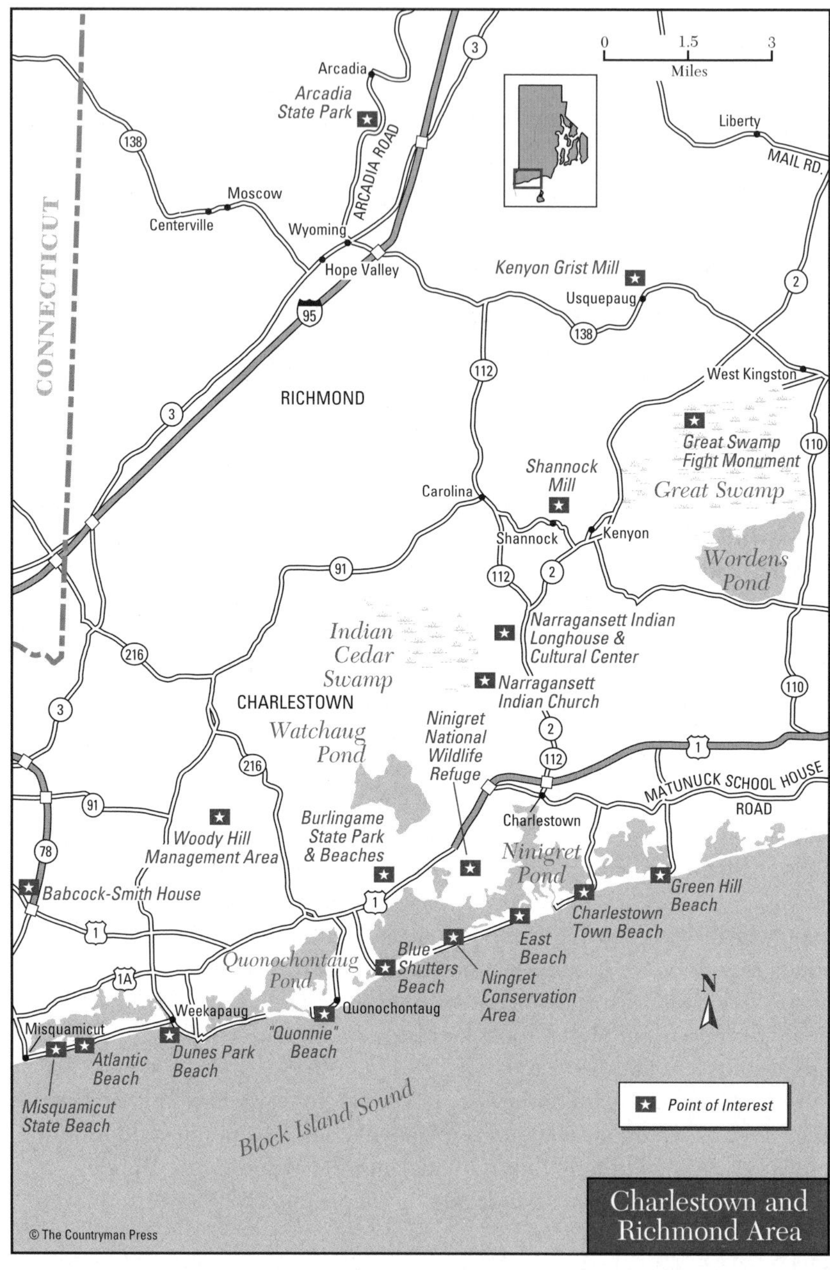
Charlestown and Richmond Area
CONNECTICUT
Arcadia
Arcadia State Park
ARCADIA ROAD
Moscow
Centerville
Wyoming
Hope Valley
Liberty
MAIL RD.
Kenyon Grist Mill
Usquepaug
West Kingston
RICHMOND
Great Swamp Fight Monument
Great Swamp
Shannock Mill
Carolina
Shannock
Kenyon
Wordens Pond
Narragansett Indian Longhouse & Cultural Center
Indian Cedar Swamp
Narragansett Indian Church
CHARLESTOWN
Watchaug Pond
Ninigret National Wildlife Refuge
MATUNUCK SCHOOL HOUSE ROAD
Charlestown
Woody Hill Management Area
Burlingame State Park & Beaches
Ninigret Pond
Babcock-Smith House
Green Hill Beach
Charlestown Town Beach
East Beach
Quonochontaug Pond
Blue Shutters Beach
Ningret Conservation Area
Weekapaug
Quonochontaug
Misquamicut
Atlantic Beach
Dunes Park Beach
"Quonnie" Beach
Misquamicut State Beach
Block Island Sound
Point of Interest
0 1.5 3
Miles
N
© The Countryman Press

GETTING THERE *By car:* Charlestown lies about 6 miles northeast of the Connecticut border and about 40 miles southwest of Providence. From Mystic take US 1 east. From Providence take I-95 to exit 9 to RI 4, and then follow US 1 into Charlestown. Automobile is really the only convenient way to get to Charlestown.

By rail: **Amtrak** (1-800-USA-RAIL; www.amtrak.com) has service from both Boston and New York to Kingston and Westerly. From either point, a taxi must be taken the rest of the way.

By bus: **Rhode Island Public Transport Authority** (RIPTA; 401-781-9400; www.ripta.com) has bus service to Kingston and Wakefield, but a taxi must be taken from both towns into Charlestown.

By taxi: **Wright's Taxi** (401-596-TAXI; 1-800-698-2941), or Eagle Cab (401-596-7300).

MEDICAL EMERGENCY The statewide emergency number is **911.**

Westerly Hospital (401-506-6000), 25 Wells Street, Westerly. **South County Hospital** (401-782-8000), Kenyon Avenue, Wakefield.

✷ Villages

Ashaway. Here on the banks of Hopkinton's Ashaway River in 1824, Captain Lester Crandall, a local fisherman, began twisting his own fishing lines with the help of a wooden wheel. Industrious and entrepreneurial, Captain Crandall was soon making fishing line for others. He built a dam to provide the waterpower to run the machinery for his production, and before he died he was selling fishing line worldwide. Today Crandall Field is a charming village green, and pretty Victorian houses line the village streets.

Carolina. This little community straddles the town lines of Richmond and Charlestown. In the mid–19th century Rowland G. Hazard bought the gristmill that stood here and turned it into a cotton mill; he named the village Carolina for his daughter, early Wellesley College president Caroline Hazard. Most of the Greek Revival and Victorian houses in Carolina were constructed by the early 20th century. The mill then closed during the Depression, and little Carolina has been largely frozen in time ever since. Among the grander homes here, all on RI 112, are the hilltop house with touches of gingerbread that once belonged to the owners of the mill; the octagon-shaped house; the imposing Italianate house; and, set back next to it, the Greek Revival house with an encircling porch. There is also the white-clapboard and Westerly granite Carolina Free Will Baptist Church, built in 1845, with a well-restored interior.

Hopkinton City. Its impressive name notwithstanding, this is barely a crossroads on RI 3 in the town of Hopkinton, but it has a handful of handsome 18th- and 19th-century houses, including Federal, Greek Revival, and Colonial structures. In the mid–19th century this was a carriage- and sleigh-manufacturing town.

Shannock. This pretty little village of white-clapboard houses near the Pawcatuck River in Richmond is situated on a road as tortuous as the river itself. In the 18th century there was a gristmill and a sawmill here. Toward the end of that century a woolen mill was constructed. Virtually abandoned years ago, the village was more recently discovered, purchased in its entirety by a developer, and restored. The project, which was planned to attract upwardly mobile young couples, largely went sour. But the restored Shannock has remained, a gem of a rural Rhode Island mill village.

Wyoming. There was an ironworks in this Richmond village in the 18th century; in the 19th century it became the site of two textile mills, and its handsome Greek Revival houses were built in this period. An old horseshoe-shaped dam here spans the Wood River.

✷ To See

HISTORIC SITES **Charlestown Historical Society**, Old Post Road (Scenic RI 1A), Charlestown (www.charlestownhistorical.org) Open July and August Wednesday 2–4 and Saturday 10–noon. Small donation requested. This one-room 1838 schoolhouse, which was in use in neighboring Quonochontaug until 1918, has an 1856 map on its wall, period primers, and a potbelly stove. As this book went to press, a town museum was under construction next door.

Fort Ninigret, Fort Neck Road, Charlestown. Boats bob in a sheltered cove below this grassy park, where an iron railing marks the site of what is believed to have been an early Dutch trading post. For many years the earthworks here were thought to have been part of a Niantic tribe stronghold. The rough stone in the center of the site is a memorial to the Niantics and the Narragansetts.

Narragansett Indian Church (401-364-7750), off RI 112, across from the Charlestown Police Station. This Greek Revival granite church burned down some years ago, but it has been rebuilt and is open for Sunday services. Further information is available from the Narragansett Tribal Council's administrative offices, situated at the junction of RI 2 and RI 112 and open weekdays 8:30–4:30.

Kim Grant

THE HORSESHOE FALLS IN WYOMING

✷ To Do

CANOEING AND KAYAKING **Breachway Bait & Tackle** (401-364-6407; www.oceanstateangler.com/breachway), 166 Charlestown Beach Road, Charlestown. Open daily year-round. Canoe, kayak and saltwater fishing rod rentals, shellfishing and saltwater fishing licenses.

Hope Valley Bait and Tackle Shop (401-539-2757), RI 3 and RI 138, Wyoming. Canoe rentals. Hunting and fishing licenses.

The Kayak Centre of Rhode Island (40-1-384-8000; www.kayakcentre.com) 562 Charlestown Beach Road, Charlestown. Open Memorial Day to Labor Day, 8-5 weekdays, noon-5 Sunday. Kayak rentals and guided trips and tours.

Ocean House Marina (401-364-6040; www.oceanhousemarina.com), 60 Town Dock Road, Charlestown. Open 7–5 most days in season; 8–4 off-season. Pontoon boats and aluminum skiffs to rent by the day or week. Fishing licenses.

FISHING, FRESHWATER A license is required for all freshwater fishing in the state, except for fishing in **Watchaug Pond** (401-322-7337), US 1, Burlingame State Park.

Ashville Pond, Canonchet Road, Hopkinton. Trout, bass, perch, bullheads, and pickerel are all found here.

Biscuit City Landing, access to Pawcatuck River. The Biscuit City Road is directly off RI 2. Angle for northern pike, largemouth bass, bullheads, pickerel, trout, and sunfish.

Dow Field, Main Street, Hopkinton, and **Grantville,** Hope Valley Road, Hopkinton. These are two of the best access points for Wood River trout fishing. There is also the **Wood River Access** in Wyoming.

Locustville Pond, Fairview Avenue, Hopkinton. Although there are no trout in this pond, calico bass are a good catch here.

Richmond Landing, Pawcatuck River, RI 91, Richmond. Catch northern pike, largemouth bass, pickerel, trout, and bullheads.

Wyoming Pond, off I-95, Wyoming. Bullheads, trout, largemouth bass, and pickerel are all here.

FISHING, SALTWATER As of 2011, the state of Rhode Island requires a license for saltwater fishing. There are also limits on take. Information is available from **DEM's Division of Fish and Wildlife**, http://saltwater.ri.gov.

Charlestown Breachway, Charlestown Beach Road. Striped bass, bluefish, tautog, and winter and summer flounder can be caught here.

Ninigret Conservation Area, East Beach Road, Charlestown. From this long stretch of state-owned beach that extends to the Charlestown Breachway, there is fine fishing for striped bass, bluefish, tautog, and winter and summer flounder.

Quonochontaug Beach, West Beach Road, Charlestown. Striped bass, bluefish, and winter and summer flounder are the prizes along this stretch of beach.

FOR FAMILIES **The Fantastic Umbrella Factory** (401-364-6616), Ninigret Park Tourist Information exit off US 1, Charlestown. Open year-round. The whole family will enjoy this potpourri of shops, gardens, a café, and a 19th-century farmyard with ducks, geese, emus, goats, and chickens. Many flower varieties grow in an untamed backyard garden, including lilies, cannas, hibiscus, dahlias, and phlox. There is also a greenhouse open spring, summer, and fall. Shops in the complex are Frills offering clothing and jewelry, Small Axe Productions selling locally thrown pots and handblown glass earrings, scarves, pocketbooks, etc., The General Store with candy, toys and gifts. Hours for most of the complex's tenants are 10 to 5 daily. Open July through September, daily 11–6, and in other months on weekends. The Umbrella Factory has a "hippie" flavor, distinctly reminiscent of the 1960s, when it was founded.

GOLF **Beaver River Golf Club** (401-539-6022), 343 Kingstown Road, Richmond. This inviting 18-hole course with a restaurant, bar, and pro shop is just a few years old.

Fenner Hill Golf Club (401-539-8000), 33 Wheeler Lane, Hope Valley. Rolling hills and rambling stone walls are part of the setting for this challenging 18-hole golf course that has a restaurant and lounge.

Laurel Lane (401-783-3844), 309 Laurel Lane, West Kingston. There's a driving range and two practice greens along with a snack bar, pro shop, and lounge at this well-maintained 18-hole course.

Lindhbrook Executive Golf Club (401-539-8700), Alton-Woodville Road (exit 2 off I-95), Hope Valley, Hopkinton. This is an 18-hole golf course on flat terrain with brooks and ponds.

Meadow Brook (401-539-6491), 163 Kingstown Road, Richmond. An 18-hole championship course set among pines and oaks with a small grill and bar.

Pinecrest Golf Club (401-364-8600), Pinecrest Drive, Richmond. This impeccably maintained nine-hole course set among pines and oaks has a grill, bar, and snack bar.

Richmond Country Club (401-364-9200), 79 Sandy Pond Road, Richmond. An 18-hole, well-maintained golf course among the pines with a pond.

HORSEBACK RIDING **Old Coach Farm** (401-783-6555), 410 Old Coach Road, Charlestown. Riding lessons and horse boarding, but no trail rides.

Sugarland Stables (401-539-2742), Hillsdale Road, Richmond. Half-hour and hour-long lessons, but no trail rides.

STARGAZING ✐ **Frosty Drew Observatory** (401-364-9508), Ninigret Park, off Scenic RI 1A, Charlestown. On clear Friday nights in summer, the astronomically inclined can study the stars at this observatory.

SWIMMING, FRESHWATER ✐ **Burlingame Picnic Area** (Watchaug Pond), Burlingame State Park, off RI 1, just 2 miles north of the Burlingame Camping Area. Shallow water and a clean beach make this an attractive spot for small children. Lifeguards are on duty. Restrooms, fireplaces, picnic areas.

✐ **Ninigret Park,** off Scenic 1A, Charlestown, has a pond that is ideal for children.

ENJOYING THE VIEW AT CHARLESTOWN BEACH

Katherine Imbrie

Kim Grant

CHARLESTOWN TOWN BEACH

SWIMMING, SALTWATER **Blue Shutters Beach** (401-364-7000), East Beach Road, off RI 1. Town beach of Charlestown is one of the most popular in the area, especially for families.

Charlestown Town Beach (401-364-7000), Charlestown Beach Road, off RI 1. Small but nicely set up beach with surf and room for volleyball.

East Beach/Ninigret State Conservation Area (401-322-0450), East Beach Road. Frequently described as one of the most beautiful and unspoiled beaches in the state, East Beach is never crowded, in part because the parking lot is small. To be sure of getting a spot, get there early.

TENNIS **Ninigret Park,** off Scenic RI 1A, Charlestown. Several courts, no fee.

✷ Green Space

Arcadia Wildlife Management Area (401-539-2356). This 13,817-acre habitat is the largest wildlife preserve in the state, offering trails through fields and evergreen forests, past wetlands and marshes. The wildlife of Arcadia includes foxes, deer, mink, snowshoe hares, ring-necked pheasants, ruffed grouse, and wild turkeys. Pheasants and bobwhites are both stocked during hunting season, and Arcadia's ponds contain warm- and cold-water fish. The Wood River, which flows through Arcadia, is Rhode Island's most impressive scenic wild river, renowned for its trout. The management area extends not only into the towns of Hopkinton and Richmond but also into Exeter and West Greenwich. Access in Richmond is off K-G Ranch Road or off Old Nooseneck Hill Road, which leads to Wildlife Management Headquarters.

Burlingame Wildlife Management Area (401-322-7994), Charlestown. Here there are 1,390 acres of forest, wetland, marsh, and agricultural land with rabbits, deer, foxes, raccoons, muskrats, and coyotes among the resident mammals, and ruffed grouse, wild turkeys, woodcock, and waterfowl also in evidence. Access is north of Buckeye Brook Road at Clawson Trail.

Carolina Wildlife Management Area (401-364-3483), Richmond. Foxes, deer, woodchucks, muskrats, otters, ospreys, and owls are just a few of the animal and bird species you might encounter on a hike through this 1,875-acre area of woodland, wetland, and agricultural land. A segment of the Pawcatuck River flows through the area. Access is possible at three locations: the hunter check station on Pine Hill Road, along Shippee Trail off Hope Valley Road, and along Meadowbrook Trail north of Pine Hill Road.

Kettle Pond Visitor Center (401-364-9124; www.fws. gov/ninigret /complex), 50 Bend Road, Charlestown. Two miles of trails through woods and overlooking the ocean and a visitor center filled with exhibits on habitat diversity and protection.

Kimball Wildlife Refuge (401-949-5454), off Prosser Trail, Charlestown. The Audubon Society runs this area, which is especially attractive to waterfowl and migrating birds.

Long Pond Woods (401-949-5454), Canonchet Road, Hopkinton. Trails wind through hemlock and around rock outcroppings at this Audubon refuge.

✐ **Ninigret Conservation Area, Ninigret Park,** and **Ninigret National Wildlife Refuge** (401-364-9124, www.fws.gov/ninigret), off Scenic RI 1A, Charlestown. These three separate areas edge both sides of Ninigret Pond. About 2.5 miles of barrier beach stretch along the conservation area on the ocean side. At the town-owned park, lifeguards watch over a spring-fed beach with freshwater swimming that is ideal for children. The park also offers a playground, 10-speed-bicycle course, and tennis and basketball courts. In the refuge you can walk through beach plum bushes and honeysuckle that shelter birds and deer, and there is access to Ninigret Pond for swimming, wading, and shelling.

✷ Lodging

HOTELS AND INNS

♿ **The Stagecoach House** Inn (401-539-9600; 1-888-814-9600; www.stagecoachhouse.com), 1136 Main Street, Wyoming. ($–$$) Back in the 18th century this inn above the Wood River in the village of Wyoming was a stagecoach stop. Over the years it fell on hard times, but it has now been refurbished to offer 12 air-conditioned rooms with fireplaces—not elegant, but comfortable. A continental breakfast is served.

The Willows Inn and Resort (401-364-7727; www.willowsresort.com), 5310 Post Road, Charlestown. ($–$$$) Open Memorial Day through Columbus Day. It would be hard to beat the setting of this hotel-motel on 20 acres above Ninigret Pond. Added attractions are a tennis court, pool table, swimming pool, and small boats for sailing on the pond. The accommodations—a motel for single-night stays, plus apartments, efficiencies, and a cottage for stays of a week or more in summer—are more ordinary than their surroundings. There is also a restaurant.

CAMPGROUNDS **Burlingame State Park** (401-322-7994; 401-322-7337), US 1, Charlestown. Open April 15 through October. Situated on the banks of Watchaug Pond, there are 755 campsites in this 3,600-acre state park, which is equipped with water, fireplaces, washrooms, showers, toilets, picnic tables, and a dumping station. Both boating and fishing are possible on the pond, and Atlantic Ocean swimming is only a few miles away. To reserve at this or any state campground: 1-877-RICAMP5; www.riparks.com.

Charlestown Breachway (401-364-7000 in-season; 401-322-8910 year-round), off Charlestown Beach Road, Charlestown. Open April 15 through October. Sites for 75 self-contained trailer units. There is a boat ramp and fishing, and swimming in the Atlantic or in Ninigret Pond. Reservations: 1-877-742-2675; www.riparks.com.

Whispering Pines Campground (401-539-7011), RI 138, Hope Valley. Open April 15 through October 15. There is space in this private campground for 30 tents and 150 trailers. Water, electricity, and sewage hookups are available, as are a dumping station, hot showers, picnic tables, firewood and fireplaces, a store and coin-operated laundry, and playground facilities. Activities offered include movies and miniature golf.

✷ Where to Eat

DINING OUT

♿ **Clubhouse Grille at the Richmond Country Club** (401-364-9292; www.richmondcountryclub.net), 74 Sandy Pond Road, Richmond. ($–$$) Open daily for lunch and dinner in-season, but call for spring and fall hours. You can overlook the 18-hole championship golf course here while satisfying your hunger with a fat hamburger or a grilled chicken sandwich, or, in the evening, feast on prime rib, fresh fish, or roast chicken at surprisingly moderate prices.

♿ **Wilcox Tavern** (401-322-1829; www.wilcoxtavern.com), 5153 Old Post Road, Charlestown. ($$–$$$) In summer, open Tuesday through Sunday from 5 for dinner. Off-season, dinners are served after 5 Thursday through Sunday. Since 1850 generation after generation of the Wilcox family has operated either an inn or a tavern in this 1730s house. The lobster bisque, prime rib, and leg of lamb are favorites.

EATING OUT ♿ **The Cove** (401-364-9222), 3963 Post Road, Charlestown. ($–$$) Open daily for lunch and dinner. Such typical ocean fare as fried clams and scallops and fish-and-chips can be found on the menu, along with pasta, sandwiches, and burgers.

♿ **Dragon Palace** (401-538-1112), 1210 Main Street, Wyoming. ($–$$) Open year-round 11–9:30 weekdays, 11–10 weekends. Japanese, Chinese, and a little Thai fare.

The Gentleman Farmer Restaurant (401-364-6202), 4349 South County Trail, Charlestown. ($) Open year-round, daily 6–8 or 9. Breakfast omelets, chocolate chip pancakes for children. Dinner entrées include such homey dishes as chicken croquettes, liver and onions, fish cakes, and honey-fried chicken.

🖍 ♿ **The Hungry Haven** (401-364-3609), 5000 South County Road, Charlestown. ($) Open daily 6:30–2:30 for breakfast and lunch; until 8 for dinner Thursday and Saturday and until 8:30 Friday. Pancakes, French toast, waffles, eggs Benedict, eggs Florentine, and omelets are breakfast specials. For children, there are silver-dollar pancakes and French toast sticks. Lunch specials include steak and cheese, veggie and turkey wraps, and homemade soups.

Nordic Lodge (401-783-4515; www.nordiclodge.com), 178 East Pasquiset Trail, Charlestown. ($–$$) At this stone hunting lodge set on a pond in the woods, you get all you can eat on Friday from 5–8:30, Saturday 4–8:30 and Sunday 3–6:30—lobster, shrimp, filet mignon, prime rib, salad, shortcakes, pies, cookies, and cakes from a buffet table. For those with mighty appetites, this is the best bargain around, even at $82 per person.

🖍 **Small Axe Cafe** (401-364-3638), the Fantastic Umbrella Factory, Ninigret Park Tourist Information exit off US 1, Charlestown. ($) Open year-round for lunch from 11–4 Wednesday through Sunday; daily in June, July, and August. Fish tacos, veggie wraps, soups, roast chicken, and much, much more—all made with locally grown ingredients—is served in this little café on the grounds of the Fantastic Umbrella Factory.

West's Bakery (401-539-2451), 999 Main Street, Hope Valley, Hopkinton. ($) Open Thursday through Saturday 6–3, Sunday 6–1. Locals flock to this little bakery for the bismarcks—raised doughnuts filled with raspberry jelly and real whipped cream—but the steak-and-cheese and cold-cut grinders are worth sampling, too.

♿ **Wood River Inn** (401-539-9800), intersection of RI 138 and US 3, Wyoming. ($–$$) The prices are surely right at this bustling, friendly, noisy restaurant. There's a special menu for seniors with smaller appetites as well as for children, and there are plenty of old favorites like shepherd's pie, fried smelts, and Grape-Nut pudding.

✷ Selective Shopping

ANTIQUES SHOP Richmond Antiques Center (401-539-2279), 320 Kingstown Road, Richmond. Open daily 10–6. Dealers rent space to show off and sell their antiques. An eclectic collection.

ART GALLERY Charlestown Gallery (401-364-0120), 5000 South County Trail, Charlestown. Open daily in summer; Thursday through Sunday in fall from 10–5:30. In winter, call for hours. Regional art and custom-made jewelry.

SPECIAL SHOPS Country Corner Yarns (401-213-6686), 5000 South County Trail, Charlestown. Tuesday through Friday 11–6, Saturday 11–5; Sunday noon–4. A large collection of yarn, patterns, and needlepoint kits.

Galapagos Boutique (401-322-3000; www.shopgalapagos.com), 5193 Old Post Road, Charlestown. Open daily 9–6 daily. This family business had its start in Ecuador—hence the name *Galapagos,* for those Ecuadoran islands renowned for their birds and animals. It sells American boutique clothing and fine lingerie for women, as well as a wide selection of gifts, cards, and novelty items. A café serving coffee and homemade pastry is a hospitable touch.

Hack and Livery General Store (401-539-7033; www.hackandlivery.net), 1006 Main Street, Hope Valley. Open year-round, but call for hours. A century ago this was a genuine livery stable. Nowadays it's full to the rafters with gift items that range from greeting cards and Christmas decorations, to women's clothing and accessories and table linens.

Hope Valley Bait & Tackle (401-539-2757), 1150 Main Street, Wyoming. Open year-round, Monday through Saturday 6 AM–8 PM, Sunday 6–6. Anything anyone could want in the way of fishing, hunting, camping, or canoeing equipment. Hunting and fishing licenses.

Mills Creek National Market (401-364-9399), 4436 Old Post Road, Charlestown. Open year-round, usually 10–6. Pottery and jewelry by local artists, recycled glassware, sea glass jewelry, pendants fashioned from Charlestown beach stones, organic foods, German wooden toys. This is an environmentally conscious shop.

Simple Pleasures (401-364-9852), 5000 South County Trail, Charlestown. Open Monday through Saturday 9–8, Sunday 10–6. Lamps, handbags and hats, soap and picture frames, birdhouses, driftwood and shell decorations are among the offerings at this eclectic store.

URE Outfitters (401-539-4050; www.ureoutfitters.com), 1009 Main Street, Hope Valley. Open Monday through Saturday 9–6, Sunday 9–5. Hikers and backpackers, hunters and anglers, birders and canoeists—all nature lovers—will find stock to explore here. Hunting and fishing licenses. In addition, there's a fine collection of books for the outdoorsperson.

FARM STANDS **Jackson's Farm Cart,** Pat's Power Equipment parking lot, Scenic RI 1A, Charlestown. Open daily in summer.

Peaches Fruit and Produce (401-364-5949), 47 Charlestown Beach Road, Charlestown. Open year-round, daily 9–6, except closed Mondays in fall and winter.

✷ Special Events

May: Richmond Memorial Day Parade (401-364-9715), starts at the Richmond Fire Station in the morning. **Charlestown Memorial Day Parade** (401-364-3878), sponsored by the American Legion and featuring the Girl Scouts, starts in the morning at the Carolina Fire Station.

May–October: Richmond Farmers' Market (401-294-6306; www.richmondrifarmersmarket.com), 5 Richmond Townhouse Road, Richmond, Saturday 9–12:30.

June–July: The **Big Apple Circus** (401-364-3878), sponsored by the Charlestown Chamber of Commerce, performs in Ninigret Park, Charlestown.

Mid-June–mid-September: Charlestown Farmers' Market, Cross Mills Public Library, 4417 Old Post Road, Charlestown. Friday, 9–12.

August: **Narragansett Indian Tribe Annual Powwow / Green Corn Thanksgiving Festival** (401-364-1100, www.narragansett-tribe.org) is held on the second weekend in August at the Narragansett Indian Church grounds on Indian Church Road in Charlestown, and includes music, dance, foods, and storytelling. The **Charlestown Seafood Festival** (401-364-3878) features clam cakes and chowder, a seafood cook-off, and live music in Ninigret Park in early August. The

Washington County Fair (401-539-7042) is a Thursday-through-Sunday midmonth event at the fairgrounds on Townhouse Road in Richmond.

September: **Swamp Yankee Days**, with crafts and food and entertainment celebrating the local country Yankee, at Crandall Field, Ashaway (401-538-0129). On the fourth Sunday in September, the Narragansett tribe holds the **Great Swamp Pilgrimage** (401-364-1100) at the Great Swamp Fight Monument on RI 2 in West Kingston, followed by special ceremonies at the Longhouse off RI 112 in Charlestown.

October: **Fall Thanksgiving Festival of the Narragansett Indians** (401-364-1100), held on the first Sunday in October, features a traditional dinner, including jonny cakes, plus an arts and crafts sale at the Longhouse off RI 112 in Charlestown.

WESTERLY AND WATCH HILL

Westerly, as the name implies, is the most westerly part of the state of Rhode Island. It shares the meandering Pawcatuck River as well as its main post office and railroad station with Pawcatuck, Connecticut.

In the 19th century, textile mills and a quarry producing good construction-grade granite and fine-grained, easily carved granite for monuments brought Westerly considerable wealth and renown. That heyday is long gone, reflected now only in a few imposing houses and public buildings, but the beach resorts of the township continue to bring it fame. And increasingly, artists from New York and Connecticut are opening studios in renovated old buildings.

Watch Hill is, after Newport, Rhode Island's most select beach resort, with arcaded shops and turn-of-the-20th-century "cottages" (less pretentious than those of Newport) set on hills overlooking Little Narragansett Bay and the Atlantic. Weekapaug, with a salt pond and a combination of rocky and sandy beaches facing the ocean, remains a place of largely remote, private, untouched natural beauty, while Misquamicut is the Coney Island of Rhode Island: young, noisy, effervescent, crowded.

When the English arrived in the 17th century, this was all Native American land (as names like *Weekapaug*, *Pawcatuck*, and *Misquamicut* suggest). The Niantic sachem Ninigret, memorialized in Fort Ninigret and by a Watch Hill statue, was then the ruler.

The first permanent white settlers are said to have been an eloping couple—John Babcock from the Plymouth Bay Colony and Mary Lawton of Newport—who fled Mary's father's wrath in an open boat that they took from Newport across Narragansett Bay. Later, other Newporters began speculating in land in the area, and Connecticut residents began making land claims. In the 18th and early 19th centuries, shipbuilding became important in Westerly on the Pawcatuck. Soon came cloth manufacturing and, in the middle of the 19th century, quarrying.

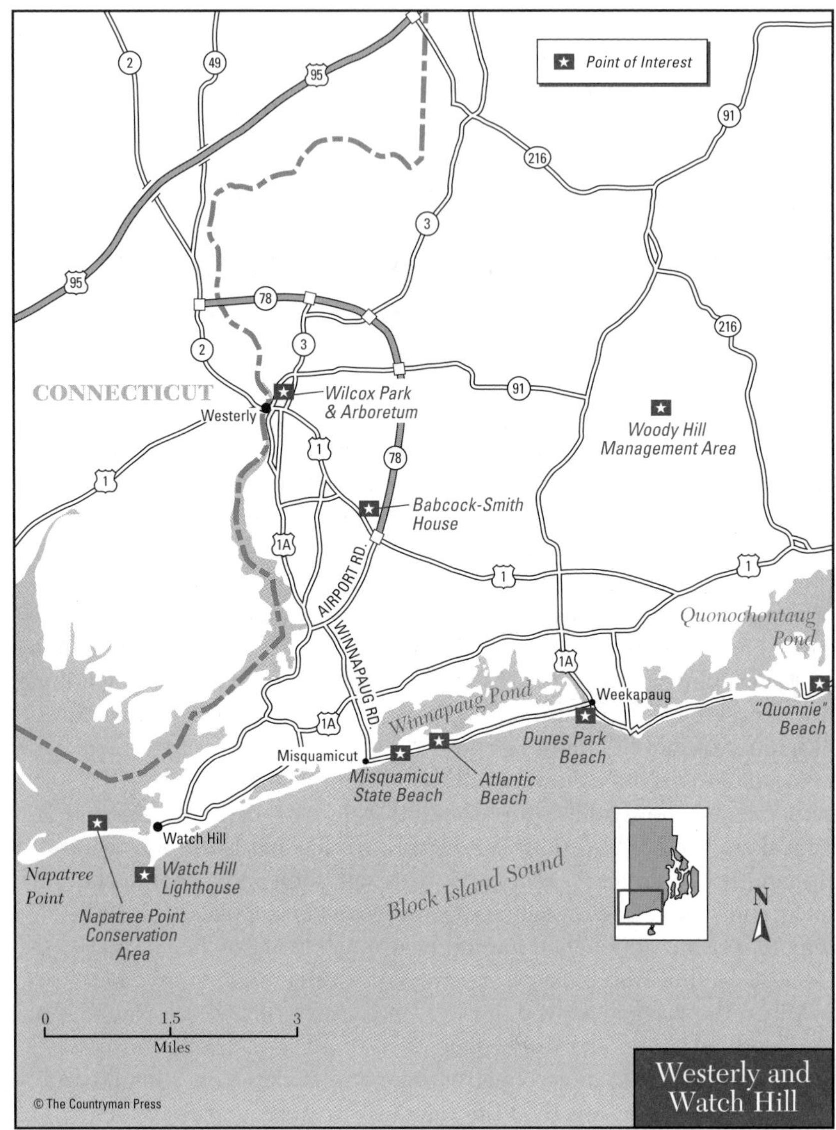
Point of Interest
95
2
49
91
216
3
78
1
1A
CONNECTICUT
Westerly
Wilcox Park & Arboretum
Woody Hill Management Area
Babcock-Smith House
AIRPORT RD.
WINNAPAUG RD.
Quonochontaug Pond
Winnapaug Pond
Weekapaug
"Quonnie" Beach
Dunes Park Beach
Misquamicut
Misquamicut State Beach
Atlantic Beach
Watch Hill
Watch Hill Lighthouse
Napatree Point
Napatree Point Conservation Area
Block Island Sound
N
0
1.5
3
Miles
© The Countryman Press
Westerly and Watch Hill

Katherine Imbrie

BOATING IN WEEKAPAUG

Today's Westerly township is a 36-square-mile area in which, as in much of Rhode Island, it is the countryside rather than the cityscape that is most appealing.

GUIDANCE **Greater Westerly–Pawcatuck Area Chamber of Commerce** (401-596-7761; 1-800-SEA-7636), 1 Chamber Way, Westerly. Publishes an annual tourist guide listing restaurants, accommodations, recreational facilities, and so on.

South County Tourism Council (401-789-4422; 1-800-548-4662), 4808 Tower Hill Road, Wakefield. This office in the Oliver Stedman Government Center can supply information about the Westerly area.

GETTING THERE *By car:* Westerly is 128 miles from New York City and 100 miles from Boston. Coming from New York, take I-95 to exit 92 in Connecticut, then CT 2 less than 5 miles to the intersection with US 1. There, turn into downtown Pawcatuck, Connecticut, and Westerly, Rhode Island. Coming from Boston, take I-95 south to RI 3, and leave it at exit 1 for Westerly.

To get to Watch Hill from I-95, take exit 92 onto CT 2, and continue to RI 78. Take RI 78 all the way to US 1, cross US 1 onto Airport Road, and at the junction with Scenic RI 1A turn left and proceed to downtown Watch Hill.

Katherine Imbrie

THE SURFING SCENE IN WEEKAPAUG

To get to Weekapaug, continue on Atlantic Avenue, crossing over the Winnapaug Breachway, and go right on Wawaloam Avenue, which leads into Ninigret Avenue and Weekapaug Beach.

By rail: **Amtrak** (1-800-USA-RAIL) has service from both Boston and New York to Westerly.

By bus: **Rhode Island Public Transit Authority** (RIPTA; 401-781-9400; www.ripta.com) goes from Providence to Salt Pond Plaza in Narragansett; from there a Flexbus goes to Westerly four times a day. The Southern Rhode Island Trolley (southernritrolley,com) also offers free service to restaurants and shops in the area from May until Labor Day.

By taxi: **Wright's Taxi** (401-789-0400) or **Eagle Cab** (401-596-7300).

MEDICAL EMERGENCY The statewide emergency number is **911.**

Westerly Hospital (401-596-6000), 25 Wells Street, Westerly.

✷ To See

HISTORIC SITES **Babcock-Smith House** (401-596-5704), 124 Granite Street, Westerly. Call for hours. Small admission fee. A two-story, gambrel-roofed, handsomely paneled home filled with old Connecticut and Rhode Island furniture, this 1734 house was built by Westerly's first physician, Dr. Joshua Babcock. Also a chief justice of Rhode Island and a major general in the Revolutionary army, he was a friend of Benjamin Franklin. Franklin was a frequent visitor and supposedly provided the lightning rods for the house roof. An engraving of the diplomat-inventor at the French court hangs over the dining room mantelpiece. An avid angler, Franklin frequently fished off Weekapaug Point. The exterior of the house is particularly notable for the hand-carved pilasters and the broken-scroll pediment over the main entrance. A 19th-century owner of the house, Orlando Smith, discovered Westerly granite. In addition to much local use, this high-grade granite was used for the Roger Williams statue in Providence and for the Rhode Island block in the Washington Monument in Washington, DC.

Flying Horse Carousel, end of Bay Street, Watch Hill. The colorful, hand-carved wooden horses with real tails and manes do virtually fly through the air with their little passengers, for the animals are suspended from a center frame. Local residents claim that this carousel, built in `1879 by the Charles W. Dere Company of New York City, is the nation's oldest. Outdoors and on the beachfront as it is, however, the carousel operates only in summer.

Ninigret Statue, Bay Street, Watch Hill. The "Guardian" of Watch Hill, legend has it, is the Niantic sachem Ninigret. Sculpted by Edith Yandell, an American artist of the early 20th century, this bronze statue kneels, a fish in each hand, in a little park in the heart of the village.

Katherine Imbrie

River Bend Cemetery, Beach Street, Westerly. Extending along the banks of the Pawcatuck, this sylvan cemetery dating from 1844 contains many a grand monument of Westerly granite.

US Post Office (401-596-2755), Broad and High Streets, Westerly. It's hard for the visitor to miss this late-Beaux-Arts building with its curved white marble facade and columns. The interior contains bronze, cast-iron, and marble decoration.

Westerly Hospital (401-586-6000), 25 Wells Street. Mementos of Crimean War nurse Florence Nightingale, who is largely responsible for modern nursing methods in military hospitals, are on display and include photographs and one of her letters. The exhibition was the gift of Westerly relatives.

Westerly Public Library (401-596-2877), Broad Street opposite Wilcox Park. Built in 1894 as a memorial to veterans of the Civil War, this yellow-brick Romanesque Revival structure houses not only one of the largest book collections in the state, but also an art gallery upstairs with changing collections in a new wing.

Wilcox Park, opposite the Westerly Town Hall on Broad Street. Open in summer, dawn–11 PM. This 18-acre park was laid out by the Olmsted architectural firm from Boston at the turn of the 20th century. It is the site of frequent outdoor musical and theatrical events.

MUSEUM ✐ **Lighthouse Museum,** Lighthouse Road, Watch Hill. Open July and August, Tuesday and Thursday 1–3. This granite lighthouse was built in 1856 to replace an earlier wooden light. The most notable rescue took place in 1872 when the steamer *Metis,* en route to Providence from New York, collided with a schooner and sank in less than an hour. Volunteers manning the one lifeboat from the lighthouse managed to save 33 of the more than 100 passengers on board. Another wreck off this site, frequently remembered because of the importance of the commanding officer, was that of a coastal patrol boat under Oliver Hazard Perry that ran onto rocks in a fog. Even when the museum is not open, its grounds are pleasant to visit.

✷ To Do

AIRPLANE RIDES **New England Airlines** (401-596-2460; 1-800-243-2460), Westerly State Airport, Westerly Airport Road off US 1, 3 miles east of downtown Westerly. Fifteen-minute flights over Block Island are offered year-round. Flights are in 10-seat, two-engine planes or six-seat four to five passenger planes and cost $89 roundtrip per person.

Kim Grant

THE LIGHTHOUSE MUSEUM IN WATCH HILL MARKS THE SITE OF MANY NOTABLE SHIPWRECKS.

FISHING **Billfish Sport Fishing** (860-741-3301; www.billfishcharter.com), Viking Boatyard, Westerly. Charter boat fishing in a 24-foot Dusky, maximum of three passengers. Stripers, bluefish, scup, blackfish, bonito.

Bonito II (401-596-6433), 13B Maybrey Drive, Westerly. Charter boat fishing for striped bass and bluefish.

Quonny Bait and Tackle (401-315-2339; www.quonnybaitandtackle.com, 5323B Old Post Road, Charlestown. Striped bass and bluefish expeditions for a maximum of three people on a 22-foot charter boat. Bait and tackle. Hunting, fishing, and clamming licenses provided.

Katherine Imbrie
FISHING IN WESTERLY

Heffernan Charters (401-364-9592; www.erinrosefishing.com), 8 Scot Circle, Charlestown. Charter boat fishing for striped bass, bluefish, scup, and fluke in a 28-foot cabin cruiser.

IN QUONOCHONTAUG POND, WEEKAPAUG
Kim Grant

Katherine Imbrie

CASTING FROM WEEKAPAUG BREACHWAY

FOR FAMILIES ✐ **Atlantic Beach Park** (401-322-0504), Atlantic Beach Park, Misquamicut. Open Memorial Day through Labor Day. Batting cages, bumper and go-carts, miniature golf.

✐ **Bay View Fun Park** (401-322-0180), Atlantic Avenue, Misquamicut Beach. Open Memorial Day through Labor Day. Batting cages, bumper boats, miniature golf, and go-carts.

✐ **Carousel** (401-322-0504), Atlantic Beach Park, Misquamicut. Some of the horses on this cheerful merry-go-round were hand-carved in 1917, others in the 1930s. Age notwithstanding, from Memorial Day through Labor Day they all spin merrily for the young at heart to music from the original organ.

✐ **Water Wizz** (401-322-0520), Atlantic Avenue, Misquamicut Beach. Open weekends Memorial Day through mid-June, then daily until Labor Day. Waterslides, serpentine slides, a kiddie slide, and high-speed slides swoop through the air and the water.

GOLF **Weekapaug Golf Club** (401-322-7870), 265 Shore Road, Westerly. This nine-hole golf course is largely on level terrain and borders Winnipaug Pond. A restaurant with outdoor seating and a fine view of the course and pond is one of its attractions.

Katherine Imbrie

SKEEBALL, MISQUAMICUT

Winnapaug Golf & Country Club (401-596-9164), Shore Road, Westerly. This is an 18-hole course on both flat and hilly terrain with a number of ponds. There's also a restaurant.

GO-CART FUN IN MISQUAMICUT

Katherine Imbrie

SWIMMING Misquamicut State Beach (401-596-9097), Atlantic Avenue, Westerly. Often crowded, this long stretch of good sand with a fine new pavilion has the feel of an old-time beach. For geographic as well as aesthetic reasons, this beach is a favorite of Connecticut residents eager to bathe in the ocean rather than Long Island Sound. To take a scenic route to Misquamicut Beach from Watch Hill, drive up Bluff Avenue, turn right onto Wauwinet, then make another right onto Ninigret to Ocean View Highway. At its end, turn right again onto Shore Road to Winnapaug Road. Turn right, then left onto Atlantic Avenue.

TENNIS Airport Road Public Tennis Courts (401-828-4450), Westerly Airport Road off US 1, approximately 3 miles from downtown Westerly. Outdoor asphalt courts, open to the public. There is no charge for their use.

Pond View Racquet Club (401-322-1100), Shore Road, Westerly. Indoor tennis courts open to the public for a fee.

✷ Green Space

Napatree Point, Watch Hill. Before the 1938 hurricane, houses stood along this 2-mile-long finger of sand. Today only the beach grass remains, where seabirds wheel and Block Island Sound thunders on stormy days. The finest spot for a Watch Hill outing, Napatree is especially inviting to explore at sunrise or sunset or when the moon is rising. On the inland side, small boats bob snugly at anchor in Little Narragansett Bay, and at the tip of the point a few walls remain of the Spanish-American War's Fort Mansfield. Access is from the municipal parking lot on Bay Street. A narrow path leads along the bay side from the yacht club past the cabanas of the private beach club. Care must be taken to stay on established paths over the dunes, as this is a conservation area.

Potter Hill Open Space Area, Westerly. A network of walking trails winds through the woods and over the fields of this 100-acre conservation area. Access is from Old Potter Hill Road off RI 3, in the northern section of town.

Wilcox Park, Westerly. Scotch elm, ginkgo, black walnut, buttonwood, and umbrella pine shade the walks and jogging paths of this pretty, 18-acre Victorian strolling park. There is a duck and water lily pond, a fountain, statues, and manicured gardens (a fragrant garden for the visually impaired among them).

Woody Hill Wildlife Management Area, Westerly. This 819-acre state management area is open only to hikers and cyclists. Much of the land is forested, but there is also hardwood swamp. Wood ducks, black ducks, mallards, and green-winged teals can be found during the hunting and fall migration season along with wild turkeys, woodcock, and ruffed grouse. Rabbits, squirrels, white-tailed deer, foxes, coyotes, raccoons, muskrats, and mink also inhabit the area. Access is along South Woody Hill Road, off US 1.

Kim Grant

WATCH HILL

✷ Lodging

INNS Breezeway Resort (401-348-8953, 1-800-452-8872; www.breezewayresort.com). 70 Winnepaug Road, Misquamicut Beach. ($$–$$$). This 55-room resort in a quiet residential area is open from the first weekend in May to Columbus Day. It is a short walk to the resort's private ocean beach or, for those who prefer to drive, there is free beach parking. There is also a pool on the property and Jacuzzis in some rooms. A continental breakfast is served, but its restaurant—Maria's—is three blocks away.

Shelter Harbor Inn (401-322-8883; www.shelterharborinn.com), 10 Wagner Road (US 1), Westerly. ($$–$$$) Open year-round. In the early 1800s this site was a working farm. The property then became a music colony in 1911. Today the old farmhouse, barn, and carriage house all have been converted into a laid-back, comfortable, 23-room country inn furnished in cozy early-American style. There's an enclosed porch-lounge, a library, paddle tennis and croquet courts, a pretty garden, and a private 2-mile-long ocean beach. Three meals a day are served year-round.

♿ **The Ocean House** (401-584-7000; www.oceanhouseri.com) 1 Bluff Avenue, Watch Hill. ($$$–$$$$). Open year-round. The original Ocean House began welcoming guests to Watch Hill in 1868 and continued to do so until 2004. Today, it has been totally rebuilt to closely resemble the original. Such architectural items as the original stone fireplaces are back in today's hostelry. This grande dame of Watch Hill sits on spacious grounds and overlooks the Atlantic Ocean and Little Narragansett Bay.

Pleasant View Inn (401-348-8200, 1-600-762-3224; www.pvinn.com), 65 Atlantic Avenue, Misquamicut Beach. ($$–$$$) This old-fashioned 112-room oceanfront inn has a pool, sauna, fitness center, and restaurant.

♿ **Weekapaug Inn** (401-322-0301; www.weekapauginn.com), 25 Spray Rock Road, Weekapaug. ($$$) As this book went to press, the inn was closed for extensive renovations under new ownership. Information on the completion of the renovations can be obtained from the website or by calling the inn number above. This sprawling, weathered-shingled, 62-room inn on 3-mile-long Quonochontaug Pond overlooks 2 miles of ocean beach.

BED & BREAKFASTS Grandview Bed & Breakfast (401-596-6384; 1-800-447-6384; www.grandviewbandb.com), 212 Shore Road, Westerly. ($–$$) Comfortable and casual, this eight-room bed & breakfast built in the early 1900s has ocean views from some of its cozy bedrooms. There's a wraparound stone porch for taking the air in the shade and a garden for sunning. A hearty breakfast is included in the price of the rooms, some of which have shared baths. Both tennis and golf are within walking distance.

Langworthy Farm (401-322-7791; 1-888-355-7083; www.langworthyfarm.com), 308 Shore Road, Westerly. ($$–$$$) This handsome 1875 farmhouse with local scenes painted on its dining room walls and a faux-book-lined library rises just opposite the entrance road to Misquamicut Beach. There are four guest rooms and three suites; some offer a splendid view of the Atlantic Ocean half a mile away. Eggs Langworthy—ham, eggs, cheddar cheese, and tomato on whole wheat toast—is among the breakfast offerings. There is also a winery on the premises.

Parkside East (401-225-6747; www.parksideeastbandb.com), 7 Grove Avenue, Westerly. ($$–$$$) This 1890s Queen Anne Victorian overlooking Wilcox Park has been restored in an inviting, modern way by its new interior-decorator owner and her husband. There is a first-floor suite with a hot tub and a third-floor suite with park view. Breakfasts include omelets and home-baked muffins.

The Villa (401-596-1054; 1-800-722-9240; www.thevillaatwesterly.com), 190 Shore Road, Westerly. ($$–$$$$)Suites with a balcony, suites with a fireplace, and suites with sheer curtains and mahogany woodwork can be found in this complex of eight suites. All are equipped with a two-person Jacuzzi, microwave, coffeemaker, and refrigerator, and there's a heated backyard swimming pool and Jacuzzi. A gourmet breakfast—at the time guests want it—is served either poolside, in the dining room, or in your suite.

Woody Hill Bed & Breakfast (401-322-0452; www.woodyhill.com), 149 South Woody Hill Road, Westerly. ($$–$$$) Open year-round, but rates vary according to the season. It would be hard to find a lovelier setting than this hilltop with informal gardens and acres of rolling fields in the distance. Though the house itself is new, it has been built like an old-fashioned farmhouse, and its three rooms with private bath are furnished largely with antiques. There is a swimming pool to escape from summer heat. Far off in the quiet countryside as it is, it's easy to forget that the mad world exists. Continental breakfasts include home-baked goods. Hearth cooking lessons also offered here.

MOTOR INN ♿ **Winnapaug Inn** (401-348-8350; 1-800-288-9906; www.winnapauginn.com), 169 Shore Road, Westerly, between Dunn's Corners and Misquamicut. ($$–$$$) A three-story motor inn overlooking the Winnipaug Golf Course, with shuffleboard, a pool, and a restaurant. About a mile from a private beach.

✷ Where to Eat

DINING OUT ♿ **Dylan's** (401-596-4075), 2 Canal Street, Westerly. ($$–$$$) Open Tuesday through Thursday 4–9, Friday and Saturday 4–10, Sunday 4–9. Casual dining in a rustic atmosphere. The all-you-can-eat pasta bar Tuesday night and the all-you-can-eat chicken bar on Sunday are local favorites. For grander dining, there are premium steaks.

♿ **Guytanno's** Café (401-348-6221; www.guytannos.com), 62 Franklin Street, Westerly. ($–$$) Open Monday through Saturday for lunch and dinner. On Sunday, only dinner is served. The seafood pasta is a perennial favorite at this intimate Mediterranean restaurant, where all the food is delicious and the wine list fine.

♿ **Olympia Tea Room** (401-348-8211; www.olympiatearoom.com), Bay Street, Watch Hill. ($$–$$$) Open daily May 1 to September 15 for lunch and dinner. In the fall, call for hours. This circa-1918 tearoom with a marble-topped soda fountain once was known for such delights as a puff pastry swan filled with ice cream and swimming in fudge sauce. But now the soda fountain has become a bar stocked with (among other things) an award-winning selection of wines. You can still get the Avondale swan and other dessert favorites like a Ghirardelli cupcake, but you can also dine on such substantial fare as a whole roasted flounder or a seafood mixed grill.

♿ **Shelter Harbor Inn** (401-322-8883; www.shelterharborinn.com), 10 Wagner Road, Westerly. ($$–$$$) Open daily for breakfast, lunch, and dinner. At this charming inn, the imaginative dishes include mango-salsa salmon as well as hazelnut chicken with Frangelico liqueur. Homey fare might include sautéed calf's liver with onions, or finnan haddie. Traditional Rhode Island jonny cakes are always on the menu, too. Since this is an inn as well as a restaurant, diners can work up an appetite with a stroll on the beach (or walk off a hearty repast). Breakfasts with banana-walnut French toast or apple buttermilk pancakes are also inviting. Brunch is served on Sunday.

♿ **Bridge** (401-348-9700; www.bridgeri.com), 37 Main Street, Westerly. ($–$$). Open daily for lunch and dinner and Sunday for brunch. The Pawcatuck River flows by this restaurant in an old stone building that in the 19th century was an addition to Westerly's Woolen Mills Company. Vegetarian grilled flatbread, vegetable black-bean burritos, and mushroom ravioli are among the many vegetarian dishes on the menu of this beautifully situated restaurant with a patio above the river that is inviting in summertime. There's live music Wednesday through Saturday evenings.

Venice Restaurant & Lounge (401-348-0055; www.venicerestaurant.com), 165 Shore Road, Westerly. ($$–$$$) Open daily 4–10 for dinner, Saturday from noon on for lunch. As its name suggests, this is a restaurant that serves Italian specialties—chicken Marsala, veal saltimbocca, but also such seafood dishes as pan-seared Stonington sea scallops. There is also a children's menu, a bar menu, and early-bird specials.

EATING OUT **Bay Street Deli** (401-596-6606), 112 Bay Street, Watch Hill. ($–$$) Open May through Columbus Day, daily 8–8. Overstuffed sandwiches, fresh as can be, and first-rate soups and pies (the apple is wonderful).

The Cooked Goose (401-348-9888; www.thecookedgoose.com), 92 Watch Hill Road, Westerly. ($–$$) Open Columbus Day–Memorial Day daily 7–3, Memorial Day–Labor Day 7–7 (table service in summer until 3; takeout until 7). Lobster salad, Thai sesame noodles, and a wide variety of salads are among the offerings at this bright and cheery little eatery where the desserts—chocolate bars and succulent lemon squares—are too tempting to be overlooked.

The Haversham Tavern (401-322-1717; www.thehaversham.com), 336 Post Road, Westerly. Open 11:30–10 daily. Two of the specialties at this casual, friendly restaurant are stuffies—stuffed quahogs—and Portuguese clams served with a chorizo sauce, but all sorts of seafood, chicken, and steak are also on the menu.

84 High Street Café (401-596-7871; www.84highstreet.com), 84 High Street, Westerly. ($–$$) Open Monday through Sunday for dinner. Lunch is served Friday through Sunday; brunch on Saturday and Sunday. A casual, friendly eatery with Formica tables and a counter. Grilled chicken, beef and vegetable focaccia, and various pastas are among the popular evening dishes.

FRA's Italian Gourmet (401-596-2888; www.frasitaliangourmet.com), Shore Road and Crandall Avenue, Misquamicut. ($) Open year-round for late breakfast, lunch, and early dinner; call for hours. Vegetarian delights as well as soups, salads, and sandwiches for carnivores. Save some room for mouthwatering Italian pastries like cannoli and cream-filled, shell-shaped sfogiatelles.

Kelley's Deli (401-596-9896), 14 High Street, Westerly. ($) Open Tuesday through Friday 7–2:30, Saturday 7–2, Sunday 7-1. There are such homemade soups as baked potato, bayou chicken and shrimp, and tomato-based chicken at this friendly little deli. Specialty sandwiches include the hefty Ninigret: turkey, ham, Swiss cheese, avocado, and a special sauce on pumpernickel bread.

♿ **Maria's Seaside Cafe** (401-596-6886), 132 Atlantic Avenue, Westerly. ($–$$) Open May through mid-September largely weekends in spring and fall, daily in summer. Although it isn't really by the seaside (it's across the road), this pleasant little café-restaurant serves many dishes from the sea along with a wide variety of pastas. Veal-filled Ravioli Maria in a cognac sauce is ever popular.

♿ **PizzaPlace** (401-348-1803; 1-877-596-7739; www.pizzaplace westerly.com), 43 Broad Street, Westerly. ($–$$). Open year-round from 11:30 AM–9:30 PM. Soups, salads, grinders, pasta, red and white pizza, children's pasta. A giant whale is the centerpiece of this spacious, welcoming restaurant.

♿ **St. Clair Annex Ice Cream Sandwich Shop** (401-348-8407), 141 Bay Street, Watch Hill. ($) Open Memorial Day through Columbus Day, in summer months 7:30 AM–9 PM; in spring and fall months 8–2 for breakfast and lunch, then until 5 for ice cream. This ice cream and sandwich shop began as a candy kitchen in Westerly well over a century ago and has been in the same family ever since. Today its specialty is homemade ice cream in more than 30 flavors. Sandwiches, clear Rhode Island clam broth chowder, and pies (strawberry-rhubarb among them) are also on the menu. A local favorite.

CAFÉ ♿ **The Bean Counter** (401-596-9999), Riverside Building, Broad Street, Westerly. Open Monday through Friday 7–5, Saturday 8–4, Sunday 8–3. Homestyle soups and salads, pastry twists, scones and muffins, cappuccino, espresso, and cafe latte.

Van Ghent Café (401-348-6026), 16 High Street, Westerly. Open Wednesday through Sunday, 8–3. Belgian waffles, crepes, sandwiches, and fine coffee, of course.

✷ Entertainment

Chorus of Westerly (401-596-8663). Several times a year this choral group holds concerts in its performance hall in the early-20th-century former Immaculate Conception Church. The structure is noted for its exceptional acoustics. In summer the chorus offers pops concerts in Wilcox Park.

Colonial Theatre (401-596-7909). Summer Shakespeare-in-the-Park presentations in Wilcox Park.

Granite Theatre (401-596-2341), 1 Granite Street, Westerly. Eight performances are given annually, March through December, in the Greek Revival former Broad Street Christian Church.

🖍 **Musica Dolce** (401-348-9453; www.musicadolce.org). This chamber music orchestra performs concerts for (and including) children and for adults throughout the year at various locations including the George Kent Performance Hall in Westerly.

✷ Selective Shopping

ANTIQUES SHOPS **Mary D's Antiques and Collectibles** (401-596-5653), 3 Commerce Street, Westerly. Six dealers display their wares, including antique and collectible Christmas decorations, buttons, and kitchenware in this shop opposite the offices of the *Westerly Sun* newspaper.

Repurposed Design and Consign (401-596-0802), 36 High St., Westerly. Antiques and collectibles and refurbishment of the old.

Westerly Enterprises (401-596-2298), 8B Canal Street, Westerly. Rare coins, estate jewelry, and antique military items from around the world can be found in this funky little shop.

ART GALLERIES **Artists' Cooperative Gallery of Westerly** (401-596-2221), 7 Canal Street, Westerly. Closed Monday. Exhibitions by artists from all over the state.

Black Duck Gallery (401-348-6500), 25 Broad Street, Westerly. Antique decoys alongside prints and paintings of marine scenes, wildlife, and sporting events.

Hoxie Gallery (401-596-2877), 44 Broad Street, Westerly. There are changing exhibits by a wide variety of artists in this attractive gallery in the Westerly Public Library.

Lily Pad Gallery (401-596-3426; 401-559-2988), 124 Bay Street, Watch Hill. Open May to Columbus Day. Oils by New England artists.

BOOKSTORES **Other Tiger** (401-596-2200; www.othertiger.com), 90 High Street, Westerly. Open Monday through Saturday 9–9, 11–5 Sunday. A wide selection of hardcover and paperback books.

SPECIAL SHOPS **Bay Breeze Interiors** (401-348-0722), 84 Bay Street, Watch Hill. Open April through Christmas. Anything and everything decorative for summer cottages, including beach-themed dishware, Simon Pearce glassware, antiques.

The Candy Box (401-596-3325), 14 Fort Road, Watch Hill. Open April through Columbus Day. Saltwater taffy, Turkish delight, candied ginger, pecan patties, fudge, and sailboat-shaped lollipops—all the favorites, domestic and imported, of a childhood of yesteryear to satisfy the sweet-toothed in summertime.

Gabrielle's Originals (401-348-8986), 1 Fort Road, Watch Hill. Open April into December. A charming collection of children's summer clothing.

Hauser Chocolates (401-596-8886; www.hauserchocolates.com), 8 Tom Harvey Road, Westerly. Delectable, innovative chocolates.

Sun-Up Gallery (401-596-0800), 95 Watch Hill Road, Avondale. Handmade glass, wood carving, and pottery by American artists as well as sophisticated, subdued women's clothing make this gallery set on the banks of the Pawcatuck River a worthwhile stop for the gift shopper.

FARM STANDS Manfredi Farms (401-322-0027), 77 Dunn's Corner Road, Westerly. Open daily June through October and November 25 through December 24.

✱ Special Events

January: **A Celebration of Twelfth Night** (401-596-8663) is offered by the Chorus of Westerly in the George Kent Performance Hall. **Westerly Artists Night** (401-596-2020). Westerly artists open their studios and galleries to the public year-round on the first Wednesday of each month. Some are in lofts; one occupies a former bank building; others have Pawcatuck River views. Music sometimes accompanies the open houses.

February: **Washington's Birthday Celebration** (401-596-7761). Sales by downtown Westerly merchants.

March or April: **Easter Egg Hunt** (401-596-7761). Easter eggs are hidden throughout Wilcox Park, and the Easter Bunny puts in an appearance. **Chorus of Westerly annual auction** in the performance hall.

April: **Rubber Duck Race** (401-596-7761). Twenty thousand rubber ducks are raced down the Pawcatuck River from the State

THERE'S NOTHING LIKE FRESH-FROM-THE-FARM PRODUCE.

Katherine Imbrie

Line on the last Saturday in the month.

May: **Memorial Day Parade** (401-596-7761) with marchers from neighboring Connecticut as well as Rhode Island. **Scottish Highland Festival** (401-596-7761) at the Washington County Fairground, with Scottish music, games, and dancers. **Virtu Art Festival** (401-596-7761), celebrating all the arts in Wilcox Park. **Spring Concert** (401-596-8663) by the Chorus of Westerly with the Boston Festival Orchestra in the George Kent Performance Hall, Westerly. Misquamicut Spring Festival (401-496-7751), Atlantic Avenue, Misquamicut State Beach. Food and games and music.

June: **Westerly Firemen's Memorial Parade** (401-596-7761), downtown Westerly. **Annual Summer Pops and Fireworks** (401-596-8663) fills Wilcox Park with musical enthusiasts in mid- to late June as the Chorus of Westerly joins the Boston Festival Orchestra. Book Fair at the Westerly Public Library.

June–October: **Westerly-Pawcatuck Farmers' Market** (401-315-2610), 85 Main Street, Westerly (behind billboard), Thursday 10–2.

July: **Shakespeare in the Park,** Wilcox Park (401-596-7909).

August: **Westerly Band Concerts** in Wilcox Park.

October: **Columbus Day Parade** (401-596-7761) from Westerly High School, with marchers from Connecticut as well as Rhode Island. Guy Fawkes Day Celebration (401-596-7751) at the Andrea Hotel on Atlantic Avenue in Misquamicut features a bonfire and costumes.

November: **Veterans Day Parade** (401-596-7761). Begins in downtown Westerly, saluting veterans of all wars with marchers from both Connecticut and Rhode Island. **Santa's Arrival** (401-596-7761), downtown Westerly. Santa makes his appearance on the steps of the Westerly Post Office, and there is an old-fashioned Christmas caroling.

December: A **Christmas Pops Concert** (401-596-8663) with the Chorus of Westerly and the Boston Festival Orchestra at George Kent Performance Hall. **Christmas Crafts Bazaar at the Babcock-Smith House** (401-596-5704). A **Luminaria and Downtown Stroll** (401-596-7761) is held in Wilcox Park. Hundreds of small white candles line the downtown streets before they are carried to the park.

Block Island

9

Kim Grant

BLOCK ISLAND

Twelve miles off the Rhode Island shore, Block Island—the Bermuda of the North—rises out of the Atlantic. It is 10.8 square miles of bayberry and blackberry tangles, moors and rolling hills, cliffs and coves. There are 365 ponds—one for each day of the year, residents say proudly—and 300 miles of stone walls rise and fall, edging the fields.

Red-roofed farmhouses perch on the hilltops, though nowadays few of them belong to farmers; Block Island has been a summer resort since the start of the 20th century. Once sultry summer days arrive on the mainland, the island's winter population of 850 more than doubles. Daytrippers on bicycles and mopeds wend their way along the winding roads; swimmers sun on Old Harbor's sandy beaches; yachters put into New Harbor. Pink and white wild roses tumble along the roadsides that lead to towering 1880s and 1890s hotels and inns, their turrets and wraparound porches overlooking the sea, open to yet another generation of visitors seeking respite from the frenetic pace of the mainland.

Block Island's history is a long one. Giovanni da Verrazzano, sent in 1524 by Francis I of France to find a shorter route to the Orient, is said to have been the first European to sight Block Island. He likened its green, undulating landscape to that of the Greek island of Rhodes, thereby giving Rhode Island its name. Block Island acquired its name from the Dutch explorer Adriaen Block, who in 1614, while sailing in Long Island Sound, stopped for a time on the island, calling it Adriaen's Eylandt.

Tranquil getaway that Block Island is for many, it has not always been so peaceful a spot. In the days of the Manisseans, the Narragansett tribe that first inhabited it and called it Manisses—"Little God's Island"—there were bloody internecine Native American as well as white–Native American conflicts. Accompanied by two white youths and two Native Americans, Connecticut trader John Oldham put into Block Island in 1636 and was murdered; his companions were taken prisoner. White men and mainland Native Americans, seeking to avenge the trader's death and free the prisoners, burned the Native tribe's island encampment to the ground.

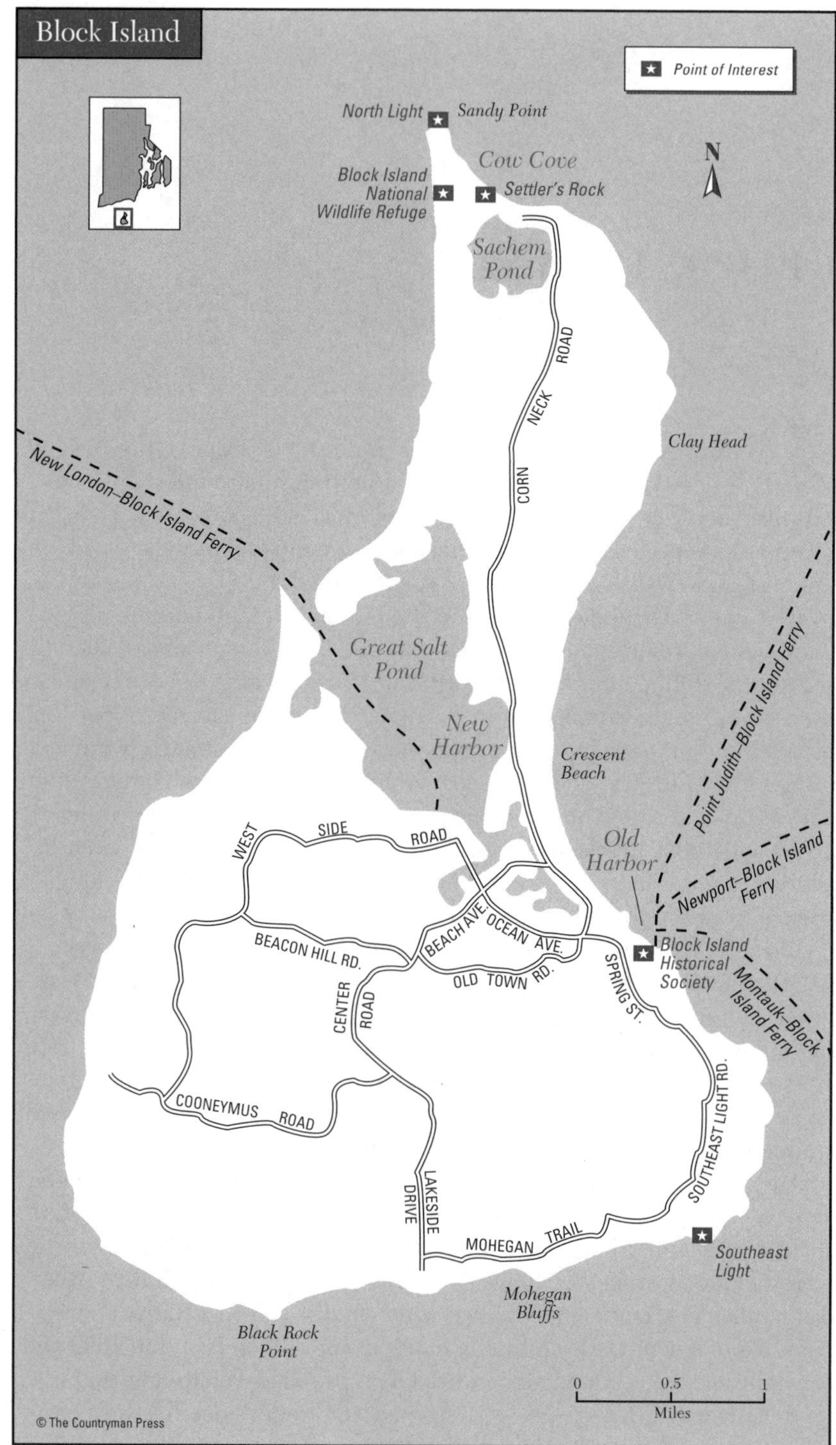
Block Island
Point of Interest
North Light
Sandy Point
Cow Cove
Block Island National Wildlife Refuge
Settler's Rock
Sachem Pond
CORN NECK ROAD
Clay Head
New London–Block Island Ferry
Great Salt Pond
New Harbor
Crescent Beach
Point Judith–Block Island Ferry
Old Harbor
Newport–Block Island Ferry
WEST SIDE ROAD
BEACH AVE.
OCEAN AVE.
BEACON HILL RD.
OLD TOWN RD.
SPRING ST.
Block Island Historical Society
Montauk–Block Island Ferry
CENTER ROAD
COONEYMUS ROAD
SOUTHEAST LIGHT RD.
LAKESIDE DRIVE
MOHEGAN TRAIL
Southeast Light
Mohegan Bluffs
Black Rock Point
0
0.5
1
Miles

Later, privateers and mooncussers came to the island to lure unsuspecting mariners onto the rocks and shoals of its waters and then loot the ships. In the 19th century a kettle of pirate gold is said to have been found, and treasure hunters still search for the chest that notorious Captain Kidd supposedly buried in a Block Island field.

For almost two centuries, from the arrival of the first English settlers in 1661 until the first hotel was built in 1842, Block Island was an out-of-the-way place where fishermen seined for mackerel and cod, shellfished, and harpooned swordfish and where farmers' cows roamed the stone-wall-bordered fields.

After 1842, visitors flocked to the summer hotels erected on hilltops and promontories, the dining rooms filled with the freshest of fish and vegetables supplied by island fishermen and farmers. In 1870 the breakwater that created Old Harbor was built, luring yachters as well as tourists.

Tourism declined after World War I, however. First came the Great Depression, followed by a 1938 hurricane that dealt the island a murderous blow. The tempest virtually cut the island in two and destroyed the entire fishing fleet.

Today tourism is regaining its former vitality. Old Harbor energetically seeks to enthrall tourists. On sunny summer days when the beach roses are in bloom or on crisp autumn days when the bittersweet is crimson and gold—and the striped bass are biting—Block Island is for sheer enjoyment.

FISHING BOATS IN BLOCK ISLAND'S OLD HARBOR

Kim Grant

GUIDANCE **Block Island Chamber of Commerce** (401-466-2982; 1-800-383-BIRI; www.blockislandchamber.com). In summer, open daily 9–5; in the off-season, Monday through Friday 10–3. Information is provided at its offices on the Old Harbor dock where the ferry comes in.

GETTING THERE *By boat:* Year-round ferry service is provided by the **Interstate Navigation Company** (401-783-4613; www.blockisland ferry.com) from the State Pier in Galilee, Rhode Island. The sailing time is approximately 55 minutes. Car reservations must be made in advance. It costs $48.75 one way to bring a car over. A one-way adult passenger fare is an additional $11.50; it's $18.75 for a same-day round-trip ticket. Children under 12 pay $5.60 one way, $8.90 for a same-day round-trip ticket. Bicycles are $2.90 each way, motorcycles are $18.70 one way. Prices are, however, subject to change on all Interstate Navigation Company routes. For those not wishing to take a car across, there is parking in Galilee for approximately $10 a day. Bus service to the ferry from various parts of the state is provided by the **Rhode Island Public Transit Authority** (RIPTA; 401-784-9500; www.ripta.com). **Amtrak** (1-800-USA-RAIL) stops at Kingston, where taxi service to Galilee is available.

From late June through Labor Day, Interstate Navigation Company also operates a passenger ferry from Newport. The one-way sailing time is about two hours. Fares are slightly lower.

From mid-June to mid-September, a daily ferry operated by Cross Sound Ferry departs from New London, Connecticut. Dock-to-dock sailing time is approximately 1 hour and 20 minutes. Car reservations must be made in advance (860-443-5281) and cost $44 one way for car and driver. Passengers are $13 one way, $22 same-day round trip. Children under 12 are $6 one way and $10 same-day round trip. Motorcycles cost $25 one way; bikes are $3. **Amtrak** (1-800-USA-RAIL) offers train service to New London.

High-speed 30-minute passenger ferry service is offered from Galilee to Old Harbor from mid-May to mid-October by the Interstate Navigation Company (www.blockislandferry.com) and is approximately $35.85 round trip; children $19.50 round trip; bicycles $6, but prices are subject to change. Reservations are recommended.

From Montauk, New York, ***Viking Star*** (631-668-5700; www.vikingfleet .com) carries passengers and bicycles—but no cars—to Block Island once a day, leaving Montauk at 10 and returning at 5 from mid-June to late September. Earlier in May and in October there is weekend-only service. The summer-season high-speed crossing takes approximately 1 hour and costs $75 round trip for adults, $40 for children, $10 for bicycles. All fares are subject to change. Parking in Montauk is about $10 a day.

By air: Year-round air service is provided from Westerly, Rhode Island, by **New England Airlines** (401-596-2460; 401-466-5881; 1-800-243-2460; www.blockisland.com/NEA) for $49 one way, $89 round trip, adult fare. Children cost $44 one way, $84 round trip, but all fares are subject to change. Parking is available in Westerly. **Action Airlines** (1-800-243-8623) offers charter service to Block Island from Groton/New London Airport in Connecticut.

GETTING AROUND *By taxi:* Taxis are generally on hand at the dock when ferries arrive. Among those operating year-round are **Oscar Berlin** (401-741-0500), **McAloon's Taxi** (401-741-1410), and **Mig's Rig** (401-480-0493).

By rental car, bike, or moped: In New Harbor, **Block Island Bike & Car Rental** (401-466-2297) offers rental cars and bikes; in Old Harbor, the **Old Harbor Bike Shop** (401-466-2029) has bikes, cars, and mopeds. For more bike and moped rentals, see *To Do.*

MEDICAL EMERGENCY The statewide emergency number is **911.**

Block Island Medical Center (401-466-2974), 6 Payne Road.

✷ To See

HISTORIC SITES Beacon Hill. Most of this 210-foot-high hill that is the island's highest point is privately owned today, but there are walking trails nearby. In Revolutionary days, when Block Island was fiercely anti-Tory, it is said that a barrel of tar was kept on top of the hill and set on fire whenever a watchman saw what looked like an "unwelcome" boatload of deserters from the mainland heading toward shore. Then it was up to the islanders to drive off the questionable visitors.

Block Island Historical Cemetery, overlooking New Harbor. Many stones here mark the graves of 17th-century settlers. On later markers, decorations include the polished black granite ball that is the emblem of part of the island's Ball family, and the pick and shovel of an islander who took part in the gold rush.

Indian Burial Ground, near the intersection of Center Road, Lakeside Drive, and Cooneymus Road. Here are the headstones and footstones of a number of Native American graves. The Manisseans were buried in a sitting position, which explains the closely set gravestones.

Mohegan Bluffs, to the west of the Southeast Light. These sandy cliffs rising 150 feet above the sea get their name from that of a war party of 40 invading members of the Mohegan tribe, who were cornered there by the local Manisseans. A wooden stairway leads down to the water.

New Harbor. Its name notwithstanding, this was Block Island's earliest harbor, but keeping the breachway open between Great Salt Pond and Block Island Sound became too difficult and expensive for the early settlers, so in 1705 New Harbor was abandoned in favor of Old Harbor. However, in 1897 a permanent cut was made, and today this is the port of call for most yachters visiting the island. On the hilltop above it sits the Victorian Narragansett Inn, and there are restaurants and facilities for yachters at Payne's Dock.

Old Harbor. Most ferries dock in this Victorian seaport. Sprawling early-1900s hotels with turrets, gingerbread decoration, and wraparound porches, as well as the half-mile-long lifeguarded Fred Benson Town Beach make this an inviting spot for the daytripper. Restaurants offer take-out fish-and-chips, lobster and clam rolls, and chowder. Little shops sell souvenirs, T-shirts, and bric-a-brac. There are also art galleries offering jewelry, stained glass, and pottery as well as paintings.

Rebecca, center of Old Harbor. This statue of the biblical Rebecca, wife of Isaac and mother of Jacob and Esau, was erected by the Women's Christian Temperance Union in 1896. At its foot sit basins kept supplied with fresh water for dogs and horses—either in memory of the gentle Rebecca's kindness to animals or because the WCTU promoted the drinking of water rather than spirits.

FRED BENSON TOWN BEACH IN OLD HARBOR IS GOOD FOR SWIMMING OR STROLLING.
Kim Grant

Settlers' Rock, Cow Cove. It is at this spot, according to legend, that Block Island's first settlers—from Braintree and Taunton in the Massachusetts Bay Colony—landed in 1661. The tale is that they pushed their cows overboard and made them swim ashore—hence the cove's name. You can walk along a sandy road from here to the North Light, but take care to stay on the road to prevent damaging the birds' nests at Sandy Point.

Smilin' Through, Cooneymus Road above Rodman's Hollow. Private. It was in this little house, one of the island's oldest farmsteads, that composer and lyricist Arthur Penn wrote in post–World War I days, "There's a little white road winding over the hill, to a little white cot by the sea. There's a little green gate, by whose trellis I wait, where two eyes of blue come smilin' through at me."

MUSEUMS **The Block Island Historical Society** (401-466-2481), Old Town Road and Ocean Avenue, Old Harbor. Open Memorial Day through mid-June, weekends 10–4; mid-June through Labor Day, daily 10–4; minimal admission fee. In Block Island's 19th-century heyday of tourism, this weathered-shingled structure was an inn called the Woonsocket House. Now its little rooms are furnished with 19th-century furniture, and there are displays of the geology of the island and of pottery and beads of the Manisses tribe. Youngsters will enjoy the birds stuffed by the late island teacher and naturalist Elizabeth Dickens.

North Light Interpretive Center (401-466-3200), Sandy Point. Open mid-June through Labor Day, daily 10–5; Labor Day through Columbus Day, daily 11–4. Hours are subject to change; call to verify. Small admission fee. Exhibits here are of the island's maritime history and old lifesaving equipment.

Southeast Light (401-466-5009), Mohegan Bluffs. Call for hours. For many years this redbrick lighthouse atop Mohegan Bluffs was the strongest light on the New England seacoast, blinking its warning to mariners as far as 35 miles away. Erosion of the bluffs finally forced its relocation 400 feet back several years ago. In its new location includes a museum of lighthouse history.

✶ To Do

AIRPLANE RIDES **New England Airlines** (401-596-2460 in Westerly; 1-800-243-2460) takes sightseers on 15-minute flights over the island, year-round, in single-engine Piper Cherokees that carry up to five people. The rate is $100 for two or three passengers.

BICYCLING/MOPED RENTALS Block Island is the ideal spot for leisurely cycling. Though it is hilly and the roads are winding, the hills are seldom arduous. The vistas invite cyclists to stop and rest awhile at the side of the road and look out across the stone walls to the sea. Because the roads are narrow and winding, automobile drivers tend to travel at a reasonable speed. Mopeds are an alternative—though considerably less safe—means of transportation. Rental rates for all modes of transportation—cars, bikes, mopeds—tend to be higher on weekends than on weekdays.

Aldo's Mopeds (401-466-5018), Weldon's Way, Old Harbor.

Beach Rose Bicycles Inc. (401-499-2035) off High Street, Old Harbor.

Block Island Bike and Car Rental (401-466-2297), Ocean Avenue, New Harbor, Adult mountain bikes, older cars and jeeps.

Island Moped & Bike Rentals (401-466-2700; www.bimopeds.com), behind Harborside Hotel, Old Harbor. A wide selection of bicycles and single and double mopeds may be rented by the day or the hour.

The Moped Man (401-466-5444), 435 Water Street, Old Harbor. At this shop located diagonally across from the ferry landing, mopeds, mountain bikes, child seats, and assorted gear for moped riders are available.

Old Harbor Bike Shop (401-466-2029), to the left of the ferry landing as visitors arrive in Old Harbor. Single and double mopeds, bikes, cars, and vans available by the day or the hour.

Seacrest Inn Bicycle Rentals (401-466-2882), at the Seacrest Inn on High Street in Old Harbor. Mountain bikes, dual-suspension bikes, 7- and 21-speed bikes.

BIRDING Block Island is situated under the Atlantic Flyway. It is said that more birds, heading north in spring and south in fall, pass by Block Island than anywhere else in New England. This and the low vegetation make Block Island an excellent birding spot. From August through early November is exceptionally good for birding, and the **Audubon Society of Rhode Island** (401-949-5454) offers a special weekend trip annually in late September or early October.

FISHING Striped bass and bluefish bite close to the Block Island shore. Offshore there are tuna, bonito, shark, and marlin; in the island's wealth of freshwater ponds, pickerel and bass are likely catches. A number of charter boats take sportfishers out to the fishing grounds in summer.

Block Island Fishworks (401-466-5392; www.bifishworks.com), Box 1373 Ocean Avenue, Block Island. Fishing for bass, blues, fluke.

Charterboat *Sakarak* (401-486-3476), New Harbor. Inshore fishing trips of three to four hours for up to six passengers.

G. Willie Makit (401-466-5151; www.gwilliecharters.com), Old Harbor. Captain Bill Gould, Box 1326, Block Island. Inshore and offshore fishing trips range in length from 3 to 10 hours.

Hula Charters (401-263-3474; www.hulacharters.com), Old Harbor. Two-hour to full day fishing trips inshore and offshore on 27-foot boat.

Old Harbor Fishing Charters (401-466-2912; www.oldharborcharters.com), Old Harbor. Two- to 12-hour inshore and offshore fishing trips.

Pale Horse Fishing Charters (1-802-379-0336) New Harbor. Three- to four-hour inshore fishing trips, with children especially welcome to fish for scup and sea bass and fluke while their elders fish for stripers and blues.

Persuader (401-783-5644), 110 Avice Street, Narragansett. Captain Denny Dillon. This mainland-based boat takes anglers out into Block Island waters on trips of 4 to 10 hours.

Twin Maples Bait & Tackle Fishing Academy (401-466-5547; www.blockislandfishingacademy.com), Beach Avenue, New Harbor. Four hours of fishing lessons for 6- to 15-year-olds.

HIKING **The Greenway** (see *Green Space*) is a 30-mile system of trails through both public and private lands. It crosses 600 acres of the island—from Great Salt Pond to Black Rock—and is open to hikers, birders, and other nature lovers, but not to cyclists. A map of the trails is available at **The Nature Conservancy** (401-466-2129) opposite Payne's Dock in New Harbor. The Conservancy also offers guided tours and children's nature programs in summer.

HORSEBACK RIDING **Rustic Rides Farm** (401-466-5060), West Side Road. Open May through October, daily 9–6; call for appointment. Guided trail and beach rides, pony rides for children.

KAYAKING AND CANOEING **New Harbor Kayak Rental** (401-466-2890), Ocean Avenue, New Harbor. Kayaks and motorboats available by the day or hour.

Pond & Beyond Guided Kayak Tours (401-578-2773 or 401-466-5105)

KITEBOARDING **Diamond Blue Kiteboarding Shop** (401-369-2297), Dodge Street, Old Harbor. Rents kiteboards and paddleboards and gives lessons.

PARASAILING **Block Island Parasail** and Watersports (401-864-2474; www.blockislandparasail.com), Old Harbor dock. Parachute flights, which rise up to 600 feet above island and sound, take off and land all summer long.

SAILING The Block Island Club (401-466-5939), Corn Neck Road, Old Harbor. Open late June through August, daily 9–4. For 30 years this club has been providing instruction in sailing, swimming, and tennis for families and individuals. The club has J-prams, JY15s, Lasers, keelboats, and Sunfish available to members. Two-week and full-season single and family memberships are available, with instruction in sports for an additional fee, but use of boats and courts is included.

***Ruling Passion* Sailing Charters** (401-741-1926; www.rulingpassion.com), New Harbor. Sunset cruises and round-the-island cruises and two-hour cruises on 45-foot trimaran.

SWIMMING Ballard's Beach, to the left as you leave the Old Harbor ferry landing. This is a clean, sandy beach adjacent to Ballard's Inn and supplied with food, beverages, and toilet facilities.

Fred Benson Town Beach (formerly Block Island State Beach; 401-466-2611), Corn Neck Road, Old Harbor. The town decided to name this section of Crescent Beach for longtime resident, raconteur, historian, and all-around favorite citizen Fred Benson. It boasts a concession stand, a bathhouse with cold showers made for rugged New Englanders, and a lifeguard.

Sachem Pond, at the north end of the island near Settlers' Rock. A fine place for youngsters to have a freshwater dip (with a touch of salt remaining from the 1938 hurricane), but there is no lifeguard on duty.

TENNIS The Atlantic Inn (401-466-5883; 1-800-224-7422), High Street, Old Harbor. Tennis courts for inn guests are available to the public for $20 an hour when guests are not using them.

Ball-O'Brien Park, West Side Road, New Harbor. Free tennis courts for public use.

The Block Island Club (401-466-5939), Corn Neck Road, Old Harbor. Access to the courts is available to members (see *Sailing*).

Champlin's Marina (401-466-2641), West Side Road, New Harbor. The public may use the tennis courts for $20 an hour when guests are not using them.

* Green Space

BEACHES Black Rock Beach, on the south shore at the end of Black Rock Road. Accessible to only the hardiest. The beach is stony, and the water is rough with an undertow. No facilities or lifeguard.

Rhode Island Tourism Division

AMBLING THROUGH THE FIELDS WITH NORTH LIGHT IN THE BACKGROUND

Charlestown Beach, Dead Man's Cove, down Coast Guard Road off West Shore Road. A west-facing beach that gets sun in the afternoon. Pebbly, so wear sneakers or beach shoes. There are no facilities or lifeguards, but the water is clear and you often have the beach almost to yourself.

Coast Guard Beach, farther down Coast Guard Road at the entrance into New Harbor. This is a fine place to watch the boats coming and going into the Great Salt Pond on Friday and Saturday afternoons. Good fishing, too.

Crescent Beach, Corn Neck Road (northeasterly from Old Harbor). Two-plus miles of sand, surf, and (cold) blue water. A must if you visit the island.

Mansion Beach, half a mile down dirt Mansion House Road off Corn Neck Road. No facilities or lifeguards, but a pleasant stretch of beach in a pretty area of bayberries and wild roses. There is often more surf here than at Benson and Scotch Beaches.

Mohegan Bluffs, south shore at the foot of the steep bluffs. Not a bad climb down, but it's a long, hard climb up. Rocky beach with rough surf. No lifeguard.

Pebbly Beach, southeast shore, off Spring Street. A sandy little beach in a cove. No lifeguard.

Scotch Beach, beyond Fred Benson Town Beach, farther to the right, opposite the Great Salt Pond. Pebbly, but a pleasant, generally uncrowded beach. No facilities or lifeguards.

Vail's Beach, south shore. Stony beach with rough water. No lifeguards or facilities.

See also *Swimming.*

WALKS **Clay Head,** off Corn Neck Road. A dirt trail called Bluestone leads to and along briar-clad Clay Head, which once was faced with good, usable clay in shades of blue, ocher, white, and red. Unfortunately, rain and sea have eroded the clay surface. This headland is the perfect spot for watching the events of June's Block Island boat race, and hikers here will find 9 miles of trails, known as "The Maze," that wander above the surf and past shimmering blue ponds and through pine groves.

Dickens Farm. This 40-acre bird sanctuary of stone-wall-edged fields begins on Cooneymus Road. Pheasants strut and swallows wheel over its grasses, and this is a favorite spot for viewing the marsh hawk. In the interest of conservation, all visitors are urged to stay on the marked paths.

The Greenway. Thirty miles of Greenway walking trails begin on Beacon Hill Road and continue to Cooneymus Road, through pastures and heath and the Enchanted Forest of Japanese black pine planted by conservationists in the 1930s and 1940s. Guided nature tours are offered twice daily in summer, and a map is available for self-guided tours from **The Nature Conservancy** (401-466-2129) in New Harbor, across from Dead-Eye Dick's. Entry points onto the Greenway from main roads are marked with posts.

Rodman's Hollow. This glacial depression that stretches down to the sea is particularly spectacular in spring, when the snow-white shadbush is in bloom, and in fall when the bayberry and poison ivy are crimson. A Greenway path meanders through the brush from Cooneymus Road to the water.

Sandy Point. One of the largest gull rookeries in Rhode Island—frequented by black-backed and herring gulls as well as yellow- and black-crowned night herons—is nestled in these dunes. Tall blond swamp grasses lie flat in the wind against the gold-brown sand. Beachcombers stroll the water's edge gathering the round, smooth, gray and white stones that rumble in from the waters of the sound. It was at this northernmost point of the island, legend has it, that the 18th-century Dutch ship *Palatine,* filled with immigrants seeking religious freedom in the New World, drifted ashore between Christmas and New Year's Day in 1752. A mutiny had left the captain and many of the officers dead and the passengers in the merciless hands of the mutineers. When they had extracted all the gold they could from the hapless immigrants, the mutinous crew abandoned ship, leaving the vessel to drift ashore at Sandy Point. In a poem criticized by Block Islanders as historically inaccurate, John Greenleaf Whittier described Block Island "wreckers" hustling down to the shore to further strip the vessel. In any case, they apparently brought 16 passengers ashore, but when a storm threatened to break up the craft, they set it afire and adrift, unwittingly leaving a woman on board—and her screams as the flames rose around her have haunted Block Islanders ever since, warning of danger.

✷ Lodging

Atlantic Inn (401-466-5883; www.atlanticinn.com), High Street, Old Harbor. ($$$–$$$$) Open Memorial Day through mid-October. This 21-room, white-clapboard hotel has sat like a grande dame on its hill above Old Harbor and the sea since 1879. Though close to town, it seems far away from the hustle and bustle of summer crowds. The pleasant rooms are Victorian in style and include a continental buffet breakfast. There is a minimum three-night stay required on weekends in high season. Two tennis courts and croquet are available for guests, and the inn's location makes its porch the ideal island spot for sunset viewing. The inn has its own dining room.

Avonlea (401-466-5891 or 1-800-992-7290; www.blockislandinns.com), Corn Neck Road, Old Harbor. ($$$) A nine-room bed and breakfast with ocean views that is open year-round.

Nicholas Ball Cottage (401-466-2421; 1-800-626-4773), Spring Street, Old Harbor. ($$$$) Open year-round. A re-creation of the 1888 St. Anne's Episcopal Church, which was blown down in the 1938 hurricane, this inn offers three rooms equipped with fireplace and Jacuzzi. All rooms have fans. This is part of the Hotel Manisses.

Blue Dory Inn (401-466-5891; 1-800-992-7290; www.blockislandinns.com), Dodge Street, Old Harbor. ($$$) Open May 1 through Thanksgiving. This 11-room Victorian-style inn, with five beach cottages, is only minutes away from the beach and the heart of Old Harbor. There is a view of the sea through the white-curtained windows of many of the rooms. Floral bedspreads and antique furniture are part of the ambience; rockers and rattan adorn the rear deck and patio. A full breakfast buffet with home-baked breads is included. All rooms have private bath; most have air conditioning.

🖍 **Gables Inn** and **Gables Inn II** (401-466-2213; 401-466-7721), Dodge Street, Old Harbor. ($$–$$$) Open late May through Columbus Day. A two-minute walk from Crescent Beach, this is an ideal spot for families with children (although the inn cannot accommodate very large families). There

Katherine Imbrie

ATLANTIC INN IS A FINE SPOT FOR RELAXING.

are barbecue and picnic facilities in the yard, and rooms have access to a refrigerator. Apartments are available by the week. The room decor is Victorian, and some rooms have a shared bath. Ceiling and dresser fans help blow away the midsummer heat.

Hotel Manisses (401-466-2421; 1-800-MANISSES; www.blockislandresorts.com), Spring Street, Old Harbor. ($$$–$$$$) The turreted Victorian Manisses has 17 rooms named for ships wrecked in Block Island waters. Guest rooms are small, but the spacious, sunny common rooms are filled with summery white rattan furniture and stained glass, and there is a Boston-style saloon bar. An attraction for families with children is the little animal farm of donkeys, llamas, goats, geese, kangaroos, camels, and ducks next door.

♿ **Payne's Harbor View Inn** (401-466-5758; www.paynesharborviewinn.com), 111 Beach Avenue, New Harbor. Open May through Columbus Day. This hilltop inn with an old-fashioned look has eight rooms and two suites through which cool breezes blow. A continental breakfast is served.

Sea Breeze Inn (401-466-2275; 1-800-786-2276; www.seabreezeblockisland.com), Spring Street, Old Harbor. ($$–$$$$) Two rooms are open year-round; the other eight, mid-April through mid-October. Overlooking Swan Pond and a field of wildflowers with a view of the sea in the distance, the weathered-shingled Sea Breeze is an idyllic honeymoon getaway. The main building was once an old-fashioned boardinghouse. There are five rooms, each in its own airy, sunny cottage with antique furnishings, pastel decor, porch, and private bath; five rooms with shared bath are in the main house. A continental breakfast of juice, coffee, and home-baked pastries is served.

Sheffield House (401-466-2494; 1-866-466-2494; www.blockisland bedandbreakfast.com/sheffield house.html), High Street, Old Harbor. ($$–$$$$) The Sheffield House is a turreted six-guest-room Victorian in the heart of Old Town. It is pleasantly furnished with patchwork quilts and family antiques, and has a welcoming, homespun look. There are some shared baths. A full breakfast is included. Fans are available.

1661 Inn and Guest House (401-466-2063; 401-466-2421), Spring Street, Old Harbor. ($$$$) Open year-round. Cottages and efficiencies in addition to the main inn. Set on a hilltop overlooking the sea, this nine-guest-room inn has an unbeatable view of sunsets over the ocean. The inn gets its name not from the year it was built—that's 1890—but from the year Block Island was settled. To further keep a historical perspective, each room is named for a notable Block Islander. The decor is eclectic, with lots of antiques to give it a tranquil, old-fashioned air, but there are also sliding glass doors in rooms where they improve the view, Jacuzzis for the aching bones of cyclists, and fans as required. Breakfast is a bountiful buffet. Dinner is offered from the third week in May to the third week in October in the imposing old Hotel Manisses across the street.

Spring House Hotel (401-466-5844; 1-800-234-9263; www .springhousehotel.com), Spring Street, Old Harbor. ($$$$) Open from April through mid-October. Since 1854 the sprawling Spring House on its promontory above Block Island Sound has been receiving guests—one of the most famous in its early days was Ulysses S. Grant. Fifteen acres of hills and dales surround the inn, and there are concerts on the grounds every other Sunday in July and August. Among the attractive public rooms are the dining room done in a restful pale pink and a sitting room furnished in Victorian fashion. The cool bar off the dining room is Victoria's Parlor. Rooms, studios, and suites are all available, and Victorian again tends to be the theme. If sea breezes don't blow through the rooms sufficiently, there are ceiling fans to help out. A complimentary continental breakfast is served in the sunroom and lunch and dinner are offered daily in the dining room in summer, with drinks on the porch.

BED & BREAKFASTS

Barrington Inn (401-466-5524; www.theinnatblockisland.com), Beach and Ocean Avenue, New Harbor. ($$$) Open early spring through mid-November. There are six sunny, airy rooms with bath and two complete apartments in this cozy, newly refurbished hostelry on the quieter part of the island. It's about three-quarters of a mile to Old Harbor and a quarter mile to New Harbor. From the back deck there are views of New Harbor and Trim's Pond. The apartments are $820–1,200 a week. Fans are available.

The Bellevue House (401-466-2912; www.blockislandbedandbreakfast.com), Old Harbor ($$-$$$) Open Memorial Day through Columbus Day. An 1880s inn with guestrooms, apartments, and surrounding cottages. For guests staying in rooms, a continental breakfast is offered.

Hygeia House (401-466-9616; www.thehygeiahouse.com), Beach Avenue, New Harbor. ($$–$$$) Open year-round. This handsomely restored, mansard-roofed house was built in 1886 by Dr. John C. Champlin, a Block Island physician who named it for a minor Greek goddess of health. It was given a new lease on life in 1999. Its 10 rooms, each with private bath, are appointed with the Victorian furnishings that have been in the house since the beginning. All rooms have a view out over either Old or New Harbor. A continental breakfast is served.

The Old Town Inn (401-466-5958; www.oldtowninnbi.com), Old Town Road, Old Town. ($$–$$$) Open May through late October. In 1825, this was Block Island's general store. Today, with 1921 and 1981 additions, it is a white-clapboard-and-shingle B&B

THE VENERABLE SPRING HOUSE HOTEL IN OLD HARBOR

Tom Gannon

set with 10 guest rooms on 4 acres of lawns and gardens. Homemade coffee cake, muffins, French bread, and scones for breakfast provide a nourishing start to a day of exploring Block Island.

Rose Farm Inn (401-466-2034; www.rosefarminn.com), Roslyn Road off High Street, Old Harbor. ($$–$$$) Open May through mid-October. Because the Rose Farm Inn is set on a rise above 20 acres of rolling hillside, the ocean can be seen in the distance from this Block Island getaway spot. The original farmhouse dates to 1897, but there is also a newer Captain Rose House with an old-fashioned look. While the deluxe rooms have fringed canopy beds, a modern touch is the Jacuzzis in the rooms themselves. An expanded continental breakfast is served on an enclosed porch with flowers all around outdoors. Fans are in all rooms.

Sullivan House Bed and Breakfast (401-466-5020; www.thesullivanhouse.com), New Harbor. ($$$–$$$$) Open June through Columbus Day. This recently restored 1904 house, situated above Trim's Pond and acres of sweet-smelling bayberries, opened as an inn in 1994. The owners are descendants of the original builder, who constructed the interior walls of knotty pine and the exterior walls of stone. Its sweeping grounds make it an ideal spot for wedding receptions, but the five rooms and spectacular situation would satisfy just about anyone's idea of a Block Island retreat.

✳ Where to Eat

DINING OUT **The Atlantic Inn Restaurant** (401-466-5883), Old Harbor. ($$$$) Open Memorial Day through mid-October, daily for dinner. Fish, of course, is a specialty of the elegant prix fixe dinner here, but all dishes are prepared with flair. A typical menu might include baked escargots en croute followed by grilled Scottish salmon and brown sugar-bourbon cheesecake for dessert. Service is impeccable. For fine dining, it's a favorite with local residents. The hilltop location overlooking the water affords the best of sunset views. Dress may be casual.

Harborside Inn (401-466-5504), Water Street, Old Harbor. ($$$$) Open mid-May through mid-September, daily for breakfast, lunch and dinner. You can eat indoors or out on the porch. Outdoors, you can watch the ferry and the passing crowds come and go. Fresh fish and shellfish are prime attractions on the menu.

♿ **Hotel Manisses** (401-466-2836; www.blockislandresorts.com), Spring Street, Old Harbor. ($$$–$$$$) Open May through October. You can start your dinner here at the raw bar, then have your main course on the outside deck or in the dining room proper. Entrées may include a bouillabaisse of local fish or a honey-braised pork shank with vegetable and potato. Among the desserts

Katherine Imbrie

OUTDOOR DINING AT THE MANISSES

are a Cambozola cheese apple tart and chocolate espresso pound cake. A fine way to end a Block Island evening out—whether or not you dine at the Manisses—is sipping an after-dinner drink or a flaming coffee at the **Victorian Top Shelf Bar** with its cool and comfortable wicker furniture.

♿ **Spring House Hotel** (401-466-5844), Spring Street, Old Harbor. ($$$–$$$$) Open daily for breakfast, lunch and dinner from July 4 to Labor Day; dinners only Labor Day to Columbus Day, except Monday. In the light and airy dining room overlooking Rhode Island Sound, the baked stuffed lobsters will put you in the Block Island mood. There are also prime steaks and chops.

♿ **Winfield's** (401-466-5856), Corn Neck Road, Old Harbor. ($$–$$$) Open Memorial Day through Labor Day, daily 6–10 for dinner. Probably Block Island's most sophisticated fare, making good use of local seafood but still including rack of lamb, Angus steaks, and tempting pasta dishes. Meals are nicely prepared and presented. Portions tend to be small.

EATING OUT **Ballard's Inn** (401-466-2231; www.ballardsinn.com), on the Harbor in Old Harbor. ($$$) Open May through September, daily 11:30–10. A one and one-quarter-pound lobster served with corn on the cob and potatoes is just one of the meals this long-time Block Island shore dinner hall (in the same location since the 1880s) is famous for. The fish-and-chips with corn on the cob is another. You can eat under an umbrella on the patio after your swim at the beach or in the big shore dinner hall itself.

The Beachhead (401-466-2249), Corn Neck Road, Old Harbor. ($) Open daily in July and August 11:30–9; spring and fall Thursday through Sunday. Fat, juicy hamburgers are the specialty at this casual little roadside eatery, but you can have clear Rhode Island clam chowder, homemade chili or sandwiches, fish-and-chips, and bountiful salads as well.

Bethany's Airport Diner (401-466-3100), Block Island Airport. ($) Open year-round, daily 6–3. Should you want a $5.50 bowl of homemade clam chowder or a $5.50 bowl of chili—literally, to fly—the Airport Diner is the place to go. If your preference is to stay on the ground and watch the hundreds of small private planes that take off and land on Block Island on summer weekends, you might want to try the Airport Diner's most popular dish, Crab Cake Benny: poached eggs on an English muffin topped with hollandaise sauce and a crabcake.

Eli's (401-466-5230; www.elisblockisland.com), 458 Chapel Street, Old Harbor. ($$–$$$) Open on a limited schedule March through May and from Columbus Day to mid-November, but usually 6–9 Thursday through Sunday and daily in summer, 6–10. For years it was the pasta that mattered at Eli's, but now this bistro-like restaurant that receives kudos from Block Islanders for its quality also has such grand entrées as grilled tuna loin. Desserts include chocolate bread pudding and pumpkin cheesecake in the fall.

Ernie's Breakfast Restaurant, Water Street, Old Harbor. ($) Open 6:30–noon May through Columbus Day. Situated on the deck above Finn's, this breakfast eatery is the perfect place to wait for a ferry and enjoy coffee and homemade muffins for under $3, or more exotic lox and cream cheese omelets for under $10.

Finn's Seafood Restaurant (401-466-2473; www.finnsseafood.com), Water Street, Old Harbor. ($–$$$) Open Memorial Day through Columbus Day 11:30 AM–9:30 PM, later on Friday and Saturday. New arrivals to Block Island can't miss Finn's, facing as it does the ferry parking lot. Go there for the memorable clam chowder, fried clams, fish-and-chips, baked fish sandwiches, lobster rolls, and broiled fish. The dining room decor is plain and simple, but there's also a deck and a take-out window.

Mohegan Cafe and Brewery (401-466-5911), Water Street, Old Harbor. ($–$$) Open mid-March through October, daily for lunch and dinner. There's a definite nautical, masculine look to the Mohegan Cafe and Brewery, where four to six homemade brews are always on tap and range from pale ales to Irish ambers and nonalcoholic ginger beer. The café is largely but not entirely casual. There's prime rib and fresh seafood on the menu along with Tex-Mex and Thai dishes. Luncheon favorites include a veggie wrap and a fried clam plate. It's noisy at night—not suited for intimate dining, but a fine place for a rollicking good time.

The Oar (401-466-8820), New Harbor. ($$) Open Mother's Day through Columbus Day for lunch and dinner, and serving everything from lobster clubs (bacon, lettuce, tomato, and lobster chunks on a roll) to hot dogs, crab cakes, lobster rolls, grilled salmon, fried chicken, sushi, and veggie burgers.

Papa's Pizzeria (401-466-9939), Corn Neck Road, Old Harbor. ($–$$) Open daily in summer. Everything from veggie and Hawaiian pizza to Chicken Cordon Bleu calzones.

♿ **Rebecca's Seafood** (401-466-5411), Water Street, Old Harbor. ($–$$) Open daily in summer for breakfast, lunch, and dinner, and featuring fresh seafood, clam cakes, and chowder. There are plenty of dishes for the landlubber, too.

Poor People's Pub (401-466-8533; www.poorpeoplespub.com), Ocean Avenue, Old Harbor ($–$$) Open year-round 11:30 AM–midnight. Pig roasts with potato salad and cornbread Tuesday afternoons in summer. Live music weekend evenings.

♿ **Sharky's Restaurant** (401-466-9900), Corn Neck Road, Old Harbor. ($–$$) Open May through November, daily 11:30–9. At this down-home restaurant, sandwiches, fish-and-chips, and burgers are always on the menu, but there are also more substantial entrées.

♿ **Three Sisters** (401-466-9661; www.threesistersblockisland.com), Old Town Road across from the Block Island Historical Society, Old Harbor. ($–$$$) Open mid-April through Columbus Day, daily 11:30–2:30 and in summer for evening fish dinners as well. The homemade soups, meat loaf, and turkey, bacon, and avocado sandwiches are among customers' favorites.

SNACKS AND ICE CREAM

♿ **Aldo's Bakery & Homemade Ice Cream** (401-466-2198; www.aldosbakery.com), Weldon's Way, Old Town. Open May to September daily 5:30 AM–11 PM, 6 AM–9 PM Labor Day to Columbus Day. Thirty-two flavors of ice cream and many frozen yogurts to choose from at the end of a long day of bicycle riding. At breakfast or teatime, you might want to sample Aldo's Portuguese sweetbread, blueberry muffins, cinnamon twists, cupcakes, and turnovers, or any kind of doughnut you can think of.

♿ **The Ice Cream Place** (401-466-2145), through the archway beside the Harborside Inn, Old Harbor. Open May through Labor Day, daily 10 AM–11 PM. The ice cream, made to order in Connecticut for The Ice Cream Place, comes in delectable flavors like French Silk (light chocolate with bittersweet bits in it) and coconut. You can have it scooped into a homemade waffle cone or topped with homemade hot fudge or butterscotch sauce and real whipped cream. There are also cookies, muffins, fresh lemonade, and fat-free and sugar-free frozen yogurts. The Ice Cream Place prides itself on being Block Island's original ice cream parlor. You can sit outside in the shade and enjoy your delicious confection.

Juice 'n Java (401-466-5220; www.blockislandcoffee.com), Dodge Street, Old Harbor. Open Memorial Day to July 7 AM–2 PM; July and August; 6 AM–6 PM; Labor Day to Columbus Day 7 AM–2 PM; Columbus Day to Thanksgiving 7 AM–noon. This was Block Island's very first coffeehouse, and it specializes in rich desserts and international coffees. On the healthy side, you can have Hawaiian shave ice and sorbet-like Acai berries topped with granola and fresh fruit. There are books and magazines to read, artwork on the walls to admire, Scrabble and chess to play and an Internet connection.

✳ Entertainment

Club Soda (401-466-5397), in the basement of the High View Hotel, Connecticut Avenue, on the way to the airport. Open year-round, Monday through Sunday 3 PM–1 AM. Bar and lounge with occasional live entertainment. Kitchen (pub food) open 4–11 PM.

The Empire Theatre (401-466-2555), Old Harbor. First a roller-skating rink back in 1882, then a theater for plays of stage and screen, the Empire fell on hard times in the 1980s when the old structure began to give way and appeared destined for demolition. But in 1993 it got a reprieve, and now the theater is all spruced up and showing first-run films in summer.

McGovern's Yellow Kittens (401-466-5855; www.mcgovernsyellowkittens.com), Corn Neck Road, Old Harbor. Year-round. This is where you go for live music on the weekends, and dancing to jukebox tunes any night of the week. There are pool tables, Ping-Pong, darts, and video and pinball games to keep you occupied from 11:30 AM until the wee hours in summer; from 4 PM until 1 AM in winter. On sunny summer days Mexican food is served on deck from 11:30 AM–5 PM. There's dinner indoors from June through Columbus Day.

✐ **Oceanwest Theatre** (401-466-2971), Champlin's Marina, New Harbor. First-run films are offered in this little theater, and on rainy days there are often matinees for the small fry. Bear in mind, though, that it has a tin roof and can be noisy.

Payne's Dock (401-466-5572), New Harbor. Once upon a time this was where the New London boat and the steamers from New York came in. Now it's a marina for private boats, but the live Irish music Wednesday through Sunday at little **Mahogany Shoals,** the bar down on the dock, is open, in season, to everyone.

✷ Selective Shopping

ANTIQUES SHOP Eylandt Fine Antiques & Furnishings (401-466-9888), first floor, Payne's Harbor View Inn at Beach and Ocean Avenues, New Harbor. Open Memorial Day through October, Wednesday through Sunday. This one-room antiques shop whose walls are covered with antique maps and seascapes gets its name from the island's old name, *Adriaen's Eylandt.* When its owner isn't on the island, he's traveling the world, collecting African carvings, Russian icons, old globes, and inlaid boxes to squeeze into his inviting shop.

ART GALLERIES Jessie Edwards Studio (401-466-5314; www.jessieedwardsgallery.com), second floor, New Post Office Building, Water Street, Old Harbor. Open Memorial Day through Columbus Day, daily 10–6 in-season; other times by appointment. Paintings, drawings, prints, and ceramics by Jessie Edwards and other New England artists.

Malcolm Greenaway Gallery (401-466-5331; www.malcolmgreenaway.com), Water Street at Fountain Square, Old Harbor. Open daily 10–9 Memorial Day to Columbus Day. Open weekends until Christmas or other times by appointment. Color photographs of Block Island by Malcolm Greenaway.

The Spring Street Gallery (401-466-5374; www.springstreetgallery.org), Spring Street, across from the Manisses Hotel, Old Harbor. Open daily Memorial Day through Columbus Day. The artists and crafters represented here are all year-round or summer Block Islanders, and the works they show and sell include paintings, photographs, jewelry, decoupage, quilting, and folk art.

BOOKSTORES Island Bound (401-466-8878; www.islandboundbookstore.com), New Post Office Building, Water Street, Old Harbor. Open year-round, 9–9 in summer; call for off-season hours. Hardcover, paperback, Block Island books. Books aplenty to keep you occupied on stormy days.

SPECIAL SHOPS The Bird's Nest (401-466-5080), Dodge Street, Old Harbor. Open April through Columbus Day, daily 10–5 and weekends until 9; from Columbus Day through Christmas, open weekends. Cheerful ceramics, art glass, aprons, and tea towels nautically decorated with seagulls, shells, and fish.

Block Island Blue Pottery (401-466-2945; www.blockislandblue

pottery.com), Dodge Street, Old Harbor. Open July through August, daily 10–6, then weekends until Columbus Day. Joan S. Mallick of Trumbull, Connecticut, has been fashioning island clay into fanciful, blue-glazed pottery for years now. You can find dinnerware and dresserware, ceramic jewelry, and mobiles with a marine air. Prices are moderate.

Blocks of Fudge (401-466-5196), Chapel Street, Old Harbor. Open mid-May through Thanksgiving, 9:30 AM–10 PM at the height of the season, until 5:30 before July 4 and after Labor Day. Closed Wednesdays off-season. For 18 years they've been stirring the kettle making penuche and peanut butter, chocolate, chocolate walnut, and turtle fudge (with caramel and pecans in the center) in this little shop for the sweet-toothed.

Golddiggers (401-466-2611; www.blockislandgolddiggers.com), Chapel Street and Weldon's Way, Old Harbor. Open May through Columbus Day, daily except Wednesday 10–6. Sea glass and beach stones are often a part of the island-made jewelry that is part of this store's stock.

Jennifer's Jewelry (401-466-2744; www.jennifersjewelrybi.com), 207 Water Street, Old Harbor. Open mid-May through Columbus Day, daily 10–6. Rhode Island–made jewelry, much of it with Block Island themes—North Light, Southeast Light, a map of Block Island.

Lazy Fish (401-466-2990), 235 Dodge Street, Old Harbor. Open mid-May through Columbus Day, daily 10–6. Vintage home accessories, estate jewelry, and Block Island photographs by K. C. Perry.

The Mad Hatter (401-466-3131), Water Street, Old Harbor. Open May 15 through Columbus Day, daily 10–9. Straw hats, beribboned hats, hats decorated with this and that, canvas hats, wacky hats, bonnets, and caps for grownups and children can all be found in this creative little shop.

Martin David Jewelry (401-466-2744), Dodge Street, Old Harbor, This off-shoot of Jennifer's Jewelry is open Memorial Day through Columbus Day, daily except Wednesday 11–4, weekends 10–5, but, off-season, call to verify hours. Block Island– and Rhode Island–made sea glass and other jewelry.

North Light Fibers (401-466-2050; www.northlightfibers.com), Old Harbor. Open Memorial Day to Columbus Day weekdays 10–12, 1–5, Saturdays 10–5; Sundays 12–4. In winter, by appointment. Yarns and rugs, alpaca throws. Tours to show how tarn and textiles are made.

The Scarlet Begonia (401-466-5024), Dodge Street, Old Harbor. Open July through September, daily 10–9; in spring and fall, open weekends 9–6. Tasteful table linens, pottery, and bric-a-brac; Block Island beeswax candles and honey; and interesting decoupage plates decorated with flowers, fruits, and beachfront scenes. A cozy, friendly gift shop.

The Star Department Store (401-466-5541), Water Street, Old Harbor. Open April through October, daily 10–5; weekends November 1 through Thanksgiving. In this cavernous, old-fashioned department store you can find shoes and socks, T-shirts and sweatshirts, stockings, guidebooks and maps, and sunglasses—just about every "essential" you left behind on the mainland, plus souvenirs.

Watercolors (401-466-2538), Dodge Street, Old Harbor. Open May through October, daily 10–9; in fall, early winter, and spring, 10–6 weekends only. The handcrafted jewelry and blown- and stained-glass items on sale here are more than just the ordinary souvenirs of a summer holiday.

✷ Special Events

Unless otherwise noted, further information can be obtained from the Block Island Chamber of Commerce (401-466-2982; www.blockislandchamber.com), Old Harbor.

February: **Groundhog Day Winter Census,** Poor People's Pub, Old Harbor.

March: **St. Patrick's Day Dinner** (401-466-5855), McGovern's Yellow Kittens.

April: **Spring Fling,** including music and dancing in Old Harbor.

May: **Annual Beach Cleanup, Islandwide. Annual Shad Bloom 10K Trail Run.**

June: **Race Week,** New Harbor. Taste of Block Island Weekend.

July: **Fourth of July Weekend Parade and Fireworks** at Crescent Beach. **Arts and Crafts Guild Fair,** Block Island Historical Society. **Steak Fry,** Fire Barn, Beach and Ocean Avenues. **Bridal Show at the Sullivan House**, Old Harbor. **Fishing tournament,** Block Island Boat Basin, New Harbor. Triathlon starts at Town Beach (401-466-3223).

August: **Arts and Crafts Guild Fair,** Historical Society. **Block Island Arts Festival,** Ocean Avenue. **House and Garden Tour** (401-466-2481).

September: **Run Around the Block,** Isaac's Corner. **Lion's Club Clambake**, New Harbor. **Taste of Block Island Weekend.**

October: **Roll Call Dinner** (401-466-5940), Harbor Baptist Church **Audubon Birding Weekend.**

November: **St. Andrew's Christmas Bazaar** (401-466-5519). **Christmas Shopping Stroll,** Artists' Guild Fair, Harbor Baptist Church. **Post-Thanksgiving 5K Turkey Trot.**

December: **Ecumenical Choir Christmas Concert** (401-466-5940), Harbor Baptist Church or St. Andrew's Church.

INDEX

B

I

N

O

S

U

V

X

Y

Z